Head On

3 5 7 9 10 8 6 4

Published in 2007 by Ebury Press, an imprint of Ebury Publishing

A Random House Group Company

Copyright © Ian Botham 2007

Ian Botham has asserted his right to be identified as the author of this Work
in accordance with the Copyright, Designs and Patents Act 1988

The Random House Group Limited Reg. No. 954009

Addresses for companies within the Random House Group can be found at
www.randomhouse.co.uk

A CIP catalogue record for this book is available from the British Library

Mixed Sources
Product group from well-managed
forests and other controlled sources
www.fsc.org   Cert no. TT-COC-2139
© 1996 Forest Stewardship Council

Printed and bound in Great Britain by Clays of St Ives PLC

ISBN 9780091921484 (hardback)
ISBN 9780091924379 (paperback)

To buy books by your favourite authors and register for offers visit
www.rbooks.co.uk

Head On

IAN BOTHAM

THE AUTOBIOGRAPHY

EBURY
PRESS

To Lady B

Contents

1	Yeovil Boy Wins Game	7
2	Everybody's Hero	43
3	A Difficult Act to Follow	82
4	A Hiding to Nothing	122
5	Botham Must Go	146
6	The War Between the Tabloids	184
7	One Foot in Front of the Other	216
8	The Reek of Betrayal	254
9	Can't Bat, Can't Bowl, Can't Field	264
10	Playing on Borrowed Time	294
11	The New James Bond	312
12	Who the Hell Did They Think They Were?	344
13	A Long Road Back	370
	Postscript	376
	Acknowledgements	378
	Index	379

Chapter 1

YEOVIL BOY WINS GAME

Two of my distinguishing features were evident almost from the day I was born. I weighed in at an eye-watering ten pounds one ounce – Beefy from the start – and from my youngest days I had an unshakeable self-confidence and belief in my own abilities ... though others might have found less flattering ways to describe it.

My parents were desperate for children but had been forced to endure the heartbreak of a succession of miscarriages. My poor mother, Marie, had miscarried four times, then almost lost me too. She was hospitalised from the third month of pregnancy and at one point was so ill that the doctors were resigned to her losing the baby yet again, and were more concerned to protect her health. What made it worse was that for much of the time, she had to endure the pain, the sickness and the mental torment on her own, for my father, Les, serving in the Fleet Air Arm as a Petty Officer, was stationed in Northern Ireland at the time.

Yet somehow she found the strength to battle through it all and on the damp, grey evening of 24 November 1955, their first child, Ian Terence Botham, was born. Les didn't see his son and heir until he arrived home on leave a week later. Our home was then in Cheshire, but my parents were so fed up with the long separations from each other that, shortly after I was born, we moved into Royal

Navy married quarters in Londonderry. I was too young to remember it but my mother later spoke of a draughty, cold and damp house on a windswept hill overlooking the city. This was in 1956, before 'The Troubles' had begun to flare once more, but it was still a place of simmering hostility between the Protestant and Catholic communities, with the British forces maintaining an uneasy presence between them.

If the surroundings were less than ideal, my parents were very happy there with the baby for whom they had waited so long. My father, Les, was tall but whippet thin, one of the characteristics I clearly didn't inherit from him. He could eat anything he liked and never put on an ounce of weight, and he always had energy to burn, organising friends and workmates for impromptu football kick-abouts in the nearest park. He was an old-fashioned, honourable man – his word really was his bond – quite fixed in his opinions and, in an understated way, a quietly determined man. If he set his mind to anything he would usually achieve it. He was also a disciplinarian though not a martinet; my mum was actually the more steely character of the two.

She was larger than life, warm, loving, gregarious and garrulous, and always enjoyed a party and a glass of wine. Although she was a keen sportswoman and took a lot of exercise, she worried about her weight, constantly taking up one diet after another, and just as constantly breaking them. 'I'm just having this as a little treat,' she'd say, tucking away another cake or chocolate.

After all the setbacks and hardships my parents had been through, probably no child was ever more eagerly anticipated nor more dearly loved. Their baby could do no wrong and throughout my childhood I was indulged shamefully, spoilt rotten, in fact. Like all parents, my mum and dad were convinced that their child was highly gifted and destined for great things, but in this case it might have had some basis in fact because I did show an unusual self-confidence and resourcefulness from the moment I could crawl. One day, Mum left me playing with some toys inside the playpen in the living room while she went to do some jobs in the kitchen. A couple of minutes later she felt a small hand on her ankle, looked down and found me crawling round her feet. Puzzled – perhaps she only thought she'd put me in the playpen – she carried me back to the living room and then went back to her work.

When I came crawling back into the kitchen again a few minutes later, she knew something was going on. She put me back in the playpen once more and then spied on me through the crack in the door. As soon as she was out of sight, I lifted up one side of the playpen, balanced it on the toy box while I crawled underneath and then put it back in position, leaving everything apparently undisturbed and no visible clue as to how the crime had been committed. When I was left outside the house in my pram, even with the brake fully on, I bounced up and down so much that it would slowly but steadily move down the hill. I managed to cover some fairly impressive distances that way but luckily everyone on the estate knew who I was and would intercept me and wheel me back to the house.

In February 1957, my mother gave birth to my sister Dale. By then I was fifteen months old and walking, greatly increasing the range and scope of my activities and the anxiety levels of my long-suffering mum and dad. The garden at the back of the house was surrounded by a wooden fence that my dad had put up in an unsuccessful attempt to curb my wanderlust; if I could not walk round or crawl under something, I would just climb over it instead. Many times my mum or dad looked out into the garden where they had left me playing happily a few minutes before, only to discover that it was now deserted. The only sign of my escape route was often the dungarees that I had snagged climbing over the fence and then abandoned. On one occasion, still less than eighteen months old, I even got as far as the driver's seat of an Army truck. The cab was so high off the ground that nobody could work out how I got there, and the fact that, having got bored with the steering wheel, I was playing with the handbrake when I was found, added a few more to my parents' rapidly increasing store of grey hairs.

My taste for adventure sometimes put me in harm's way, and in Londonderry I made the first of several trips to hospital after falling off a wall and cracking my head. I was kept in hospital for four days for observation, and though I was eventually given the all-clear, the doctors there were sufficiently concerned to suggest that I should wear protective headgear for a while. Dad made me a foam-rubber helmet to protect my head, though a full body-suit might have been a better idea; it would certainly have saved him from at least some of the subsequent trips to the casualty department to treat my latest cuts, abrasions and broken bones.

Then, as now, I chafed at any restrictions that others tried to impose on me, and my hyper-competitive instincts also came to the surface. After eighteen months in Northern Ireland, my dad's tour of duty there ended and we went back to Cheshire where, during a toddlers' race at the naval base's sports day, I eliminated most of the opposition by the simple expedient of barging into them and knocking them flat. The race was mine for the taking, but instead of hightailing it for the tape, I stopped to see what the others were up to. As a result, virtue had its just reward, and having got back to their feet they all went roaring past me, leaving me well down the field when I finally reached the tape. Those who have batted with me over the years will confirm that running twenty yards or so never became my strong point.

In 1958, after just one year in Cheshire, we moved again, to Yeovil in Somerset, when my dad reached the end of his term of service with the Fleet Air Arm. He was offered promotion if he signed on for a further term, but he opted instead for civilian life, and a job with Westland Helicopters in Yeovil. The job gave him financial security but it also meant that he was home a lot more often and I think that was at least as important a factor in his decision; he had been away a lot when I was very young. From then on, he was always available if

I wanted to play cricket or football. He'd bowl to me endlessly or go in goal while I practised my penalty-taking technique, and he'd referee seven- or eight-a-side games that he'd organise, rounding up all the kids and heading down to the local playing fields – the Mudford 'Rec'.

Everywhere my dad went, I went as well; he even made me a special cut-down golf club so that we could play golf on the local course together. Whether because he didn't feel qualified to do so, or because he didn't feel it was necessary, he never really coached me in any sport I played, but gave me the most important thing: his time. My dad and mum never went overboard with praise and always played it down when I'd played well, letting me know that, well as I'd done, there was always room for further improvement. But I had their wholehearted support and encouragement in anything I did, and that was all I needed. The time we spent together and the sacrifices that they made for me are things I remember to this day with pride and gratitude, and when I look back and try to trace the roots of my success in sport, I always return to my mum and dad. They gave me the platform from which I could launch myself.

Our first home in Yeovil was at 64 Mudford Road, a house with a large garden including a small orchard and huge ash and horse chestnut trees. There was even a small wood beyond the hedge. My childhood there was a time when – at least through the rose tints of middle-age – there was no rain or cloudy skies and the sun always shone on Mudford Road. I played for hours on end in the dappled shade, exploring the wood, building dens, damming the stream and climbing trees, though when I got myself high up in the ash tree I discovered a previously unknown aspect of my character: I was scared of heights. Climbing up had been easy but coming down again proved to be impossible. I clung to the trunk, absolutely petrified, until my dad appeared with a ladder and rescued me. I've been scared of heights ever since; I can't even look over a parapet without a certain dampness of the palms.

Even our garden and the wood beyond wasn't always large enough to contain me and, like the proverbial chicken, I had an irresistible urge to cross the road. Mum's first intimation of this was when a neighbour told her that Dale and I were playing "chicken" by dashing to and fro in front of the traffic. For the first time in my life, I was spanked and sent to bed as punishment. It didn't cure my wanderlust but it did at least make me approach the road with a bit more care in future.

I continued to be accident-prone and Mum practically had her own chair in the waiting room at Yeovil General Hospital. I had my first operation there at the age of four. I was out in town when I collapsed with a terrible stomach pain. I was rushed to hospital and had surgery to repair a hernia. To keep me company, Mum and Dad brought in my teddy bear, Mr Khrushchev, a name inspired by the influence of television in my early upbringing, when the bear-like Soviet leader regularly featured on TV news bulletins, on one memorable occasion banging his shoe on a desk at the United Nations, by way of emphasising the point he was making. The nurses pretended that Mr Khrushchev had had the same operation as me, and even bandaged him up to sustain the illusion.

I must have enjoyed the experience of being in hospital and all the attention from the nurses because, for a while, I toyed with the idea of being a doctor when I grew up on the impeccably logical grounds that, since the nurses did all the work, to be a doctor had to be job heaven. However, by the time I went in for another hernia operation four years later, I had abandoned the idea of medicine in favour of a career as a professional sportsman, though my first paying job was in an unrelated field: as a choirboy at St John's Church at Yeovil. I earned five bob a week and seven and sixpence for weddings – a much better rate than a paperboy's – though my voice, if loud, was so rarely in tune that I was under standing orders from the choirmaster to mime the tricky parts of any hymn we were singing.

Both my parents had been good at sport and both were highly competitive; it must run in the Botham genes. Marie had played badminton, hockey and, unusually for the times, women's cricket, to a good standard. Les was also a keen cricketer, had run in middle-distance events for East Yorkshire and played football for the Combined Services. He had a trial for Hull City when he was a boy and also had an offer to join Bolton or Blackburn as a professional footballer. With the financial rewards available in football these days, it wouldn't be a hard decision to make, but it was a very different world back then. My dad thought long and hard about it but, tempted though he was, the modest wages of a football player and the lack of security and prospects when his brief career was over made him turn down the offer; if he stayed in the Navy, he'd at least get a pension when he retired.

With my parents' sporting background, it was probably not entirely surprising that I proved to be something of a sportsman myself. I can't remember a time when I didn't have a cricket bat in my hand and I'd been bowling daisy cutters at the garage door since I was six and playing impromptu games of cricket in the local park at every opportunity. I would have preferred a brother to a sister so we could have played sport together and – according to my mother; I've somehow erased this from my memory – I punished Dale for being the wrong sex by insisting on calling her John, and making her talk in a deep voice and play cricket and football with me.

Like most siblings, my long-suffering sister and I were constantly fighting when we were kids, and Dale even had to learn to treat my rare displays of brotherly love with caution. After the shed at the bottom of our garden burned down in mysterious circumstances, arson was suspected and my parents lined up the two principal suspects – Dale and me. I gave her hand an encouraging squeeze as we waited for the interrogation to begin and it was pure coincidence that the box of matches I'd been holding somehow found their way into her hand at the same time. One of the rare examples of brother–sister co-operation in our youth came at the end of every summer, when we collected the apples from our orchard, set up a table at the end of our drive and sold them to passers-by.

Beyond the hedge at the rear of our house was a little lane leading to the woods and on the other side of the lane were the Yeovil Grammar School playing fields, where I often went to watch the older boys playing cricket. I even made a couple of holes in the hedge to give me easier access, which may not have endeared me to the assistant groundsman who often rounded me up and carted me back home in his wheelbarrow; but once he and the school teachers realised that I could play a bit, they were happy for me to watch, and to field and to bowl to the boys in the nets, though chances to bat were very few and far between.

My love affair with sport grew stronger in September 1962 when, aged six and three-quarters, I moved from Miss Wright's private school at Penmount to Milford Junior School. I went home for lunch at first but when I found out that kids who ate school dinners were allowed to play football afterwards, I managed to persuade Mum and Dad to let me stay at school for lunch. I was only in my first year and officially you were not allowed to play football until the second, but Richard Hibbitt, the deputy headmaster who was also in charge of games, saw how keen I was and asked my parents to allow me to play for the school team. That was all the encouragement I needed, and as young as seven, my mum found me one day, my tongue protruding from the corner of my mouth as I wrote my name over and over on a piece of paper. 'What on earth are you doing, Ian?' she said.

'Well, people are going to be asking me for my autograph one day,' I said, 'so I'm just practising it.'

The school was newly built in typical 1960s style – concrete walls, flat roofs and huge windows that made it sweltering in summer and freezing in winter – and I hadn't been in her class more than a few weeks when my form mistress, Mrs Olwyn Joyce, was telling my parents that she wished the school had been built with rather less panoramic windows. I spent most of my time staring out of them, watching the other kids doing games and wishing I was out there as well.

Mr Hibbitt was my great ally. A sports nut, he recognised and encouraged my talent, and didn't even make a fuss when I broke a school window since I'd done it by hitting a cricket ball for six. He also gave me my first earnings from sport when he put piles of coins on a good length on the cricket pitch and told us that any coins we managed to hit were ours. I needed no further encouragement and collected the cash in very quick time.

There was one potential block to my emerging prowess as a cricketer: I was colour-blind. It was first suspected at school where they noticed that, unlike those of my peers, the skies in the pictures I painted were rarely blue. The diagnosis was confirmed when I had the standard eye test, trying to pick out numbers among dots of contrasting colours, and I couldn't see them at all. It's a very common condition in males – as many as one man in three suffers from it – and it usually manifests itself as a difficulty in distinguishing green from red. In theory that presents a sizeable obstacle in a sport played with a red ball on a green grass pitch, but in fact the actual pitch is usually colourless and the sightscreen against which you're spotting the ball is white. In any case, if you're standing at one end of a pitch with a bat in your hands and a small round object is approaching you at high speed, whatever colour it might appear to be, it's probably a pretty good idea to try and hit it.

Mr Hibbitt excepted, I had problems convincing my teachers that even though I was two or three years too young for the age group of the team, I was more than good enough to play. This was to be a recurring and frustrating problem throughout my youth and beyond, but once I was given an opportunity, I rarely needed more than one chance to win over the doubters. Mr Hibbitt had raided the school funds for a couple of new cricket bats, one of which, he made clear, was for my exclusive use, and perhaps helped by the new bat, I went from strength to strength as a batsman. In Under-11 cricket it was very rare for a team to total much more than fifty or sixty and an individual score of twenty was worthy of special note. Yet I was regularly scoring centuries in inter-school games. If people needed any confirmation that I had a special talent, then this was it; I and they could see that there was a gulf between myself and my contemporaries.

I was also a big hitter. I didn't do any exercises or weight training to build up my strength, but my natural physique and the endless hours I spent out of doors, climbing up trees – though not down them – and constantly playing sport of all kinds, developed my fitness and strength until I could hit the ball harder and farther than most adults. During one school match I hit a six over mid-wicket that cleared the roof of the school building and landed in the car park on the far side. My only regret was that it had somehow missed all the cars. A beaming Mr Hibbitt paced it out and then told me that he reckoned it would have carried the boundary at Somerset's county ground at Taunton, or even at Lord's.

I could also field a bit. On the school sports day I took part in the throwing the cricket ball competition. The teacher doing the judging took up station a safe distance away down the playing fields and several of my peers took their turns. Then it was my go. The teacher must have been glancing down at his clipboard as I ran up and threw the ball, because after waiting for a few seconds, he shouted: 'Well come on then, Botham, we haven't got all day. Get on with it.'

'But I've already thrown it, sir.'

Frowning, he peered at the ground between us and to either side of the target area. 'Then where on earth is it?'

'About twenty yards behind you, sir.'

He stared at me in disbelief, then looked behind him, did a double-take and began pacing out the extra distance to where the ball was lying in the grass. The best throw by any of my schoolmates was barely half as far. As a result of this feat, Mr Hibbitt then entered me in an Under-13s throwing the cricket ball competition in London – the Crusaders' Union National Sports Day at Motspur Park. Like the teacher in Somerset, the judges could not believe their measurements of the distance I achieved with my first throw, so they made me throw again. They measured this one with even greater care but the result was pretty much the same, a record throw of just over 207 feet, which remained unsurpassed for many years. I won the Victor Ludorum and took a shiny silver cup back to Somerset with me, the first trophy I had ever won.

I enjoyed my success. The parents of my contemporaries probably had me down as an arrogant little so and so, and they might even have been right, but if it sometimes made me a precocious, bumptious child, that self-belief was also what made me a fierce and successful competitor at whatever I turned my hand to. People at school sometimes called me a bighead but I used to think, 'No I'm not. I'm just very good at this, a lot better than you, as a matter of fact. So I'm going to keep enjoying it and I'm going to keep doing it. Get used to it.' Each time I went up to a higher level or an older age group, I did pause to wonder if I would be good enough to succeed, but each time I realised that I was as good as, and usually far better than, anyone else playing at that level.

My dad also began taking me along to his cricket matches for the Westland Helicopters' Second XI. He was easily good enough to have played for the first team but he didn't want to commit the time because it would mean him being away from home too much at weekends, so he captained the second team and we set off together on Saturday mornings, walking down the road with our bats and the Tupperware box in which Mum put our sandwiches. If either side was short – which often happens in club cricket, especially at second team level – I would volunteer to make up the numbers. I was heart-broken if both teams were at full strength, but most weeks I'd get a game and from the age of eight onwards I was not only playing against full-grown men but more than holding my own.

By the time I began secondary school at Buckler's Mead in Yeovil – then much smaller than the massive school it has now become – my strengths and weaknesses were recognised by everyone, including myself. I was good, very good, at sport, but my lack of prowess in the classroom was acknowledged by the nickname my mates gave me: 'Bungalow' – nothing upstairs. Despite the nickname, I wasn't unintelligent, but I simply had no interest in anything that would not further the aim I had already set myself of becoming a professional sportsman. Nor did my lack of academic ability prevent me displaying my trademark self-confidence when it came time to sit the 11-plus exam. When I came home from school that day, my mum was waiting on the doorstep. 'Well?' she said. 'How did it go?'

'Dead easy,' I said. 'I don't know what all the fuss is about.' It therefore came as something of a shock to my parents when a letter arrived a few weeks later to say that I'd failed by some distance. If the 11-plus had been a quick single, I'd have been stranded halfway down the wicket.

I got into a few scrapes and scraps at school, and in general took my punishment without complaint, but my woodwork teacher and I were on a collision course from the start. Woodwork wasn't exactly my forte. My joints were always too tight or too loose, the legs on my coffee table were so constantly shortened to try and level them up that in the end I turned it into a tray instead, and even my attempt at a toy cricket bat was a disaster. The end came when one of my classmates was fooling about behind me and, having wrongly identified me as the culprit, the woodwork teacher cracked me on the head with a T-square. I don't know whether the blow or the injustice of it riled me more, but I was shaking with rage and was tempted to flatten him there and then – and even at that age, I was powerful enough to have done so. Instead I thought about it for a few seconds and then told him, 'I'm going to do you a favour and leave the room now.' I went straight to the headmaster, told him what had happened, and then said, 'I'm not going to go home and blab about what's gone on today, but nor am I ever going in a class with that teacher again.' It did the trick; that was the end of my woodwork lessons. Looking back now, it seems remarkable that a schoolboy in that much more deferential era should have had such self-confidence and self-possession, but for whatever reason, that was the way I was.

Even as a boy, once I'd got past the brief flirtation with the idea of being a doctor, I had no doubt where my future lay: in professional sport. The careers master at Buckler's Mead wouldn't have been doing his job if he hadn't made some efforts to point out the pitfalls, like the lack of security and the small percentage who actually made it, but I had already been through all this with him, and my mum and dad, on several occasions, and I saw no point in covering the same well-worn ground again.

'Morning, Ian,' he said, as I turned up at the library for yet another session. 'Any thoughts since last time?'

'No. I'm still going to be a professional sportsman.'

He gave me an indulgent smile. 'Of course you are. Every schoolboy has the same dream. But what are you really going to do for a living?'

'I've just told you what I'm going to do,' I said. 'Why won't you believe me? There are loads of boys behind me in the queue who don't have the faintest idea what they're going to do. They're the ones who need your help, not me. I know precisely what I'm going to do, so there's no point in me coming to any more of these sessions.'

Just as I had with my woodwork teacher, I told the careers master that I wouldn't be coming to see him again, and then walked out, but once more I took the precaution of going straight to the headmaster's office and telling him what had happened. When I'd explained my unshakeable belief in the career that awaited me and the total pointlessness of going to careers advisory sessions with a master who ignored what I said and started recommending all sorts of other, wholly unsuitable occupations, the headmaster said, 'Fair enough. Next time there's a careers session, come to my office instead.' I did so and the headmaster and I sat and talked about cricket until the bell rang for the next lesson.

I was very good at most sports at school, but rugby was one that passed me by. I love to watch it now, but back then the rules might as well have been written in Latin for all I knew about them. We were a football school, but when a new games teacher arrived – a Welshman – he brought part of his Celtic heritage into play and told us we'd have to play rugby for half the year from then on. We were willing to give it a go, but none of us had ever played the game in our lives and our first and, as it turned out, our only game of rugby was a complete shambles. Whenever most of our players had the ball in their hands – and that wasn't often – and saw someone coming to tackle them, they threw the ball blindly over their shoulders and ran for it.

The other side had one star player, a hammer thrower who'd represented England Schools, who was a great big lump of a guy and ran straight through us every time he got the ball. I tried to tackle him, but he just steamrollered me out of the way and, as an afterthought, whacked me on the head as he went by – and not just a hand-off, a blow with a clenched fist. After this happened for the second time I went to the referee and said, 'Is he allowed to do that?'

The ref just said, 'Get on with the game,' so I thought, 'Fair enough,' and the next time the big guy came at me, I got my retaliation in first and did a football-style sliding tackle on him. Then I was off, running like hell with the gorilla in hot pursuit. He never caught me though. I mightn't have been the fastest runner around, but I was much too quick for him. That was the end of the school's rugby experiment; from then on we stuck to football.

When I was ten we moved to a larger house on the top of town with views out to the Mendips and Glastonbury Tor. At the foot of the terraced garden was a small wood and open fields sloping steeply down to the stream that ran through the bottom of the valley, a perfect slope for winter sledging. My bedroom window faced Yeovilton aerodrome and on the days I was ill, I lay in bed watching the aircraft and helicopters taking off and landing, though there weren't many days like that; I hated missing school because it meant missing a game of cricket or football as well. On the rare occasions when my mates and I were not playing sport, we'd be doing what country boys used to do: fishing, damming streams, or going off to try and pot rabbits with our air rifles. I got my first air rifle after having a couple of teeth pulled out at the dentist. I was put to sleep while they were taken out and when I came round, a brand new air rifle was lying across my lap … either the tooth fairy was a fully paid-up member of the NRA, or my mum had been round to the dentist's the day before with it so that I would have it as soon as I woke up.

My dad drew some concentric circles on a piece of wood and nailed it to a tree at the bottom of the garden so that I could prac-tise my shooting, but he had to intervene hastily when I found a more challenging alternative target. I was just drawing a bead on the backside of our next-door neighbour as he stooped to weed his vegetable patch when my dad followed my gaze and knocked the barrel of the air rifle up just as I was about to fire.

I didn't really discover girls until I was fifteen or sixteen; before that, as far as I was concerned, they just got in the way of playing sport. An abrupt change in my attitude was signalled when I sidled up to my mum in the kitchen, and as casually as I could manage, asked her to get me some Lifebuoy soap next time she went shop-ping. Mum weighed me up for a moment and then came straight to the point. 'Who is she and what's her name?'

I blushed. 'Her name's Margaret.'

'And what's the big attraction?'

'She can run faster than me.'

'When you get a bit older, Ian,' my mum said, 'that'll cease to be an attraction.' I had so much to learn...

My subsequent attempts to attract the interest of the opposite sex led to one or two fashion disasters. My bright orange shirt with a huge collar, blue flared trousers and platform shoes certainly ensured that I caught the eye of the local girls, but not necessarily in the way I'd have liked.

Although we had our moments, I think my teenage years were probably less traumatic for my parents than most, mainly because my dad and especially my mum laid down clear rules about what they expected from me and were willing to back them up with strict discipline. On the one occasion we had a really big row, ending with me threatening to leave home and go to London to see the bright lights, my mum simply called my bluff by packing my bags and leaving them in the hall by the front door. Shamefaced, I carried them back upstairs and that was the last empty threat of that sort that I issued.

The major source of arguments with my parents was my determination to make sport my career. As any parent would, they worried about what would happen if I failed to make the grade. It was not a thought that had ever troubled my mind; I knew I was going right to the top. The only doubt that I harboured was whether I should be a professional cricketer or a professional footballer. I played as a central defender for my school football team and I was good enough to be picked for the county schools team as well. I also played for Ilminster Town, scoring a hat-trick for them in one game and then scoring four a couple of games later – not bad for someone who was primarily a defender. I was spotted by scouts from various clubs and in due course I had an offer from Crystal Palace – then a top-flight football club – and from five other clubs in the lower divisions. The approaches were always made to my dad, not to me; I think it was illegal to sign players below a certain age, so the scouts would talk to the parents, and if any cheques changed hands, they always had a parent's name, not the son's, on them.

In my case it never got to that stage. When the offers started to come in I sat down with my dad and asked his advice. He thought about it for a few moments and then said, 'Right, son. I think you're a better cricketer than a footballer,' and that was it, the decision was made, though had Chelsea been one of the clubs chasing me, it might have given me serious pause for thought. I'd been a Chelsea fan ever since I first saw them. I started supporting them for no better reason than that I liked the colour of their shirts, and my bedroom was decorated in the team's blue. I even gave my mum a Chelsea rosette so that she could match the shade exactly when she was buying the paint, wallpaper and bed covers, though she drew the line when it came to the carpet. When Chelsea beat Leeds United in the 1970 Cup Final replay at Old Trafford, I drew a picture of the trophy on my bedroom wall.

As I grew older, I recognised the wisdom of the advice my dad had given me. There was a lot more money to be made in football than cricket at the time – there still is – but my dad saw that, while I was a competent footballer and certainly good enough to have enjoyed a moderately successful professional career, I did not stand out from those around me as being a special talent. I was just one of the team, neither the best nor the worst player in it. In cricket, on the other hand, I was definitely the most gifted player in any team in which I played, and not just slightly better than the others, but miles ahead of them. This wasn't bigheadedness – though I certainly wasn't short in the ego department – it was a cold recognition of the facts.

My success at cricket was all the more remarkable because, although I played the game incessantly whenever enough people could be rounded up to make up the numbers, I rarely practised, least of all in the nets. That was partly because of my low boredom threshold, but it was also because I always suffered badly from claustrophobia whenever I went into the nets. It sounds ridiculous but it was true, and it was even more curious because I've never suffered from claustrophobia in lifts, cellars or any other confined areas, but

I genuinely used to hate being in the nets, especially the indoor ones; they felt like prisons to me. Perhaps it was the noise, the endless squeal of rubber-soled shoes on wood floors as bowlers turned and ran up, and the crack of bat and ball from adjoining nets that always made me flinch and want to duck just as I was facing my own delivery. When I was bowling, I used to fall away to the side after delivering the ball and always found myself heading straight for the side netting. Whatever the reasons, I had a particular aversion to nets and would go some way to avoid them. If I had to go into them and bat – and if I was going to make a career as a cricketer, a certain amount of time in the nets was unavoidable – I tended to start smashing the ball around as soon as I got in there, probably in the hope that it would shorten the ordeal if I did so.

As was so often the case with me, I was covering up my genuine fears and insecurities with a display of sheer bravado, but I also felt most fired up when my back was to the wall. From my earliest days, some of my best performances came when I felt that I had no other option than to come out with all guns firing. It was as vital a part of my armoury as my self-belief and my ultra-competitive nature. Without that I would never have achieved anything, and as a kid I had it in abundance. I simply had to win at everything I did, whether it was football, cricket, Monopoly or a game of I-Spy to while away a long car journey, and that burning desire to be better than the rest – a winner – at anything I do has never left me.

However, it was also reflected in my inability to admit to a mistake. The idea that I might have bowled a bad ball, played an injudicious shot or misfielded simply never occurred to me. If I bowled a long hop and was hit for four, it wasn't a bad ball, it was all part of my tactical masterplan and the next delivery would get him out for sure. If I dropped a catch, or was bowled or caught, I had an everlasting list of reasons at the ready – the sun was in my eyes, someone in the crowd had chosen that moment to take a flash photograph or rustle a newspaper, a midge had flown into my eye, or whatever it took to preserve my pride and self-belief. It must have been irritating as hell to my teammates and coaches, but it did the job for me. I grew more and more successful as a player and the occasions when I needed to trot out those hoary old excuses grew fewer and fewer.

In 1969, aged just thirteen, I made my debut for the Somerset Schools Under-15 side against Wiltshire. We won the toss and batted but were soon in trouble, with four or five batsmen back in the pavilion quite cheaply, and when I got to the wicket, I was surrounded by a very attacking field ... which left plenty of gaps in the outfield. My dad had bought me a brand new Stuart Surridge, Ken Barrington-autographed bat especially for the occasion. A Surrey and England batsman, Barrington was my cricketing hero. Most people would probably think of him as a pretty dour and dogged player – the Geoffrey Boycott of southern England – but I liked the uncompromising attitude he showed and the way he wore his colours on his chest.

I had one other sporting hero, an England fast bowler, and when his county played at Taunton, my dad took me round to the back of the pavilion to join the small group of kids waiting for autographs. When he arrived, the England bowler pushed straight past us, saying, 'I'm not signing autographs now, come back at lunchtime.' When we did, he told us, 'Come back at tea,' and then, 'Come back after close of play.'

When he finally emerged from the pavilion, he made straight for his car, and when we followed him across the car park, he turned round and gave us a foul mouthful. As I hesitated, my dad, who had been waiting in the background, called out, 'Come here, Ian, you don't want the autograph of a man who behaves like that.' In my later years, I always tried to keep that incident in mind if I was tempted to be impatient with fans waiting for me.

Unlike that fast bowler, Ken Barrington was always polite and patient with fans and autograph hunters, and my bat was my most treasured possession. It was the first time I'd used it in a competitive match. I put it to pretty good use, smashing the bowling to all parts of the ground. I scored 80 very quickly and we won the game with something to spare.

My dad had struck a deal with me that he'd pay me 6d for every run I scored – not that I needed any added incentive to do well – and my innings ensured a £2 jackpot. He paid up with a smile but made sure that he never risked anything like the same amount again. The next day, I had another nice bonus. For the first time ever, I made headlines in the local paper, the *Weston Gazette*: YEOVIL BOY WINS GAME. I was on my way, and as well as achieving my fifteen seconds of local fame, it led to me being snapped up by the Yeovil cricket club, which played in a higher league than my dad's Westland team. I moved on with his blessing and suddenly I was in the big league, travelling to the furthest reaches of the known world ... like Poole and Bournemouth.

In 1970, the year after I'd played for Somerset Under-15s as a thirteen-year-old, I was selected to represent the south-west at the trials for the England Under-15s; inevitably I'd been told that I wasn't old enough to play the year before. The trials to decide who would play for England Schools against the Public Schools XI were held in Liverpool. Dad came with me and saw me play a blinder. During the long train journey up from Somerset, I'd spent a lot of time thinking about the field I was going to set and how I was going to get batsmen out and get myself noticed. When I came on to bowl, I set a field to fit the plan I'd evolved and picked up a wicket straight away when I beat the batsman through the air and had him caught at mid-wicket. I took five more wickets that afternoon and left the field very happy with my performance and sure that I would be picked for the final XI.

That confidence was increased when I then scored 80 with the bat; how could they possibly leave me out? Quite easily as it turned out. Not for the first time and certainly not for the last, a panel of selectors saw things in a very different light. My dad had been sitting near enough to them to overhear their conversations, and when I took my first wicket, he heard one of them say, 'Ignore that. It was a fluke.'

When they read out the team that they had chosen, my name was not among those selected. I went straight up to the chairman of the selectors and said, 'Why haven't I been picked?'

He did a bit of a double-take – schoolboys, and especially fourteen-year-old ones, were clearly expected to be seen rather than heard – but then told me, 'Well, we thought the opposition you faced was not as strong as some of the other teams.'

'Is that so?' I said. 'Well, who else scored as many runs and took as many wickets against them?'

Once more, he looked taken aback and he had no answer for me, but I still didn't make the team. He did mention that they considered me a batsman rather than a bowler; I suppose they hadn't heard of all-rounders. I suspected then and still believe that the real reasons they didn't pick me were a) that I was a yokel from the south-west and b) that a couple of them had already made up their minds to choose someone else that they thought was a better player, and who just happened to come from the Home Counties, like them.

My dad was fuming, and when the selectors added insult to injury by offering me the exalted role of substitute's substitute – thirteenth man – we both said 'No thanks' and set off for Lime Street Station and the train home. I think the rebellious, anti-Establishment side of my nature was born there and then, but I also began to learn a bit of the street wisdom that a country boy like me badly needed to acquire.

That trip to Liverpool taught me a lot, not least that sometimes you have to be better than anybody else, just to be treated the same. That wasn't just my prejudice; I met there two other future professional cricketers whose experiences were very similar to mine. Graham Stevenson, a Yorkshire lad, who was a future

England fast bowler, and Paul Romaines, who came from the north-east and played for Gloucestershire for many years, were similarly ignored. The kids from the wrong side of the tracks just didn't make it. I now began to realise that life was not always going to be fair and square. That didn't put me off at all; it merely spurred me on. Whatever obstacles were put in my way, I was going to overcome them. It would just make me even more determined to succeed.

I hadn't caught the eye of the selectors of the England Under-15s, but before long there were the first stirrings of interest from the Somerset county team, and I was invited to attend a practice session with a few other promising youngsters from the county. My heart was thumping as I entered the Taunton ground for the first time as a player and looked around. Even now, it has something of the feeling of one of those farms where extensions and buildings have been tacked on over the years as needed – there are still a couple of corrugated iron sheds shrouded in chicken wire at one side of the ground. Back then it definitely had a quirky, almost organic feel to it, though the red sandstone spires and pinnacles of the churches of St James, St George and St Mary visible behind the ramshackle, weather-boarded pavilion, the ancient yew and pine trees in St James's churchyard and the sweep of the Quantock Hills rising in the distance also gave it a timeless quality.

I could almost feel the history of the place as I crossed the greyhound track that then encircled the ground and walked across an outfield that seemed to go on for ever. The grass was manicured and the square looked as flat as a billiard table. Countless cricketing greats had played on this ground; in 1895, the great Archie MacLaren had smashed 424 runs to all corners of it. I could feel my fingers tightening on the handle of my bat, desperate to get out there myself and score some runs on that perfect surface and maybe launch a six into the muddy waters of the River Tone drifting by beyond the far boundary. One day, I told myself, one day …

I joined a group of tongue-tied boys clustered around the Somerset coach and two sun-burned, weatherbeaten senior pros, Merv Kitchen and Tom Cartwright, who were there to run the rule over us. I did well enough at that first practice session but the fact that Somerset continued to show interest in me over the next couple of years was largely due to Tom Cartwright. He had been an excellent all-rounder with Warwickshire, Somerset and England over the years, and I think in many ways he saw me as a younger version of himself. Although he was now well into the veteran stage, he was still a very skilful bowler, and for a medium pacer, which is all he was, he was quite exceptional, with great control and nagging accuracy but also variety and a very subtle change of pace.

After watching me that first time in the nets at Somerset, he called me over and had a chat with me. I was known primarily for my batting then, but he saw how desperate I was to become an all-rounder, and my enthusiasm must have struck a chord, for he said, 'You're a decent bowler. Get out there and bowl.' From then on, with Peter Robinson, the coach at Taunton, he was my mentor. He really helped and encouraged me, taught me the art of swing bowling, and continued to champion me in the face of opposition from some other figures within the county who thought I was no more than average. Tom had seen enough in me to form a different opinion and though he used to hold his head in his hands sometimes as I persisted in bowling bouncer after bouncer rather than following the advice he had given me, he had enough belief in me to keep the faith and not give up.

I was grateful for the coaching and advice that Tom and Peter gave me, but I didn't take it quite so well when I was in a bit of a bad streak with my batting and my father began to offer some unsolicited advice. 'Ian, what you should be doing...' was as far as he got before I interrupted him. 'Listen, Dad,' I said, 'I don't come down to Westland and tell you how to do your job...'

I'd left school at the legal minimum age – I think both sides realised that there was no point in prolonging the agony any further

– and I didn't even look back as I walked out of the gates for the last time. School was over; it was time to start making my way in the world, and the only world I was interested in was that of professional cricket. I received a huge boost not long afterwards when, at Tom Cartwright's instigation, Somerset recommended me to Len Muncer, the chief coach of the Lord's ground staff, the traditional apprenticeship to a career in the professional game. My first visit to Lord's took place at the end of August 1971. Dad was busy at work and couldn't come with me, so I travelled up with Mum for the trial. We got off the train at Waterloo and took a cab, at huge expense, to Lord's. Walking into 'the cathedral of cricket' for the first time should have been an unforgettable moment, but I was so hyped up and focused on the trial for the ground staff that neither Lord's nor even London really registered on me. It was only on my second visit that I really began to take notice of my surroundings.

My mum sat in the rose garden behind the pavilion while I went off to try and prove what I could do. I was fifteen and the youngest boy there, and though I bowled and batted pretty well, I was up against boys who were all a good bit older than me, and I was more than a little startled when Len Muncer took me to one side and told me, 'We want you to start on Saturday.'

I didn't have any stuff with me other than my cricket gear and the clothes I'd come up in, so I arranged to go home to get my things and then come back on my own on the Monday, providing that I'd managed to overcome my parents' reservations. Even though Mum bought me dinner on the train going home to celebrate and Dad had pointed me towards cricket rather than football as a career, my parents still harboured serious reservations. They worried about what sort of life I would have if I failed to make the grade and ended up as an unemployed seventeen- or eighteen-year-old cricketer with not a single qualification to my name. It took a conversation with Roy Kerslake, a member of Somerset's cricket committee, to finally convince my dad.

Roy told him that boys who didn't make it as county cricketers often used their Lord's ground staff experience to get jobs as cricket coaches at the independent and public schools, and that was enough to persuade my parents to let me take my chances as a cricketer. Throughout my entire life until that point, they had given me unflagging encouragement, support and sound advice. Without them I would never have been able to set foot on my chosen path, but now I had to travel it alone. I had been given my chance and it was up to me to take it.

There were only three weeks of the season left by the time I got back to Lord's but it was enough time to demonstrate to myself and to Len Muncer that I was good enough to shine even in this relatively exalted company and I was at once invited back for the following summer, 1972.

My time at Lord's, brief as it was, had also opened my eyes to the wider world beyond Somerset. When I first arrived I was the original country bumpkin, young and totally naive about life in a big city that never slept. In Yeovil the town centre was deserted five minutes after the pubs shut; London's West End seemed as busy at four in the morning as it was at four in the afternoon. The older ground staff also introduced me to the dubious delights of Soho, including my first ever visit to a strip club. I stood there transfixed; such was my naiveté, I hadn't even known there were such things. Once more, I had much to learn...

The gulf between the haves and have-nots was also eye-opening for me – the rich men with their expensive suits, beautiful companions and chauffeur-driven limousines, and the down-and-outs sleeping in shop doorways or under bridges. Even that short spell in London was enough to convince me that I wanted to be one of life's successes, not one of its casualties, and professional cricket would be my means to achieve it, but first I had to get through the winter.

I returned to Somerset – life was cheaper there – and went to the local labour exchange to look for work to tide me over. I wasn't proud, I'd do anything that paid a few quid, and I was never out of work the whole winter. I enjoyed physical work and I threw myself into it with the same energy I showed on the cricket field. As a result, working as a plasterer's mate and keeping two plasterers supplied at once, I earned more in five days during some weeks than I did in a whole season of playing cricket. It not only put some money in my pocket, it also made me appreciate the cricket season all the more when it came, and made me even more determined that there was going to be more to my life than mixing plaster. My new mates couldn't understand why I was going back to cricket when I was making such good money working with them, but I said, 'Look, lads, you've got to see the bigger picture here. This'll have long-term benefits; one day it'll pay off.'

When I arrived back at Lord's full-time the following spring, I had to readjust to earning a lot less money while paying out a lot more in rent and other expenses – at that age, mostly beer. As a ground staff member I was paid just £12 a week. Out of that I had to pay for my accommodation, and St John's Wood certainly wasn't the cheapest place to be looking for digs. I finished up paying five guineas a week – the fact that the rent was in guineas says a lot – for a half share of a dingy, damp and decrepit basement. By the time I'd paid for food and laundry, not that there was much of either, there was very little left. We were paid on Thursday and by Sunday we were all skint.

My reappearance at Lord's had been greeted by the kind of ritual that goes with the turf in professional sport: the initiation ceremony. The older boys marched into the junior dressing room, pounced on the newcomers, pinned them down, de-bagged them and gave the 'meat and two veg' a generous coating of whitewash – not over-sophisticated perhaps, but the strength of the resistance you offered dictated your future status. Although still only sixteen, I was a powerful lad and it took about half a dozen of them to hold me down and get the job done. When the initiation was over, I was in with the in crowd...

My best mate on the ground staff was Rodney Ontong, who had come to Lord's from South Africa and later went on to play for Glamorgan. In its different way, his home town of East London was as much of a sleepy country town as Yeovil, and as two country boys, we immediately struck up a friendship. We also had the same confidence and ebullience and approached cricket in the same fashion: play it hard on the pitch, and then play even harder afterwards. Every time I went home to Yeovil I came back with as many plastic containers of scrumpy – rough cider – as I could carry, and we blended it with Onty's South African brandy. It was frighteningly cheap and a very acquired taste, but it provided more bangs per buck than more sophisticated and expensive drinks, and as impoverished ground staff boys, value for money was all-important.

There were also a lot of practical jokes like setting fire to the back of newspapers as people were reading them, or putting bits of fruit or a festering prawn in the corner of someone's cricket bag or one of the fingers of their gloves just before they went out to bat. I carried on playing such pranks throughout my career; I derived enormous pleasure from them, though I'm not sure if my colleagues always found them quite as amusing.

Sometimes the pranks went too far, particularly on one wet, miserable day when I decided to perk up the dressing room and picked up a glass jug of water to give one of the juniors, a lad called Anwar Muhammad, first use of the showers. As I threw the water over him, the jug came away with it, leaving me holding a broken handle. The broken jug hit him and cut his hand so badly that he nearly lost a finger, and my wrist was bleeding so much that I was afraid that I'd never play cricket again. There was blood everywhere and an ambulance was called but luckily neither of us was seriously injured.

There was more broken glass when Onty and I staged one of our impromptu games of football in the hallway of our digs. The land-lady was dour and humourless, with an expression set in permafrost, and failed to see the funny side when Onty let fly with a screaming shot that beat my despairing dive and went straight through the window and into the road. We were well behind with the rent and had already received several final warnings; this time we were turfed out without further ado.

Luckily, we scrounged some floor space at some friends' place for a couple of weeks, and when we'd outstayed our welcome there, we slept at Lord's, something a few of the gentlemen in 'egg and bacon' ties have also done over the years. Security was poor to non-existent in those innocent days, so every night we sneaked in after dark and got what passed for a night's sleep curled up in one of the baths in the junior changing rooms.

Although Onty committed his fair share of crimes and misdemeanours, he made sure that he stayed on the right side of the coaches, Len Muncer and his assistant Harry Sharp, whereas I struggled with Len, who was a military type, with razor-sharp creases in his flannels and immaculately whitened boots. Apart from my occasional bad behaviour, most of the friction between us arose because he'd made up his mind almost from the start that I couldn't bowl. Somerset had recommended me as an all-rounder, but Len didn't see it that way and had me down as a batsman, pure and simple.

He didn't much like me, thinking I was much too full of myself, and who knows, he may even have been right. Our relationship deteriorated even further after I broke one of the unwritten rules by which he set great store. It was the practice to give your wicket away as soon as you had reached 50, in a suitably subtle fashion – it didn't do us any harm and it was a nice boost for the bowler's ego. However, I'd been having a bad run of form with the bat and when we played the City of London School I failed to follow the normal tradition and, having reached 50, instead of giving my wicket away, I proceeded to fill my boots and make a century. I left the field in a stony silence and was then taken to one side by Len and given a savage tongue-lashing.

Fortunately, Len's assistant, Harry Sharp, nicknamed 'The Admiral' on the predictable grounds that he had been an able seaman during the war, didn't share Len's assessment of my character or my talent and gave me a lot of encouragement. He took up his position behind the nets while I was batting, and kept up a running commentary between puffs on the cigarette that was always dangling from his bottom lip: 'Bloody awful shot that one, Botham ... but if you keep hitting it, son, you keep on playing it.'

Despite my aversion to nets, most of my bowling had to be done there, not only for practice but also because it was the place to escape from some of the more tedious tasks that were part of the job of the ground staff, including cleaning out the dressing rooms. However, my feud with Len meant that I also lost out on one of the perks. Every weekend, MCC teams played matches all over the country, and players would often pull out at fairly short notice. When that happened, a member of the Lord's ground staff would deputise, getting not only a game of cricket, but his expenses, a free lunch and tea and often a few drinks as well. From one match we could not only eat like kings but, by claiming the train fare and then hitchhiking to the ground, we could also double our £12 wages for the week.

Unfortunately, because I'd locked horns with Len, I was very rarely picked for these trips, though at least I did manage to eat at the games the ground staff team – known as 'The Nippers' – played against London schools and cricket clubs. During the tea interval we put away more food than was humanly possible and for good measure we also stuffed any leftovers into our bags for later consumption. A forgotten, festering pork pie or green-tinged chicken drumstick would sometimes turn up in a dark corner of my cricket bag a couple of weeks later. The matches were taken fairly seriously, but everyone also understood that as the evening shadows began to lengthen the aim was to get the game over and hit the bar as quickly as possible. For our home matches we had the invaluable assistance of an umpire called John Collins. Even with his back to the pavilion, John could tell when the towels were coming off the beer pumps and from then on any appeal, no matter how optimistic, was likely to be greeted with a broad smile and an upraised finger. 'And that's your lot,' he'd say happily as the last dumbfounded batsman was sent packing and John would then lead the charge for the bar, revealing a turn of speed that would have done credit to a man half his years.

Over the course of that summer, Somerset called me back a number of times to involve me with the second team. The club didn't have a lot of money in those days and if they had injuries they were scratching around for players, so when one of the Somerset committee mentioned to the captain, Brian Close, that there was a Somerset youngster on the Lord's ground staff, Brian said, 'Well, let's have a look at him, then.'

A report from Lord's on my progress arrived ahead of me and I was lucky that Brian preferred to form his own judgement, otherwise my promising career might have been still-born because the report, signed by my nemesis, Len Muncer, stated unequivocally 'Ian Botham will never make a first-class cricketer'. Brian and a few other people at Somerset disagreed with that opinion, and although I was due to return to Lord's for the whole of the summer of 1973, in the event I spent hardly any time there at all because during that season I became a regular in the Somerset second team.

When not playing I made myself useful around the Taunton ground, fetching and carrying and bowling in the nets, and it was on one of these occasions that I first met John Arlott. Somerset were playing a home game and the great cricket writer and broadcaster had arrived to commentate for BBC radio. As I was passing the back of the pavilion, the Somerset secretary, Jimmie James, called me over, pointed to a large wicker basket and said, 'Ian, I'd like you to take Mr Arlott's luncheon basket up to the commentary box for him.'

When I picked it up, I found it was a hell of a weight – the clinking and chinking of bottles coming from inside it as I carried it across the ground suggested the reason for that. To get to the commentary box in those days, you had to climb a rickety set of stairs – though 'ladder' would be a more accurate description – and then cross a narrow gantry perched on top of the stand. I struggled up there with my burden and John followed. I helped him unpack his lunch, including cheeses, cold meats, two kinds of bread and four bottles of Beaujolais. It was only ten-thirty in the morning but he got busy with the corkscrew straight away and said, 'Sit down and have a glass of wine with me.'

'Thank you, Mr Arlott,' I said, 'but I don't really know much about wine.'

'Well,' he said, 'the first thing you need to know is that you call me "John", not "Mr Arlott", and second, if you're interested, I'll tell you a little bit about wine. Now this is Beaujolais…'

I had a glass of wine with him and listened fascinated as he talked about it with the same enthusiasm, insight and authority with which he talked about cricket. I then reluctantly had to go off and bowl in the nets and do my jobs, but at the close of play I went back up and carried the basket – now considerably lighter since the bottles were empty – back down for him. It was the start of a friendship between us that continued throughout the rest of John's life, and it was also the beginning for me of a lifelong love of good wines.

Towards the end of that season, I made my first appearances with the first team squad, first as twelfth man before being blooded in a couple of Sunday League matches. It was largely thanks to Tom Cartwright's powers of persuasion that Somerset gave me a chance in those games. My match fees were very modest but the mileage rates were better, especially as I hitchhiked to both games. In the first of them, a televised game against Sussex at Hove, I was pretty unsuccessful with bat and ball. When we batted I found myself going in for my first ever innings for Somerset with the score on 39 for five, and didn't improve matters much. I did at least manage to get off the mark but was then out lbw to Mike Buss for 2. When we fielded, I bowled three indifferent overs for 22 runs and no wickets, but then pouched a skier in the deep to dismiss Tony Greig off Brian Close's bowling, and I think it was that, as much as anything else, that convinced one or two sceptics at the club that I might have the temperament to make a professional cricketer. We lost that game by six wickets and in the next, the last of the season, against Surrey, I was again out for 2, caught and bowled by Intikhab Alam, but took my first wicket, one for 14 in four overs, though we again went down to a 68-run defeat. Played two, lost two; batting average 2.00, bowling average 36.00, was not quite the start I'd envisaged, but I was offered a one-year contract for the 1974 season, guaranteeing me the princely sum of £250 for the next five-month season. I was joining an elite group: Somerset only had about fourteen full-time pros back then; everyone else was drafted in as required and paid a match fee plus expenses.

Quite a few of my mates at Lord's also went on to county cricket careers. In those days being a member of the ground staff was a recognised step on the way to the professional game and counties often sent registered players there to further their cricketing education. These days the counties sign them younger and keep them to themselves, perhaps fearing that someone else may poach them, and I don't often hear of players now who've made that jump from the Lord's ground staff to professional cricket.

I was never going to play for any other county than Somerset. It was where I had lived for years and played all my cricket and in any case, county cricket operated under a completely different system then. There were virtually no scouts scrutinising junior teams and passing on recommendations that would today lead to large payments for boys to sign up before they'd even hit their teens. Back then, there was no queue of cheque-waving agents and managers, and I and most other young cricketers felt a definite loyalty towards the county that had nurtured us.

Young players at Somerset were being introduced into the senior side gradually, so it was never a case of being a club cricketer one day and a full-time professional the next. There was a definite pecking order and the junior players had to know their place. It amazed me in later years to watch fresh-faced seventeen-year-olds march in on the first day and demand: 'Where's my sponsored car?' In those days you did as you were told and – on cricketing matters at least – you kept your mouth shut unless asked for your opinion, and you wouldn't be holding your breath waiting for that to happen. Anyone who breached this unwritten rule would usually find one of the senior players shaking him warmly by the throat while telling him a few home truths.

I clearly had learned something from my time at Lord's and my confrontations with Len Muncer, because when I broke into the Somerset first team, I decided to act like a dumb country yokel, though some of my schoolfriends would have said that I didn't need too much preparation to get into character. I reckoned that if I was seen as a thick hick from the sticks, I'd be no threat to anyone, and I'd be able to get on with working on my game without attracting too much unwelcome attention. It seemed to work and because the rest of the team thought I didn't have a brain cell in my head, there was also never any danger of me being drawn into Somerset 'office politics', which could be as complicated and poisonous – though rather less affluent – than a medieval court. While everyone else was deep in discussion and argument, I could just concentrate on playing cricket and having a beer or two afterwards, though I had already decided my objectives. My first aim was to break into the county side and stay there. Next, I wanted my county cap, and then, even at that stage, I was looking towards claiming an England Test place.

However, before any of that, I had to find somewhere to live. My first digs were in Greenway Road, Taunton, sharing with another Somerset new boy, Dennis Breakwell, a slow left-arm bowler who had just joined us from Northamptonshire. It was called a 'club flat', but that was overstating it a little. It was close to the county ground, but that was its only good point; it was so damp and dingy that you could have grown mushrooms on the carpets. The electricity and water had been cut off the previous summer, and supplies had never been restored, though it did have a functioning outside tap. We also had the luxury of a toilet, also situated outside, and since there was no running water to that either, it could only be flushed with a bucket of water.

There was an open fireplace in the living room, but we had no money for coal or logs, so our only source of heat was burning rolled-up newspapers and bits of scrap wood salvaged from skips. There were no cooking facilities at all, so we had to eat out or raid the milk float that woke us every morning as it rattled down the street. We dreaded returning to our digs at the end of the day, and postponed the awful moment as long as possible, first by staying in the pub till closing time – the heat and light were as much of an attraction as the beer – and then going on to a club. By the time we got back, we were so tired and/or drunk that we fell asleep in our sleeping bags on the floor without even noticing our dismal surroundings.

Fortunately by the start of the 1974 season our situation improved somewhat. My salary had been doubled – to the vast sum of £500 per annum – and Dennis and I found a slightly more comfortable and salubrious flat, in St James Street, right next to the county ground. We also had a new flatmate to share it. I'd been picked for Somerset Under-25s in a one-day game against Glamorgan at the Lansdowne Cricket Club in Bath, and another highly rated young player was also appearing that day. Len Creed, a bookmaker in Bath who was a keen Somerset supporter, had been holidaying in Antigua when he heard about a young cricketing prodigy and went to take a look. What he saw impressed him so much that he used his own money to pay for the young man – Isaac Vivian Alexander Richards – to come over to England. Len then got on the phone and persuaded Somerset to take a look at him. I'd heard stories about this hugely talented young West Indian, who had been playing as a pro in the Bath League that summer and scoring a shedful of runs, and he'd also heard about me, but because I was playing my cricket in Taunton and he was in Bath, we'd never met, nor even seen each other in action until the day of the game against Glamorgan.

He strolled in, looking nonchalant, dumped his cricket bag in a corner of the dressing room and glanced around.

'I'm Ian,' I said. 'You must be Viv. I've heard a lot about you.'

He smiled. 'I've heard a lot about you too.'

We sat talking as we waited for our turn to bat and the friendship that formed that day has endured and grown ever since. Our performances during the game were a total role-reversal. Viv, the new superstar batsman, went in at first wicket down and one ball later was on his way back to the pavilion, clean bowled for a golden duck. I came in at number five and promptly scored a century, but when Glamorgan batted, I failed to take a wicket and was hit to every corner of the ground. Viv then turned his arm over and took five for 25 with his occasional off-spin. As we strolled off the field at the end of the day, I said, 'Listen, Viv, from now on, you take the wickets and I'll score the runs.'

Our careers proceeded in parallel from then on and we were soul buddies from that first meeting onwards. I think we recognised in each other the same self-belief and relentless will to succeed. Viv had the best eye of any cricketer I've ever seen and he made full use of his immense talent. He felt that any moment of a match when he was not batting was wasted, which probably came from his childhood in Antigua, when so many hundreds of kids were always awaiting their turn to bat in the daily cricket game on the beach. If you got out, it might be days before you got another chance.

I admired his obsessive drive to perfect his skills but, although I was also single-minded about succeeding, I didn't take things to quite the same extremes. He actually slept with his bat next to his bed, though not necessarily so that he could practise his strokes. We lived in a fairly dodgy area at the time and when my mum paid a visit to our flat, she found Viv huddled up in bed, wearing several layers of woollies to ward off the English cold, and clutching his bat. 'What are you doing with that?' she said. Viv shrugged. 'Anyone tries to break in, Mrs B, they'll have to get past me first.'

Our shared flat was pretty basic and had no washing machine, so at the end of each week we piled all our dirty washing into the back of the car, drove over to Yeovil and called on Mum. She always greeted us with a hug and a world-weary smile and said, 'Nice to see you boys. All right, you can bring it in now.' Having dumped the lot on my long-suffering mother, we'd set off for the Gardener's Arms. When Viv bought a really nice flat near the ground in Taunton, over-looking Roy Marshall's pub – almost too handy – I moved in with him. I then rented a place of my own, but when Viv sold his flat, he came and lived in mine while he was waiting to complete on the house he was buying.

Chapter 2

EVERYBODY'S HERO

I made my County Championship debut against Lancashire at Taunton on the opening day of the 1974 season, and once more it was not a particularly auspicious start. The wicket was damp and the skies overcast, and I was out for 13, steering a short-pitched delivery into David Lloyd's huge hands. When we took the field, conditions had improved and I was entrusted with only three overs, taking none for 15, as the Lancashire openers, Barry Wood and David Lloyd, put on 265 for the first wicket. Lancashire had the better of the game but it ended in a rain-affected draw. I doubled my highest score to 26 in the next game against Sussex, but still didn't take a wicket, and finally broke my duck in our third game against Gloucestershire, though match figures of one for 91 and innings of 2 and 1 scarcely suggested a star in the making. I hadn't done myself justice and, though bitterly disappointed, I was not surprised when Brian Close told me that I would be returning to the second team to continue my cricketing education. My only consolation was that he made it clear that it was only a temporary exile, and it only increased my determination to make it count the next time I was picked for the first team.

I sat out the next two county games and I was only picked for Somerset's Benson & Hedges quarter-final against Hampshire in

June 1974 when our first choice, fast bowler Allan Jones, was ruled out with a leg strain. The call to join the first team came just a few hours before the game. I packed my kit and hurried to the Taunton ground. The dressing room in those days had a concrete floor, reached by a narrow, precipitous flight of steps. The green floor paint was so chipped and scarred by players' spikes that it was down to the bare concrete everywhere except under the benches. A doorway led to another room with some less-than-fragrant urinals along one wall and a communal plunge bath against the opposite wall. Beyond that was a little physio's room with a couple of couches that were used far more often for sleeping than for treatment; Somerset didn't even have a physio in those days. On hot days Merv Kitchen's mountainous dog, Thumper, which went everywhere with him, would lie panting on the cold concrete floor between the dressing room and the bathroom, an immovable obstacle that you somehow had to negotiate if you wanted to use the loos or have a kip in the physio's room.

It was a perfect summer's day, scorching hot, with the sun glinting from the gilded weather vane on top of the church spire and hardly a breeze stirring the trees in the churchyard. There was a tremendous atmosphere and a capacity crowd, the biggest I had ever seen, let alone played before, with the gates closed long before Brian Close won the toss and put Hampshire in. They made a solid start until I bowled their finest batsman, the South African Test star Barry Richards. Our wicketkeeper Derek Taylor was standing up to the stumps – practically an insult to someone who considered himself a fast bowler – and Richards stayed at the crease for a few moments, unable to believe that the ball that had bowled him had done enough to hit the stumps without rebounding from Derek's pads. I took another wicket without addition to the score, and with Graeme Burgess chipping in with a couple more for no runs, Hampshire had collapsed from 22 for none to 22 for four. They recovered well to 182, thanks mainly to Trevor Jesty's 82, but I was reasonably pleased with my bowling and fielding. That was just as well, because I'd been picked as a bowler and was well down the batting order, at number nine. By the time I walked out to the wicket, windmilling my arms to loosen up and taking some deep breaths to calm my nerves, the game was as good as lost. We were 113 for seven, needing 70 runs from the last fifteen overs, and with only three wickets to take, Hampshire were long odds-on to go through to the semi-final.

The last of our recognised batsmen, my unofficial mentor and bowling coach Tom Cartwright, was at the crease and he walked over to me as I came out to the middle. 'All right young 'un?'

I nodded.

'Don't try to knock the cover off it straight away. Play yourself in, we've still got a few overs in hand.'

Unfortunately Tom immediately departed, caught at mid-on for a duck, and was replaced by Hallam Moseley, a definite tailender. I farmed the strike as much as I could and with an odd boundary and a few nudged ones and twos from me and a few lusty blows and flying edges from Hallam we had whittled the target down to 38 runs by the time the lightning-quick West Indian fast bowler Andy Roberts returned to the attack. I hadn't played against him or even set eyes on him before that day but I was well aware of his fearsome reputation. He had been terrorising English batsmen all season and had put several of them in hospital with broken arms and broken jaws.

He'd removed a couple of our batsmen in his first spell – I think he scared one of them out as much as got him out – but I had no intention of showing him too much respect. I was well set by now and when he dropped one short, I was on it at once, swivelling to hook it over square leg for six. Roberts stood there, hands on hips, glowering at me – and he had a very penetrating stare, his eyes burning holes right through me – then snatched the ball as it was returned from the boundary and stalked off back to his mark.

We now needed 32 runs. I told myself to put the last ball out of my mind and play the next one on its merits. Tapping my bat lightly,

I settled at the crease and watched Roberts running in again. I saw the ball as it left his hand, the sun glinting slightly on the polished side, the white stitching along the seam a few degrees from the vertical. I didn't see it again until it was about a foot from my face. In those few tenths of a second some part of my brain had recognised that this was another short one and I had rocked on to the back foot, shaping to hook this one too, but there was one crucial difference: this was the fastest ball I had ever faced. Halfway through the shot, I realised I was way too late on the ball. Before I had fully digested that alarming fact, the ball had smacked into my face, and in those far-off days batsmen did not wear protective helmets.

In an instinctive act of self-preservation, I'd thrown up my gloved right hand towards my face and that absorbed some of the impact, but the ball still smashed my hand into my mouth with savage force. I dropped my bat and backed away, cursing and spitting blood, then realised that I was not just spitting blood, but bits of teeth as well. Two teeth had been knocked clean out and another two broken off at the gum line. Even more alarmingly, they were on opposite sides of my mouth, and the ones in between were noticeably looser than they'd been a few moments before. My right eyebrow was also cut where the ball had ricocheted on to it after striking my hand, but that was a minor problem – I didn't even notice that until the next day.

I was staggering around the pitch and so groggy that I almost slumped to the ground. Peter Sainsbury, the Hampshire left-arm spinner, ran up to me and said, 'Are you all right?'

'Fine,' I said, though it was more an instinctive than a considered reply. Meanwhile, as good fast bowlers should, Andy Roberts paused at the end of his follow-through only to give a quiet nod of satisfaction and fix me with another of those meaningful, penetrative stares. Then he turned to pace back to the end of his run-up, ready to deliver the next thunderbolt. As he did so, I spat out the last fragments of tooth, took a few sips from the glass of water that the physio – actually the twelfth man – had brought out, and then let him assess the damage. Believing that the game was now lost, he and some of the crowd wanted me to retire hurt to avoid further punishment, but doing that had never entered my mind.

The doctor who examined me after the game told me that I had suffered mild concussion from the blow, which might explain the curious sense of detachment I felt as I brushed off the twelfth man's restraining arm, picked up my bat and walked back to the crease. The umpire held out his arm for an unduly long time, partly to ensure the twelfth man had left the field before play resumed, but partly also, perhaps, to give me time to change my mind before unleashing Andy Roberts once more.

I declined the opportunity. I felt no pain from my teeth then – perhaps I was still in shock and certainly the adrenalin was pumping – and I was strangely calm and relaxed as I watched Roberts moving in, accelerating smoothly as he approached the wicket, the arm whipping over and the ball arrowing towards me. This one was a very full length, noticeably slower than the previous delivery, but still fast enough and with a little late inswing to help it spear in towards my toes. But I had already gambled that he would follow such a vicious short-pitched delivery with a yorker, and I managed to get enough bat on it to clip it away for three runs through mid-wicket. Normally I blanked out the crowd and was only dimly aware of the noise they were making, but this time there was no mistaking the roar that went up as I began to run.

I really must have been mildly concussed because while I was running the three runs, I had a curious floating sensation, as if I was hovering a few inches above the ground. As I stood at the non-striker's end, I muttered to myself, 'Come on, you've got to snap out of this.' We now needed 29. I kept farming the strike as much as possible and we had put on another 22 runs – I hit another six and even whacked Andy Roberts for a couple more fours – making our partnership worth 63 from thirteen overs, when Hallam missed one ball too many and was out for 24. There were now just 7 runs needed to win from sixteen balls but our last man, number eleven Bob Clapp, was walking to the wicket, a sight that usually had bowlers and fielders licking their lips in anticipation, and the bartenders taking the towels off the beer pumps. Bob was a very useful bowler and no slouch in the field, but his career batting average was in the low single figures – to misquote a famous football manager, he was often lucky to get none – but on this occasion he did all that was required, blocking, leaving or playing and missing without losing his wicket, while I kept sneaking singles and then a three in which Bob had to dive full-length to make his ground and avoid being run out. He later told me that he reckoned he'd been run out by a good twelve inches. Had there been a third umpire using slow-motion replays in those days, the game would have been over there and then, but luckily the umpire at the bowler's end had to use his own judgement and he gave him not out.

Those watching must have found the tension almost unbearable, but my concentration was now so total that I was no longer aware of their existence, though my nerves must still have been jangling for, having brought us to within two runs of victory, I then played and missed three times in a row against Herman before connecting with a flowing drive to a half-volley outside off-stump. As I saw it speeding away, beating the despairing dive of the cover fielder and smacking into the boundary boards, I raised my bat over my head and heard the loudest roar I had ever heard. I'd scored 45 out of the 70 we'd made with the last two wickets to win the game. Bob Clapp was nought not out, and if he never played another innings in his life, he had fully earned his winning bonus with that one. We ran from the field together as the crowd poured across the boundary ropes, forming a backslapping gauntlet that we had to pass through to reach the safety of the pavilion.

I was on the biggest high of my life so far; we'd won the game and I collected the Gold Award for player of the match, though perhaps I should have shared it with Andy Roberts. If he hadn't smashed my teeth, we might never have won. I needed some emergency dentistry, but that could wait for now. The broken teeth were not yet sending out pain signals so I showered and changed, then went straight to the Stragglers' Bar to join in the celebrations. People I'd never seen before were wringing my hand, slapping me on the back and offering to buy me drinks, but I took most pleasure and satisfaction from the quiet nod of approval I got from the Somerset captain, Brian Close, as he caught my eye across the bar. He then followed it up with some no-nonsense cricketing advice. 'Know why you got hit?' he said, immediately answering his own question. 'Because you took your eyes off the ball. Your head can move faster than any other part of the body, so providing you actually know where the bloody ball is, you can always get your head out of the way.'

As I was pouring my first pint over my smashed teeth and swollen gums, two old Somerset professionals, Bill Alley and Kenny Palmer, called me over and gave me some more fatherly advice. 'Today, you're everybody's hero,' they said. 'Just remember that tomorrow they'll have forgotten you again.'

I thanked them for their wise words, though in truth I didn't want anyone raining on my parade that night, but in time I came to appreciate how right they were; as the old saying goes, today's headlines are tomorrow's fish and chip wrappers. Those headlines also gave me a small problem when I strolled into my local, the Gardener's Arms, later that evening. Expecting at the least a pint on the house and a bit of mild hero-worship, I got a cold shoulder instead. 'The usual, please,' I said as I approached the bar.

I would have had a warmer welcome from an iceberg. 'And just what is your usual?' the landlord said.

'You know what it is,' I said. 'The same as it's been for the last year and a half.'

He gave me another frosty glance, then picked up the evening paper and dropped it on the bar in front of me. The headline read:

17-YEAR-OLD SOMERSET YOUTH PLAYS A BLINDER. Then, as now, the legal drinking age in Britain was eighteen. There was a beat of silence, then he winked and said, 'Must be a misprint. The usual then?' and pulled me a pint. In fact it *was* a misprint. I'd been eighteen since the previous November ... though I'd also been a regular at the Gardener's for rather longer than that.

When the pub closed, Dennis Breakwell, Viv Richards and I went on to a club and were drinking till two in the morning. When I woke up the next morning I was in agony and for once it wasn't the hangover to blame. My jaw and the lower half of my face were a mass of bruises and the inside of my mouth looked like an out-take from *The Texas Chainsaw Massacre*. I went straight to a dentist and he patched up the hole where one tooth used to be and put temporary crowns on the broken ones, and gave me some powerful painkillers.

My next call was at a newsagent to pick up the papers. The sports pages were full of my exploits, swelling my head even further. BRAVE IAN'S GOLDEN DAY, BOTHAMS UP, YOUNG BOTHAM THE SOMERSET HERO, and so on. I read them all several times before reluctantly handing them over to my mum for the scrapbook she had already started to house my cuttings. To swell my head even further, I received a case of champagne from a Somerset supporter living in Devon, with a note reading 'In appreciation of your great "recovery innings" today, the best I've seen since I started watching cricket in 1912'.

My mum soon had to buy another scrapbook because that narrow, impossibly dramatic victory had catapulted me into the public eye and given my fledgling career an enormous boost. From a nobody, I was now an overnight sensation. The *Sun* included me in a feature on "Young England hopefuls" and whenever and wherever I played for the next few weeks, crowds were turning up to take a look at this new prodigy. I could sense and hear a definite buzz when I next went out to bat – but had that been my only moment of fame, I would have faded from public view as quickly as I appeared. I had now set a standard for myself and every time I took the field I would be expected to live up to it. I was still only a novice, feeling my way in professional cricket, but everyone – spectators, reporters and commentators, as well as opponents – was now aware of me and what I could do. I had to live up to the billing. Had I been left entirely to my own devices, my swell-headedness could easily have been my downfall, and I was lucky that two men in particular, Tom Cartwright and Brian Close, had the time and the patience to coach, cajole and encourage me through this crucial period in my career.

The Somerset captain, Brian Close, deserved the major share of the credit for turning the county from a non-achieving side into a successful one. Somerset had always been the ultimate "social" team – the county hadn't won anything in its entire 104-year history – but the arrival of Brian signalled that there would be a very different attitude from then on. A granite-hard Yorkshireman, he was still playing professional cricket at an age when virtually all his peers had long since retired to tend their roses. Even in his forties, he was still a very good player and unequalled as a captain: a fearsome disciplinarian, a brilliant tactician and leader. He was the most fearless and ferocious competitor in the game, and respected, even revered, in the Somerset dressing room.

When he was just eighteen years old, Brian did the 'Double' of one thousand runs and one hundred wickets in a season and played his first matches for England. If his record in Test matches since then had not been the record-breaking one that many had predicted – and his unwillingness to suffer fools in silence cost him many caps – no one could ever doubt his talent, nor his dedication and will to win. His professional career spanned four decades and his approach to the game never wavered in all that time. He had an absolute confidence in his own ability and an unshakeable belief that if you weren't prepared to do anything and everything necessary to win, then it would be better if you didn't turn up to play at all.

Nothing infuriated him more than people who, no matter how

talented they might be, lacked the guts, the 'ticker', to tough it out when things weren't going well. During a one-day game against Nottinghamshire at Trent Bridge he actually sent off one of his own bowlers, Allan Jones, because Brian was incandescent about what he perceived to be Jones's lack of heart and appetite for the task. To the great amusement of the Somerset players, he then had to call Allan back again as he was making his way to the pavilion, when Mervyn Kitchen said, 'Hang on Closey, he's still got four overs to bowl and he's the only bowler we've got left.'

Brian was not afraid of anything or anyone. Picked to face the West Indies in the 1963 Test series, he enjoyed his finest moment in the second Test at Lord's. No one who was there or who watched it on television will ever forget the courage he showed against a brutal bowling assault by Wes Hall and Charlie Griffith. He came out to bat as Colin Cowdrey was being helped off after having his arm broken by a short-pitched ball. The light was poor, the pitch was green and the ball was rearing from just short of a length but Closey defied Hall and Griffith for almost four hours and took England to the brink of what would have been an incredible victory. Jaws chewing rhythmically on a wad of gum, his bald head unprotected by any helmet and with no padding of any sort to shield his ribs, he took every blow to his body – and there were plenty – without complaint, not even deigning to rub the affected areas, lest this gesture give the slightest heart to the bowlers.

Even more extraordinary, he advanced down the wicket towards them, giving himself even less time to see and play the ball, but showing his complete disdain for anything that they could bowl – or throw – at him. He was eighth out, bottom-edging a catch to the wicketkeeper as he advanced once more down the pitch, with England just 15 short of victory. After the ninth wicket fell 9 runs later, Cowdrey had to show his own courage by coming out again, ready to bat one-armed to see out the final over, though in the event he did not have to face a ball as the match ended in a draw with England still 6 runs short of victory. Closey had scored 70 – his highest Test score – but it was an innings that ranked alongside any double or triple century that any England batsmen had ever scored, and for sheer heart and guts, the greatest that has ever been played.

Close's abrasiveness, however, later cost him the England captaincy. With the series already lost three-nil, Brian was called up to add some fighting spirit and Yorkshire grit to the dispirited England team in the final Test against the West Indies in 1966. He did just that and led them to victory by an innings. He then captained England to series victories over India and then Pakistan the following summer, but after his Yorkshire side used time-wasting tactics to guarantee a draw against Warwickshire, he was booed off the field. The MCC, never known for their fondness for uncouth Yorkshiremen at the best of times, used it as the pretext to strip him of the captaincy. His record of six wins and one draw from the seven Tests in which he led England remains unequalled.

Nine years later, aged forty-five, after seeing the England team battered, bruised and beaten by the West Indies' fearsome pace attack, the selectors turned to Close once more. Rather than telling them what they could do with their invitation, Brian accepted without hesitation, his unconquerable self-belief convincing him that even at his age, he still had the technique, the reaction speed and above all the heart to slug it out toe to toe against the short-pitched barrage from the new generation of West Indies pacemen.

Dismissed cheaply in the first innings at Old Trafford, Closey walked out to open the batting in the second innings facing an impossible victory target of 552 on a pitch that was helping the seamers and in murky, overcast conditions. Although he scored only 20, he defied Michael Holding, Wayne Daniel and my own nemesis, Andy Roberts, for more than two and a half hours. As their frustration grew, they bowled faster and faster, and shorter and shorter, and

Brian took a battering. Even the West Indies captain, Clive Lloyd, later conceded that his bowlers had lost the plot and gone well beyond what was acceptable.

Brian didn't care. He wore his bruises from that day as badges of honour and if his insistence that, though Muhammad Ali might shade a verdict against him over fifteen rounds, he would be damned if the champ would knock him out, was a standing joke in the Somerset dressing room, none of us doubted that he meant it, and few would have bet against him proving it.

Plenty of people can talk the talk but then you don't see them for dust when the going gets hard. Closey not only said it, he did it as well, and he was absolutely fearless on the field of play. Anyone who saw it won't soon forget the occasion when he was hit on the head with a full-blooded hook shot while fielding at short-leg, a blow that would have poleaxed most mortals. Brian's only reaction, as the ball cannoned into the air, was to shout 'Catch it!' I saw him take another vicious blow at Cardiff, when Alan Jones, the Glamorgan opener, was facing Tom Cartwright. Tom bowled his one and only half-volley of the year, on leg-stump, and Jones whipped it off his legs. It hit Brian, once more fielding at short-leg, a yard and a half away, full on the shin. I was standing at slip and said to the wicketkeeper, Derek Taylor, 'Christ, that's got to hurt.'

Brian didn't even flinch. He didn't rub it, he didn't do anything, he just settled back down in his stance, ready for the next ball. Twenty minutes later, when we went off for lunch, there was blood coming out of the lace holes of Brian's boots. When he pulled up the leg of his flannels, he had a livid bruise and a four-inch gash on his shin. He still didn't say anything, he just had it stitched, put on a clean pair of flannels and socks and led us back out after lunch as if nothing had happened. The regularity with which Closey was hit by the ball when batting or fielding prompted Eric Morecambe to joke that 'you know the cricket season has arrived when you hear the sound of leather on Brian Close'.

Brian's raw courage was also allied to a very shrewd cricketing brain and he was a master of 'kidology'. There was a famous occasion when Gary Sobers came out to bat against England. Closey, fielding as usual at short-leg, waited until Sobers had reached the crease and then called out to the bowler, John Snow, 'Drop one short at him, John. The "cavalier of cricket" won't be able to resist hooking it. If he top-edges it, square leg'll catch it, and if he bottom-edges it, I'll catch it.'

Sobers stared at him in disbelief, then settled at the crease. The first ball was indeed short and the 'cavalier of cricket' did indeed try to hook it, no doubt intending to shut the big mouth of the cocky Englishman at short-leg. Instead, he bottom-edged it and Brian, who as usual had neither flinched, moved, nor taken his eye off the ball, pouched the catch: Sobers, caught Close, bowled Snow, 0.

Starting out with Closey played a vital part in my subsequent success as a cricketer, because he taught me so much about mental attitude … and we had at least one thing in common, because Brian's never, ever been wrong about anything in his life. He was the toughest man I ever played sport with or against, and although at one time or another every single member of the side had their rows with him, he inspired us because he would never give up and he would never ask us to do anything that he wouldn't, couldn't and almost invariably hadn't already done himself. I'm sure that I had Closey's example in the back of my mind in the aftermath of Andy Roberts's dental treatment in that Benson & Hedges quarter-final.

The Somerset side that Close led was developing into a fine one. Tom Cartwright came to the county soon after Brian, and won countless matches for us with his bowling, and we also had fast bowler Allan Jones, a solid run accumulator in Merv Kitchen, and Derek Taylor, a wicketkeeper/batsman who was good enough to have played for England, but was unfortunate enough to have been playing in the same era as Alan Knott and Bob Taylor. Around this core of experienced players Brian was bringing on some very good young players. Apart from myself and Viv, there was Brian Rose, Peter Denning, Vic Marks, Phil Slocombe and Peter Roebuck. Viv also recommended Joel Garner to Somerset and he arrived a couple of years after him. What an athlete he was – he said he was six foot eight but I'm sure it was more like six foot ten – a magnificent bowler, and a very fine fielder as well; unusually for such a big man, he was very agile and had lightning reflexes.

There was a great blend of youth and experience at Somerset, but the man who put it all together and turned Somerset from seaside donkeys into thoroughbreds, and genuine contenders for every trophy, was Brian Close. If you sat Viv Richards and me down and asked us where everything came together for us during our cricket careers, when we first successfully harnessed mental attitude, discipline and application to our natural talent, we would both give you the same answer: at Somerset under Brian Close. I think he saw something special in Viv and me – he knew that we could both play – and so he was willing to look out for us and go the extra mile with us, something that he certainly wouldn't have done for less talented and dedicated players.

His one and only argument with me on the field came a few weeks after the game against Hampshire in the B&H. We fell out not because I had got out to a poor shot – though there was no shortage of those – nor because I'd dropped a catch or bowled like an idiot, but because I'd run someone out without thinking through the consequences if I'd missed the stumps with my throw. We were playing Surrey in the quarter-final of the Gillette Cup and I was bowling to Geoff Howarth, who straight-drove the ball back past me and called his partner for a quick single, but I fielded it with my back to the pitch, spun around, let fly and threw the stumps down.

As it turned out, there had been a communication breakdown between Howarth and his partner and they had both ended at the far end of the pitch together. Instead of hurling the ball at the stumps, I could have strolled up and knocked off the bails, and

Closey gave me a bollocking for, in his view, playing to the crowd. 'For heaven's sake,' he said, 'use your bloody nut. All you needed to do was an underarm throw.'

'But no one called to let me know what was happening,' I said, bristling at the rebuke. 'I had no idea where the batsmen were.'

'But you should have known,' was all he said.

When I calmed down again, I realised that he was absolutely right. That incident taught me to keep cool and think even when the pressure was on, and it was a lesson I never forgot.

Our victory over Surrey put us into the semi-final against Kent. Despite the heroics against Hampshire, I was still young and insecure enough to be uncertain whether I'd even be picked, and I asked Merv Kitchen if he thought I'd make the team. He eyed me up and down for a moment, deadpan, then smiled and said, 'Yeah, I think you might make it, mate.'

It wasn't a success for us, we lost by three wickets, but I won a personal battle with Colin Cowdrey, one of the legends of the game. Closey always told me that, whether batting or bowling, I should never worry about the reputation of an opponent; in his view, great players imposed their will on their opponents, however illustrious they might be. My natural self-confidence and Closey's advice combined to ensure that I approached bowling to Cowdrey with the same attitude I had to a county number eleven: I'm better than you and I'm going to get you out. I did, cheaply.

I became a Somerset first team regular over the rest of that 1974 season, ironically helped by the injuries that kept my mentor Tom Cartwright sidelined for much of the remainder of the year. I didn't set the world on fire with my performances, scoring 400 runs in County Championship games at a modest average of just over 17, but I hit my first half-century – 59 against Middlesex – and took my first five-wicket haul against Leicestershire. I was cementing my place in the Somerset side and slowly building my cricketing reputation, but I was also now a local celebrity and people were beginning to recognise me around the town. I was aware that girls were showing more interest in me and it was certainly mutual. I liked the fame and fortune that went with being a well-known figure and there were only rare moments when the public attention became wearying. I did find it frustrating that we almost never seemed to be able to have a drink or meal in peace. I always tried to oblige anyone who asked for an autograph or wanted a few words – they were, after all, paying my wages – but it used to drive me mad when we'd sit down in a restaurant and people at a neighbouring table would clearly recognise me and stare at me, but not say anything. Then, twenty minutes later, just as our food arrived, they would come over and ask for an autograph or want me to pose for photographs. And I'd be thinking: 'You've been sitting there staring at me for twenty minutes, why the hell couldn't you have come over then?'

The occasional brushes with local 'Jack the lads' who wanted to prove how tough they were by punching the famous Ian Botham were more tedious than alarming. I'd always been brought up to believe that if someone tried to hit you, then you had to hit them back. When I started at school, on my very first day a fight started in the playground and next thing I knew, the school bully was coming straight at me. I was in the first year and he was in the fifth, but I was big for my age and I nailed him, and my 'street cred' around the school went up straight away. If he'd have beaten me, he'd have been kicking my arse around the school for the next six months.

So I wasn't fazed when people tried the same stuff on me as adults, and it seemed that every time I went to a pub – and that was frequently – there would be some local hard case wanting to prove his manhood by having a go at me. Some people can just count to ten and walk away, but I always had difficulty getting past one. After a few pints in Taunton one night, Dennis Breakwell and I were returning home when two yobs appeared out of nowhere and one of them ripped a handful of hair out of my head. I wasn't going to waste time asking why or waiting for him to pull a knife or bottle on me, I just hammered him while Dennis kept his mate occupied, telling him: 'If you want any trouble, pal, you can have it as well.'

However, because I was in the public eye, I soon learned that any incident was going to attract attention and the next day's headlines would always be BOTHAM IN PUB BRAWL, not DRUNKEN YOB ATTACKS BOTHAM, and once the press have attached a label to you, it stays with you wherever you go. The same kind of morons often had a go at Viv and he also had to bear a lot of racist crap as well. He was a tough person anyway, but I think those early experiences hardened him even more. We also looked out for each other. I've straightened out a few cretins who muttered racist epithets behind Viv's back and he was also there for me. One night he was standing at the bar minding his own business when he overheard two blokes talking about 'that Ian Botham' standing at the far end of the bar. One of them bet the other £10 that he wouldn't dare stand on my foot. I was completely unaware of all this and, unusually for me, didn't react when a total stranger trod on my foot and strolled off without even apologising, but when he got back to the other end of the bar to collect his winnings, Viv stepped in front of him. 'Ian seems to be feeling a bit dead tonight. How about dealing with a live person instead?'

Viv, Dennis and I lived the bachelor life to the full that summer of 1974, but on 26 June of that year something happened that was to change all that, for one of us at least. We were playing Leicestershire in the Benson & Hedges semi-final at Grace Road, Leicester, and Brian Close had invited Gerry and Jan Waller and their daughters Kathryn and Lindsay to watch the match. Gerry and Jan were two of Brian's oldest and closest friends; when he was being hounded by the press after being sacked from the England captaincy, he went to earth at their house for a few days.

Gerry and Lindsay got there first, having driven down from their home in Thorne, near Doncaster. The other two had been working and didn't arrive until six o'clock, by which time rain had wiped out the rest of the day's play. Kath hadn't wanted to come at all – she was worn out after a business trip, and had been planning a quiet weekend with her boyfriend – but she agreed to drive her mother down to Leicester and perhaps stay for a drink or two. By the time they arrived, we were all sitting around in the bar. Kath already knew some of the Somerset lads through Brian, but we had never met, although I had certainly noticed her at a match at Weston-super-Mare, when she turned up wearing a striped top, a pair of navy blue hot pants and long white boots. I confided to Peter "Dasher" Denning that she was 'a bit of all right'. She clearly didn't know me from a bar of soap because when I sat down next to her and started chatting, she asked me whether I had seen any of the match before the rain started. 'You could say that,' I said, 'I was playing in it.'

We got on really well, and as Dennis and I were starving and about to head off to the Chinese for something to eat, I asked Kath and Lindsay if they wanted to join us. As we walked out through the main gates, Kath started looking round for her car. 'Funny,' she said. 'I thought I left it just here.' While Dennis and Lindsay went to a pub for a drink, Kath and I began wandering right round the outside of the ground looking for the car. I didn't mind how long that took; I was very happy to be spending time getting to know Kath. That feeling even survived the downpour that began when we were at the farthest point of the ground, soaking us to the skin by the time we got back to the gates, where we found Kath's car twenty yards from where we'd started, hidden from sight by a large van parked next to it.

By the time we said goodbye that night, I'd extracted Kath's address and phone number from her, together with a promise that she'd come to our game at Derby the following Sunday. I knew I had serious competition – she'd told me about her boyfriend, a student at Cambridge University, so we weren't exactly identical types – but I kept up the pressure, constantly ringing her and sending her flowers.

Whenever I had two or three days off, I'd hitchhike from Taunton to Thorne to see her, and I gradually wore her down. A few weeks later Jan, Gerry and Kath all travelled down to Taunton to watch the match and have a meal afterwards with Closey and me. As they set off home the next day, Jan turned to Kath and delivered her verdict: 'What a nice, quiet young man.' Clearly I wasn't the only one who had so much to learn.

Whether as a result of that assessment or not, the Cambridge student was soon off the scene and Kath and I were a serious item. Kath was working as a rep in her father's business selling top-of-the-range drums, drumsticks and cymbals used by some of the biggest names in rock music at the time, like John Bonham of Led Zeppelin and Phil Collins. She travelled the country promoting the equipment and, as our relationship grew, it was astonishing how many times her business trips to places like Sussex, Kent, Nottinghamshire and Warwickshire happened to coincide with Somerset matches against those counties. Never has a young woman read the County Championship fixture list with such interest and enthusiasm...

In September 1974, just three months after we met, I proposed. Kath recalls the moment far more vividly than I do, but then she wasn't as drunk as I was at the time. She had come down to Somerset for the weekend and we ended up at a nightclub, Carnaby's in Yeovil. I can't dance to save my life, and while Kath spent most of the evening dancing with one of my oldest friends, I was at the bar. Whether it was Dutch courage or just jealousy at the amount of time she was spending with my friend, when she returned from another lengthy session on the dance-floor, I took her hand, fixed her with the most intense look my bloodshot eyes could muster and said, 'I've decided. We'll get married.'

She didn't say much more than 'That's nice' at the time, probably reckoning my drunken bravado would have evaporated by the following morning, but as we sat down to breakfast the next day she said, 'Do you remember what you said last night?'

'Of course I do.'

'And did you mean it?'

'Absolutely.'

'All right then. Let's get married.'

I was just eighteen at the time and Kath a year older, but we were convinced it was the right thing to do. However, when I told my parents the news, my dad burst out laughing. 'Married? You're joking, aren't you? How are you going to manage that on £500 a year?'

Kath's father, Gerry, adopted a more subtle approach, smiling and giving us his blessing, while no doubt privately hoping that we'd either think better of the whole foolish plan or at least opt for a long engagement first. However, he did give me a hint that he didn't think me entirely unworthy of his daughter when he eased my winter financial worries after the abrupt end to my employment as a floor-tiler at the new Yeovil Hospital by taking me on as one of his sales reps. I sold quite a few sets of drumsticks and things for him though not in one shop where I kept getting the brush-off from an under-manager. He kept me waiting for well over an hour, and when he finally deigned to see me he kept drumming his fingers on the desk and gazing out of the window, and then said, 'Well, quite frankly we don't really deal with little companies like yours.' I lost my temper at being messed around like that and gave him a verbal blast. 'Well, to be honest,' I said, 'we've got standards too. So you can piss off, because we're not interested in selling to a crap shop like this.'

I spent most of the return journey wondering how I was going to tell Gerry that I'd just lost him a customer for ever, but when I got back he came out to meet me, beaming all over his face, and said that the father of the man I'd had the bust-up with had phoned to apologise for his son's behaviour and then placed a big order with Gerry as compensation.

If breaking the news of our wedding plans to our parents had been daunting, telling my Somerset captain, Brian Close, was decidedly scary – so unnerving that we got Kath's mum and dad to pave the way. They broached the subject while they were on an evening out with him and he went spare; it ruined the whole evening for everybody as he hauled Jan and Gerry over the coals for not vetoing the whole marriage plan from the start. 'They're far too young to be making such a commitment,' he said, 'and I'm very concerned about Kathryn being married to a man who's going to be away from home so much of the time.'

We gave him another forty-eight hours to calm down before we braved an encounter with him ourselves, and then waited until Brian was comfortably settled with a drink in his hand and a smile on his face. Kath went first, as I hovered in the background. 'Uncle Brian? You've heard that Ian and I have got engaged, haven't you?'

The result was completely predictable: Closey exploded again. 'Now then, listen here you two bloody young fools,' he said. He turned to me first. 'For heaven's sake, Ian, your mind should be on bloody cricket at the moment. A marriage this young might damage your career before it has properly begun.' He went on in the same vein for a few minutes, paused to see if this was having any effect, then gave a sigh of resignation. 'All right. If you're set on this, I can't stop you, but I'll tell you this: Kathryn is a wonderful girl and if you do anything to hurt her, I'll skin you alive.'

Next it was Kath's turn for a stern lecture. 'Ian is a bloody marvellous cricketer. He will play for England some day' – I liked that bit – 'So Kathryn, you mustn't do anything to stop this. If you interfere with his career in any way, I'll tan your arse. He must be single-minded and dedicated; you'll have to accept that, and if you're determined to go ahead with this crackpot scheme, it will have to be on the understanding that cricket comes first.' He paused. 'And another thing, Kathryn, he's not good enough for you.' I'd like to think he was joking…

We listened respectfully to all the sound advice from Brian and our parents about postponing our marriage plans until we were older and wiser, and then proceeded to ignore it. We had originally intended to wait for three or four years before marrying, but when we went to a friend's wedding a few weeks later, my impetuosity once more got the better of me. 'Let's get married as soon as possible,' I said.

On 31 January 1976, we were married at Thorne Parish Church. As well as our family and friends, Closey, Peter Denning and a lot of my Somerset teammates were invited, and there were 120 wedding guests in all, a pretty large number for a small village like Thorne. Once the local B&Bs and hotels were full, the rest of the guests were billeted all over the place. I spent the night before the wedding at Kath's aunt's house. Most men make do with a stag night or perhaps a stag weekend. As far as I can recall – and my memory is perhaps understandably blurred about this – I'd had a stag week with my mates. Kath's aunt took one look at me the next morning as, head pounding, I listlessly tipped some cornflakes into a bowl, and then she disappeared into the next room. She came back with a bottle of whisky in her hand and poured it all over my cornflakes. 'Hair of the dog' was all she said. I can't recommend the flavour, I would definitely have preferred milk, but one of the ingredients – was it the cornflakes or possibly the whisky? – seemed to do the trick.

It was a beautiful winter's day, cold but clear, with the sun shining from a bleached blue sky. I was shaking as I waited at the altar; I didn't feel nervous but I was certainly cold. It was absolutely freezing in the church and Kath was almost half an hour late. It's traditional for brides to be a few minutes late, but this was getting ridiculous, though there was a good reason. While having a photo taken with her dad before setting off for the church, she'd got the veil of her wedding dress caught on a rose bush, and it was so badly hooked up that it took fifteen minutes to disentangle it without tearing the veil to shreds.

We went to the Lake District for our honeymoon, staying at Pooley Bridge on Ullswater. We were only going to stay for four days, as that was all we could afford, but at the wedding reception one of the guests, a friend of Kath's parents, pressed a £20 note into my hand as a wedding present and we decided to use that to pay for a fifth night.

I'd always wanted to live in the north; I liked the people and the 'broad acres' and even though we'd only ever lived in Northern Ireland, Cheshire and Somerset, my parents were both from Yorkshire: my dad came from Beverley and my mum from Bradford. They talked about it often and I felt a Yorkshireman at heart; maybe having that archetypal 'Tyke' Brian Close as one of my mentors at Somerset also helped.

Given the insecurities of a career in professional cricket, it also made sense to base ourselves close to Kath's work and my off-season employment in Yorkshire. It might have seemed a strange choice of location for a man contracted to play cricket for Somerset but it wasn't quite as weird as it looked. Although the commute to home games was a long one, for almost every away game it was much more convenient to travel from Yorkshire than Taunton. In terms of geography and transport links, Somerset wasn't ideally placed for the county circuit. With the exception of the games against the nearby counties like Gloucestershire and Glamorgan, every away game involved something of a marathon trip, whereas from Yorkshire, using the M62 and the M6 or the A1 and M1, I could be at almost any of the other cricketing counties much quicker than from Somerset.

Nine months before we got married Kath had found us a house, not quite in Yorkshire but a handful of miles over the Lincolnshire border. The sleepy rural village of Epworth was in the middle of the 'Bermuda Triangle' south of the River Humber, where few tourists and visitors ever penetrate and most of those get lost. Our house was in Mowbray Street, near the birthplace of the Methodist John Wesley. It was a tiny two-bedroomed farm-worker's cottage, sandwiched between two grander farmer's houses, and set at right-angles to the road. It had no garden, just a front yard barely big enough to park the car, but it was right across the road from the pub, the Mowbray Arms. This was dangerously handy, but the pub also had a large garden that we used for *al fresco* entertaining of our friends and family. Jan and Gerry gave us the deposit on the house as a wedding present and Kath's grandfather gave us our first sofa and chairs. The rest of the furniture was begged and borrowed and, with the help of another friend, I even managed to install a central heating system.

Having made the move to the north, there was only one problem with living a few hours' drive from Somerset: I'd never learned to drive, so Kath set out to teach me. With L-plates attached to her company car, I made my first drive from south Yorkshire to Taunton with growing confidence, although after a while Kath did point out to me that driving at ninety miles an hour with L-plates on wasn't necessarily the best way to avoid police attention.

I'd clearly absorbed a few tips from the Brian Close School of Motoring, because I also put a few dents in Kath's car from time to time – especially irritating for her, as her battered old Austin 1100 had just been replaced by a shiny new Ford Escort. Kath claims that by the time the car came to be sold, the only original body work left was the bonnet and the passenger door.

It was a miracle I avoided further damage while driving to Bath for another game. I was well behind schedule and knew I'd be in serious trouble with Closey if I turned up late. We were on a road with bollards down the middle. The traffic was very heavy going our way but very light in the other direction, so there was only one thing to do. Hazard lights flashing, horn blaring and still with L-plates firmly attached, I swerved on to the wrong side of the road and accelerated away, squeezing between the bollards and the oncoming motorists, whose Doppler effect horns came and went all the way to the head of the queue, where I squeezed back on to my own side of the road, accompanied by more irate blaring and tooting of horns ... but at least I made the ground in time.

The facilities at Bath, like many of the smaller grounds on the county circuit, were a nightmare. The pitches were sometimes, though far from always, OK, but dressing rooms and the other facilities were a joke. At Weston-super-Mare the dressing room was so small that you couldn't get more than four or five people in there at a time, and the wooden floor had been so chewed up by players' boots over the years that it was a minefield of splinters. Often I'd be bowling and would come to a juddering halt as a splinter trapped between the two pairs of socks that I wore was driven into my foot. If you played at Weston, a pair of tweezers for pulling out splinters was an even more vital piece of kit than a thigh-pad or a box, and there was never enough hot water in the showers. I liked to have a couple of pints after the day's play, unwind, cool down, reflect on the game, have a chat, and then have a shower, and by then, if there ever had been any hot water, it was always stone cold.

The dressing room smelled stale and musty, as if we were the only people who used it all year, and the pitch was unofficially known as 'Dogshit Park' by the players because that's what the outfield was littered with. People didn't 'poop-scoop' in those days, and there were clearly a hell of a lot of dog-owners in Weston-super-Mare who used the park as their dog toilet.

Even Taunton wasn't perfect then, but it was a damn sight better than the other county grounds and has since been improved enormously. Despite one or two minor problems like the leak in one corner of the "Away" dressing room – we never told the ground staff because we didn't want it to be repaired; anything that made the opposition a bit more uncomfortable was definitely to be encouraged – Taunton was by far the players' favourite ground, and not only because it housed the Somerset Stragglers' Bar, just to one side of the pavilion. There was a great deal of opposition from some of the county members to the idea of abandoning Weston and Bath and concentrating all the fixtures on the county ground at Taunton, but there wasn't a single player opposed to the change. We all wanted top-class facilities for ourselves and the paying spectators and scattering the games around the grounds was neither welcomed by us nor remotely cost-effective for the county. I have some great memories of matches at Bath and Weston-super-Mare and the people who came to watch them, but I don't have any affectionate memories of the facilities – nor the dog shit – that we had to endure in order to play there.

The crowds at Taunton were larger too and I always wanted to be playing in front of a big, noisy crowd; I hated the occasions on the sleepier reaches of the county circuit when we played out a meandering draw in front of two old men and a dog. It was partly ego, of course, but also a genuine desire to entertain. I always equated us with actors on the stage; we were there to put on a show for the public, to entertain and excite them. If they were enjoying it, they would come back; if they weren't, they wouldn't. Without major surgery you could never have Test cricket at Taunton because, even after the ground improvements, it's just not big enough, but for county cricket, the atmosphere from the ten thousand or so supporters it held was always fantastic. It was a terrific place to play … if you were from Somerset. Other counties hated to play there, because the crowd were so close that they felt like they were right on top of you and the noise and the fervour of the home support would intimidate them; they were halfway to losing before they'd even taken the field.

Still only twenty, newly established in the Somerset First XI and even more newly married, I knew that the real work on my cricket career was only just beginning. This was the crucial moment for me. In cricket as in any other field of human activity, there are stories without number about young prodigies who burst upon the scene, flourish briefly and then fade from view, their decline as rapid as their meteoric ascent. Talent alone wasn't enough; it had to be linked to dedication, application and the self-belief and iron will to win that someone like Brian Close embodied. I used to travel to and from games with him and learned a huge amount about cricket from talking and listening to him, but unfortunately his cars proved to be much less unbreakable than his will, and Closey really was an appalling driver. He went through three Ford Capris in the course of his benefit year alone, and he once took his car into a garage for crash repairs, collected it and then brought it back a few minutes later, having crashed it again. He drove off the forecourt to a round-about fifty yards away and in full view of the mechanics and panel beaters who had just finished patching it up, ploughed it straight into the back of a lorry. He exchanged names and addresses, turned around the roundabout and limped back to the garage to have it mended again.

Even more alarmingly, he drove up and down the motorway between games at eighty or ninety miles an hour, with a flask of coffee between the front seats, the sandwiches that his wife, Vivienne, had made for him on the dashboard and a transistor radio on the seat or in the footwell. Many a time he'd have the *Sporting Life* spread open in front of him across the steering wheel as well. As he poured his coffee – or sometimes he'd make tea, using a Heath Robinson contraption that plugged into the cigarette lighter on the dashboard – he'd also be studying the form, and it was in very small print, casting only an occasional glance at the road ahead. The Royal Society for the Prevention of Accidents could have used video footage of him, uncut, as a perfect example of the way to guarantee an accident. I used to sit in the passenger seat scared witless and offered to drive many times, but in the car as on the cricket field, Brian liked to be in control.

After one game at Bath, I was following him – at a safe distance – in another car along the Fosse Way towards Taunton. As usual Brian set off like a Grand Prix driver and disappeared in a cloud of dust, while we followed at a slightly more sedate pace. The road runs absolutely dead straight for about five miles, then there is one gentle curve and another endless straight beyond it. When we reached the one and only bend, we found that Brian had failed to negotiate it; his car was now perched on top of the hedge. Although he denied it furiously, it was obvious that he'd been fiddling with his transistor radio, trying to tune it in to get the racing results, and had only looked up when his car was already off the road and heading straight for the hedge. As usual he emerged unhurt, but facing another hefty bill for repairs.

After surviving a few months of near misses and minor accidents, I decided to start making alternative travel arrangements. It was just as well; had I accepted a lift with him after our game against Surrey at Guildford, my cricket career would have come to a premature end. Brian offered me a lift back to the team hotel but I was having a pint with Pete 'Dasher' Denning and told Brian I'd go back with one of the other players later on. On our way back that evening we saw the wreckage of Brian's car wrapped around a lamp post. The area around the passenger seat had been totally stove in – it would have taken oxyacetylene gear to cut me out if I'd been sitting there – but as usual, Closey's side was undamaged and he'd emerged from the wreck with not a scratch on him. When we got to the hotel we found him perched at the bar, enjoying a nightcap, as if nothing out of the ordinary had happened ... which, given his driving record, was probably the case.

When he wasn't putting my life at risk in his car, Closey was now doing his best to push my claims for an England place. My record as a batsman would not have frightened anyone; I had not yet learned to build an innings at this level and several promising starts were wasted when I got myself out having done the hard work. In the whole of the 1975 season I started twenty championship games for Somerset, but scored only 499 runs, with a top score of 65 against Derbyshire; but my bowling was definitely on the up. I picked up fifty-eight wickets in the season and also strengthened my all-rounder claims by pouching eighteen catches. Newspapers reported that, along with Gloucestershire's Andy Stovold, I was 'very much in the forefront of the England selectors' thoughts', but my name didn't feature that season where it would really have counted: on an England team sheet.

1976 was my real breakthrough year. I had my first ten-wicket match against Gloucestershire, and had four five-wicket innings, with a best of six for 16. I hit 56 against the touring West Indians – including Andy Roberts – in May, one of six half-centuries I scored that season. My maiden century almost arrived in our game against Sussex at Hove in May, but on 97 I was bowled trying to smash a delivery from Michael Buss into the pavilion to reach my century in style. Michael was a left-arm slow bowler whose pace was so gentle that the ball barely had enough strength left to knock off the bails by the time it got to the other end of the wicket. I probably had time for two or three swings at the delivery that got me out and somehow managed to miss all of them. You sometimes get done for pace by a bowler, but this was the first time I'd been done by lack of it.

My first century finally came in Somerset's victory over Nottinghamshire at Trent Bridge at the beginning of August. Set 301 to win in three hours and fifty minutes, we got there with seven overs to spare 'due to the sparkle of Botham', as *Wisden* later kindly remarked. I'd already made 80 in the first innings before holing out, going for another big hit, and I more than doubled that in the second innings, reaching my maiden century with something to spare by hitting six sixes and twenty fours in an undefeated 167. I scored 1,000 runs for Somerset that season at a respectable average of 34, took sixty-six wickets and was awarded my county cap.

I'd now achieved two of my three original aims in professional cricket: I'd gained and held a place in the Somerset first team, and I'd now been awarded my county cap. The next step was selection for England, and a press campaign calling for me to be given my chance was now beginning to gather momentum. There is nothing that the press hates more than the status quo – there are no banner headlines in 'England pick same team again' – so they were always looking around for the next rising star in English cricket. They'd fasten on to a promising young player and then push his claims until the clamour for his inclusion became irresistible. If he was a success, their self-congratulatory copy would remind us where we read it first; if he failed, he was promptly rubbished by the very people who'd been calling for his selection, and a fresh bandwagon would begin rolling for someone else. In August 1976, it was my turn to be flavour of the month. Brian Close had been recalled by England to face the West Indies' pace attack in that infamous Test series, and as well as batting like a hero himself, I'm sure he'd also put in a good word for me with the England captain Tony Greig.

I didn't make the Test team that summer, but I did receive an England call-up for the one-day series that followed it. My delight at being picked for the first one-day match against the West Indies at Scarborough on 26 August 1976 was mixed with a few flutters of nerves. Confident though I was in my own ability, this was a real step up in class for me, because the 1976 West Indians were an awesome team and their quick bowlers – as Andy Roberts had already demonstrated to me – could be devastating.

My England one-day debut was pretty anticlimactic. I'd seen Andy Roberts before at very close quarters, but this was my first sight of Michael Holding from the other end of a wicket and it was a pretty impressive sight. His run-up was as easy and languid as David Gower with a bat in his hands, but the smoothness of his approach belied the speed with which the ball was delivered. On his day, Michael Holding was as fast as anyone, and this was clearly one of his days. I got off the mark, but that was all I managed to do and I lasted just seven balls before I was caught by Roy Fredericks off Holding for 1. Tony Greig was out injured and Alan Knott was captaining the side, and when we fielded he didn't say a word to me and didn't call on me to bowl. Having been very pumped up, I'd completely relaxed until five minutes before tea, when he suddenly said, 'OK, take the last over before tea.' All I could think was 'Why the hell didn't you tell me to loosen up a few minutes ago?' I bowled that one over and then two more after tea, taking just one wicket for 26 as the West Indies cantered to a six-wicket win. I missed the next game but returned to score 20 and take one for 31 at Edgbaston as the West Indies wrapped up the three-match series 3-0.

I hadn't set the world on fire in my first couple of one-day games for England, but I felt I'd done well enough to be picked for the tour that winter and the England captain Tony Greig clearly agreed, because he told me, 'Pack your bags, Ian, you're off to India and Australia for the Centenary Test in Melbourne.' But I was listening to the sports bulletin on the radio when the names of the touring party were announced, and my name was not among them. Tony was just one voice on the committee and clearly the other selectors didn't agree with him. There wasn't too much adventure about the select-ors in those days; there still isn't, come to think of it. I felt that I should have been playing for England a good eighteen months to two years before I was finally picked, and I definitely should have gone on the tour. On performance I was certainly better than anybody else around at the time – including Chris Old, the Yorkshireman who went on the tour as first-choice all-rounder – but the selectors obviously felt I was too young and would benefit from an extra year's experience.

One of the biggest bugbears throughout my early career was that people were always saying I was too young – 'Give him another year, there's plenty of time for him.' As far as I was concerned if I was good enough, then I was old enough, and it drove me mad that I had to step aside for players who I knew were nowhere near as good, but were selected just because they were older. I wasn't picked for the Under-15 side when I was eleven because they thought they should leave me for another year, and at every age group it was the same story. I still feel for young players when I hear the same old story now. 'We haven't picked him because he lacks experience.' How the hell can he get the experience if you don't pick him? It drove me up the wall and, even more frustratingly, I see the same thing happening to my youngest grandson now, another hugely talented player who keeps being told he's too young to play with the big boys, even though he's clearly better than any of them. It would drive any talented kid mad.

When I reached the senior levels of the game, I found that not just my age but also my background counted against me. The era of English cricket when only amateur players had their initials recorded on the scorecards and where some grounds even had separate entrances for Gentlemen and Players – no wonder some of the bacon and egg ties at Lord's found the apartheid regime in South Africa so attractive – was only just fading when I began coming into consideration for the national team, first at schoolboy level and then as a professional. It is not prejudice or northern 'chippiness' to suggest that, like many others, my path would have been easier had I been playing my cricket in the south-east rather than 'in the sticks'.

I had just about got used to the idea that I wouldn't be going away that winter when I received a phone call from Donald Carr, the secretary of the Test and County Cricket Board. 'I've got some good news, Ian,' he said. 'You've been selected for the Whitbread young player scholarship to Australia.' Four young players who were thought to be future England stars – myself, Mike Gatting, Bill Athey and Graham Stevenson – were to be given the chance to further their cricket education on a three-month, expenses-paid trip Down Under. I was thrilled to be chosen, of course, but it was by no means certain that I could afford to take up the offer. The scholarship was usually given to young single players but I had a young wife and mortgage to look after and, generous though the offer of my air fares and living expenses was, it didn't help me to meet my mortgage payments while I was away. Even though my county salary had been doubled to £1,000, it was nowhere near enough without supplementing it with some winter income.

Having thought about it and talked it through with Kath, I called Donald back and explained my predicament. 'Leave it with me,' was all he said. Twenty-four hours later, he called back. 'Problem solved,' he said. 'In view of your special circumstances, Whitbread have very generously agreed to an additional payment of £100 a month to you.'

I thanked him profusely and put down the phone. The next couple of weeks flew by. I must have packed and repacked my bags a dozen times before I was satisfied that I'd included everything I would need. On 27 December 1976 I met the other boys at Heathrow and we flew out together. It wasn't the winter tour I had been hoping to make, but it was a very good second and I've always been very grateful to Whitbread for giving me that chance. Five days after I arrived Down Under I discovered that a tour of Australia wasn't the only new experience I'd be having.

Back in England, Kath had been experiencing a few bouts of morning sickness and a pregnancy test confirmed the good news. Her first thought was obviously to share the news with me, but there were no mobile phones in those days and as I was in Australia and staying in cheap digs with no phones in the rooms – my budget didn't stretch to hotel accommodation – she had no idea how to get hold of me. In desperation, she telephoned Colin Cowdrey, who had chaired Whitbread's selection panel, and explained why she needed to get in touch with me. He then made several calls to Australian cricket officials and eventually found a number at which she could reach me.

The legendary English fast bowler Frank Tyson, who had emigrated to Australia after retiring, had kindly offered to put me up for a couple of weeks and I was just settling into bed that night when Frank knocked on my door and summoned me to the phone down the hall.

'Ian?' Kath said. 'It's me. I'm pregnant.' After a few moments' silence, she tried again. 'Ian? Did you hear what I said? I'm pregnant.' There was still no response. 'Ian? Are you still there?'

I was there all right but I'd been struck dumb, speechless with delight. Every father will know the emotions that raced through me; my only regret was that I was ten thousand miles away. Once I'd found my voice, we talked for an hour.

I now had an even more powerful incentive to reach the top in my chosen career. I've always thought that it's much harder to get into the England side than to get out of it – and I think that's still the case – but if I'd gone to India, I felt that I would have forced my way into the Test side. So it was doubly frustrating and annoying to miss out but there was nothing I could do about it and in some ways going to Australia on the Whitbread Scholarship probably did me more long-term good than joining the England tour in India. At a very young age, I'd been given the chance to experience playing in Australia, to get a feel for the conditions there – the different light, the way the pitches respond – and the Australian approach to the game, especially their determination and will to succeed. Aussies only know one way to play – to win. It was an attitude that I already had, but the time in Australia sharpened my own competitive instincts even more. To this day, a lot of Aussies tell me that I'm more like an Australian than an Englishman and I take that as a compliment.

I played with and against some very talented young players, including Graham Yallop, Rodney Hogg and Trevor Laughlin who all went on to play for Australia, and after the cynicism of Britain, I also saw at first-hand the strength of the Aussies' loyalty to their flag and their country. Being Australian really meant something to them and some of that rubbed off on me; when I went back to England I took even more pride in representing my country. I learned a lot about life in those three months in Australia and it was one of the best times of my life, because Aussies play hard off the field as well as on it, but it also stood me in very good stead for the rest of my career and gave me a little bit of an edge over some of the other young English players.

The highlight of the trip came when Graham Stevenson and I were given the job of looking after the England dressing room during the Centenary Test at Melbourne. We just had to make ourselves useful to the players, getting towels, food, cups of tea and anything else they wanted, but we absolutely loved the chance to sample the dressing-room atmosphere during a Test and it also gave us the opportunity for a couple of beers with the players at close of play. The dressing room has changed now, but then it was like a vast underground dungeon with a long flight of stairs up to a viewing room looking out over the pitch. It was a very impressive sight with a hundred thousand spectators packed in. As I looked around it, I thought to myself, 'I want to be here for real next time, as part of the England team.'

I'd managed to stay out of trouble most of the time I'd been in Australia, but I did get involved in one punch-up during the Centenary Test, with Ian Chappell. After stumps one evening the players of both sides were drinking in a bar when Chappell started rubbishing England. I don't know if Chappell was intentionally goading me, or just mouthing off for the sake of it, but if there's one thing I hate it's a loudmouthed Aussie insulting my country. I gave him three official warnings, all of which he ignored, so the next time he started I just flattened him. He went flying over a table and crash-landed on a group of Aussie Rules footballers, spilling their drinks in the process.

Chappell clearly didn't fancy any more of the same treatment because he made a bolt for the exit, but he couldn't resist stopping in the doorway to give me a final mouthful. The red mist had now descended and I at once set off in hot pursuit, chasing him down the street and even hurdling the bonnet of a passing car. I was closing fast when I saw a police car cruising towards us and decided to make a tactical withdrawal. Punching Chappell hadn't been the wisest of things to do and I was lucky that there were no journalists in the bar at the time. When I calmed down I resolved to use a bat and a ball to make the Aussies pay in future.

*

That winter in Australia also witnessed the greatest upheaval in the long history of cricket. Tony Greig was England captain during that tour, but he was also moonlighting as the principal headhunter for Kerry Packer's World Series Cricket. The South African-born Greig was a tremendously aggressive cricketer, a fine bat, a bowler of medium-pace seamers or off-breaks, a brilliant close catcher and a very shrewd captain. He was also a showman who put "bums on seats" at cricket grounds around the world yet, like all cricketers at the time, the rewards he obtained for doing so were pitifully small. Cricketers were among the paupers of international sport, so when the Australian television magnate Kerry Packer wanted Greig to be one of the ringleaders of a new form of cricket – heavily sponsored and marketed as a major television sport, with vastly increased financial rewards for the players – he did not have to work too hard to convince Tony to come on board. Together they drew up the plan to use Packer's wealth to strip the Test-playing nations of their brightest stars by recruiting the best players from every cricket-playing country, and set up a rival competition – World Series Cricket – in direct opposition to the traditional game.

The split in the game was bitter and rancorous and a few lifelong friendships were ended by it. The game as a whole suffered wounds which took a long time to heal, but it was undeniable that the rewards for professional cricketers, whether they sided with Packer or the cricketing establishment, were massively increased. In order to compete, the Test and County Cricket Board simply had to raise more revenue, forcing the introduction of commercial sponsorship, previously anathema to the diehards at Lord's. Pay rates for cricketers were vastly improved, and a long-overdue recognition that cricket was part of the entertainment industry and could only survive by competing in that marketplace was forced upon the game's administrators. The way was paved for innovations like coloured clothing and day-night matches, that caused thromboses among cricket traditionalists at the time but are now commonplace and have played their part in bringing new audiences to the game.

Too junior to be courted by World Series Cricket, I was merely a spectator while the 'Packer Affair' unfolded, but I gained from it in three ways. My earnings shot up as the administrators acted to stop the haemorrhaging of talent to Packer, and the defection of senior players created gaps in the England ranks that I was as well placed as any to fill. In particular, if the current England all-rounder Tony Greig was going to defect to Packer, in my eyes and those of most other observers, I was the obvious choice to replace him in the England Test side. Packer brought one further benefit to myself and other young players like David Gower and Mike Gatting: the defections of the leading players from the other international sides made our early Test match careers a little less testing than might otherwise have been the case.

The 1977 season was shaping as a make-or-break summer for me. My early-season form, particularly with the ball, was very good. I faced the old enemy – Australia – for the first time in mid May and scored a half-century off only thirty-eight balls, including 20 from one over by spin bowler Kerry O'Keeffe. I followed it up with 39 not out in the second innings, and also got four top-order batsmen out in their second innings. It was enough to earn me a second crack at them for the MCC team at Lord's at the end of the month. I picked up three wickets, though in my eagerness to impress I was probably guilty of bowling too short, and after being not out for 10 in our first innings, I got my first duck against the Aussies when Jeff Thomson had me caught behind. I was still hopeful of Test selection, but missed out on the first two Tests in which England took a 1-0 lead in the series. As the implications of the Packer Affair and Tony Greig's part in it began to sink in – the players had known that it was happening for a long time but, for once, the news was slow to leak to the media – change was in the air. I had no doubt that I was ready to make the step up in class to Test cricket, but I wasn't sure if the England selectors shared my opinion.

I was playing for Somerset in a Sunday League game and was on my way to the Taunton ground when I heard on the car radio that I'd been selected for my first Test – the third of England's Ashes series against Australia at Trent Bridge, beginning on 8 July 1977. I still couldn't quite believe it, but when I got to the ground, the Somerset secretary confirmed that I'd been picked. I didn't hear from any of the England selectors at all, though as this was the era before mobile phones, they would have had difficulty in tracking me down even if they'd wanted to let me know in person.

Even though I was half-expecting it, no matter how much you might have been anticipating something like that, it was still a wonderful moment, one that I'll never forget. I'd already played in a couple of one-day internationals, but this was something else entirely, my first Test match, and an Ashes Test at that. As I walked across the Taunton outfield, lots of Somerset players and supporters who had also heard the news kept coming up to me and saying 'Well done'. Brian Close, waiting in the dressing room, shook my hand and gave me some typically pithy advice: 'You've earned your chance, now don't fuck it up.'

The day passed in a bit of a blur – press interviews before the match, the game itself and then the celebrations in the bar afterwards. My mum and dad were there, almost bursting with pride, but unfortunately, amid the celebration drinks, congratulatory calls and the euphoria of the moment, I completely forgot to phone Kath and tell her the news. She hadn't been listening to the radio or watching TV that day, so the first she had heard about it was when my mum phoned and said, 'Isn't it wonderful news about Ian?'

'What?' Kath said.

My mum stumbled her way through an apology. She and my dad had come to the ground for a celebration drink and then gone home and had been certain that I would have rung home to tell Kath by then – as any normal husband would have done. The atmosphere when, prompted by an urgent call from my mum, I finally did ring home, more than a little the worse for wear, was understandably frosty. 'Sorry, love,' I said. 'The lads bought me a couple of drinks and I got carried away.'

Chapter 3

A DIFFICULT ACT TO FOLLOW

My Test selection was formally confirmed by the arrival of a bulky envelope containing an official letter and a lengthy document entitled 'Conditions of Acceptance and Notes and Instructions of Test Matches'. Among its sixteen sections, I discovered that the playing fees were £210 per cricketer per match, but that the twelfth man had to make do with £116, but only if he was 'on duty throughout the match'. The insurance package was impressively comprehensive, covering everything from my life – £30,000 – down to my big toes, £1,600 each, and my little toes, a bargain at £600 each. A quick mental calculation told me that if I lost a foot, I'd earn the equivalent of almost twenty Test match fees.

There was also a lengthy list of clothing to be issued and the dire penalties that would ensue for mislaying or mistreating the precious items. I would be issued with a cap, tie, sleeveless and long-sleeved sweaters. I would also receive a blazer, but was warned that a new one was only issued to a cricketer who had been playing for England for over eight years. If I lasted that long, mine was going to be a little threadbare by then.

The day before any big game, Kath left me alone as much as possible because she knew that I was so hyper. I was a complete Rottweiler as a big match was looming. For my first Test, I was even worse than usual, and it must have been a relief for her to kiss me goodbye, wish me luck and shut the door behind me. Nowadays the England players assemble two or three days before a Test but back then we just turned up on the afternoon before the game. When I arrived at Trent Bridge there was a blur of activity. I went to the dressing room where the captain, Mike Brearley, welcomed me – the only new cap – and introduced me to my teammates. I knew most of them from the county circuit and my previous games with the England one-day side, but there were a couple I'd never crossed paths with.

I was issued with my England kit and then got changed, once I'd established which peg in the dressing room I could use. I was the twenty-one-year-old new boy in the team and I didn't want to get off on the wrong foot with any of my teammates by pinching their jealously guarded place in the dressing-room hierarchy, though the democratic approach to man-management adopted by Tony Greig and his successor, Mike Brearley, made this much less likely. Even though this was the match when the legendary Geoffrey Boycott was to make his long-awaited return to Test cricket after three years of self-imposed exile, Brears made it clear that seniority conferred no special privileges on anyone.

Even so, I waited until the senior players had all claimed their spots and then put my bags in the corner, with Bob Willis on one side of me and Mike Hendrick on the other. Like all players, I had a few superstitions and dressing-room rituals. Mine was always to put on my left boot before my right one, and my left pad before the right. I've no idea now how or why it started but it became an unshakeable habit. I also always had to use the same peg in the Somerset dressing room. If a young player pinched 'my' place – often because one of my teammates, as a joke, had told them to use it – I told him to shift somewhere else. Other players had a talisman that they carried in a pocket, or would tap their bat or their pads in a certain way, or would never pass an incoming batsman on the left side, and so on. The Gloucestershire and England wicketkeeper Jack Russell had so many twitches, rituals and superstitions to complete before he took the field that it's a miracle that he made it out there at all.

Players also arranged their kit in entirely different ways. I was the original dressing-room slob, with all my kit – bats, flannels, gloves, shirts – dumped in an untidy heap. Most fast bowlers seem to be the same. If you walked into the England dressing room now, I'd wager that 'Fred' Flintoff would be one of the untidiest people in the dressing room. A batsman like Chris Tavaré represented the opposite extreme. Every item of clothing, even his socks, was scrupulously folded and put on a hanger, and his pristine kit was laid out in neat rows, which he arranged and rearranged as fastidiously as the hostess of a particularly formal dinner party.

When I'd got changed, I sat tight and kept pretty quiet. It wasn't my normal nature, but as the newest kid on the block, I didn't want to be shooting off at the mouth. I couldn't stay silent for long, however. As one of the new boys, I was then ushered into the pre-match press conference where batteries of British and Australian media asked me endless variations on the same question: 'What's it feel like to be the new boy?' We had a brief practice and then a team dinner that evening but once more I hardly said a word; I just listened to the others and tried to take it all in. I had a couple of beers with some of the guys afterwards and then went to bed. The whole day seemed to have passed in a blur and I wished afterwards that I could have rewound the whole of it and played it again in slow motion, just to savour it.

To my surprise, even though I was both nervous and excited, I slept well that night, but I was again uncharacteristically quiet in the Trent Bridge dressing room the next morning, mainly because I was a bundle of nerves. No matter how confident you may be in your own ability, you never really know whether you can be a Test cricketer until you go out on the field. The history of cricket is full of great county players who never made the grade at Test level. I went to my allotted corner, dumped my kit in its usual shapeless heap, then looked guiltily around, but no one was complaining about the mess. The kit of the other fast bowlers, Bob Willis and Mike Hendrick, was almost equally untidy.

I put on my shirt, flannels and boots, and we went on to the outfield for a bit of fielding and catching practice, a chance to shed a few nerves. Then we returned to the dressing room to get ready for the match. I was like a kid on his first day in a brand-new school. Everything seemed to be happening at top speed. I've no doubt that a thousand and one people came up to me to wish me luck, but I simply cannot remember a single word anyone said. In the remaining time before play began, Brears encouraged us to talk about the game, and every single player, whether they were making their first appearance or their forty-first, was asked to contribute, but I still kept silent. I was barely capable of speech at all; I had a knot in my stomach as big as a fist and my mouth was as dry as the dust on the dressing-room floor.

In those final tense minutes before taking the field, it helped that I had so many minor details to keep me occupied, like checking whether I'd put my jockstrap on under my flannels rather than over them. My tension was eased a little when Mike Hendrick, perhaps spotting that I was very wound up, came and sat next to me and started discussing shooting with me. Talking about something other than cricket helped to take my mind off things a little, but no matter how hard I tried to remain calm and focused, my nerves simply wouldn't go away.

I was desperate for us to field first, not because the pitch was a seamer's paradise – quite the reverse, it looked full of runs – but the thought of having to sit around for several hours waiting for my turn to bat set my nerves jangling even more. No one could ever accuse me of excessive patience at the best of times and on this occasion I just wanted to get out on the field and into the thick of the action as soon as I could. So I was probably the only person in the England dressing room who was delighted when Brears signalled from the pitch to tell us that Greg Chappell, the Aussie captain, had won the toss and decided to bat. It was a great feeling as I pulled on the England sweater and followed my teammates down the steps and out on to the field, to be greeted by a huge roar from the capacity crowd. I glanced around, taking in the packed stands and terraces, the TV cameras and press photographers and, outside the ground, the people lining every window with a view of the pitch. What a moment that was; for the first time, I truly felt that I was an England player.

Once the first ball was bowled, I relaxed a little – it felt good just to be running around the outfield, making a couple of stops – but as the time passed and I knew that some time soon Brears was going to toss me the ball and tell me to have a bowl, my nerves returned. The longer the wait, the worse it got, and by the time I was finally given my first spell in Test cricket, I was as tightly wound as a watch spring. As I paced out my run, I tried to keep in mind Closey's advice never to be intimidated by anyone or any situation, but the harder I tried, the worse I felt. I was about to bowl my first ball in Test cricket. I had imagined this moment countless times since I was a kid bowling daisy cutters at our garage door in Yeovil, yet now it was finally here, I was almost paralysed by nerves. I could feel a bead of sweat trickling down my forehead and brushed it away with an impatient gesture. I could delay no longer; there was nothing for it but to take a deep breath and go for it.

I paused at the start of my run and glanced at the close catchers around the bat – two slips, wicketkeeper and short-leg. Brears had consulted me on what field I wanted, but when I asked for another slip, he told me, 'Just get yourself loose first.' I switched my gaze to the batsman, the Australian opener, Rick McCosker, frowning in concentration as he watched and waited. The ball was still fairly new, hard and shiny but scuffed in places from a couple of impacts with the boundary boards. I laid my fingers over the seam, canting it to the left – I'd start with my stock ball, an outswinger. Then, my mouth dry, my heart banging in my chest, I started my run. I was only dimly aware of the crescendo of crowd noise as I reached the wicket; everything was focused on the batsman and the spot on that twenty-two-yard strip of sun-bleached grass where I hoped to pitch the ball.

Despite my nerves, it was a good first delivery, pitching on a good length and with enough late swing to defeat McCosker's hesitant defensive push. The ball flicked the edge and flew at catchable height, straight through the vacant third slip position. If I had been my usual hyper-confident self, I would have insisted to Brears that he bring up a third slip, and I made a mental note that, junior member of the team or not, from now on I would insist on setting the field that I wanted. My first spell in Test cricket had almost started in the perfect way, but it fell away rapidly after that. I was still much too pumped up and trying too hard, and as a result, my accuracy suffered. Brears had soon seen enough and told me, 'Thanks Both, have a "blow".' I felt bitterly disappointed that I hadn't done myself justice and I was desperate to put things right the first chance I had.

The Australians had been largely untroubled in reaching 101 for one at lunch. They had moved that on to 131 for two not long afterwards when, seeing how fired up I was, Brears threw me the ball again and gave me a second spell. As he did so, he said, 'Both, when you played for the MCC against these guys at the start of the tour, you bowled far too many bouncers. It's a weapon that's much more effective if you use it sparingly. Do what you do best, pitch it up and give it a chance to swing and use the bouncer only as a very occasional surprise. If I think you're using too many, I'll take you off straight away. All right?' He slapped me on the back and jogged off to take his place in the slips – and this time there were three of them.

My first ball was no more than a loosener, and not a very good one at that. It was a 'buffet ball' – help yourself – a long-hop wide of off-stump, and Greg Chappell went to force it through the covers off the back foot. Ninety-nine times out of a hundred he would have hammered it to the boundary for four, but this was the odd time out. He misread the bounce a little and instead of cracking it through the covers he bottom-edged it on to his stumps. He stared at his wicket in disbelief for a moment and then began the long, slow trudge back to the pavilion. As I was engulfed by my team-mates, I was desperately trying to be cool, as if a Test wicket – even my first – was no big deal, but all the time my heart was beating so wildly it felt like it would burst right out of my chest. It had been a lucky dismissal, but I didn't care. My first Test victim was one of the greatest batsmen in the game.

Any first-match nerves had now completely evaporated. I was steaming in to bowl and took three more quickfire wickets to get rid of Doug Walters, Rod Marsh and Max Walker. In just thirty-four deliveries, I'd now taken four wickets for 13 runs. The Aussies slumped to 155 for eight before the tail wagged and took the total to 243, but I then rounded things off by getting Jeff Thomson caught behind to finish with figures of five for 74 – my first five-wicket haul in Tests at the very first attempt. Once more, it all happened so fast that I never really had a chance to savour the individual moments, though I'll never forget being presented to the Queen during the tea interval. Taking five wickets and meeting the Queen in the year of her Silver Jubilee, all on the first day of my first Test match, was going to be a very difficult act to follow, though strangely the memory that has remained most vivid with me down the years was not of those great events but that nerve-jangling, unforgettable moment when I first set foot on the field, an England player at last. At the press call at the end of that first day, I was asked what I'd be doing to celebrate and told the assembled hacks that, though I might have a quiet pint or two to celebrate later, I first had to call Kath because, as I said at the time, 'My wife was eight months pregnant when I left home this morning ... I hope she still is.'

I also wanted to seek out and thank Mike Brearley, who had made a big contribution to my initial success. As he proved by entrusting me with the ball at a crucial juncture of the match, he had a great knack of recognising how each player could best be handled and exactly what was needed to get them playing at the peak of their game. He was also as shrewd and astute an observer of the game as I ever saw, as he showed by his remarks as he handed me the ball for that second spell. He'd noted in the MCC game against the Australians at Lord's that I'd been overdoing the bouncer, filed it away for future reference and then used it at just the right moment at Trent Bridge. When I bowled out the Aussies that day, I hardly sent down a single bumper, but if Brears had not had that cautionary word with me, the combination of my nerves, eagerness and sheer bloody-mindedness might have had me sending down two or three an over, most of which would probably have disappeared into the crowd at square leg. He was worth his place as a captain alone – perhaps just as well, because his record as a batsman didn't put him in the top rank of England openers.

The next day, as Brears and Boycs went out to bat, the rest of us passed the time while waiting our own turn to bat in different ways. I've never been very good at watching the game – ironic in view of my career these days as a commentator – and sitting and watching absolutely every ball of a six-hour day would wear me out. When the late, great Kenny Barrington was a player, and later the England team manager, he used to sit on the balcony or in the corner of the players' dressing room and watch – and live – every single delivery. He must have been exhausted by the end of each day. I usually watched the first couple of balls of the innings and then I'd be off, looking for something to do, and I'd pass the rest of the day at the back of the dressing room, playing cards, reading a magazine or sleeping – anything but watch every ball. If there was an exciting finish then of course I and everyone else watched, but in general play I wouldn't be on the balcony at all.

I was also very laid-back about getting ready when I was next man in. Some players would be out there fully kitted-up, sitting on the balcony, adjusting to the light, scrutinising the pitch for signs of movement, and so on, and they might have to sit there for hours like that if there was a lengthy partnership between the batsmen before them. I put my pads and thigh-pad on but I never got the rest of my stuff until the previous batsman was actually out and on his way back to the pavilion. That always took a couple of minutes and it was plenty of time to get my box into place, pick up my gloves and bat, and be out of the door in time to pass him coming up the pavilion steps.

I always had the same routine going out to bat, windmilling my arms and looking up at the sky as I crossed the outfield, though what I was looking for, I was never entirely sure. I took guard: 'Two please' – middle and leg, the one I used at the start of my career. Later, after a spell when I was getting out lbw regularly, trapped in front as I shuffled across my stumps, I discussed my guard with the then England team manager Kenny Barrington. He thought that since my natural movement was towards the offside, I'd be better taking a guard of 'One' – leg stump. I found that sorted the problem and suited me better and I then kept the same guard for the rest of my career.

I'd go for a wander down the pitch, tapping imaginary lumps down with my bat – we'd all do that even if cricket pitches were made of concrete – and then have a quick word with the batsman at the other end before settling to face my first ball. I was more nervous waiting to go in than facing the first few deliveries. I was out first ball a number of times, but I don't think it was because of nerves. I'm one of those batsmen who likes to feel the ball on the bat, so I wasn't a big leaver of balls outside the off-stump. As a result, I sometimes played at deliveries I should have left alone and ended up caught in the slips, but once I got past the first ball or two I'd be fine. I also much preferred to face a fast bowler when I went in; far better a big, nasty quick bowler than a spinner with three or four men clustered round the bat. It got the adrenalin going as well – a short-pitched, high-speed delivery going past your nose wakes you up a bit.

I didn't score a debut century that day, but I did manage a respectable 25, and with Boycott inevitably marking his Test return with a century, and Alan Knott adding another, we had a sizeable first innings lead. It was the first time I had seen the legendary Boycott at close quarters and I was shown the best and worst sides of his character in the course of that innings. He was an absolutely brilliant batsman – to see the joy on the Australian faces on the rare occasions when they got him out cheaply showed how highly they rated him – but I also thought he was extremely selfish. All top sportsmen need to have that quality to an extent – and Kath would confirm that I had it in spades – but in my opinion and that of many people who played with Geoff Boycott over the years, his selfishness was sometimes to the detriment of the teams for which he played.

In our first innings, we were struggling at 34 for two when Boycott played the ball into the covers and set off for what would have been a comfortable single had he not hit it straight to a fielder. Derek Randall tried to send him back but Boycs just kept on coming and, in front of his home crowd, Randall had to set off on a hopeless attempt to make his ground. He was run out by several yards. Boycott's attitude, then as always, was that even if he was at fault, as he was the team's best batsman, the man at the other end should always be the one to sacrifice his wicket.

In this case, as in several others over the years, Boycott remained at the crease and went on to make a tremendous century. Alan Knott also scored a hundred. Boycs then scored another 80 not out in the second innings, putting on 154 for the first wicket with Brears, and we cruised to a seven-wicket victory and a 2-0 lead in the series. 'Test cricket,' I thought. 'What's not to like?'

My very first Test match had earned me a match fee of £210, but the next one paid five times as much. In between those games, a cricket-loving industrialist, David Evans, contacted the TCCB and told them, 'I don't want any more England cricketers to defect to Kerry Packer,' and provided enough money to pay England players £1,000 a Test from then on. There was one other immediate tangible benefit from my England debut: I got my first sponsored car. Tony Greig – demoted as captain for his involvement with Packer, but still an England player for the moment – was chatting to me in the dressing room and suddenly said, 'Have you got a car?' I shook my head. He made a few phone calls and a week or so later I took delivery of a bright red Triumph TR. It was a fine car, but a two-seater was not necessarily ideal for a professional cricketer with a wife, a baby on the way and a couple of bags of cricket equipment to transport around. Fortunately I always managed to squeeze everything in somehow and never had to face the impossible choice between Kath and the cricket kit.

There was one sad irony to my successful debut for England in that Trent Bridge Test. While I was bowling out Australia, the man who had done so much to develop my talent and forge my attitude to the game, Brian Close, was announcing his retirement from first-class cricket. Kath and I often talked about what might have happened if I had had the benefit of Closey's guidance on and off the field for a while longer. He was a great stabilising influence on me, and when he felt I needed reining in there was no mistaking the message, but I respected him for it. As my career progressed, there were several occasions when a stentorian few words from Brian – probably along the lines of 'Don't be such a fucking idiot' – might have saved me from myself. Left to my own devices, my motto was 'Beefy knows best', and in my more reflective moments, even I was aware that that was far from always the case.

My first Test match had only strengthened my determination to rise to the very top of the game and I could see the financial rewards that would be available as the top players in sports like football and cricket became more widely recognised beyond the confines of their own sport. I intended to make sure that one of them was me; I wanted to be the best there was.

After Trent Bridge, my selection for the fourth Test at Headingley was a formality, and there I and the team took a further opportunity to rub Australia's collective nose in it. Brears won the toss and chose to bat – a decision he may have regretted since he was out at once for a duck – but Boycs and Bob Woolmer then set about building a big total. Boycs followed up his Trent Bridge heroics with another century, a massive 191, and in the process became the first player ever to score his hundredth first-class century in a Test match. In front of a sell-out crowd of fervent Yorkshire Boycott-worshippers, he simply ground the Aussies down. When he reached his hundred there was a roar that could probably have been heard in Epworth, as his fellow Yorkshiremen celebrated. As a local newspaper put it the next day, it was 'not merely another triumph against Australia, but another victory in the greatest and most long-running battle of them all – Yorkshire against the rest!'

After waiting my turn to bat for hours while Boycs was piling up the runs, I then got a bit carried away by the feverish atmosphere and tried to hit the third ball I faced from Ray Bright out of the ground. Had I connected it would have cleared the stand with something to spare, instead I missed and was bowled for my first Test duck in only my second Test innings. We totalled 436 and I then redeemed myself with the ball, taking five for 21 as the Aussies, who probably felt by now as if they had been bowling at Boycott non-stop since the moment they stepped off the plane at Heathrow, crumbled to 103 all out. I was wicketless in the second innings but only Rod Marsh with 63 put up much resistance and we eventually crushed them by an innings and 85 runs.

I also had a less pleasant reason to remember the match. While fielding in the deep during Australia's second innings, I found a particularly stupid way of getting injured by treading on the ball as I tried to field it. I felt a searing pain in my left foot straight away, but like an idiot, I continued to field and even bowl on it, and it was not until after the match that I found out I'd broken a bone, a stress fracture that had been further aggravated when I kept bowling. As a result, my Test career came to a temporary halt and I was ruled out of the last match of the series at The Oval, though it was some consolation when I was named as Young Cricketer of the Year by the Cricket Writers' Club.

When I got back to Somerset, the team doctor had a look at my foot and then sent me to see a specialist at Musgrove Park Hospital in Taunton. On my way for an X-ray, I was taken through a children's ward where, among a roomful of sick or heavily bandaged kids, I saw four perfectly normal-looking youngsters sitting around a small table playing Monopoly. 'What are they doing here?' I asked the specialist.

'They're suffering from leukaemia,' he said. 'Two of them have very little time to live.'

In that moment all my feelings of self-satisfaction evaporated. I'd never even heard of leukaemia but I listened intently as he explained exactly what happens to a child's body when he is suffering from the disease. I was aghast. How could these normal-looking children, playing so happily in front of us, be on the point of death? I thought of Kath and the baby we were expecting, and what such a devastating blow would do to us. When the specialist told me that a shortage of funds meant that the hospital could no longer hold the party they always held whenever a child was dying – the last happy memory he or she would ever have – I didn't need a second to make up my mind what to do. It wasn't a huge amount of money, just £50 for some sausage rolls, crisps, 'fizzy pop', party hats, and that sort of thing, and I wrote out a cheque straight away. It was the start of a lifetime involvement with the fight against that terrible disease. I paid for a lot of parties after that – sadly, far too many – and I then began to cast around for a way I could help to prevent the disease, rather than just help those who were already beyond hope.

A few days later I was back in hospital for a far more pleasurable experience and I had cause to be grateful for that foot injury because, had I not been injured, I would have been on Test match duty and would have missed one of the great moments of my life: the birth of my son, Liam. I had to wait a long time before I could hold him in my arms, because the birth was far from straightforward.

In the early hours of 24 August, Kath told me that her waters had burst and by mid-morning we were driving to the maternity ward. Originally I had told her that I wouldn't be there for the birth. Call me old-fashioned, call me a coward, but I felt I would just be getting in the way, so I dropped Kath off, kissed her goodbye, went home to feed the dog and give her a walk, in case it was a long time before she got another one, and then went to a pub to wait, but not for long. Soon afterwards, Jan called me to say that Kath was really suffering badly. I went straight back to the hospital and was at her side from then on.

When I got to the delivery room, I found Kath crawling around on her hands and knees and screaming out in pain. I ran to get hold of the midwife. The woman who turned up to take care of Kath greeted me by saying, 'I don't want you fainting at the sight of blood. If you're going to do that, get out of the way now, because I don't want to be stepping over your prone body for the next hour or so.'

She then turned her charm on Kath. After examining her, she said, 'Don't make such a fuss, everything's perfectly normal. You're just getting hysterical for no reason. Now stop being silly.'

You tend to assume that medical personnel know what they're talking about so, even though she could have been a bit less patronising and a lot more pleasant, I let it go. I was holding Kath's hand, and as the labour went on I was trying to get into the spirit of things by telling her, 'Come on now, push,' which clearly wasn't helping because all I got in reply was a mouthful that would have made Brian Close blush.

Finally, a doctor appeared and after examining Kath he at once diagnosed that Liam was in an inverted position in her womb. Far from being 'hysterical' and 'silly', Kath had genuinely been in agony. I was still there when Liam was finally born at 3.50 on 26 August, although by that stage Kath was almost too exhausted to care; she'd been in labour for over twenty-six hours. Fortunately there were no long-term repercussions from Liam's prolonged and, for Kath, very painful birth.

I was now a proud dad, but with a winter tour of Pakistan and New Zealand looming, I didn't have too long to reflect on the joys of fatherhood. I went for a fitness test at Edgbaston on my injured foot, a rather less scientific process than it would be now. Charlie Elliott, the former umpire and Test selector, watched me bowl a dozen balls in the indoor nets and then said, 'All right?'

'Fine,' I said, and that was the fitness test over.

I was duly named in the England touring party, heralding the start of another long separation from Kath. Having been away from her the previous winter on the Whitbread Scholarship, I was now disappearing again only a couple of months after Liam's birth. If there was a hint of irritation in Kath's voice when she told me 'You're like a kid getting ready to go back to boarding school' as I checked and packed my kit, it was entirely understandable. She would be left literally holding the baby, while I was off enjoying myself.

My rise from cricketing zero to hero had been so sudden that, while it brought obvious benefits, it also led to frictions between us. When we got married, I wasn't even certain of my place in the Somerset first team. Yet within six months I'd been picked for England's one-day side and twelve months after that I was playing a starring role in the England Test team. It transformed both our lives in ways that we couldn't have imagined and we both found it a hard adjustment to make. If we'd been starry-eyed in love when we married, the romance had now turned a little sour. Parents and friends who had all told us 'You're too young' would have been perfectly entitled to say 'I told you so', because we could easily have been divorced almost as quickly as we were married.

Kath had been warned in advance that the life of a cricketer's wife is seldom easy, but being the wife of a twenty-one-year-old Ian Botham was harder than most. It helped her that, having known Brian and Vivienne Close all her life, she was already aware of what life with a professional cricketer would be like before she married me. There were long separations, but far more damaging than those was the inattention, bordering on indifference, that I displayed towards her at times. I was undoubtedly immature and still approaching life like a single man, and I was also so focused on my cricket career and so self-centred in that respect that Kath often came well down my list of priorities. During our courtship, I'd watched for her arrival at the ground and been so keen to see her that I was invariably the first one changed and out of the dressing room at the close of play. Now, I'd often be in the bar for an hour or so after the close of play and if Kath complained that I was putting my teammates before her, my customary response was to tell her, 'You're talking nonsense, Kath. Now cheer up and get on with it,' which cannot exactly have helped.

I had neither the time nor the patience to sit down with her and talk over our problems, and instead we just rowed constantly. We were both very strong-willed, and neither of us would back down in an argument. After we'd finished shouting, we'd relapse into an angry silence. On one occasion, driving the twenty-eight miles from my parents' house in Yeovil to a match at Taunton, we barely exchanged a single word. It tortures me now to look back and see how insensitive, callous and downright boorish I was then, but I was so focused on attaining my goals in cricket that everything else seemed secondary, almost unreal.

Now I was leaving for several months and Kath would not only have to deal with Liam on her own but also cope with an ever-increasing workload. She was running our business and she was the one who had to deal with the floods of correspondence, offering endorsements and public appearances, fan letters, hate mail, and all the rest. She found it particularly hard to deal with all the hundreds of requests from charities, all doing very good work in their own field. How could she possibly recommend that we support some and not the others? In the end, we were both very grateful for the advice given by that great and very kind-hearted man the late Eric Morecambe, who sat next to Kath at Lord's on the one and only time she was invited to attend a function there. In the course of conversation he said, 'Now, how are you coping with the sudden fame?' and when Kath mentioned the agonies she was going through about the charity requests, he said, 'Just choose one charity that's close to both your hearts and put all your energies into that.' It was wise advice, and we followed it.

When the day arrived and I set off on tour with England for the first time, I was determined that this was going to be the start of something big, but despite my successful introduction to Test cricket under his captaincy, I soon found out that I still had something to prove to Mike Brearley. Early in the tour, I had a private chat with him about how he saw my role. As usual I was full of myself and wanting to be heavily involved but felt I was being underused. 'Why am I not playing more?' I said.

Brears shrugged. 'Well, I consider Chris Old to be my premier all-rounder and I've chosen to go with him in the Tests.'

I was gobsmacked – it was bullshit then and it's still bullshit now. 'No way is he the best all-rounder and I'll prove it to you once and for all,' I said. 'I'll make you eat those words.' That was easier said than done because on any tour, once the first couple of games are out of the way, the "fringe" players have few opportunities to impress. Nor did my aversion to nets help me to catch Brears's eye. Players like Geoffrey Boycott would bat in the nets all day and still not have had enough; he even went in the nets for an hour before he went out to bat in the middle. I used to say to him that he did it so that he could play all his shots and get them out of his system before he went out to bat.

I much preferred to practise in the middle. If I had a problem, I'd round up a couple of teammates and go and work on it out on the cricket field rather than the nets. In the early stages of the tour, I kept being no-balled for overstepping the crease in my delivery stride. It was hard enough taking wickets in Pakistan anyway without taking them with deliveries that turned out to be no-balls, so I resolved to sort out the problem there and then. I worked on it until I'd cracked it and for the rest of my career I never bowled another front-foot no-ball. The umpire who called me for two in a crucial match years later obviously disagreed, but the videotapes of the game showed that he was wrong.

Having sorted out that problem, I was itching for a chance to get on the field and prove Brears wrong, but he was spared any immediate confrontation with me because Mike Hendrick and I were then laid low with amoebic dysentery. Mike and I shared a room, which was unfortunate since there was only one toilet and dysentery does not really lend itself to politely waiting your turn. It was not a pleasant illness to have in the heat of Pakistan and it got so bad that at one point I really thought I was dying. The disease was so virulent that I lost the whole of my stomach lining, and it has given me problems ever since. I have to take medication daily, even to this day.

Both Mike and I had lost stones in weight by the time we were cured and were as weak as kittens, but we were still determined to give it our best shot to try and establish ourselves in the side, and even tried to fool the management. Reporting for duty, pale-faced, hollow-eyed and trembling, but protesting our one hundred per cent fitness on the morning of the final warm-up match before the Test, we managed about fifty yards of one lap around the ground under the sceptical gaze of Brears, his fellow selectors and physio Bernard Thomas before collapsing in shattered heaps.

Being unable to get on the field and give it my all was enormously frustrating, but when I was finally passed fit to play, I showed no ill effects from the disease and came back in style, scoring heavily and taking plenty of wickets in the last two one-dayers in Pakistan and the first ones in New Zealand. Whether even that would have been enough to persuade Brears to include me in the Test team ahead of Chris Old, I'm not sure, but in the event, Brears broke his arm in the last one-dayer in Pakistan and went home.

Geoffrey Boycott took over as captain for the New Zealand leg, and I was straight back in the team for the first Test at Wellington, one of the strangest I ever played. After winning the toss, Boycs put New Zealand in and they made 228. In reply, Boycs then embarked on a personal go-slow, scoring just 10 runs in the first hour, 12 in the second, 6 runs in the third (and 4 of those came off one shot), and 12 in the fourth. By then I'd long since stopped counting and fallen asleep – if counting sheep won't cure your insomnia, I can guarantee that counting Boycott singles will – but, according to those who managed to stay awake, it took him well over three more hours to add his final 37 runs before he was at last mercifully out for 77. In all, he faced 304 balls and his innings lasted seven hours twenty-two minutes.

We were only 13 behind on first innings and got the Kiwis out for 123 second time around, leaving us a very modest victory target of 137; but many of us must still have been in a Boycott-induced trance, because we completely fell apart, scoring a humiliating 64 all out to lose by 72 runs. I didn't exactly cover myself in glory, scoring only 7 and 19 in the match, as Richard Hadlee twice tempted me into the hook and had me caught, at square leg in the first innings and then at deep backward square leg in the second. It was the Kiwis' first-ever win over England in forty-eight years and forty-eight Tests between the two countries and, Boycott-style boredom apart, the main factor in their win was the brilliant bowling of Hadlee, who took ten wickets for 100 in the match.

Having just been defeated, it was neither the time nor the place to complain – we didn't want to be 'whingeing Poms' – but the dubious quality of some of the umpiring did not help our cause at all. Neutral umpires were not used in those days and there's no doubt in my mind that the Kiwis benefited from far more than their share of 'home' decisions. In his first over, Bob Willis found the edge of opener John Wright's bat. It was a thickish edge and flew wide enough for wicketkeeper Bob Taylor to have to dive in front of first slip to take the catch. Yet our appeal was met with a shake of the head and when Bob asked the umpire at the end of the over, 'What was wrong with that, then?' his reply was 'Well, umpires have to get their eye in as well.' That particular decision didn't cost us too much – Phil Edmonds got Wright out caught and bowled for 4 as soon as he came on – but more than a few other decisions went New Zealand's way in the rest of that series and arguably cost us at least one Test, if not the series as a whole.

Boycott's behaviour in the second Test at Christchurch was even more mystifying. We were determined to level the series and after our first five wickets fell fairly cheaply, I set myself to play a big innings. Our 'keeper Bob Taylor kept me company for almost five hours while we added 160 for the sixth wicket but, with my maiden Test century in sight, I then repaid him for his support by running him out, Boycott-style. Becalmed on 99, my nerves eventually got the better of me and I called him for a suicidal single. After he was out, I duly reached my hundred, but I owed Bob a big apology when I got back to the dressing room.

It was not the most spectacular innings of my career but my maiden Test hundred was one of the most satisfying. In my early career, batting had been a very straightforward business – 'Get out there and smack it' – but if I was going to succeed at Test level, there would be times when I would have to show a bit more guile and patience. My experiences in the first Test at Wellington, holing out twice to Richard Hadlee, also helped me make that century at Christchurch. I remembered the lesson and when Hadlee dropped short this time, I just let the ball go. It was still an aggressive innings, but it was controlled aggression. It was a fantastic feeling, and when I was out for 103 – I had a rush of blood and edged one to the wicketkeeper as soon as I'd reached my hundred – I just wanted to go out there and do it all over again.

We eventually reached 418 all out and I then took five wickets for 73, and with Phil Edmonds chipping in with four for 38, we bowled them out for 235, just failing to enforce the follow-on. We needed quick runs to give us enough time to bowl them out a second time and win the match. As captain, Boycs should have led from the front, but as usual he seemed so obsessed by his own innings that he failed to see the urgency and didn't get the scoreboard moving at all. In the end he batted for two hours and faced eighty balls but scored just 26 runs.

The tense atmosphere was made worse after the Kiwi seam bowler Ewen Chatfield produced a shocking piece of gamesmanship. As he reached the wicket to send down a delivery, he suddenly stopped and removed the bails. Derek Randall was backing up and slightly out of his ground and when Chatfield appealed, the umpire had no option but to give him out, but as every schoolboy cricketer in New Zealand and anywhere else the game is played could have told Chatfield, such actions are just 'not cricket'. It would have been acceptable if Derek had been trying to steal an advantage by sprinting out of the crease too soon, but even then it's customary to give a warning before carrying out the threat to run him out. Derek was just backing up in the normal way, and Chatfield's action led to some seriously bad feeling between the sides.

I was next in, promoted up the order to try and pick up the pace. I first let Chatfield know what we thought of him and then exchanged a few words with Boycott. 'We're going a bit slow, Boycs,' I said.

'I know. I'm trying my best, but I just can't seem to get the ball off the square.'

'Don't worry, Boycs,' I said. 'I'll sort everything out.'

I was as good as my word. I hit the ball into the offside and, once more in true Boycott-style, called him for a suicidal single. He never stood a chance and was run out by half the length of the pitch. He stared at me aghast, muttered, 'What have you done? What have you done?' and then began the long walk back to the pavilion.

What I'd done was to follow to the letter the instructions I'd been given by Boycott's vice-captain Bob Willis. Tearing his hair out at the slowness of our scoring rate, he had sent me on my way to the crease with the clearest if most unusual of instructions: 'Go and run the bugger out.' He probably knew I was the man for the job because he'd seen me do it to Bob Taylor in the first innings ...

I was only too happy to oblige, and after getting rid of Boycs, by close of play I had reached a swift 30 off thirty-one balls. We now had a lead of 279, probably more than enough in a low-scoring match, but when I got back to the dressing room, Boycs was in a sulk, lying on a bench with a towel over his head and refusing to talk to anyone, least of all me. The *omertà* continued the next morning, when the only player he would talk to was his Yorkshire teammate and close ally Geoff Cope, with whom he spent the early morning pacing the outfield as he agonised over the timing of the declaration and his future as captain.

In the end, he declared at our overnight total. Bob Willis then blew the New Zealand top order away and I mopped up the tail and the Kiwis were all out before lunch, squaring the series 1-1. The morning session ranks as one of the stranger ones of my entire career. Boycs was now talking to the rest of the team but still not to me so when I was bowling and he wanted to communicate with me he had to use a go-between. Boycs would summon cover or mid-off and they would then jog over to me to say, 'Boycs wants to know if you want another slip.' I'd say 'Tell him that would be nice,' and he'd then jog back to pass on the message. After the match was over and won, Boycs suddenly regained the power of speech and began regaling the assembled press men with a blow-by-blow account of the victory he had overseen.

Clive Radley scored 153 and there were half-centuries from

Boycs, Graham Roope and me as we took a first innings lead of 114 in the final Test at Auckland, and I had another five-wicket haul in New Zealand's, but Geoff Howarth scored a century in both innings to steer New Zealand to the safety of a draw, leaving the series shared 1-1. It hadn't been the most successful tour in English cricket history but from a personal point of view, after a terrible start when I'd lost the Pakistan leg of the tour to dysentery and been told by Mike Brearley that Chris Old was his first choice in my position, I'd seized my chance in New Zealand and taken what I hoped would prove an unshakeable grip on that England all-rounder spot.

By the time I got home, I hadn't seen Kath and our new baby for three months. In those days I and most of the other players simply couldn't afford to bring our wives and kids out for even part of the tour. The buffers' brigade at Lord's weren't going to go out of their way to help us; they preferred the wives to be safely out of the way back in England. So we not only had to pay their fares ourselves if we wanted them out there, but also – insult added to injury – we had to pay a supplement on our room charge. We shared rooms with a teammate in those days, so if Kath had come out, I'd have had to pay for her flights and the cost of another room for my ousted teammate. They organise things rather differently now: wives and girlfriends are flown out and accommodated in the same hotels as the players, all at ECB expense, and they even get a 'shopping allowance'.

Returning home after so long away always required a period of adjustment for both of us. Kath had got used to her routine without me, Liam didn't even recognise this strange, long-haired and moustachioed man who'd suddenly appeared in his life, and I had to get used to the fact that, after three months living in hotel rooms, there was no longer a maid service. I had to pick up my own wet towels and clean up after myself now. Kath had also hardly been out for a few months and was keen to resurrect our social life, but I was exhausted from the tour, sick to death of hotels and restaurants, and just wanted to enjoy my home and my family. When the dust had settled, we both vowed that we would never again be apart from each other for so long.

As soon as he could crawl, Liam displayed the same venturesome spirit that I'd shown as a child. Kath once found him hanging upside down from the garden gate, caught by the straps of his dungarees as he made a bid for freedom, and when he was a little older he was always disappearing to one of the neighbouring farms, where he'd help to feed the calves and even try to drive the tractors.

Back at Somerset for the new season, I renewed acquaintance with Viv Richards, who had just returned from the West Indies. It was a pattern that both of us were to follow for many seasons: winters touring with our national sides, summers playing for Somerset. In those days there were no central contracts for Test players and no rest periods between games; professional cricket was a relentless seven-day-a-week treadmill throughout the season. Many times I'd finish a Test match at six in the evening and have to leave at once to drive a hundred miles or more to be ready for a county game starting the next morning. It doesn't happen now; with central contracts from the ECB and an ever-expanding programme of Tests and one-dayers, their counties are lucky to have Test players for a handful of games a year. Back then we were with our counties until the day before a Test match started and then back with them the day after it finished.

I was already well on the way to establishing myself in the England team, but the summer Tests against Pakistan offered me the chance to make the all-rounder spot my own. In the first Test at Edgbaston, my old rival Chris Old returned figures of seven for 50 in the Pakistan first innings, but I riposted with another century, exactly 100, in our first knock, and with Clive Radley also scoring a ton and David Gower notching a half-century on his debut, we posted a big first innings lead and cantered to victory by an innings and 57 runs.

During the game I also had my first experience of the controversies that seemed to dog England-Pakistan matches in which I was involved over a number of years. The Pakistan players and management were unhappy with Bob Willis's bowling to their night-watchman Iqbal Qasim after they had followed on. Qasim saw out the last over on the Saturday evening, and then dealt with a few lifting deliveries from Bob on Monday morning without any apparent problems, but when Bob switched to bowling round the wicket, he hit Qasim in the mouth with a ball that reared sharply from short of a length. He had to retire hurt and the Pakistan manager, Mahmood Hussain, then accused Bob of unfair tactics.

Mike Brearley, back in harness after recovering from his broken arm, didn't agree, arguing that Qasim was a competent enough batsman to play the short stuff and had just been unlucky to be on the wrong end of a particularly spiteful delivery that might have done the same thing to any Pakistan batsman. After my early experiences against Andy Roberts, I felt able to discuss being hit in the mouth by a short-pitched ball with some authority, and as I saw it, the problem was not Qasim's lack of ability but the fact the visitors were heading for defeat by an innings inside four days. The way Qasim had batted up to that point proved he was no rabbit. Nonetheless in the interests of fairness and to avoid animosity between the teams in the remainder of the series, a compromise was reached between the two managements. As a result we went into the next match at Lord's with a total of five players classified as non-batsmen, who would be spared trial by bouncer. Our pace bowlers Bob Willis and Mike Hendrick were given protection and three Pakistanis – Qasim, Sikander Bakht and Liaqat Ali – were also guaranteed a bouncer-free Test.

The new arrangements made no discernible difference to the result, another emphatic English victory in a match that also gave me my best-ever Test match figures. I scored 108 – my third Test century in the last four Tests – and with solid half-centuries from

Graham Gooch, David Gower and Graham Roope, we reached 364. Bob Willis then took five wickets and Phil Edmonds four for 6 as Pakistan collapsed to 105 all out and had to follow on, but second time around it was my turn to shine with the ball. I was put on at the Nursery End to allow Bob to change ends and got into my rhythm at once. I always liked bowling at Lord's, particularly from the Nursery End, where the slope exaggerated my natural movement away from the bat, and on this occasion I took seven wickets in the morning session and eight for 34 overall, as their last eight wickets fell for 43, to give us victory by an innings and 120 runs. My figures were the best by any England bowler since Jim Laker took nine for 37 and ten for 53 against Australia at Old Trafford in 1956. The final Test, at Headingley, ended in a rain-ruined draw, giving us a 2-0 series victory.

New Zealand were our next opponents in that 'split' summer of 1978, and perhaps mercifully for the sake of relations between the teams, Ewen Chatfield did not make the tour party and New Zealand umpires were not involved. Although my batting tailed off slightly from the heights of the first series, my bowling more than compensated for that. During the three-match series, I took six for 34 in the second Test at Trent Bridge, including my fiftieth Test wicket, and followed that up with six for 101 and five for 39 in the final Test of the summer at Lord's, making a total of twenty-four wickets in the three-match series, as we completed a 3-0 whitewash that also marked the end of my first year as a Test cricketer. The apprehensive debutant had come of age and I could be proud of my record: eleven Tests, three centuries, eight five-wicket hauls and one bag of ten wickets in a match.

As far as the public was concerned, the void created by Tony Greig's defection to Packer had now been well and truly filled. West Indian batting line-ups in the 1950s had been dominated by the 'Three Ws' – Everton Weekes, Clyde Walcott and Frank Worrell. English cricket had now seen the emergence of the 'Three Gs' –

Mike Gatting, Graham Gooch and David Gower. Gooch had been a Test player since 1975, but both Gatting and Gower made their first appearances in that year of 1978. They were three characters who differed in just about every degrees, but they had two things in common: they were all future England captains and they were three very prolific run-scorers.

Graham Gooch was the elder statesman of the three, who made his Test debut against Australia at Birmingham in 1975. It wasn't the most auspicious of starts – he was out for a pair, caught behind off Max Walker in the first innings and off Jeff Thomson in the second – and the portly, rather shy Gooch looked anything but a Test cricketer on that occasion. He played only one more Test before being exiled to the international wilderness for three years and did not play his next until 1978, in the Lord's Test against Pakistan, securing his place with a half-century in an innings victory. One of his greatest strengths was his determination and dedication to improving his game. Criticised for his weight, Gooch went on a fitness campaign that continued for the rest of his long career – his last Test came twenty years after his first, once more against the old enemy, Australia, at Perth in 1995. Along the way he scored an English Test record of 8,900 runs at an average of 42.15, and hit twenty Test centuries with his highest score a triple century – 333.

When he began, Gooch was a ferocious hitter with a bat that felt like a breeze block, but he adapted his game as he went on, and almost uniquely among cricketers seemed to keep on getting better and better the older he got. He often virtually carried the England batting on his own, and as opening bat, he took on the most fast and ferocious bowlers in world cricket, including the West Indies legendary pace attack, when they were at their freshest, played them all fearlessly and probably scored as many runs as anyone against them. No one who saw his magnificent, match-winning 154 not out against the West Indies on a seamer's wicket at Headingley in 1991 will ever forget it.

Off the field he was never an easy man to read; always private, in adversity he could often be morose and introspective. His decision to join the first South African rebel tour – one of the few young players to do so – cost him three years of his Test career. The English cricket establishment took a long time to forgive him and it could be argued that they only appointed him Test captain when all other candidates had been tried and failed. He did well at first, his fitness and hard work regime bringing a new sense of purpose to the side and with it improved results, but when things started to go wrong, his only response was to up the physical workload even more and that rapidly became counterproductive. In my opinion it cost us the 1992 World Cup. His treatment of David Gower was also baffling. They were poles apart as characters, but to spurn Gower's talent as a batsman was foolish and short-sighted in the extreme.

David Gower was the most languid of characters. When on his game, no one made batting look easier and his strokeplay, his flair and his sheer genius had crowds around the world on the edge of their seats whenever he went out to bat. My antipathy to watching cricket from the pavilion was well known, but David and Viv Richards were the only players for whom I would make an exception. I sat for hours watching David bat, wondering how the hell he could produce such brilliant strokeplay and make it look so effortless that one could almost imagine him yawning as he despatched yet another perfect cover drive to the boundary. He was also a superb athlete and one of the most brilliant cover fielders I've ever seen. He hated nets, training sessions and all the other trappings of the 'modern approach' to the game, took remarkably little exercise, and was a gourmet, wine connoisseur and bon viveur as well, yet he was one of the most naturally athletic, as well as the most naturally talented, players in the world game. His golden locks might have brought Shirley Temple to mind, but any fast bowler thinking Gower might be a soft touch would soon find themselves being smashed all over the ground by a batsman who wasn't even breaking sweat.

He made his debut in the first Test against Pakistan in 1978 and in true Gower style seemed to have hours of time in hand as he slid on to the back foot and rifled a pull for 4 off the first ball he received in Test cricket. He went on to make a half-century in that first Test innings ... though he was rather outshone by an all-rounder who hit a bruising century!

Those who saw only the surface impression often thought him too laid-back, diffident, even indifferent, and commentators would lavish praise on his strokeplay but in the next breath berate him for getting out with a 'careless' shot. The hard facts are that in the course of his career he scored a then English Test record of 8,231 runs at an average of 44.25 and you don't achieve those sorts of figures without having a core of steel beneath the cavalier exterior. Had the England management's obsession with work-rate and suspicion of someone with such apparently effortless gifts not deprived him of at least two more years' Test cricket when still at the height of his powers, he would probably have passed ten thousand Test runs. He now sits alongside me in the Sky TV commentary box and is as good and apparently effortless at that as he was with a bat in his hand in the middle.

Mike Gatting made his debut a few months before Gower, in Karachi on the tour of Pakistan in January 1978. He was probably a more talented all-round sportsman than either of the other two – he was a good golfer, footballer, and squash player – but he wasn't quite in their league as a batsman. Although far less prolific than Gower and Gooch – he scored 4,409 Test runs at an average of 35.55 – Gatt's career statistics don't tell the whole story of the man. He began and ended his Test career with a run of low scores, but for five years when he was at his peak in the mid-1980s, he scored as heavily as any England batsman. He was as different in every way from "the Golden One" as it was possible to imagine. Gatt was gutsy, industrious, pugnacious, an NCO, not an officer, but a man who would fight to his last breath for England ... and he could certainly eat for England too.

Where Gower was a gourmet, Gatt was definitely a gourmand – plenty of everything – but if you ever had to choose one man to go into the trenches with you, Gatt would be an automatic selection.

His courage was exemplified by his reaction to having his nose splattered all over his face by a ball from Malcolm Marshall. Doctors were worried that the force of the blow might even have done permanent damage to Gatt's sight; his only concern was how quick he could get back on the field to resume his innings. His build didn't exactly scream 'athlete', but the strength in his forearms was unbelievable – blistering pulls, hooks, cuts and back-foot punches of the ball through the offside were Gatt's trademark – and very few people played spin as well as Gatt. In fact, he didn't just play it, he usually murdered it.

Brought into the England side as a twenty-year-old, it took him seven years and thirty-one Tests to record his first Test century, at which time his Test batting average was a lowly 23.65, but he made up for lost time after that with ten centuries in total and a highest score of 207, and averaged well over 40 throughout the remainder of his career.

As England captain, he led from the front, and although he only won two Tests as captain, it was enough to secure the Ashes in 1986-87 and he played a huge part in that success. He was wise enough to allow the senior players a good measure of personal responsibility, saying, 'I'll trust you to do what you think you need to do.' It was a dramatic contrast to the Gooch approach, but it paid off. Team spirit was high, the tour was very enjoyable, but crucially the results prove that Gatt's approach worked. We were given no chance before the tour, but came home with the Ashes.

However, the England selectors were soon gunning for Gatt after his notorious row with Pakistani umpire Shakoor Rana later that year and they found an excuse to sack him six months later after tabloids published accounts of an alleged affair with a barmaid. An embittered Gatt captained a rebel tour to South Africa in 1989 and though he played on for England until 1995 – his last Test, like Gooch, was against Australia in Perth – the England captaincy was never restored to him.

If Gooch, Gower and Gatting were the rising stars of the England batting line-up, I hadn't been doing too badly myself and my great year was capped by the announcement that I'd been named as one of *Wisden*'s Five Cricketers of the Year. Fleet Street was busily proclaiming me the new 'superstar' of English cricket, and offers of sponsorship deals, product endorsements, newspaper columns and personal appearances were flooding in.

It brought us a very welcome boost to our family income, but my spare time was increasingly taken up by events and functions – sportsmen's dinners, celebrity golf tournaments, shop openings and so on – and Kath must often have felt like a single parent. She never complained, though as any parent knows, looking after a baby is pretty exhausting even with two people sharing the load.

It was obvious that I was going to be picked for the Ashes tour that winter and I'd made a solemn promise to Kath that we'd be together in Australia for part of the tour. However, we had just discovered that she was pregnant again and her doctor told her that she could only undertake the long flight to Australia in the early stages of the pregnancy. If she was going to come at all, it would have to be right at the start of the tour. The TCCB had never been keen on wives coming out on tour, least of all at the start of one, but I wrote off with a formal request and was told that I would be notified of their response in due course.

Having taken soundings with his committee, the TCCB secretary Donald Carr rang me at home one evening. 'Sorry Ian,' he said, 'the answer is no.'

'Well I'm sorry too, Donald,' I said, 'but that's not good enough. I suggest that you do everything in your power to get that decision changed.' The threat was unspoken but obvious: if I didn't get the right answer, England would be going into an Ashes series without their first-choice Test all-rounder.

He went away for further consultations and then called back – the answer was still no. We spoke several more times that evening but were getting nowhere fast, so I finally made the threat explicit. 'Donald, I'm not bluffing here. If you won't allow Kath to join me on the tour, I'll have no option but to withdraw from it.'

I left him to sleep on it and early the next morning I took yet another call from him. 'Hello Ian,' he said. 'On reflection, the TCCB have decided that Kath will be able to join you in Australia after all.' It was the result I wanted, but I might have been storing up trouble for myself in the future. I had put a few people's backs up on the committee and they had long memories.

After all this, I nearly missed the tour anyway after injuring my hand in a freak accident at a send-off party in my local pub. I was walking through to the pool room from the main bar when someone behind me shouted out, 'Ian? Just a minute?' I turned my head to see who it was, putting my hand out to stop the door swinging shut. Unfortunately, it was a glass door on a strong spring and as it swung back, my hand went straight through it. Even worse, I instinctively jerked my hand back towards me, doing further damage on the broken glass. There was blood everywhere and I couldn't move my hand. I was taken straight to hospital and spent a sleepless night, afraid that the accident had ended my career. The next morning, I had an operation to investigate the damage and try to repair it. It was done under a general anaesthetic so I knew nothing until I came round in the afternoon. Still groggy, I pestered the nurse to find the specialist, who arrived at my bedside a few minutes later. I'd severed two tendons, and come within a whisker of severing a nerve too, but the good news was that there was no permanent nerve damage and the injury would only take a few weeks to heal.

When Kath picked me up from hospital, she told me that I was not the only one who'd had a sleepless night. She'd answered a knock at our front door in Epworth the previous evening to find two reporters – to call them 'reptiles' would be an unfair slur on cold-blooded creatures – from a tabloid newspaper standing there. 'Evening Mrs Botham,' one said. 'Can you confirm a report we've had that Ian has been badly injured in a pub brawl and is out of the England tour?'

We'd already been warned by Donald Carr not to say anything about the incident until the TCCB had issued its own press statement, so Kath just said, 'I'm afraid I've got no comment to make.'

'Come off it, luv,' the other one said – as they do. 'We've already got the story and whatever you say, even if you say nothing at all, we're still going to print it. Why don't you just come clean and tell us what happened in your own words?'

'Sorry,' she said, 'there's really nothing I can add to what I've said already.' They tried a bit longer and then stalked off into the night. The next morning, as threatened, the paper duly ran a story alleging that I'd been involved in a punch-up in a pub. We'd seen the tabloids at work when they were building me up, now we had to realise that there was another side of the coin: what goes up, must come down.

We arrived in Australia together at the end of October 1978 and my tendons had healed and I was ready for action a fortnight before the first Test in Brisbane. The night before the Test, Kath and I visited a celebrated seafood restaurant just outside town and I put away a plate of Oysters Kilpatrick. I don't know about Patrick, but they certainly did a job on me. I was commuting between the bog and the basin and beginning to have flashbacks to the dysentery on the tour of Pakistan, when Kath called the England physio, Bernard Thomas. He got a doctor to come straight away. The England team always had a doctor on stand-by and he injected me with a powerful sedative. Bernard then stayed with me for most of the night, first putting me in a cold bath to bring my body temperature down and then waking me every two hours, to rehydrate me, bathe me and change my bedding – I was sweating so much from the fever that my sheets were soaking wet. Liam, bouncing up and down in his cot on the other side of the room, thought it was a great game and wanted to join in himself. The food-poisoning, combined with the sedative, eventually put me into a sleep so deep that the doctor might well have pronounced me dead if he'd returned for a second visit. Bernard finally managed to shake me awake at ten the next morning and I eventually arrived at the Gabba just twenty minutes before the start of play.

It was a very unfamiliar Australian team that faced us, defections to Packer having removed some of the biggest stars in the game; but we'd lost key players too and we knew that any Australians pulling on the baggy green caps would be far from easy beats. Mike Brearley, now with a full chin of beard and promptly christened 'The Ayatollah' by the locals in honour of the Iranian leader, Ayatollah Khomeini, lost the toss and the Aussies decided to bat. It turned out to be a good toss to lose: the Aussie opener Cosier had a rush of blood and was run out with only 2 on the board and they then slumped to 26 for six and then 53 for seven, before struggling through to 116 all out. Bob Willis took four wickets and I chipped in with three for 40 and then scored 49 as we built up a 170-run lead, Derek Randall top-scoring with 75. Aussie paceman Rodney Hogg began what was to be a milestone series for him with six for 74. The Aussies did better in their second innings, with Graham Yallop and Kim Hughes both scoring centuries and sharing a big partnership for the fourth wicket, but once they were parted, wickets fell at regular intervals and we were left with a modest 170 to win the match. We knocked them off for the loss of three wickets, Derek Randall again top-scoring with 74 not out.

Kath had to fly home before the next Test, my thirteenth for England. I'm not a superstitious person but for the first time I came out of a Test without a wicket and match figures of none for 100. I only scored 11 and 30 when we batted but it made no difference to the result. Despite a ten-wicket match haul for Rodney Hogg, we won by 166 runs to go two-nil up in the series. We went into the third Test, the traditional Christmas holiday match at Melbourne, fancying our chances of making it 3-0, but instead Brears suffered his first defeat as captain in sixteen Tests as Allan Border started his Test career on the winning side. With Rodney Hogg taking his fourth five-wicket haul in five innings, we were tumbled out for 143 in the first innings. Although I was back among the wickets with three for 68 and three for 41, we were soon in trouble at 6 for two in our second innings chasing 283 to win. We eventually capitulated for 179, losing by 103 runs, with Hogg taking yet another five wickets to end with his second ten-wicket match haul in a row.

It was a big shock for the whole party. We had been so dominant in the first two games and now were battling to regain our momentum. In the fourth Test early in the New Year on a spinner's wicket at the Sydney Cricket Ground, I top-scored with 59 out of a disappointing first innings total of 152 and by the end of the first day the Australians looked to be cruising at 56 for one. On the second day, we dug deep and restricted them to a total of 294 and a first innings lead of 142 runs. Once again we were soon in trouble in our second innings with Boycs out first ball – his first duck for England in nearly ten years – but Derek "Arkle" Randall then began a salvage operation with a brilliant 150. The Aussie crowd gave Arkle heaps for the slow scoring rate but we didn't care, it was a crucial innings for us. Rodney Hogg could only manage four wickets this time giving him a modest total of six for the match, the rest falling to the spinners.

On the last day the Aussies needed 205 to win in 265 minutes, a reachable target under normal circumstances, but the wicket was beginning to crumble and John Emburey and Geoff Miller had the Aussies in all sorts of trouble as they collapsed to 111 all out. We were now 3-1 up and back in the driving seat. At Adelaide, we collapsed to 26 for five before Geoff Miller and I staged something of a recovery. Geoff hit 31, I top-scored with 74, but with Rodney

Hogg – inevitably – among the wickets, we were still hustled out for 169. I then took four for 42 as we turned the tables on the Aussies and grabbed a psychologically important first innings lead of just five runs. With wicketkeeper Bob Taylor playing his best-ever innings for England – he was cruelly out for 97, just three runs short of a maiden Test century – and good support from Boycs, Geoff Miller and John Emburey, we set Australia a victory target of 366, which was well beyond them. Our 205-run victory meant that Brears was the first England captain since Douglas Jardine in the infamous 'Bodyline' series of 1932-133 to win four Tests on an Ashes tour.

For the last Test of the six-test series we returned to the SCG. Brears was not yet in the mood to let us relax and urged us on to what would be a record-breaking victory. 'The series may be in the bag,' he said at the team meeting before the match, 'but the job isn't done yet.' Graham Yallop won the toss and decided to bat. It was a good choice from a personal point of view – he scored 121 – but his ten teammates could only muster 77 between them, and five of those were extras. I collected another four wickets as they were all out for 198.

We batted solidly all the way down the order to total 308, and with the wicket increasingly taking spin, Australia could manage only 143 at the second attempt, leaving us a target of only 34 to win, which we knocked off for the loss of one wicket. Australia had been humiliated 5-1, the worst losing margin in an Ashes series that they had ever endured. Some critics said the victory was devalued by the weakness of an Aussie side stripped of some of its leading players by defections to Packer, but they ignored the fact that we'd lost some great players of our own. In any case, you can only beat the eleven that are out on the field, and we'd certainly done that. Had it not been for Rodney Hogg, the defeat would have been even more emphatic. Despite taking only one wicket in the last Test, he finished the series with an astonishing aggregate of forty-one wickets at just 12.85 runs each.

I had now played eight matches against the Aussies and won seven of them, and even better than that, I now had a daughter, Sarah, born during the final Test. One of the British papers kindly wired a photograph of her out for me – a reminder that the press had a good side as well as a bad. Brian Close had had a big influence on my early life and he would now have the chance to do the same with the next generation, as he and his wife Vivienne accepted our invitation to be Sarah's godparents. When I flew home in mid-February after almost four months away, I met my daughter for the first time and spent a few precious weeks with my family before the treadmill of the domestic season began to turn again.

The first half of that summer of 1979 was taken up with the World Cup. On our home turf, we felt that we'd never have a better chance of winning the trophy, and after crushing Canada and Australia – again – in our group matches, and squeezing home against Pakistan, we beat New Zealand in a nail-biting finish in the semis to set up my first appearance in a final at Lord's. Our opponents were the West Indies, who had been in awesome form all the way through the tournament. Viv Richards took us apart, as only he could, scoring a majestic 138 not out, and then shared a devastating partnership with Collis King, who even outscored Viv with a searing 86 from just sixty-six deliveries, to take the West Indies to a daunting total of 286. Although Brears and Boycs put on 129 for the first wicket, we were always behind the clock, and with Joel Garner impossible to get away, we collapsed from 183 for two to 194 all out. I was gutted to lose, of course, but when I reflected on it a little later, I knew that we'd been beaten by the better side, and I was still young enough to look forward to other chances to win the World Cup.

In the four-Test series against India that followed I got back to close to my best form. I took a back seat at Edgbaston as 155 from Boycs and 200 from David Gower took us to a huge first innings score of 633 for five but picked up five wickets in the Indian second innings as they went down to defeat by an innings and 83 runs. I grabbed another five wickets in the first innings at Lord's where a shell-shocked India were blown away for just 96. We piled up 419 for nine declared, but India then ground out a draw with centuries from Vengsarkar and Viswanath. There was a personal milestone for me in that innings: when Mike Brearley brilliantly caught Sunil Gavaskar, low down and left-handed at first slip, he gave me my one hundredth wicket in Tests and in the shortest time on record – in my nineteenth Test, two years and nine days after my debut.

Headingley has always been a favourite ground of mine and events during the third Test there did nothing to change that. On a rain-interrupted first day we had struggled to 80 for four by the close and Derek Randall was out the next morning without adding to his overnight score, but by then the sun was shining and I decided to make a little hay. Nine not out overnight, I smashed the bowling to all corners of the ground and went to lunch on 108 not out, my only disappointment being that I had missed joining the very exclusive club of batsmen who have scored a century before lunch in a Test match by just one run. I ended with my highest Test score to date, 137, scored at almost a run a ball. Rain ruined the rest of the match – India did not even complete their first innings – and we went to the last Test 1-0 up in the series.

That match, at The Oval, also marked another personal milestone in my Test career. I began my twenty-first Test needing just 3 runs to reach the landmark of a thousand runs and a hundred wickets in Test cricket quicker than anyone had ever done before, and I soon collected them, forcing Bishan Bedi away backward of square, on my way to 38. I then took a couple of wickets and clung on to two catches, the second a truly bizarre one. Vengsarkar had batted beautifully for three hours when he edged Bob Willis to the keeper. David Bairstow, diving to his right, could only parry it goalkeeper-style. The ball ricocheted off Brears's boot as he stood at first slip and flew upwards, and with the burly figure of Bairstow scrambling down on me for a second go at it, I stuck up a hand and pouched it one-handed at second slip.

We took a first innings lead of 103 and extended it to 437 thanks to a fine century from Geoff Boycott and a typically pugnacious 50 from David Bairstow. My own innings was rather less successful – I was run out for nought. No prizes for guessing my batting partner at the time: Geoffrey Boycott had finally gained his revenge for his run-out at my hands in Christchurch, New Zealand.

Set 438 to win, India made it look all in a day's work with a double century opening stand, and Sunil Gavaskar went on to score a memorable 221 to take his side to within reach of their target. They were 304 for one at tea and 365 for one when I put myself in the doghouse by dropping Vengsarkar on the boundary. However, I then made amends by taking the catch he offered just one run later and after Bob Willis had disposed of Kapil Dev, I took the key wicket of Gavaskar. As India inched towards their target, I had Yajurvindra Singh and Yashpal Sharma out lbw in successive overs, and in between ran out Venkat. With two wickets in hand, the Indians eventually needed 15 runs from the final over to square the series. All four results were still possible with three balls to go but in the end they were forced to settle for the draw, giving us the series 1-0. Anyone who says that drawn games are boring can't have been at that one – it was one of the most exciting that I ever played in.

Although I'd finished on the losing side in the World Cup Final at Lord's, I enjoyed success in another final there that year, one of two winners' medals I collected that season. Somerset County Cricket Club had been in existence for over a century without winning a single trophy, but in one incredible weekend in September 1979 we won two of them, thanks to dazzling performances by our two West Indian stars. We first beat Northamptonshire at Lord's by 45 runs to win the Gillette Cup. Viv Richards scored a brilliant century to set Northants a victory target of 270 and Joel Garner then squeezed the life out of them with six for 29 in 10.3 overs. The next day we transferred operations to Trent Bridge for our final Sunday League game of the season, where Peter Roebuck's excellent first half-century in the competition and more stingy bowling by Joel, myself and Colin Dredge helped us to a 57-run victory and the title. They were the first of five trophies we would land in the next five glorious years; Taunton had never seen anything like it before, or since.

Chapter 4

A HIDING TO NOTHING

The winter of 1979–80 began with a tour to Australia followed by a one-match trip to Bombay for the Indian Golden Jubilee Test. Sadly for us, the Aussies had now got their best players back together after the Packer Affair, not least the legendary fast bowling partnership of Lillee and Thomson, and though I picked up eleven wickets in the first Test at Perth, a second innings 115 by Allan Border steered them to a 138-run victory. The pitch for the next Test at the Sydney Cricket Ground was saturated after days of continuous rain. It was a real 'green top' and even though Jeff Thomson was missing, no one was looking forward to facing the Australian pace attack of Lillee, Dymock and Pascoe on such a surface. Having taken a look at the state of the wicket, Geoff Boycott suddenly announced, 'My neck's stiff, I don't think I'm going to be able to play.' Brears gave him a very dubious look and packed him off to the nets, where he looked in perfectly good shape to us, but Boycs was adamant: 'My neck's still sore. I'm not playing.' At this point Brears lost it completely. Puce-faced with anger he looked ready to belt Boycs. Instead he stuck to his guns and eventually Boycs was forced to play.

Whoever won the toss was bound to put the opposition in; it was our misfortune that Greg Chappell called right. Dennis Lillee and Len Pascoe weren't far off unplayable on that surface and both took four wickets as we collapsed to 123 all out; from 79 for seven we did quite well to get that far. I took four for 29 as we restricted Australia to a 22-run first innings lead, but despite a beautiful innings of 98 not out from David Gower – he ran out of partners with his century there for the taking – we couldn't prevent Australia cantering to a six-wicket win and taking an unassailable 2-0 lead in the series.

In the final Test at Melbourne Graham Gooch hit a magnificent 99 and then, overcome by nerves, ran himself out before reaching his maiden Test century. We totalled 304 but the Aussies scored heavily all the way down the order and with Greg Chappell hitting a beautiful century, they led by 171. I scored an undefeated 119 in the second innings but the Aussies knocked off the modest victory target of 103 for the loss of just two wickets. They felt they had now made their point. They were thrashed 5-1 just twelve months before, but now, with their Packer players like the Chappell brothers and Dennis Lillee back in their ranks, they had slaughtered us 3-0.

We approached the Golden Jubilee Test in Bombay determined that we would win, but we were equally determined to let our hair down off the field. The lack of decent beer on the subcontinent at the time – the situation is much improved these days – was a major obstacle to this and we took the precaution of importing as much Aussie beer as we could cram into our hold baggage on the flight from Australia.

It was my first visit to India and a huge, jaw-dropping culture shock but also an unforgettable experience. On our first night in the Taj Mahal hotel my roommate, Derek 'Deadly' Underwood, decided to be helpful by leaving my blue leather shoes outside the bedroom door to be polished. It proved to be the last time I saw them. I was still giving men in blue shoes filthy looks and staring accusingly at their feet for many years afterwards.

Off the field, Deadly was working on a book with his ghostwriter

Chris Lander, but progress was proving slow ... partly because Deadly's roommate insisted on dragging one or both of them off for a drink at every conceivable opportunity. The more they tried to avoid me, the more relentless I was in my pursuit, and after three or four king-size cocktails in the hotel bar neither of them were in good enough shape to get back to work afterwards.

I really got to know Chris Lander well, nicknaming him 'Crash' after he and Deadly had yet again tried to give me a body-swerve. This time they tried a double-bluff, telling me that they were going to get down to work and then hiding out at a corner table in the hotel's penthouse bar, on the grounds that it would never occur to me to look for them there if I thought they were working. The double-bluff failed and within ten minutes I was at the bar buying us all a stiff drink. Things went downhill from there and a few hours later Lander was on stage, performing a karaoke routine in front of a slightly bemused audience of hotel guests. Singers sometimes indulge in a bit of 'crowd surfing' by throwing themselves on to their fans; carried away with his performance, Crash did the next best thing, tripping up and falling head first into the audience. By the time he got back to his seat, I'd given him his new nickname.

On the night before the Test we decided on a quiet night in, and settled down in front of the television, with only two bottles of brandy and some room-service tandoori chicken for company. The TV remote control didn't work, and after trying and failing to adjust the set I lost my rag and threw a chicken drumstick at it. It missed – my fielding clearly needed some work – bounced off the wall and got stuck in the back of the set, at which point the television mysteriously started working.

It was another very late and liquid night and the next morning Crash woke up with a pounding head to find that someone had tastefully arranged the remains of his tandoori chicken on his pillow like a halo around his head. Too hung over to contemplate going to the Test match he was supposed to be covering, he struggled across the room, turned on the television to watch the cricket and fell back on his bed. As he took in the action he nearly fell off the bed again. Apparently unscathed by the previous night's binge, Ian Botham was tearing through the Indian batting like a knife through, well, tandoori chicken. While he was still trying to process this information, Crash smelt burning and saw a plume of smoke rising from the TV set. Fearing the worst, he dived for the TV, only to discover that the same helpful person had stuffed a few more pieces of tandoori chicken in the back of the TV, where it was (over)cooking in the heat.

Despite my own prodigious hangover, and the similarly savage ones I suffered after each subsequent night of the match, I took six wickets in the Indian first innings, seven in the second and scored a century in between as we won the match by ten wickets. Perhaps I should have been preparing for all my Test matches the same way.

Although, to say the least, I wasn't an over-analytical cricketer, most of my captains thought enough about my knowledge of the game to seek out my opinion on our own players and those of the opposition, and to discuss tactics with me. During the tour to Australia and India, Mike Brearley brought me on to the England selection committee, ranking me ahead of a number of more senior players. He had already decided that he did not want to tour with England again, as he wanted to concentrate on his training for a career in psychoanalysis, so it was obvious that a new captain would have to be in place within the next twelve months.

I didn't go out of my way to put myself in the frame, but nor did I rule myself out, though I never really thought I would be given the chance. However, Brears had long repented of his preference for Chris Old ahead of me on the tour of Pakistan and now told me that he saw me as his successor. His and my preference would have been for him to carry on as captain for at least the first part of the 1980 home series against the West Indies, and it would certainly have helped me grow into the job had that happened, but the England selectors had different ideas. Brears was left out of the team altogether, while I was summoned to Lord's to be told that I was being named as England captain, albeit only for the one-day series.

In the eyes of the selectors or the public, I don't think that there were too many other contenders for the role, though some of my fellow players might have disagreed. Brian Close, who was one of the selectors at the time, was the only one who publicly begged to differ. He was implacably opposed to giving me the captaincy, not because he thought I would never be capable of it but because, at the age of twenty-four, I was not yet mature and experienced enough to cope with it. I might also lose form with bat and ball under the strains and responsibilities, and since in Brian's not altogether unbiased opinion I was often carrying the team on my shoulders, it could be a disaster for England's Test match fortunes.

Needless to say, I did not agree with any of this, but when Brian realised that he was going to be outvoted by the other selectors, he tried to persuade me not to take the job. He bought me a pint and then sat me down in a quiet corner and said, 'Listen, Ian, the England selectors are going to offer you the captaincy. Turn it down.' He held up his hand as I started to protest. 'Just hear me out first. You can't do everything. You're taking wickets, you're getting bloody runs, you're taking catches. If you took your performances out of the England side at the moment, there'd not be much left. You can't do all that and also take on a job where you're responsible for everyone else's performances as well. The captain's got to know how to look after each player – and they're all individuals with different talents, different mental attitudes, and all the rest of it. You're not ready for that yet. And I'll tell you another thing. Mike Brearley has a good record as England captain but that's because he's been taking on sides without their Packer players; he's been playing the second teams. They're all back on board now and that means that the West Indies and Australia are at full strength.

'You've just been hammered in Australia and the next three series are the West Indies home and away, followed by Australia again. With all their fast bowlers, the West Indies are a great side at the moment. Brearley hasn't improved anybody in that England team while he's been captain, and the side is nowhere near good enough to have a prayer against the West Indies. So nobody in their right mind would want to take the England captaincy on now because they'll be on a hiding to nothing.'

He studied me for a moment and I think he knew he'd been wasting his breath, but he tried once more. 'You can't do it all and make others play at the same time. Let them give the captaincy to a more experienced player now. It'll come your way in time anyway, make no mistake about that, and you'll be a better captain then for being a bit older and a bit wiser. You'll make a great captain in four or five years, but if you take the job now, it'll be the worst bloody year of your life.'

With the wisdom of hindsight, I have to admit now that Closey was right on all counts. Terms like 'man-management' and 'motivation' were a foreign language to me. I couldn't understand why anyone should need motivating to play for their country and my approach to man-management was pretty basic: buy 'em a pint in the bar if things were going well, and give 'em a kick up the arse if they weren't. Yet despite my personal failings and the misgivings of others, if I was to be offered the England captaincy I remained absolutely convinced that I could do it. There is no greater honour than to lead your country and, whatever Closey might have said, if I was offered the chance, I wasn't going to say, 'Thanks, but can you come back in three or four years' time?' I was going to snap their hands off.

The omens for that critical season in my career were not good. In April 1980, on one of those freezing spring days when the wind feels like it's blown all the way from Siberia, I was playing for Somerset against Oxford University at The Parks, one of the most beautiful of all cricket grounds, when I felt a slight twinge in my back. I hadn't taken the trouble to loosen up sufficiently before starting to bowl and I put the stiffness in my back down to that. It didn't trouble me that much to begin with – I bowled twenty-five overs – but on the final day it was giving me so much pain that I was reduced to bowling off-spin.

X-rays showed that I had a deformity of the spine, but the specialist deferred an operation on the scarcely encouraging grounds that if he operated it might put extra strain on the adjoining vertebrae and cause permanent damage. He also gave me the grim warning that one day it might just give out altogether. From that spring day in Oxford onwards, I was always in pain when I was bowling. Some days it barely hurt at all, some days it twinged a bit and on some it was agony.

I tried to put it to the back of my mind as I began my reign as England captain with two one-day matches against the West Indies at the end of May 1980. We lost the first, a rain-affected game at Leeds, where the West Indies batted first and scored 198 all out in fifty-five overs. In reply, Chris Tavaré top-scored in the match with 82 not out and I hit 30, but from 38 for four we were always facing an uphill struggle, and we were eventually all out for 174, losing by 24 runs.

The next match was at Lord's. I won the toss, again chose to field and we restricted the West Indies to 235 for nine, mainly thanks to some fine bowling by Vic Marks. Geoff Boycott and Peter Willey then laid solid foundations for our reply – 135 for the first wicket in thirty-three overs. After they were parted, we lost four wickets for 25 runs, but when I arrived at the crease, I scored 42 not out and even made the winning hit off Joel Garner to give us victory by three wickets with nine balls to spare. Although the series had ended 1-1, the West Indies took the trophy on a higher scoring rate over the two matches.

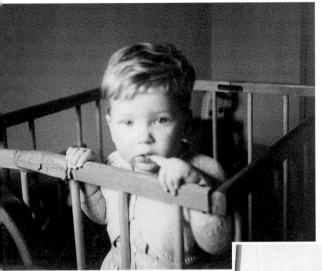

Me, aged around 18 months, trying to work out how to get out of my playpen. The answer I finally discovered was to balance the underside on the toy box and crawl under.

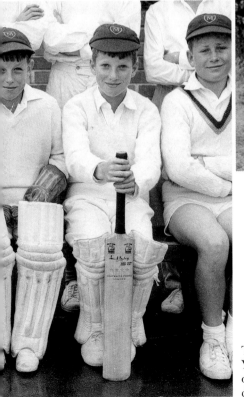

Swing bowler: out in the back garden at Mudford Road. My fearless desire from an early age for danger and adventure was a source of constant anxiety to my parents and led to more than one trip to the hospital. Dad finally made me a foam-rubber helmet.

The Milford Junior School cricket team in Yeovil. I'm showing the self-confident smile of someone who knows he's going to be doing this for a while.

© PA Photos

Me in my recently acquired England whites and my dad Les in an Aussie cap pose for a publicity shot. He was my original mentor - always generous with his time, encouraging my talents, but never going overboard with his praise. I owe so much of my success to him and Mum.

An early trophy: being presented with the ball after I took what would be the only hat-trick of my career during the first day's play of the MCC vs. Middlesex at Lords in early summer, 1978.

Photocall at Somerset County Cricket Club, May 1976. An honour to stand behind captain Brian Close (bottom-left). A colossus both as a player and a man, he is probably the single biggest influence on my career.

An early courting shot of me and Kath. Kath agreed to marry me just three months after we first met in 1974. Everyone, particularly 'Uncle' Brian Close, thought we were barmy to marry so quickly.

Our wedding at Thorne Parish Church, January 1976, with Kath's parents, Gerry and Jan Waller. My hangover after the stag do was so pronounced that Kath's aunt poured whisky on my cornflakes for some 'hair of the dog'. I do look a little pale.

am's christening in 1977, with god parents Viv Richards and Dennis Breakwell in tendance. Just months after his birth I'd be whipped away on a winter tour of Pakistan and ew Zealand. By the time I returned Liam barely recognised me.

Introducing the Queen and Prince Philip to the team before the start of the first day's play in the second Ashes Test at Lords in 1981. It was a brief respite from both the press, who were calling for my head, and from my dire performances with the bat. It wouldn't get any better as I was about to record back-to-back ducks and resign the captaincy.

How fortune can change: the now famous shot of me leaving the field of play at the end of the fourth day at Headingley, 145 not out.

Myself, Geoff Boycott and B Taylor struggle off the pitch miraculous conclusion of the day's play at Headingley.

Taking plaudits
from the press and
public at the end of
the Headingley Test
with Mike Gatting,
Chris Old, Peter
Willey and Graham
Dilley. Fred Truman
is about to make me
man-of-the-match.

True happiness –
waiting for the victory
presentations after we
had finally clinched
the Ashes at Old
Trafford in 1981,
winning the match by
103 runs.

It's smaller than my can of XXXX, but still the biggest prize in cricket. David Gower and I start to celebrate winning the urn after an innings victory in the sixth test at the Oval in 1985.

After no silverware in a century of play, I was part of a team that won five trophies at Somerset in the golden era between 1979 and 1983. Here I am holding the NatWest trophy aloft after our 24-run victory against Kent at Lord's in 1983.

The life and soul of the party – one of many celebrations I enjoyed at Somerset.

My son Liam accompanying me to net practice at the Oval before the Third Test against New Zealand in 1986. A chip off the old block, he would go on to play cricket and rugby professionally himself.

The 1986/87 Ashes in Australia were possibly my favourite tour, largely because Kath and the kids – Liam, Sarah and a very young Becky – came along for the whole four months. At my own expense, I might add.

I'd had to make my own choice early on between football and cricket, but I was still lucky enough to play a few professional league games for my local team Scunthorpe. I'd originally started training with them to get fit after an injury.

Viv and I flanking my one-time manager Tim Hudson at a benefit match at his 'Birtles Bowl'. You never quite knew what was real and what was spin with Tim, but I certainly fell under his Hollywood spell for a while.

© PA Photos

You know you're a star when you've made it into wax. Me and my Madame Tussaud's likeness in 1986.

Likewise when you make it on to *Wogan* or *This Is Your Life*. I was in an England team meeting for the upcoming trip to India in 1981 when Eamon Andrews appeared with his Big Red Book. I presumed he was there for Geoff Boycott. What would he want with me – I was still in my mid-twenties.

It had not been a bad start and I waited with impatience to see if the selectors felt that I had done enough to be given the Test captaincy as well. I didn't have long to wait. The following day, 31 May, Alec Bedser called to let me know that the job was mine. It wasn't altogether a surprise – I'd been canvassed about it in advance – but it was still a wonderful moment and I was supremely confident of making a success of the job, even though I was the youngest England Test captain since Ivo Bligh in 1882-83. That wasn't necessarily a good precedent: the defeat of Bligh's side was what prompted those famous Melbourne ladies to burn the bails and present the ashes to him in an urn.

By coincidence, the day I was given the news Middlesex were at Taunton for a county game against us, ensuring that the new captain of England was in opposition to his predecessor. Alec Bedser had already phoned Mike Brearley to tell him the news and he came straight into our dressing room to offer his congratulations.

The England captaincy gave my profile another boost, and with it came more offers of commercial endorsements, more requests for interviews, and more well-wishers, back-slappers and hangers-on. It would have been very easy to get carried away with my own importance, but I had one great advantage: the wisdom, good advice and, when she thought I needed it, the gentle mockery of my wife, to keep my feet on the ground. Many people in the public eye are surrounded by toadies and yes-men. Kath would always put on a united front with me in public, but she was never an uncritical supporter of the Botham party line, and if she felt I was wrong about anything – and it has been known – she would not hesitate to tell me so in private. In my younger, headstrong days, my motto was always "Beefy knows best", but as I grew older and a bit wiser, I came to realise how valuable and how wise was the counsel that Kath gave me.

It's an old cliché that behind every great man there's a woman. It was and is true for the Bothams too, but that doesn't mean that Kath lives in my shadow. She has a great business head and has always run our business affairs and our company and kept our finances on an even keel – not an easy task given my impulsive nature and free-spending habits. If it had been left to me, we'd have been bankrupt within weeks.

She decided from the start that she didn't want the limelight. She's got no interest in being a Z-list 'celebrity', always available to attend the opening of anything from an envelope upwards. Those people and that world are too phoney for Kath. She doesn't like the limelight, hates having her photo taken, and she's not interested in schmoozing celebrities. We do count some famous names among our friends, though they're not friends because of their fame but because they're good people, and Kath treats them in just the same way she treats everyone, with warmth, friendliness and kindness.

She's unbelievably generous with her time and it was typical of her that when I was away on tour with the England squad, she was the one who had the idea of getting all the wives and girlfriends together for a girls weekend back at home, and then provided the venue – our house – and organised and catered for it. It was the first time that it had ever been done and it worked really well. They had a great time together and drew a lot of strength just from discussing their problems with other women in the same position. It became a regular thing, and Kath's still good friends with many of them today. It wasn't like the football WAGs we see now, they weren't interested in the limelight, or changing outfits five times in the course of one morning just to keep the paparazzi interested, they were there as a mutual support group, and Kath was at the heart of it.

There was only one occasion that she regretted her involvement with the other 'England wives', when a woman Kath had counted as a friend inferred in a book that she was nothing but 'a little wife from north Yorkshire' who existed only to jump and come running when-ever I snapped my fingers. It was an utterly false description of her and it really hurt her. Kath is a feisty, strong-willed and self-contained woman. The fact that she doesn't want to play the London celebrity game – existing only to be seen in the right places, wearing the right outfits – does not make her a mousey northern housewife, it makes her a woman with the intelligence to decide who she is and what she wants to be for herself, and the self-confidence to go ahead and do it. She's worth a dozen shallow, vapid celebrity junkies. The one good thing that came out of it was that it inspired Kath to write her own book, and the advance she got for it paid the deposit on our house in north Yorkshire.

My first Test as captain was at Trent Bridge and by then my back had got so bad that I had to wear a corset just to get on the field at all. Even without that added handicap, I was under no illusions about the task facing us against a mighty West Indies side. Post-Packer, Bob Woolmer and Alan Knott were back in the England team for the first time in three years, but the West Indies also had all their Packer stars back in the fold. The batting was frightening enough, with Gordon Greenidge and Desmond Haynes opening, and a middle order of Viv Richards, Alvin Kallicharran and Clive Lloyd, while the fast-bowling quartet of Malcolm Marshall, Andy Roberts, Joel Garner and Michael Holding was one of the most formidable in the entire history of Test cricket … and if any of them were injured, Colin Croft was a more than adequate replacement.

I made a good start by winning the toss and decided we should bat. All the top-order batsmen got a start, but all of them, including me, then failed to capitalise on it. I top-scored with 57 as we made 263, but I felt it was 40 or 50 runs short of what we should have achieved, as the West Indies then demonstrated by replying with 308. Viv Richards and Deryck Murray both hit 64, I picked up three wickets for 50 and Bob Willis four for 82. Second time around we made 252, Boycott top-scoring with 75, and we set them a target of 208 in just over eight hours. As the pitch was wearing by now we felt we were in with a great shout, but a typically flamboyant Viv

Richards knock of 48 from just fifty-nine balls put the West Indies on the front foot. Desmond Haynes's 62 was much less dashing but in the end it was to prove crucial.

When the last day started the West Indies needed only 99 to win with eight wickets in hand and few spectators paid to watch the last rites, but those who did saw a wonderful day's play with fortunes swaying first one way and then the other and the result in doubt until the very last ball. Bob Willis bowled beautifully, finishing with five for 65, and at one point the West Indies had slumped to 180 for seven and, even though Haynes was still playing the anchor role, I felt victory was within our grasp. Two dropped slip catches didn't help but we were still in the driving seat until yet another dropped catch all but sealed our fate. There was probably no more brilliant fielder in England than David Gower but even the best fielders miss an occasional catch and this was one of those days for David. When Andy Roberts spooned a delivery from Bob Willis into the covers, I was already mentally popping the victory champagne when the groan from the crowd and David's agonised reaction told me that he'd spilled it. It's unfair to single David out for that – he won us enough games with his batting and fielding – but it was a crucial error at the decisive moment of the game. Andy Roberts survived and went on to make 22 not out, but the Windies were still not home and hosed because with just 3 needed to win, Desmond Haynes was brilliantly run out after a direct hit on the stumps by Peter Willey. Des left the field in tears, afraid he had cost the West Indies the game he had worked so long and hard to try and win for them. His 62 took over five hours but without it the West Indies would have lost by a distance. In an atmosphere of almost unbearable tension Michael Holding came to the wicket and watched as Andy Roberts hit the winning run off the bowling of the England captain.

My first Test as captain had ended in defeat; the second, at Lord's, was a rain-affected draw, with only half an hour's play possible on the final day. I again won the toss and chose to bat but 269 all out was again well short of what we should have scored on a fine Lord's wicket. The West Indies put our effort into its proper perspective by amassing 518 for a first innings lead of 249. With no hope of victory we would have had to bat for the best part of two days to save the match – just the sort of challenge that Geoff Boycott relished – but in the event the weather came to our rescue and we had reached 133 for two when rain ended the match. We were lucky, but we were also going well in our second innings and Boycs seemed positively aggrieved not to have had the chance to build on his 49 not out scored in three and a half hours.

The weather again dominated the third Test at Old Trafford. This time Clive Lloyd won the toss and invited us to bat – not an invitation we were pleased to receive – and we collapsed to 150 all out. We restricted the West Indies to a first innings lead of 110 and batted far better in our second innings, reaching 391 for seven before the Mancunian weather once more brought the proceedings to a damp close.

We maintained the improvement at The Oval, where we took a first innings lead for the first and only time all summer. Along the way I bagged my hundred and fiftieth Test wicket – all the sweeter because the victim was Viv Richards. Yet we then did our best to snatch defeat from the jaws of victory with a dismal second innings performance. The whole of the third day's play had been lost to rain, but there still looked to be plenty of time for the West Indies to secure an improbable win when we collapsed to 20 for four by the end of the fourth day, and then 92 for nine before lunch on the last morning, though Peter Willey and Bob Willis then staged one of the great rearguard actions, batting together for almost three hours in an unbeaten last-wicket stand of 117. I declared at 209 for nine as soon as Peter passed his century, but there was no time to force a win and the West Indies were now two up with one to play. As any golfer will tell you, that means game over.

The weather in that miserable summer was even worse at Headingley where the first and fourth days of the final Test were completely wiped out by rain. Clive Lloyd again won the toss and put us in and once more we were rolled over for a very modest score – 143 all out. David Bairstow hit 40 and I scored 37; no one else got more than 14. Our bowlers again laboured long and hard to restrict the West Indies' lead to 102 runs, and we had reached 227 for six in our second innings when time, perhaps mercifully, ran out. My own performances that summer had been modest – thirteen wickets and 169 runs in five Tests was scarcely the stuff of legends – and that was one of the factors, but only one, in my first series as captain ending in defeat. Those who wished to prove that the burden of the England captaincy would affect my performance had been given at least some ammunition, but as far as I was concerned it was pure coincidence. Until that time, my career had been a continuous success story and I was bound to have a poor run of form somewhere along the line; it was just unfortunate that it happened to coincide with my being awarded the captaincy.

The Test match season was not yet over, for the Australians had now arrived for the Centenary Test at Lord's. We warmed up for the game with two comfortable one-day victories over them at The Oval and Edgbaston, but once again in that rain-ruined summer, the weather intervened to spoil the big day at Lord's. Because of rain inter- ruptions, the Australian first innings was spread over virtually all of the first three days, with Graeme Wood hitting 112 and Kim Hughes 117 as Australia declared at 385 for five. We were hustled out for 205, with Dennis Lillee blasting out the top order and Len Pascoe then blowing away the tail, and the Aussies then rattled up 89 for four declared to set us a stiff victory target of 370. We were well on course at 244 for three, with Geoff Boycott on 128 not out and Mike Gatting on 51, with the captain next man in, but time ran out and it finished as a draw.

The rain interruptions had spoilt what should have been a great occasion and a breathtaking finish, and the match was further marred by a fracas between an MCC member, who had probably imbibed rather too freely during the lunch interval, and umpire David Constant. The natives at Lord's were getting restless about the failure to restart the game promptly after yet another rain break, and Constant, Dickie Bird, Greg Chappell and myself had just returned from yet another pitch inspection when the MCC member tried to give Constant his personal assessment of the situation. Greg and I had to act as peacemakers – not my normal role, I confess – and when play eventually did start the umpires were given a police escort through the Long Room. Having heard some of the crusty old gentlemen in bacon and egg ties complaining about yobs and football hooligans, it would have been interesting to hear what they made of this behaviour by one of their own.

My first season as England captain had come to a fairly inglorious end, and as the winter tour to the West Indies didn't begin until after the New Year, I kept myself fit by playing football for my local team, Scunthorpe FC. I had started training with them the previous winter and had a few games for the reserves. Coach John Kaye then recommended me to the manager Ron Ashman, and I played a couple of end-of-season first-team games for them. I made my debut as a second-half substitute in a 3-3 draw at Bournemouth on 25 March 1980, and also played in the next game, a 3-1 home defeat by Wigan.

Despite disapproval from Lord's, I continued to train with Scunthorpe because I enjoyed it and I socialised with a few of the players as well. I got on really well with the goalkeeper, Joe Neenan, and went as his guest on the team's Christmas night out on the town. Joe certainly needed cheering up that night because he'd conceded a penalty that afternoon, giving non-League Altrincham a 1-0 win in a second round FA Cup replay. Defeat was bad enough, but it was made much worse by the knowledge that had Scunthorpe won, their third round opponents would have been Liverpool at Anfield – a once-in-a-lifetime opportunity for players from the lower leagues to appear on one of the greatest stages in the game.

Earlier that evening Joe had been given a hard time by some disgruntled Scunthorpe fans, and when he went to the gents there had been a bit of push and shove, but I was at the bar at the time and remained in blissful ignorance about it. We ended the evening at a nightclub, but when we went outside to get a taxi home, the same troublemakers were waiting and had another go at Joe. He was not the sort to back down and I had to pull him away from one particularly mouthy character who just kept on baiting him. Finally, our patience snapped and we chased them down the road. The football training must have been doing me some good because we covered about six hundred yards before we caught up with them. Joe cornered his chief tormentor in a 'ten foot' – the local name for an alley – and thumped him. Honour was satisfied and we walked back and caught a taxi home. That was not to be the end of it; the next day, the papers splashed the story under the banner headline IAN BOTHAM BEAT ME UP.

Joe and myself were then interviewed by the police, cautioned and charged with 'assault occasioning actual bodily harm', and had to appear before the Scunthorpe magistrates. Joe couldn't afford to take his chances in the Crown Court, and reckoned he had no choice but to plead guilty, pay a fine and forget it. He was duly fined £100 plus costs, but I was determined to clear my name and I pleaded not guilty and elected for trial in the Crown Court. It caused me a few problems. The TCCB were not exactly thrilled that the England captain was on trial for assault, and as I was due to leave for the West Indies in a few days, there was a real danger that a trial might be set for a date when I was supposed to be captaining England in a Test match. Fortunately my solicitor, Alan Herd, managed to persuade the court to delay the trial until after the tour and I was able to leave for the Caribbean with the rest of the team, albeit with the court case still hanging over me.

When I eventually appeared at Grimsby Crown Court, it came out that the man Joe had punched had previous convictions for assault and criminal damage. Two of the witnesses for the prosecution – his friends – also had records for theft and criminal damage and one of them for assault causing actual bodily harm. The police evidence had described them as 'typical Scunthonians' ... I was eventually acquitted; it was ridiculous that the case had ever gone to court at all.

One of my first duties as tour captain had been to sit as a member of the selection panel to choose the rest of the touring party, and it was a real eye-opener for me. I was absolutely amazed at the amount of horse-trading that went on between the selectors. They sat around the table and argued for a while and then one of them would say, 'Well, all right, if you're so set on having A [a player on the fringes of the Test squad], then I'm having B [and he named a promising but unproven player who had recently been built up by the tabloids as the next 'Great Hope' of English cricket].' The focus should have been on putting together the best possible team to do the job in hand, but instead there were guys pushing favourites or players that the press had been boosting – and three or four times a season they'd start a 'Player X for England' campaign, often on the flimsiest of grounds.

I always had a pretty clear idea of the team I wanted, and in any case, in most tour selection meetings around thirteen of the sixteen players would pretty much pick themselves. But the wrangles over the other three would take hours. That's when the trade-offs started and eventually I found myself saddled with players who I didn't want, didn't rate, and who weren't up to the job, just because a couple of the selectors had struck a deal to back each other's 'pet' players. I'd like to think that it doesn't happen as much now as it used to, but I don't know if that's true. I'll have to ask Freddie Flintoff or Michael Vaughan.

On the 1981 West Indies tour, the biggest wrangles were over the Middlesex batsman Roland Butcher. I really wanted him in the tour party because I felt that he had the technique and stroke-making ability to counter the extra pace and bounce we would face on the West Indian wickets. He had played there before and as well as his batting skills he was also a brilliant fielder. However, some of the other selectors were adamant that the place had to go to Bill Athey, and I had to fight like hell before they grudgingly agreed to accept Butcher, with Athey as first reserve. When Brian Rose returned home injured, the selectors got their wish and Athey joined the tour party, but he scarcely set the place on fire, scoring just seven runs in four Test innings.

If I wasn't happy with my co-selectors, I was delighted with the choice of coach. Kenny Barrington was not just my boyhood hero and role model, he was a legend in the game. You could break rocks on his craggy profile and he knew only one way to play the game: as tough as you could. He had been a relentless competitor and accumulator of runs in his playing days, and was well respected in the West Indies, where he'd played some of his finest innings. We shared the same attitude to the game and we always got on really well. On our days off we'd go golfing and he was as competitive at that as he was at cricket, but the thing I and my colleagues most respected him for was that, unlike certain famous ex-players, none of us had ever heard him preface any remarks with the words 'In my day …'. He appreciated that it was a different era and that no young player wants some old fart telling him how things were tougher/better/harder or whatever in the old days, and that automatically set him in high esteem among us.

His only problem was that he was one of life's obsessive worriers, who found it very hard to relax. Watching the cricket – and he never missed a ball – he would sit chain-smoking with a mound of butts growing ever higher in the ashtray at his elbow, shaking his head and muttering to himself. Everything that happened to his players, Kenny felt as acutely as any of them, living every moment out on the field.

He took a lot of the load off my shoulders, but it was a heavy burden to bear, because the tour was beset with difficulties from the start. In the first seven weeks we had only seventeen days' cricket, with torrential rain turning the practice pitches into mud-heaps that were more typical of England than the Caribbean. When we did manage to get some play, we began with three wins in a row, first over the Young West Indies in Trinidad, and then in two one-day games in the Windward Islands. In the first one-day international in St Vincent, bowlers were on top throughout. We thought we had done well to restrict the West Indies' glittering batting line-up to just 127, with only Mattis and Haynes reaching double figures, but when we batted that soon seemed a mammoth total. We collapsed to 15 for four, but David Gower and I then staged a rescue act and, with some stubborn help from the tailenders, took us to within 14 runs of victory with three wickets in hand before Colin Croft had me caught behind for 60. In a nail-biting finish, we fell short by just two runs. Colin Croft was the principal destroyer, taking six for 15.

The first day of the first Test at Port-of-Spain in Trinidad was interrupted by more bad weather but the West Indies were well in control at 144 without loss at the close as we felt the absence of our main strike bowler, Bob Willis, who was struggling with a knee injury. Gordon Greenidge and Desmond Haynes were both out in sight of their centuries the next day, but useful knocks from Viv, Clive Lloyd, Deryck Murray and, more surprisingly, Andy Roberts allowed them to declare on 426 for 9. It could have been much worse, but John Emburey bowled really well, sending down fifty-two overs in searing heat to return figures of five for 124.

Colin Croft then ripped through our top order, taking five for 40 as we collapsed to 178 all out and had to follow on. We did no better at the second attempt, Andy Roberts and Michael Holding making the inroads this time as we were dismissed for 169 and crushed by an innings and 79 runs. Geoff Boycott's 70 was the only real resistance. I was pilloried for trying to hit Viv Richards out of the ground and holing out to Michael Holding for just 16, but I felt that the team would be best served by my playing my normal game. It had paid off many times in the past and would do so to spectacular effect in the future, but on this occasion it got me out.

We had fallen at the first hurdle and, even worse, we would have to play the remainder of the series without our vice-captain and principal strike bowler, Bob Willis, who finally had to concede defeat in his battle with his knee injury and fly home for treatment. It was a huge blow to the team and to me personally, because he was not only an inspirational figure but a good friend and a shoulder to lean on as well. I now had to find a new vice-captain who would lead from the front and command the respect of the players. I soon produced a short-list of two: Peter Willey and Graham Gooch. In my eyes, the senior professional on the tour was Peter Willey. He was my kind of guy: he only knew one way to play – to win – you needed dynamite to get him out and he never took a backward step, no matter what was thrown at him.

While we were in Guyana, we had a chat one evening. We talked first about the cricket and he came up with some solid suggestions for ways to improve the team's performance and my own as captain, but one of the things he said took some swallowing for me. 'You've always been one of the lads, Both, but you're captain now and you can't be everybody's buddy in the bar and still expect to be able to crack the whip when it's needed. You need to get a bit of distance yourself a little – go off and do your own thing – because by mixing with the rest of the lads I think you're unconsciously undermining your authority as captain.'

I didn't like it at all, but when I thought about it, I could see that 'Will' was right. However, although I could have had no shrewder adviser than Will, I realised that giving him the vice-captaincy was unnecessary. Because of the type of player he was, Will was already playing to his absolute capacity and he was generous in sharing his insights on the game. Whether or not I made him vice-captain he would continue to do that. Whereas I felt that a player like Graham

Gooch, although he already had a very good cricketing brain, needed additional responsibility to raise his game to a new level. If I made him vice-captain I was confident that he would not only contribute even more to the team and our strategies and tactics, it would also make him an even more prolific contributor as a batsman.

Having clarified my own thoughts, I then discussed things with the tour managers A.C. Smith and Kenny Barrington – A.C. was in charge of the overall administration while Kenny and I concentrated on the playing side. They agreed with my analysis, so I next approached Graham himself to find out how he felt about it. He was delighted; problem solved. However, when we notified the TCCB, purely as a courtesy, the chairman of selectors, Alec Bedser, just said, 'No. Geoff Miller will be the new vice-captain.'

I couldn't believe my ears. 'Geoff won't even be playing in all the games,' I said, but Bedser and the rest of the stuffed shirts at Lord's were immovable. The decision made by the captain and management who were actually in the line, aware of the situation and the needs of the team on the field had been overturned by people thousands of miles away, some of whom would not have known what day it was if they hadn't had a calendar to consult. There was apparently nothing I could do. Alec Bedser and the other selectors had made an irrevocable decision, and the fact that they refused to give me a reason was even more irritating. They categorically refused to discuss it and to this day I have no idea why they were so keen to have Geoff Miller as vice-captain. It certainly wasn't to groom him for the captaincy in the future, because he was never offered it.

Having swallowed that bitter pill, I then had to tell Graham that, though I wanted him to be vice-captain, I'd been overruled by the board. He was disappointed but philosophical about it, and I did my best to reassure him that his time would undoubtedly come. Next I tracked down Geoff Miller and told him that he was to be our new vice-captain. I told him the circumstances – there was no point in pretending otherwise – and his principal emotion was embarrassment.

He was taken aback. 'It could be a bit tricky, Both,' he said. 'I reckon I won't be picked for some of the Tests' – the same point I'd already made to Alec Bedser.

We all had to put up, shut up and get on with it, but it led to some farcical moments with Geoff volunteering to leave the room during selection meetings so that we could first decide whether he was going to be in the team at all, before we got around to choosing the rest of the side.

The tour contract meant that I was gagged and prevented from revealing the board's myopic interference in the team's affairs. None of it would happen now because, though still some way from ideal, the system has changed, but back then, that was just another of the things that we had to put up with. All the other players knew what had happened and it can only have further undermined my authority as captain.

Our next problem arrived with Bob Willis's replacement, Robin Jackman. A local journalist in Guyana claimed that Robin's inclusion was a clear breach of the Gleneagles Agreement – the boycott that had made South Africa a sporting pariah nation. Because Robin had played and coached in the Republic – as many English cricketers, including other members of the tour party, had done, earning some money and getting some winter sunshine during the English close season – his name was on a United Nations blacklist. The Guyanese authorities then withdrew Robin's visitor's permit and demanded that he leave the country at once.

British officials argued that Robin's actions were irrelevant because the Gleneagles Agreement was targeted at teams and nations, not at individuals, and in any case it was unfair to single out Robin when some of the other players had also played in South Africa and been accepted without any problems. The Guyanese remained unmoved.

A.C. Smith took soundings with me and the players. We were unanimous that we stood or fell together; the Guyanese could not tell us who to pick and not to pick. I was delighted by the way he supported us in this. He may have had the urbane manner of a diplomat and the rounded vowels of a true MCC man, but he earned our respect by backing us to the hilt and not bowing down to the pressure the Guyanese authorities were exerting. He next cleared the course of action he was planning with Lord's, and then told the Guyanese that, since they were making it impossible for us to select the team we wished, we would refuse to play the second Test.

Robin Jackman bore himself with great dignity during an impossible situation. When I first played against him I had wanted to flatten him because he struck me as an arrogant poser, but when I got to know him better I discovered that he was a great team man who would bowl his guts out for the cause. However, the row over 'the Jackman Affair' was making the atmosphere in Guyana increasingly poisonous for him and the rest of the team and we were now virtual prisoners in our hotel, unable to go out for fear of being harassed, spat upon or worse by mobs stirred up by the increasingly inflammatory coverage in the local media. The stress was equally great on the England management, and glancing at Kenny Barrington one evening, I could see how it was gnawing away at him. None of us had been sleeping well, but Kenny was grey-faced with fatigue and the stress had etched even deeper lines into his already craggy features. I said to him, 'You've got to switch off and try to relax,' and he nodded and said, 'Yes, I know, you're right, you're right,' but it was clearly easier said than done for him.

It was hard to focus on cricket with all the political rows going on around us, but in the midst of the stand-off we played the second one-day international in the up-country town of Berbice. The teams travelled there by military helicopter, and after the England chopper had left without me – I'm sure it was an oversight rather than anything more sinister – I piled into the West Indian one and flew up there chatting to Viv and his teammates. We played the game, lost by six wickets, and were clambering on to the helicopters for the flight back to Georgetown almost as soon as the umpires had removed the bails.

The second Test was eventually cancelled and we made ready to leave Guyana. There were few regrets. Even after we'd boarded our flight for Barbados, we still had to endure a long delay before we finally took off, to the accompaniment of loud cheering from the England players. It had been a very unpleasant ten days in Guyana but as soon as we touched down in Barbados the atmosphere – and team morale – began to lift. AC and Kenny were still locked in tense negotiations about the future of the tour, but Barbados and the other islands were desperate to see it go ahead and an agreement to see the rest of the tour through was formally announced a week later, on 4 March 1981.

Apart from all these off-field problems, I was still struggling with the captaincy, particularly in my least favourite area: man-management and motivation. My worst problems in that respect were probably with Chris Old. The Yorkshire all-rounder had genuine talent, but I always felt that his attitude and his appetite for the fray – in short, his 'ticker', in Brian Close's phrase – was suspect when the pressure was on. The wicket for the third Test in Bridgetown looked ideally suited to his bowling, and Kenny was very keen to include him in the team, but I was unconvinced. I felt Chris's attitude, and some of his comments to me, suggested that he was not up for it at all, but Kenny was adamant.

The team was announced with Chris Old included, but on the morning of the match, just forty minutes before we were due to take the field, Chris sidled up to me and said, 'Sorry Both, I can't play.'

I did a double-take. 'What? What do you mean?'

'I've been stung,' he said, shifting from foot to foot like a naughty schoolboy in front of the Head.

'By what exactly?'

He shrugged. 'I don't know.'

'Well, where have you been stung? The arm? The leg? The arse?'

'Just somewhere,' he said and, still not having met my eye once in the whole conversation, he turned and began to walk away.

I could cheerfully have strangled him and I let loose a mouthful at his retreating back. A captain from the Mike Brearley school of man-management would no doubt have put an arm round Chris's shoulders and coaxed, flattered and cajoled him into playing but I had no desire to play amateur psychologist. As far as I was concerned Chris Old was just another player who was letting his talent go to waste. In subsequent games we chose another Yorkshireman, Graham Stevenson, in preference to Old, and if there were any doubts about the size of Stevo's ticker they were dispelled by his performance in Antigua, where he bowled thirty-three overs despite heavy strapping on a torn thigh muscle.

Chapter 5

BOTHAM MUST GO

Disaster is a much overused word in sport, but for once, in Bridgetown, Barbados during the third Test, it was appropriate, not for anything that happened on the field but for what occurred off it. The first two days of the game pretty much followed the pattern of the tour so far. The pitch was bone-hard but with a good covering of grass – a pace-bowler's dream and a batsman's potential nightmare – and when I won the toss, I had no hesitation in putting the West Indies in to bat. With the Windies on 65 for four, I was entitled to feel quite pleased with my decision, but Clive Lloyd and Larry Gomes then took the game away from us, adding 154 for the fifth wicket with Clive scoring exactly 100. When they were parted, I ran through the tail, but 265 all out, though lower than any previous West Indian score this series, looked a very good total on such a bowler-friendly track.

Our innings then began with one of the most remarkable opening overs ever seen in Test cricket. For sheer sustained aggression, coupled with absolutely blinding pace, nothing I've encountered came close to the first over Michael Holding bowled to Geoff Boycott. Geoff was jerking and jumping this way and that, trying to get out of the way of a barrage of short-pitched deliveries that seemed to be on him almost before they'd left the bowler's hand. I doubt if any of us – and maybe no batsman alive – could have played Holding in that mood, and Boycs did well to survive the first five balls of the over, even though he never managed to get so much as an edge on any of them. He didn't hit the sixth one either, which scorched straight through his understandably hesitant defensive push and shattered his wicket. Never has a duck been so hard-earned.

None of us looked exactly comfortable when it was our turn to face the music and we were bowled out before the close of play for just 122, with Graham Gooch and I joint top-scorers with a modest 26. Although Graham Dilley got Gordon Greenidge for a duck before the close, the West Indies were now long odds-on to secure the victory that would give them the series.

That evening, 14 March 1981, I went out for dinner with Kath who had just flown out to join me. We got back to our room about eleven that evening and soon afterwards the phone rang. I was expecting a call from my mum back in the UK, but in fact it was A.C. Smith. 'Ian? I've got bad news. Kenny's had a heart attack. I'm afraid he's dead.'

Kenny had had a heart attack many years before, at the end of his playing days. He'd recovered from that one, but he was still a chain-smoker and an obsessive worrier, and nothing could change that. Now he'd had another heart attack, this time a fatal one, and whatever the doctors might say, the stresses of the tour and in particular the fracas in Guyana must have contributed to his untimely and tragic death. I lay awake far into the night, remembering Kenny Barrington. My childhood hero, he was also a great friend and a wise counsellor to me in later years.

I met AC early the next morning and we walked along the beach near our hotel as we discussed what to do. The most pressing problem was whether we should go ahead with the Test. Having already called off the previous one in Guyana, cancelling this one would probably have finished off the tour, but that mattered less to both of us than that we should do the right thing by Kenny and by the England players. In the end we decided to break the news to them and see how they reacted before making a final decision. They were absolutely devastated, but after a long discussion we decided to play the match, purely because we were convinced that it was what Kenny himself would have wanted. When we arrived at the Bridgetown ground later that morning, there was no atmosphere at all. Even the normally ebullient Barbadian crowd was unnaturally silent.

Before play started the two teams lined up, wearing black armbands, and stood with the capacity crowd of fifteen thousand for a minute's silence – and there was not the faintest sound, not a cough, not a murmur. Players on both sides had tears in their eyes. It was the most emotional experience I'd ever had on a cricket field, but I felt that I could not show my feelings. I had to mask it, put on the brave face and lead from the front, and as play began I kept saying, 'Come on, let's do it for Kenny.'

That evening, I spent a long time with Ann Barrington, who was due to fly home with Kenny's body the next day. There's little anyone can do to ease the pain in such circumstances but we sat and talked about Kenny and what he had meant to us, and I think and hope that it helped her a little to talk about him. I was later honoured to be asked to read the lesson at the memorial service for him, held in London after our return.

The match seemed almost irrelevant, but in the event the West Indies coasted to another win. Viv Richards hit a majestic 182 not out as the West Indies reached 379 for seven declared, and faced with an impossible victory target of 523, we slumped to 224 all out and a heavy defeat. Only David Gower with 54 and Graham Gooch really troubled the scorers, but Gooch's superb 116 was a fitting tribute to Ken Barrington, an innings that Kenny himself would have been proud to have played.

We tried to put our grief behind us as we went to Antigua for the fourth Test where I won the toss for the third time in the series and took first use of a good-looking batting track, but the West Indies pacemen again pinned us back, with Colin Croft once more the destroyer in chief with six for 74. Peter Willey played with typical guts to score an undefeated century but, though healthier than our previous totals against the Windies, 271 didn't look quite as good a score when they responded with 468 for nine declared, with Viv Richards scoring another century – 114. The fourth day was lost to rain and Gooch and Boycott's first-wicket stand of 144 in our second innings then made certain of the draw.

The fifth Test was at Sabina Park in Jamaica, and for the first time in the series, I lost the toss. We were put in to bat, but Gooch and Boycs picked up where they had left off in Antigua. They put on 93 for the first wicket and after Boycs had departed for 40, Gooch continued his sensational innings, smashing our nemesis, Colin Croft, out of the attack and scoring so freely that when he was fifth out at 249, he had scored 153. We eventually reached 285, but once again, it was not enough as the West Indies replied with 442. At 32 for three in our second innings, we looked down and out, but after a three-hour rain break, Peter Willey and David Gower then made the game safe with a century partnership, and Gower went on to a majestic 154 not out. My second Test series as captain had ended like the first in defeat, 2-0. I had only scored 73 runs in the four Tests but I was England's leading wicket taker with fifteen victims at an average of 32.80, and despite all the problems on and off the field, we had given the West Indies a battle. Gooch, Gower, Boycott and Willey had all played superb innings and to come up short against the finest team in the world – perhaps the finest of all time – playing at their very peak on their own turf was nothing to be ashamed of.

I remained confident in my ability both as an all-rounder and as a captain, but my approach to captaincy remained resolutely unanalytical. I didn't believe in spending too much time worrying about the opposition. We'd have a brief discussion of their individual strengths and weaknesses, the flaws that might get them out, but my view was always that if we performed to our own capabilities, we were good enough to beat anyone, so let the opposition do the worrying. As far as I was concerned, the captain was just the man who made the decisions; he was still part of the team. Maybe, as Peter Willey had suggested to me, it's easier to make tough decisions, like which players to pick or drop, if you've distanced yourself a little more from your teammates, but I never had any problem in making the hard calls. If a guy wasn't performing or wasn't good enough, I had no problem in saying, 'Tough, you're out of the team.'

As captain on that tour, I was happy to pick a side, then just go out on the field and play the game, but that uncomplicated approach did not go down well with everyone ... particularly Chris Old. Motivation and man-management were never my strong points, and certainly not at that stage of my life. Playing for my country, pulling on that shirt, was what I had dreamed of ever since I was a kid and no matter how many times I did so I never lost that pride and the drive to do my very best. I really couldn't understand why anyone needed more than that to bust a gut for his country. If his heart wasn't bursting out of his chest with pride, then to hell with him. Nor was I inclined to be too 'touchy, feely' with players who screwed up. If someone dropped a catch or got himself out for a duck with a lousy shot, my first instinct wasn't to say, 'Oh well, never mind, bad luck, well tried,' it was to give him a bollocking, just as I'd expect one if I did the same thing. Some players were upset by this approach; they wanted an arm round their shoulders and some soft words of encouragement, but that wasn't the way I'd been brought up to play the game. I couldn't imagine Brian Close ever using soft words to get any of his players to perform. He'd tell them what to do, most likely in blunt Anglo-Saxon phrases, brook no arguments about it, and give them a savage tongue-lashing if they messed it up.

The other thing that really drove me mad was when players developed a mystery injury just before a big game; it happened then and it still happens now with certain players. They'd complain about a twinge in their back or their leg or whatever it was, and then say, 'But I'll be all right, Skip. I'll just have an injection and I'll be as right as rain.' What they were really doing was giving themselves a parachute, a get-out clause, so that if they played badly, they could blame the injury. It used to make me furious. I'd guarantee that every time we had a real pressure game, one or two of the people I played with and a couple of the ones who are playing now would go up to their captain and start complaining about a little niggle. If they then went out and played like a wanker it wasn't their fault, it was the injury's fault. You could almost set your watch by the time when these mystery injuries would suddenly appear.

A good man-manager like Brears would probably butter such guys up and coax a good performance out of them by saying, 'Come on, you'll be fine. Take it easy today and you'll be in great shape tomorrow.' My reaction was more likely to be, 'If you don't want to play, fine. Fuck off and we'll get someone who does.' I think that surprised a couple of players. It wouldn't have won me any prizes for diplomacy and it obviously wasn't the right way to get the best out of some players who if they were flattered or cajoled might then have gone out and played a blinder, but that just wasn't my way. I genuinely couldn't understand the mindset of anyone who had to be treated in that way, and even with the wisdom of hindsight, I wouldn't change my approach. I see no point in pandering to those sort of players. If the only way they can play is to have a parachute for when things go wrong, then maybe they should go and get themselves some other job.

After the series defeat in the West Indies there was inevitable criticism in the press, both of the team and of my performance as captain, much of the latter concentrating on my loss of form since assuming the role. There were rumbles from Lord's too and I had a growing feeling that, slowly but surely, the rug was being pulled from under my feet. Yet despite the mounting criticism, I was appointed captain for the one-day games against Australia at the start of the 1981 summer series. My only chance to take a look at Kim Hughes's side came in their match against Somerset towards the end of May, but rain ruined the match, though I put one over on Graeme Wood by getting him out for a duck. In between the showers, they reached 232 for eight declared and we replied with 25 for no wicket, before yet more rain brought the match to a damp conclusion.

I kept up my good run with the toss in the first one-day international at Lord's. I put Australia in to bat and we held them to 210 for seven from their fifty-five overs. After Gooch and Boycott put on 86 for the first wicket, we were always cruising and we reached the target for the loss of four wickets, with Boycs 75 not out. Two days later the Aussies got their revenge in a thriller. I again won the toss and put them in, but this time they scored a healthier 249 for 8, and though we looked in control at 224 for five with five overs to go and Mike Gatting batting superbly, a spectacular catch by Geoff Lawson to get rid of Gatting for 96 swung it Australia's way and they eventually got home by two runs.

The decider was at Headingley. Once more I won the toss and asked Australia to bat, but a gritty 108 from Graeme Wood steered them to 236 for eight. We needed a similar knock from Boycs but this time he couldn't oblige, out for 4, and only Gooch, Gatting and Willey offered much resistance as we went down to defeat by 71 runs.

My record as England captain wasn't looking too impressive. We'd lost the one day series to Australia, 2-1, following two Test series defeats against the West Indians, but those defeats were by 1-0 and 2-0, not 5-0 'blackwashes', and the Windies were a formidable side. However, there was now a mounting campaign in the press for a change of captain. The argument was still that the pressures of captaincy were affecting my form, particularly my batting, and that lifting the burden from me would restore me to my best form and give team spirit a boost as well. I didn't agree with that diagnosis at all. It was true that I'd been struggling for runs in the last few Tests, but everyone has a bad patch at one time or another, and I was in the batting form of my life for Somerset. In my view I'd come good sooner or later, and whatever the causes of my loss of form for England, it had nothing to do with the captaincy. I was still young and learning on the job, but I'd grow into the captain's role over the next year or so … providing I was given the time.

That was looking in rather short supply, after the England selectors announced that I would be appointed as captain only on a match-by-match basis. The implication was clear: if we made a poor start to the Ashes series, I'd be out of a job. When I got back home after fielding endless hostile questions at the press conference, Kath gave me a quizzical look and then said, 'It's not worth the candle, is it, Ian? Why don't you just give it up?' She was right, of course, I should have resigned there and then, but I loved captaining my country and it's not in my nature to give up without a fight, so I swallowed my pride and carried on.

My luck with the toss ran out at Trent Bridge for the first Test. Kim Hughes won it and put us in to bat and we were all out for 185 soon after tea. Although Australia were in dire trouble at 89 for six, Allan Border, given a life when only on 10, then marshalled the tail to bring Australia to within 6 runs of our total. Our second innings began badly and did not improve. I top-scored with 33 but a total of 125 was nowhere near enough. We made the Aussies fight for every run but they eventually got home by four wickets. I felt the result could easily have gone the other way, but you can't argue with the scoreboard and that now read 'Australia 1, England 0'.

The uncertainty about my future and the stress of the constant criticism in the press were having an even greater effect on Kath than they were on me, to such an extent that she'd lost a stone in weight. We were moody and short-tempered with each other; the captaincy issue was now tainting our lives. It wasn't fair on either of us to let the uncertainty drag on any longer. After further deliberations, the selectors appointed me captain for the second Test at

Lord's, but by then I had already told Kath that if they were going to stick to their 'one match at a time' policy, I would quit. It was very tough to take. Until that point my sporting life had been one continuous success. I wasn't used to failure at anything and it was not an experience I wanted to repeat.

As I walked through the Grace Gates on the first morning of that Lord's Test, the first thing I saw was a newspaper hoarding: BOTHAM MUST GO. For once the tabloids and I were in full agreement. I lost my last toss as England captain and we were put in by Kim Hughes. The decision looked to have backfired. Gooch and Boycs put on 60 for the first wicket and though I was out for a duck, a pugnacious 82 from Peter Willey saw us to 311.

Round One to us, but after crumbling to 82 for four, the Aussies then again fought their way back to a first innings lead of 34.

Geoff Boycott and David Gower put us in a strong position in our second innings but delays for bad light and rain had eaten into the game time, and I promoted myself in the search for quick runs that might give us a chance of a result. However, it might have been wiser not to have tried to sweep the very first ball I received, from Ray Bright. I missed and suffered the ignominy of being bowled behind my legs for a golden duck. Even worse, it was my second duck of the match.

It was not the greatest shot I had ever played, but as I made the slow walk back, I might have expected a modicum of sympathy from the ranks of bacon and egg ties lining the pavilion. Fat chance. Some suddenly became very fascinated by the headlines in their afternoon newspapers, or the contents of their bags. Others, with even more charm, ostentatiously turned their backs as I passed them on my way up the steps. It was a frigid reception that I never forgot. My declaration set Australia 232 to win. At 17 for three they were reeling, but Graeme Wood batted for over three hours for 62 not out to steer them to the safety of a draw.

If I'd had any doubts beforehand about giving up the England captaincy, the attitude of the MCC members had crystallised my thoughts. I could either continue, limping from game to game until the selectors pulled the plug on me, or I could go out with dignity on my own terms. It was a no-brainer, and I told my teammates in the dressing room at once, 'Boys, I'm resigning. It's a ridiculous situation, it's no good for you, it's no good for me. So I've decided to put an end to it.' I'd already written my resignation letter before I got to the ground that morning, so all I had to do was hand it in.

As I walked away from the office, I felt that I was now at the lowest point of my life. I couldn't imagine that things could get any worse, but within fifteen minutes I had been proved wrong. As soon as he received my resignation, Alec Bedser, the chairman of selectors, summoned the cricket writers from the press room to attend a hastily convened press conference. As soon as they were seated he told them the news of my resignation and then added, 'But we were going to sack him anyway.'

I will never understand why he felt moved to do that. We'd had our differences of opinion about selections and particularly about the issue of the vice-captaincy in the West Indies, but whatever I thought about his actions on that occasion, I respected him as a man and as one of the great Test bowlers. I expected the same respect from him, but instead he resorted to petty point-scoring when a more dignified, civilised man, having achieved what he wanted anyway, would have kept his mouth shut.

This was typical of the hidebound attitudes of the TCCB that Bedser personified; players, from the England captain down, like Victorian children, were expected to be seen and not heard. While Bedser was free to have a pop at me, I was reminded that my TCCB contract forbade me from commenting at all. It was perhaps fortunate that my path did not cross with his again that day; in my fury and bitterness at his actions, I might have done something that I would later have regretted.

As I packed up my kit in the now-deserted dressing room, I thought back to what Brian Close had said to me, when he was trying to persuade me not to accept the England captaincy. 'Turn it down,' he had said. 'If you take the job now, it'll be the worst bloody year of your life.' Not for the first time, he'd been absolutely spot on. Kath and my parents had been at Lord's throughout the Test, and she was waiting in the car when I sprinted out of the pavilion, dodging the waiting reporters. As I jumped into the car, I said, 'That's it. I've resigned.'

'You don't say,' she said, drily, gesturing to the phalanxes of reporters and photographers surrounding the car. 'I'd never have guessed.' It was an attempt to lighten the mood, but I was too mired in a black depression to be dragged from it so easily.

Kath had arranged that her parents and our nanny Diane would look after the kids for a few days so she could be with me in Somerset, but I was adamant that I wanted to go there on my own. We drove to the hotel car park in a bruised and angry silence, and we said the most terse of goodbyes before I screeched off, leaving her staring after me. Until I condescended to get in touch, she would have to pick up what information she could from the television news and the press, or second hand from other people. Even though I was at the lowest possible ebb, there was no excuse for my pigheadedness and selfishness and it left scars on our marriage that lasted for years.

I'd arranged to meet Viv Richards in the Four Alls in Taunton that night, fresh hurt for Kath – I could make time for Viv but not for her. It was hard for her to understand why I would choose the companionship of my friend rather than discuss my problems with her, but living, eating, drinking, batting and bowling together over a period of years, it was inevitable that Viv and I had grown to know each other inside out and this was a cricketing problem and I needed another cricketer's input to help me solve it. As I paused outside the pub, I realised that I had no idea what sort of reception I would receive. I soon found out – my friends were out in force to support me.

It gave me a great boost, but later that evening Viv and I took ourselves off somewhere quieter and sat down to talk through the events of the past few days and weeks. As we talked, I began to get a bit of perspective on what had happened. It was a bitter blow, of course, no point in trying to deny that, but I was still the same player, the same person I had always been. I was no longer England captain, but nobody had died and life would go on. The best thing I could do was get back to doing what I did best, scoring runs and taking wickets.

The following morning I received another huge morale boost. I got to the Taunton ground early and even at nine-thirty it was already close to half-full. As I began to walk across the outfield, I could see people turning to look my way, nudging their neighbours. There was a momentary silence and then people began to applaud, a few at first, then more and more until it seemed as if everyone there was on their feet, clapping, shouting and cheering. After the black times I had endured, this was the most wonderful antidote.

It was a great moment, but because of my pigheadedness, Kath was not there to share it with me. She only heard about it when my mum phoned her the next day and gave her chapter and verse about it. 'It was wonderful, Kathryn,' she said. 'You should have been there,' unwittingly twisting the knife even further in Kath's wounds. I don't regret many things about my life because I believe that stuff happens for a reason and that there's no point looking back over your shoulder and pondering on "what might have beens". You have to look to the future and press on, but I'll always regret that I shut Kath out then and prevented her being at Taunton to share that moment with me.

Bitter as I was at being effectively forced from the England captaincy, it was undeniably good to be able to leave someone else to worry about the captaincy from now on and concentrate on regaining my own form. I had always been blessed with total self-belief, but after the events of the past twelve months, even I was beginning to have a few doubts about myself. I had felt in good shape, but since my half-century in my first game as England captain, I had played twenty Test innings with a top score of only 37, and there was more than my usual dose of stubbornness in my refusal to acknowledge that I was struggling for form, particularly with the bat. I still talked the talk, but I hadn't walked the walk for quite some time.

The England selectors had once more called up Mike Brearley as a stopgap captain, and he contacted me before the third Test at Headingley. 'Beef,' he said, 'I know what you must have been through in the past few weeks, so are you sure you want to play in this Test? Don't get me wrong, you're the best all-rounder we have and I want you in the side, but if you don't feel ready to play, I'll fully understand.'

Ray Illingworth had no doubts about whether I was ready to play. In an interview in the *Sunday Mirror*, he told the world that I was 'overrated, overweight and overpaid. He should be dropped from the team.' I knew that some of the selectors had also been arguing that I should be dropped, but curiously, I didn't share that opinion. I'd never had a moment's doubt that I was worth my place and that I wanted to carry on playing for England. The day that I didn't would be the time to quit the game altogether. 'Of course I bloody want to play, Brears,' I said. 'I have a good feeling about this Test,' I added. 'We can beat this shower.'

'That's great,' he said, deploying the psychology once more. 'I think you'll get 150 runs and take ten wickets.'

Our main strike bowler, Bob Willis, almost missed the game. He had had a chest infection during the second Test at Lord's and it had a big impact on his performance – he sent down a staggering total of thirty-two no-balls during the game. His form and the selectors' concerns that he was increasingly injury-prone and perhaps not up to the demands of top-level fast bowling any more had put his Test career in jeopardy. To ensure he was fit, Bob had opted to miss Warwickshire's next county game, but the selectors read his absence as proof that he wasn't fit to play at Headingley. They reasoned that if he wasn't fit enough to play in the championship he was certainly not fit enough to play for England and chose Mike Hendrick in his place. They even sent out Mike's official invitation.

When Alec Bedser rang him to pass on the news, Bob blew his top. He explained why he wasn't playing and told Bedser that if he wanted Bob to prove his fitness, he'd turn out in a second team game the next day. Fortunately the team had not yet been announced but after the selectors had a hasty rethink, Bedser then had to phone the Derbyshire CCC office and get them to intercept Mike Hendrick's mail, so that he would not receive the official invitation to play that had already been posted to him.

I didn't have any problems about coming back into the England dressing room as one of the 'other ranks'. Graham Gooch and a few of the other players had written me supportive letters since I resigned the captaincy and, as ever, I felt proud to be pulling on that England shirt. I took my normal peg in the dressing room, chatted to a few of the players and then went out to take a look at the wicket. As was often the case at Headingley then, it didn't look too good a surface for a five-day Test, with movement for the seam bowlers but also uneven bounce.

Kim Hughes won the toss and chose to bat, a decision that we should have made him regret but our bowling was not up to the mark and a grafting century from John Dyson and Kim Hughes with a captain's knock of 89 laid the foundations for a big Aussie total. Brears used me as third change bowler and I barely bowled at all on the first day, but I got a long stint on the second and returned figures of six for 95. I'd been experimenting with a modified bowling action, in which I sidestepped just before releasing the ball. I thought it might help me swing the ball more, but Brears felt it was affecting the pace and bounce I could generate and urged me to go back to my natural style. He reinforced the message by calling me 'the sidestep queen'. I did as he suggested and my bowling figures suggest that he was right, but it wasn't enough to stop Australia building what looked like a match-winning score of 401 for nine declared. It was well in excess of what they should have reached on a pitch that, as expected, had made batting a struggle from the start. Hughes called 400 runs on that wicket 'as good as a thousand' on a better one and he wouldn't have found many to argue with him.

Their innings had taken almost all of the first two days, leaving Gooch and Boycs only a couple of overs to survive that night. They negotiated those safely, but Gooch was out early the next morning, signalling the start of a traditional England collapse. The score was 87 for five as I came out to bat. Given the state of the wicket, which made even survival something of a lottery, I decided to swing the bat. It had failed miserably at Lord's but here it paid off, and I had reached 50 from fifty-four balls when I gloved a brute of a delivery from Dennis Lillee. It almost cleared Rod Marsh behind the stumps but he took off like a goalkeeper to take it high above his head. It was a fitting way for him to pass a personal milestone, becoming the most successful wicketkeeper in Test history with 264 victims to his name in just seventy-one Tests.

The tail quickly folded and we were all out for 174, with Lillee, Alderman and Lawson sharing the wickets. After the misery of Lord's where I'd scored my first ever Test match 'pair' it was good to be back in the runs, but it was the only satisfaction to be gleaned from a match that saw us trailing by 227 runs on a wicket that was only going to get worse and worse.

Kim Hughes enforced the follow-on and Dennis Lillee got Gooch out for a duck before bad light brought play to a merciful end. Poor Goochie had managed to get out twice in the same day for a total of just two runs. So far, the change of captaincy did not seem to be having much effect; we'd been outplayed since the first over and were staring down the barrel of a very heavy defeat that would give the Aussies an almost impregnable lead in the series. I'd developed a tradition of hosting the 'Botham barbecue' for both teams on the Saturday of every Headingley Test – my 'home' Test – and both teams duly arrived at our house on the Saturday night. The Aussies were naturally full of themselves, while we were about as low as the proverbial snake's belly, but a relaxing evening and a few drinks helped to cheer us up a little, though even the most incurable optimist among us couldn't find any ray of sunshine in the clouds gathering over Headingley.

Sunday was a rest day and rather than spend the day brooding over the fate of the game, I went down to the pub for a couple of pints. When I set off for the team hotel that evening I said to Kath, 'I'll check out in the morning and be back home some time tomorrow afternoon, or early evening at the latest.'

Resuming at 6 for one, still 221 behind, we were 41 for four before Boycs and Peter Willey fashioned a stand of 64. Peter was then out for 33, bringing me to the wicket. As I walked out to the wicket, I took in the familiar scene: the sightscreen and tiered seating at one end, all painted duck-egg blue, with the heads of the spectators just visible above the high backs of the rows in front; the stand separating the cricket and rugby league grounds and the low, raked terracing to either side, with trees, red-brick houses and the spire of St Michael's church visible beyond them. Given those low, almost open sides, and the spaciousness of the ground, it was amazing how much atmosphere the passionate Yorkshire fans could generate there, but on this morning Headingley had all the atmosphere of a funeral – appropriately enough, because the small crowd gathered there had come to watch the last rites of this match and the inevitable Australian victory.

The local hero, Boycs, and I added a few more before Alderman at last trapped him lbw for 46. It had taken him two and a half hours to score his runs, but for once I didn't begrudge him his slow scoring rate. Bob Taylor fell two runs later, bringing Graham Dilley to the wicket at about three o'clock. At 135 for seven, still 92 runs short of making the Aussies bat again, with three hours' play left before stumps and a full day still to come, we were goners. The ground was emptying fast as the dispirited England supporters slunk away and the bookmakers were so desperate for business that they were offering England at 500-1 against. Even at those unprecedented odds, very few punters were willing to take them on. When I saw the odds chalked up on a board, I did think to myself, 'Bloody hell, that's got to be worth a punt,' but I didn't have time to do anything about it. Unlike Dennis Lillee and Rodney Marsh, who reportedly tried to get their teamates to put £50 of their team fund on us, and when they howled them down, slipped the team bus driver a tenner to put on for them.

When I'd gone out to bat, as far as I was concerned the match was over. I wasn't even particularly aware of the score – it just didn't seem relevant – and I wasn't alone in writing off the game. Brears had showered, changed and packed his bags ready for a quick getaway after the last rites, though he had put on a clean cricket shirt so that anyone, spectators or TV cameras, looking at the dressing room would see no visible sign of the English surrender.

Graham Dilley was newly arrived on the Test scene and in a reasonably comfortable position: since no one regarded him as anything more than an out-and-out tailender and the game was already as good as lost, he reckoned that he had nothing to lose by swinging the bat. He connected a few times, but the Aussies weren't overly concerned at first; his luck would run out soon and the Ashes would then be in the bag. Down the other end, I was quite enjoying the show, but not reading anything more into it than that, but as Graham kept on clouting fours, some off the middle and some off the edge, I decided that I'd better come to the party as well.

It came as something of a shock when I glanced at the scoreboard and realised that we were within striking distance of making the Aussies bat again. The runs kept coming, and when we passed 227, we had our noses in front. Our score still had no more than nuisance value – even the handful of punters who'd taken the odds couldn't really have expected that they would ever collect – but we had at least got up the Aussie noses a bit, made a game of it and staunched the haemorrhage of supporters from the stands.

Slowly, imperceptibly, the mood of the two teams changed. Graham and I were having the time of our lives, smiling and laughing as we chatted in the middle of the wicket between overs, but, from their expressions, the Australians weren't getting the joke at all. They were deadly serious now, but we were still carting them all over the ground. From the time we passed their total I can't remember playing a single defensive stroke. I hooked, pulled, cut and drove, and if I flashed, I flashed hard. The sight of a few edges whistling through or over the slip cordon did us a power of good and wreaked further havoc with Aussie morale. It wasn't exactly the noble art of batsmanship – Mike Brearley described it as 'pure village green stuff' – but it certainly did the job. I glanced up to the balcony at one point, expecting to see him urging restraint, but instead he was miming even wilder and more extravagant strokes. I tried to oblige, hitting one four off Alderman that TV watchers heard Richie Benaud describe thus: 'No need to look for that one … it's gone straight into the confectionery stall … and out again.' My own favourite was a square cut off Dennis Lillee that had cannoned off the boundary boards before any of the fielders had moved. I don't think I ever hit a more perfectly timed and executed shot in my entire career.

By this time the television and radio commentators were practically giving birth, and even I was getting a bit carried away by it all – we couldn't really save this match or win it, could we? Possibly not, but we could at least make them wait until the last day to seal their victory. For the first time I told Graham Dilley to keep it going as long as he could. That was probably a mistake for, having reminded him of his responsibilities, he was out soon afterwards for 56 – his first Test match fifty and one he'd never forget. We'd added 117 for the eighth wicket in just eighty minutes of mayhem. At that stage we were 252 for eight, still in effect only 25 for eight, but at least we had ensured that Australia would have to bat again. They were now becoming seriously angry about the lengthy delay to their victory celebrations and Geoff Lawson so lost his cool that he bowled two chest-high 'beamers' at me. As Lady Bracknell might have said, one might be an accident but two smacked of carelessness. I stored the information away in the memory banks for future reference the next time Lawson was batting and I was bowling.

If I was angered by it, it also showed that the Aussies were under pressure and getting rattled. Their pacemen certainly bowled with ever greater speed and aggression as the rearguard action continued, but they also started to lose control and I was surprised that Hughes kept them on as long as he did before trying a spinner. When Ray Bright finally came on, he almost got me out straight away. Had he done so that would have been game over, but my mishit didn't find a fielder and I breathed again.

Chris Old was next man in, sent on his way by Brears as he left the pavilion with a 'Just hold it together and keep an end up.' I'd had reason to disparage Old's lack of commitment in the West Indies, but I could not fault his efforts here in front of his home crowd as he scored 29 and helped me to add another 67 for the ninth wicket. Along the way I passed my century. I'd scored it from eighty-seven balls, with the second fifty taking just thirty deliveries. The atmosphere was now absolutely explosive. Far from leaving the ground, spectators were now streaming back in. Every run was cheered to the echo and every four celebrated as if it was the winning hit … and the Aussies had suddenly gone very quiet indeed. Even their sledging seemed half-hearted. 'What's up boys?' I said at one point. 'Are you not enjoying this as much as me?'

Bob Willis, last man, had replaced Old at the other end and was content to give me the strike whenever possible, and I kept smashing the bowling all over the ground. We had added another 31 runs when the umpires brought play to a close for the day with England on 351 for nine, 124 runs ahead. It speaks volumes about the extent of the deflation of Aussie morale in the space of three short hours that they seemed far more relieved than us to be trooping off the field.

I was left not out 145 overnight, my highest Test score to date … it was probably fair to say that I had regained my batting form. The atmosphere back in the dressing room had been transformed from the morgue I had left earlier that day. Now people were cracking jokes, laughing and shouting, while from the Aussie dressing room we could hear only a brooding silence, punctuated by the occasional angry curse. I flopped down, put my feet up, lit a cigar and struggled to make sense of what had just happened, but I rapidly gave up trying; all I knew for sure was that the 'Botham *Boys' Own* Story' was now firmly back on track. The reporters clustered outside the dressing room were keen to get a few quotes, but after the way I had been hounded out of the captaincy I was in no rush to help them out. I was not at the hastily convened press conference and, though they chased me to my car, I kept my mouth firmly shut.

We'd already checked out of our hotel that morning, assuming we'd be on our way home before nightfall, so we all had to check back in again. We should have been celebrating with champagne and lobster, but the job was not yet done so we settled for a fish and chip supper and a couple of pints instead. That evening, unlike the previous one, my mind was fully focused on the job in hand. If Bob and I could somehow put another seventy or eighty runs on the board, I felt we'd be in with a genuine chance, but it was a hell of an ask for a number eleven batsman.

The following morning, the headlines were all variations on the theme of BOTHAM'S MIRACLE and the copy was full of frenzied speculation about what the day might bring, but in our more rational moments none of us really believed we could do it – or at least no one admitted to feeling that way. That was reinforced when our hopes of building a really challenging total were torpedoed when Allan Border caught Bob off an outswinger from Terry Alderman with only five added to our overnight total. I was left high and dry on 149 not out. Australia now needed 130 to win.

At the start of the Australian second innings, Brears indulged in a bit more of his trademark psychology. As our main strike bowler, Bob naturally expected to take the new ball, but on this occasion Brears waved him away and gave it to Graham Dilley and me. It was partly because he thought that Graham and I might still be on a bit of a roll after our partnership, but he also thought it might help to gee up Bob. In that at least he was right. When Bob finally got his hands on the ball, there was steam coming out of his nostrils. Before the match he had been talking to me and a couple of the other senior pros and saying, 'This might be my last ever game for England. After the West Indies tour, I never thought I'd play cricket again, let alone Test cricket, but if I don't get wickets here, I'll be on the scrapheap.'

If this was going to be his last hurrah, Bob was determined to make it a memorable one. I'd never seen him run in with more pace, passion and commitment than he did that day.

I got Graeme Wood caught behind by Bob Taylor – 13 for one – but John Dyson and Trevor Chappell then took the score to 56, just 74 short of the target with nine wickets in hand. Bob had been bowling up the slope and not liking it, and Brears now switched him to the other end. It paid immediate dividends as Trevor Chappell, pinned to his crease by a vicious bouncer, could only glove it to Bob Taylor behind the stumps. Two runs later, in the last over before lunch, I held on to a screamer from Kim Hughes at slip and the Aussie captain was back in the hutch for a duck. Just to make sure they really didn't enjoy their lunch, Bob then had Graham Yallop caught fending off another bruising lifter to Mike Gatting at short square leg. At 58 for four they should still have been slight favourites but they certainly didn't act that way.

As we came out after lunch I glanced along the balcony and saw the expression on the Australian faces; the words 'rabbits' and 'headlights' sprang to mind. After five days' wear and tear, the pitch had deteriorated even more, and our tails were well up. Chris Old picked up the next, crucial wicket, clean bowling Allan Border for a duck –

the Aussie middle order of Hughes, Yallop and Border had made precisely nought between them. 65 for five. Bob Willis suckered the obdurate Dyson into hooking early at a slightly slower ball and he top-edged a catch to Bob Taylor – 68 for six – and Rod Marsh then repeated the trick for Graham Dilley to take the catch – 74 for seven. Geoff Lawson was next out, giving Bob Taylor his fourth victim of the innings, once more off Willis – 75 for eight.

The Australians had just lost seven wickets for 19 runs, turning the match on its head, but now, with the most unlikely of victories almost within our grasp, this extraordinary game took yet another turn. The Aussies still needed only 55 to win. On this wicket it was a huge ask, but Ray Bright and Dennis Lillee wiped the anticipatory smiles from our faces with a series of improvised shots and wild slogs that somehow eluded the fielders. They added 35 in only four overs to leave the Aussies needing just 20. You could feel the mounting tension and the frustration gripping us as the Australians edged towards their target, but once more Bob Willis was equal to the challenge. He pounded in again and speared in a 'toe-crusher' at Lillee. 'DK' tried to go for the big hit but only succeeded in spooning the ball up in the air off the leading edge. It looked safe at first because Mike Gatting was standing quite deep at mid-on. He had a long way to go to make the catch and normally accelerated like a fully loaded double-decker bus ascending a steep hill. Everyone, players and spectators alike, froze as we watched Gatt rumbling up through the gears. The ball was well past the peak of its arc and descending inexorably on an empty patch of turf when, drawing on reserves of pace that neither he nor we had ever suspected he possessed, the blurred, diving figure of Gatt scooped up the ball a fraction of a second before it hit the turf and clung on to it despite a collision with the ground that must have rattled the glasses in the Members Bar.

If ever there was a match-winning moment, that was it, but Australia were still only nine wickets down. Terry Alderman joined Ray Bright at the crease and for a few minutes it seemed as if the gods might yet favour Australia. Fielding at third slip, the unfortunate Chris Old put down first one sharp chance and then another. Games have swung on such moments before, but on this occasion we – and Bob Willis – were not to be denied. He had already sent down fifteen overs at searing pace and began his sixteenth with another guided missile – a perfect yorker that went through Bright's defensive push before he'd even registered that the ball had arrived and shattered his stumps, rounding off the most magnificent spell of sustained hostile bowling it has ever been my privilege to witness, and probably one of the greatest bowling performances ever seen. Australia were all out for 111 and Bob Willis had taken eight wickets for 43 in 15.1 overs.

Having pushed our way through the hordes streaming on to the pitch, we reached the sanctuary of the dressing room to find that it was complete bedlam as well, awash with photographers, reporters and the well-wishers and back-slappers that always fill a winning dressing room … but are never to be seen in a losing one. After the emotions and the teeth-grinding tensions of that last day, we were all mentally and physically exhausted. Bob Willis, who had made talk of dropping him look absurd, was too tired even to crack a smile. However, we recovered our equilibrium soon enough and then the search was on for some victory champagne. The Aussies had bought theirs in advance but it now remained unopened behind the closed and locked door of their dressing room as they began the inquest into what had gone wrong. When we sent our dressing-room attendant, Ricky – later to become a caddy for top golfers like Ernie Els, whose bags he carried on Els's two US Open triumphs – to ask if we could beg, borrow or steal some of their champagne, it was suggested to him, in suitably undiplomatic Australian language, that he might like to consider going away. Eventually the England management entered negotiations with their opposite numbers and, after a bit of haggling, bought a dozen bottles which we downed in record time. Peter Willey, who in his nineteen-Test career had only ever tasted winners' bubbly when it had been offered to him by the other side, poured himself a glass, took a sip, rolled it appreciatively around his mouth and said, 'That's better. All the other stuff I've drunk over the years has made me want to puke.'

As we took calls and messages from friends and heard snippets of TV and radio coverage, we began to realise that our epic comeback had caught the imagination of the entire nation. Never in British industrial history had quite so many people phoned in sick or neglected to return from their lunch breaks, and never had so few shares been traded on the Stock Exchange. Even in Scotland, where as a rule cricket barely causes a flicker on the national radar, some friends told me that the traffic had ground to a halt in the streets of Glasgow and, in those pre-Sky TV days, huge crowds had gathered around television shop windows.

We had also gained a crucial psychological edge over the Aussies. From now on, even if they were in a winning position, there would be a little voice of doubt whispering in their inner ear, 'What if lightning strikes twice?' They feared Bob Willis, no doubt about that, and would not relish further encounters with him, and if he was nearing the end of his career, I was still in my prime and I was now the stuff of Australian nightmares. Every time I walked to the wicket, or picked up the ball, they would remember Headingley 1981 and wonder if it was about to happen again.

The conclusion reached by most observers about my startling return to form was the obvious one: the England captaincy had placed such a burden on me that I was simply unable to perform. Only after that burden had been removed could I do myself justice as a player with bat and ball. I didn't – and still don't – agree with that for one minute. Even when I was making a pair at Lord's, I was still convinced that it was only a matter of time before I hit a big score again. I was just sad that the time had come one Test too late.

The series was now tied at 1-1 but we held a huge psychological advantage. Australian morale had taken a hell of a battering, and this was the time to make it count. The fourth Test at Edgbaston was another low-scoring game and proved to be another absolute nail-biter. Our first innings was a disaster. Brears won the toss and chose to bat – the obvious decision on a pitch that looked full of runs, with a lightning-quick outfield. We should have scored at least 400; in fact we were all out for 189. There were no excuses, it was just poor batting. Of our batsmen, only David Gower failed to get a start, but none of us, including me, built on it to fashion the big innings we needed. Terry Alderman once more caused us most problems, his nagging length and late movement giving him five for 42.

We fought back and held Australia to a score of 258 thanks largely to John Emburey, who took four for 43 in 26.5 overs, but once more, no one got on top of the bowling in our second innings and a total of 219 left Australia needing just 151 to win with two days to play. The only straw we could clutch at was that the target was 21 more than at Headingley; but we couldn't pull off another miracle, could we?

Australia were 9 for one overnight and Bob Willis again bowled superbly the next morning but this time without much luck. Allan Border blocked up one end and nudged and glanced singles and twos to keep the scoreboard moving, and though Dyson, Hughes and Yallop could not stay with him, Australia reached 105 for four without too many alarms, and needed only another 46 to win, with six wickets in hand.

Unusually for me, I wasn't clamouring for a spell with the ball because I felt the pitch was more likely to help the spinners, and I suggested to Brears that he give Peter Willey a try at the other end from John Emburey. Peter gave it a real rip and I thought he might trouble the left-handed AB by bowling into the rough outside his off-stump. Umpire Dickie Bird was also eager to see the spinners in action, but not because he thought they might bowl us to victory. When Brears asked him, 'What do you think?' Dickie, with one eye on getting home to Yorkshire before dark, said, 'I think it's all over, skipper. Best thing you can do is put on the twirlers so we can get off early.'

In the next over, John Emburey upset both my and Dickie's calculations by getting Border out with a ball that lifted from a good length, and looped to Mike Gatting off AB's glove. Willey was already loosening up, ready to come on at the other end, when Brears played one of his hunches and tossed me the ball instead.

I still don't know what was in his mind, or why his hunch paid off – there was nothing in the pitch for me, any more than there had been for the other fast bowlers – but something certainly seemed to work. The score was 105 when Border was out. It was 114 for five when I clean-bowled Rod Marsh. Ray Bright went at the same score, leg before for a duck. Dennis Lillee then chased a very wide one – I was trying to bowl an inswinger, but it went the other way – and snicked it to a diving Bob Taylor who juggled it and then hung on at the third attempt. Lillee out for three – 120 for eight. I bowled Martin Kent one run later, and finally, as the crowd went crazy, I put a quicker one straight through Terry Alderman's defensive push to bowl him for a duck. I had just taken five wickets for one run in the space of twenty-eight deliveries – my overall figures were five for 11 from fourteen overs – and we had taken a 2-1 series lead. I had bowled well – fast and straight – but on that wicket it should not have been enough to make the Aussies crumble that way. The only explanation I could find was that they had bottled out. The psychological edge that we – and I – had got over them at Headingley was proving an insuperable barrier for them.

When we went to Old Trafford for the fifth Test, the Aussies looked in the same shell-shocked state. They were being pilloried in the Aussie press – which could be just as unforgiving as the British tabloids when things did not go Australia's way – and I think they knew that the series and the Ashes were lost and just wanted to slink away home.

We won the toss and batted first, but Lillee and Alderman took four wickets each to reduce us to 175 for nine, and the only evidence of my Midas touch this time was that I was out for a golden duck, caught in the gully off Dennis Lillee. However, Paul Allott, who scored a fine 52 not out in front of his home fans, added 56 for the last wicket with Bob Willis – how the Aussies must have been sick of seeing him – and once more we got off the hook, reaching a respectable 231 all out. We bowled out the Aussies for 130 – Willis four for 63, Botham three for 28 – but we then struggled against more tight bowling from Terry Alderman, who picked up another five-wicket haul in the innings. I came in to bat with the score on 104 for five, 204 ahead. It was a handy lead but not yet an insuperable one.

I had a good feeling as I walked out to bat – some days you just feel that way. Chris Tavaré was at the other end and we went pretty slowly at first. I was playing myself in, ready to take on Lillee and Alderman as soon as they took the new ball. When they did, the assault began, and everything I tried paid off. Dennis Lillee was bowling very fast, but three times I went for hook shots off deliveries by him that were heading straight for my head, on each occasion I connected, and each time the ball sailed high into the crowd for six. I also hit one straight drive back over his head that was going like a howitzer shell. Dennis made an instinctive move to try and catch it, but then, discretion triumphing over valour, thought better of it and let it go. Despite the big hitting, this wasn't a 'slogathon' like Headingley. I can only remember playing one false shot in my entire innings, an inside edge that flashed past the stumps on its way to the fine-leg boundary.

I scored 118 and it was probably the best innings I ever played, though I would not have had the chance to do it had Chris Tavaré not held up the other end. He was barracked and slow-handclapped by the crowds and pilloried by the press for his slow scoring during his brief Test career, but he'd been brought in to solve a crisis at number three in the batting order – Bob Woolmer, Brears and David Gower had already been tried there earlier in the series without success. 'Tav' had been told to just stay there, closing up one end while others played their strokes. It can't have been any fun for him at all – he was a natural stroke player – any more than it was for the spectators, but he performed his appointed task to perfection, and no matter what was said in the press or on the terraces, there wasn't a word of criticism from inside the dressing room, where we all knew the value of what he was doing.

He took four and three-quarter hours to make 69 in the first innings and was even slower in making 78 in the second – his innings took seven hours and three minutes in all, included the slowest fifty in Test cricket history, 304 minutes. Of the 149 we added together for the sixth wicket, Tav made just 28, but his innings was just as crucial as mine. He broke the Aussie hearts and ground them into the dust, and after I was out he shared two more big partnerships with Alan Knott and John Emburey who also both passed fifty. All out for 404, we set the Aussies a target of 505. Even on a pitch that was playing better and better as the game went on, it was an impossible total.

Graham Yallop and Allan Border both scored hundreds as they made a real fight of it, but the task was too great, and though they scored 402 all out, a remarkable fourth innings score and enough to win many Test matches, it was not enough for this one. The Ashes were ours. It had been an incredible turnaround from those early summer days when both I and my team had looked down and out.

The celebrations continued on the Sunday after the Old Trafford Test when, batting in a Sunday League match against Hampshire at Taunton, I made a century in sixty-seven minutes. The official timing for the second fifty was nine minutes, although I made it seven.

After all that had gone before it, the sixth and final Test at The Oval ended in an anticlimactic draw, though it did include another personal milestone, my two hundredth Test wicket. I took six for 125 in the Aussie first innings, including the wicket of the Aussie captain, Kim Hughes, who trod on his leg-stump as he pulled the ball through mid-wicket. He was halfway through his third run when we helpfully pointed out to him that he should save his energy as he'd already been out for a couple of minutes. It's always an unfortunate way to be dismissed and pretty much summed up his disastrous series as captain. I could sympathise with him: I had very recent experience of what he was now going through. Bob Willis continued his own golden summer with four for 91, but helped by a fine unbeaten century from Allan Border they reached 352 all out.

Geoff Boycott hit 137 in reply, but from 246 for two we crumbled to 314 all out, with Dennis Lillee making the most of the second new ball to finish with seven for 89. I made it a ten-wicket game with four for 128 in the second innings after another marathon bowl – altogether I got through eighty-nine overs in the match – as the Aussies declared at 344 for eight, setting us 383 to win. Any thoughts of ending the summer in a blaze of glory were eliminated when Boycs was out for a duck in the first over and Tav went at 18. At 144 for six, we were in some danger of defeat, but Alan Knott with 70 not out and Brears with a fifty in his last Test innings saw us to safety.

Brears had already announced that it would be his last match and he was given a standing ovation as he left the field for the last time. After Brian Close, Tom Cartwright and Kenny Barrington, Brears was the fourth in a quartet of major influences on my cricketing career. He gave me my head when he felt the situation merited it, but he wasn't afraid to call me to heel when I was getting carried away. If I overdid the short-pitched stuff – not entirely unknown during my career – Brears would simply say, 'I'm taking you off. You're bowling like a pillock.' I wouldn't have taken that from everyone but I took it from him because I had the utmost respect for him. He was the best England captain I ever played under … and that included Ian Botham!

It was the end of the most turbulent year of my life, and if I was back on top for now, the experiences of those twelve months had taught me one vital lesson: you're surrounded by friendly faces when you're on the way up, but it's the ones who are still around after the shit has hit the fan who are the true friends. I was astonished to discover how many of my so-called mates had dropped out of sight since my feet of clay started showing; that hurt me as much as anything. Now that I was flavour of the month again they all started reappearing, but this time I had their measure.

The 'Botham summer' of 1981 was now over, but it had changed my life for ever. Before then I was reasonably well known in Britain and in cricketing circles abroad, but unknown elsewhere; now I was internationally famous. Even in America, where cricket was virtually unheard of, I made the cover of *Sports Illustrated*, the first cricketer ever to do so. It was hard to keep my feet on the ground at the time, with the phone ringing off the hook with offers of endorsements, advertising campaigns, book deals and personal appearances.

I also made a surprise television appearance, as the subject of *This Is Your Life*. Kath had obviously been in on the secret from the start and she'd vetoed the original list of people that the programme's researchers had come up with. They wanted to fill the programme with celebrities and people that I'd barely even heard of and Kath said, 'No. If you do it that way, it won't be a true reflection of Ian's life up to now. I'm not having him portrayed as if all he wants to do is hang around with celebrities, because he's not that type of person at all. If Ian's going to do it, he'll want his real friends and his family to be there, not all these other people.'

She dug her heels in and got her way in most of the arguments, so people like Charlie Martin, a Scots ghillie who had taught me to fish, were there – the first time in Charlie's life that he had ever been outside Scotland. The only exception was Gary Sobers. Kath had wanted Brian Close to be the final guest because he had been such a big part of both our lives. Though we became good friends later on, I barely knew Gary at the time, but he was a huge name back then and the TV company insisted on making him the last guest, so he came on stage with Liam and Sarah.

I had no inkling that it was being planned – Kath had sworn everyone to secrecy – though I was a bit puzzled why conversations kept fading away as I came into the room and why she kept sneaking off to the phone box while we were on holiday just before I was 'ambushed' for the programme. I was in an England team meeting ready for the trip to India when I saw Eamonn Andrews appear with that trademark rictus grin on his face and his Big Red Book clutched in his hand. I was sitting there thinking, 'Wonder who he's going to get – Boycott? Willis?' When he gave me the book I was gob-smacked. If I'd known in advance that he was coming for me, I would have told him, politely of course, what he could do with it; a lot of people say that, I know, but I really mean it. The idea of somebody saying 'This is your life' to someone in their mid-twenties was quite ridiculous. However, when it actually happened, I knew all my friends and relatives would be waiting backstage and would be bitterly disappointed if I pulled the plug on it. So I bit my tongue and went ahead with it, and I must admit it was touching to see all the people who had given up their time to come and say nice things about me ... but it was still an absurd idea.

In the story of my life, it may sometimes seem that Kath only gets mentioned when things have gone pear-shaped and she's having to rein me in, give me a bollocking or clear up the mess I've made, but that would be to denigrate her. She is the heartbeat of our life, our work and our family. Strong-willed, quick-witted and a real grafter, she could have had any career she chose, but like many women, she preferred to put her family and her children first. It was never easy. My fame as a cricketer and as the target of numerous tabloid exposés left our kids open to playground taunts – and, as we all know, kids can be very cruel. Our parents also had to deal with the media pressure and face their friends and neigh-bours after the latest tabloid 'outrage', and our own friends and relations were all affected by the three-ring media circus that kept revolving around us.

Yet despite the pressure-cooker world we came to occupy, Kath shielded the children from media pressures and intrusions, and kept them grounded and free from the swollen heads and self-indulgence that blight the lives of many children of famous people. The result, and the greatest tribute to Kath, is that our three children have all grown up to be self-confident and successful, but also likeable, decent human beings, with their feet fixed firmly on the ground.

If I managed to keep some sense of perspective about my new-found fame and all the adulation and money that came my way, it was partly through Kath's wisdom and good advice, and partly because my experiences earlier in the year had taught me that there was another side to the celebrity coin. I was now a very tall poppy and there were plenty of people out there looking to cut me back down to size.

With Mike Brearley retired and my name not even considered, the England selectors turned to Keith Fletcher of Essex to lead the winter tour of India in 1981-82. It was very nearly called off before it had started. There was no general international consensus on how the Gleneagles Agreement should be applied, and although Britain had signed up to its pledge to combat 'the evil of apartheid' in sport, the opposition of the patriarchs of Lord's to apartheid was very much more muted than that of the ruling bodies in India, Pakistan and the West Indies. Several England players, including Geoff Boycott and Geoff Cook, were on a UN blacklist because, like Robin Jackman, they had played or coached in South Africa.

Things came to a head in October 1981 when the Indian authorities imposed a ban on Boycott and Cook because of their South African links. The TCCB responded by insisting that they would not bow down to political pressure and change the team, and it looked inevitable that the tour would be cancelled. However, Indira Gandhi, the Indian Prime Minister, then made a personal intervention and at her insistence the ban was lifted and the tour went ahead. I can only speculate about what she thought four months later when the news broke that Boycott was leading a party of England cricketers on a rebel tour of South Africa. To add insult to injury, the whole thing had been put together in secret and the players recruited by Boycott while they were on tour in India.

When he first sounded me out I was interested enough to find out more. I was not a very political animal, but I knew enough about South Africa to know that apartheid stank. I did not want to be seen to be doing anything that could be construed as condoning it – you still have to look yourself in the eye while you're shaving in the morning – but when you have a wife and family to support you also have to look at every angle.

Professional sport is a short-term, high-risk occupation. Form can be fickle and all sportsmen are also only one bad injury away from an abrupt end to their careers. I was one of the top players in world cricket yet I was earning only £1,000 a Test match – £5,000 for a five-Test series. Somebody was now willing to pay me ten times that amount just to play cricket for two months; I'd have been a fool not to have given it some thought.

The subject of a rebel tour had been briefly discussed during the previous winter in the West Indies, but everything else was over-shadowed by the sudden death of Kenny Barrington and by the time we got home I'd forgotten all about South Africa. Boycott hadn't, however, and he was hard at work helping to lay the groundwork for the tour. He even bought an off-the-shelf company which would contract cricketers to play in South Africa. He had made a few discreet enquiries during the English season, but he really got to work as soon as the England tour party arrived in India. It was all very 'Spy versus Spy' – code words, muttered conversations and meetings in corridors and dark corners.

I had talked it over with Kath who was vehemently opposed to me having anything to do with the rebel tour, and she was in my solicitor

Alan Herd's office when I phoned to ask him to come out to Bangalore with my agent, Reg Hayter, to discuss it. It showed that I was giving the idea some serious consideration, but even before they arrived I was having second thoughts. Just after the Edgbaston Test back in August 1981, rumours of a rebel tour had first reached the TCCB and they had fired off a letter warning players that 'any cricketer who takes part in any such international and/or representative matches in South Africa could thereby make himself ineligible for future selection for England'.

The most important thing to me was my continuing career with England, and though £45,000 was a lot of money, I didn't want to jeopardise my England future for the sake of it. My growing off-the-field income would also be at risk if I went to South Africa: the companies with whom I was dealing all had international operations and could not afford to be seen endorsing someone tainted by association with the apartheid regime.

Reg probably wished he hadn't made the journey. He set off down to the hotel pool in Bangalore to have a swim – wearing a pair of boxer shorts as a substitute for trunks – but was then chased by half-a-dozen wild dogs and had to beat a hasty retreat back to his room. Reg was in his seventies, and quite overweight, but he conjured an impressive turn of speed out of those blue-veined, little white legs of his; I don't think I've ever seen him move faster as he beat the dogs to his room by a short head.

Alan and Reg had taken some discreet soundings before they left and were convinced that if I went to South Africa I would almost certainly be banned from playing for England, in which case my value to the companies currently seeking my endorsement would plummet. Nike and the sports equipment specialists Patrick were both chasing my signature and neither wanted their brand associated in any way with the apartheid regime.

The South Africans were aware of at least some of the problems and were offering an 'insurance policy' as part of the deal: any players who lost their Test status because of their involvement in the rebel tour were offered the chance to return to South Africa for two more years at the same inflation-proofed fee. However, Reg and Alan insisted that, first of all, the tour was far from guaranteed to happen. The South Africans had been very careful to deal through intermediaries and 'front companies' throughout. If the tour collapsed, for whatever reason, they could step back into the shadows, but the players had no such protection and would have to carry the can. Second, if I did go, I would not only gain very little, if anything, by doing so, since I would certainly lose my endorsement and sponsorship deals, I would also be banned from the England Test team for the foreseeable future. That was the clincher for me, and I made up my mind to say no.

I would obviously have been one of the major draw-cards for the rebel tour – 'Botham's Match' in the 1981 Ashes had made sporting headlines around the world – but I was far from the only big-name player involved and the South African cricket fans were also so starved of international competition that they would have turned up in droves to watch any England XI that took the field. However, Boycott was still desperate to include me and asked Alan to meet him again to discuss it. When Alan turned up Boycott handed him the telephone and put him on to a sports promoter who almost doubled the previous offer to me if I would join the tour. Alan passed that on, but I'd made my mind up and wasn't going to change it, even for £85,000.

A number of other younger players, including David Gower and Mike Gatting, also turned down the South Africans. For players like Boycott, who was close to retirement anyway, it might have made economic sense to take the money and risk a Test ban, but for the younger ones, the risk was just too high, even for the substantial sums on offer. I certainly never regretted the decision to turn them down.

Boycott may have been the man with the keys to a safe full of

South African gold, but some of his other actions in India alienated every player in the tour party, despite him scoring a hundred in the third Test at Delhi to overtake Gary Sobers and become the highest run scorer in Test history. In the middle of the fourth Test in Calcutta he left the ground claiming he was too ill to field. He then proceeded to spend the afternoon on the golf course – what amazing powers of recovery. After we took him to task for skiving off while we were running ourselves into the ground in the heat and dust of a Calcutta afternoon, he announced that he was quitting the tour alto-gether. Terrified that he might change his mind, we immediately got him to sign a piece of paper to that effect ...

It was not a great series for us on the field. I had a good personal match in the first Test at Bombay. I took nine wickets in the match and when I had scored 16 in our second innings I passed two thousand runs in Test cricket, becoming the third all-rounder after Gary Sobers and Richie Benaud to complete the 'Double' – two hundred wickets, two thousand runs. However, India had the better of a low-scoring match, and set 241 to win, we fell short by 138 runs. Having gained the upper hand, India were helped by their groundsmen who produced a succession of slow 'featherbed' wickets in the remaining five Tests, and with Gavaskar and Viswanath in princely form we never came close to a victory as all the remaining Tests were high-scoring draws – I batted six times and made a century and four half-centuries. Off the field this Indian tour was a wonderful and, at times, very humbling experience. The size of the crowds that greeted us wherever we went was incredible; thousands of people set up camp outside our hotels, yet all they wanted was a glimpse of us. One family travelled for two days in their horse and cart just to hand me a garland of flowers and take a souvenir photograph. They were back on the road five minutes later, on the two-day journey home again.

There was only one problem. In those days Indian beer was not entirely to English tastes, but, moderate beer being better than no beer at all, we were fuelled during most of the tour by the delightfully named but less delightfully flavoured Rosy Pelican London Lager. Its least appetising aspect was the thick layer of glycerine on top of the beer – it was used as a preservative – and you had to pour that away before you could get at the lager. Some cynics in the tour party suggested that the flavour was actually improved if you poured the beer away and drank the glycerine instead. However, a couple of weeks before Christmas I was voted BBC Sports Personality of the Year, and during a live interview with the programme I happened to mention that we would sell our souls for a few pints of English beer. A few days later a huge shipment of bitter arrived from a Yorkshire brewery. The precious load was put in the care of Govind, the baggage master on England tours of India over many years, whose proudest boast was that he had never lost a piece of luggage. He didn't lose any of the beer either, and once suitably refrigerated, it kept us going happily for the rest of the tour.

I'd almost forgotten about the rebel South African tour by the time I got home, but the arrival of the party in South Africa on 28 February 1982 exploded into the headlines. Despite his leading role in organising the tour, Boycott did not captain the team. That dubious honour went to Graham Gooch, one of the few younger players in the party who in my opinion had been badly advised. Of the others, players like Geoff Boycott, Peter Willey, Chris Old, Derek Underwood, Bob Woolmer, John Emburey, Alan Knott, Mike Hendrick, Dennis Amiss and John Lever were much nearer the end of their careers. As they had threatened, the TCCB at once imposed three-year Test bans on all those involved. Boycott never played Test cricket again, but I suppose he was happy to take the money and pay the price. Boycott later had a go at me, accusing me of hypocrisy for saying in a press statement I wasn't going on tour because 'I could never look Viv Richards in the eye again'. On the face of it, Boycott was correct – it would have been hypocritical if I had said that. But in actual fact I never uttered the words. I'd already made it clear to him that my decision was made, at least in part, for financial reasons.

What had happened was, when news of the tour broke, my press agent, Reg Hayter, was besieged by reporters wanting the Botham take on the tour. I wasn't even in the country at the time but, knowing my close friendship with Viv, in good faith but without consulting me, Reg put out the statement in my name. It was true in one way – had Viv ever said to me 'Don't go on that tour, man' I would have turned it down for that reason alone – but I also knew my own mind on the subject. Although the fragility of a career in professional cricket always made me listen to financial offers very carefully, the bottom line was that apartheid was apartheid, and I was not going to support or condone that.

Chapter 6

THE WAR BETWEEN THE TABLOIDS

In case we hadn't already seen enough of the Indians after playing six Tests against them that winter, we went straight into a three-Test series against them in the early summer of 1982. Much was made in the press about the rivalry between myself and the Indian equivalent, Kapil Dev, and we both did pretty well in the first Test at Lord's, though even I was forced to admit that Kapil Dev had just about won the personal duel. He took five for 125 as we reached 433. I scored 67 of them, but Derek Randall took the batting honours with 126. I then took five for 46 as Kapil Dev scored 41 in India's poor first innings total of 128. They did much better after following on, with Vengsarkar's majestic 157 and another fine knock of 89 from Kapil Dev taking them to 369, but, set just 65 to win, we knocked them off for the loss of three wickets – all to Kapil Dev – to go one up in the series.

Next time around, at Old Trafford, I took the batting honours with 128 in England's 425. Early in the innings I was hit on the toe by a fast full toss. It was agony – I thought I'd smashed it beyond repair – and I was hobbling for the rest of my innings. Since I didn't much fancy running between the wickets, I decided I'd better get my runs in boundaries and hit nineteen fours and two sixes before I charged Shastri once too often and was bowled as the ball squeezed beneath my bat and trickled on to the off-stump. Kapil Dev scored another half-century – actually making 65 – as India fought back from 173 for six to the safety of 378 for eight before rain, which had already caused several delays, wiped out the whole of the last day.

We went to The Oval needing only a draw to take the series and that was never in doubt from the moment we won the toss on a belter of an Oval track. We were nicely placed at 185 for three when I walked to the wicket and Allan Lamb and I then put on 176 for the fourth wicket. Lamby was run out for 107 – never risk a run with Ian Botham at the other end – but Derek Randall and I then added another 151. I reached my highest Test score, 208, my first and only Test match double century, including nineteen fours and four sixes, one of which smashed a few tiles on the pavilion roof; but then I tried to reverse-sweep Doshi and was caught. I was furious with myself because I was in such good nick that, if I'd just kept hitting it down the ground, there's no telling how many runs I might have scored that day.

During that innings, I also eliminated India's finest batsman, Sunil Gavaskar. I knew Sunil well – we'd played together at Somerset – and when he stationed himself at silly point, I said to him, only half-joking, 'Are you sure you want to stand there, Sunil?' Doshi had tossed a few up well wide of off-stump, tempting me to have a go. I let a few go, but when he did it again, I smashed it away and it hit poor Sunil full on the shin. Even Brian Close would have been pushed to have carried on as if nothing had happened after that; Sunil was carried off with a broken leg and took no further part in the series. With Randall out just short of his century, we were all out for 594. Kapil Dev was unlucky to miss a century in reply, making 97 as India batted all the way down the order to total 410, and once they had avoided the follow-on it was only ever going to finish as a draw. India were 111 for three, chasing a notional target of 376, when both sides called it a day.

I had been in prime batting form, scoring 403 runs at an average of 134 in the three Tests, and I scored some rapid hundreds for

Somerset too, including a century in fifty-two minutes against Warwickshire, but I did less well in the next three-Test series of the summer against Pakistan. Once more the press were talking up the all-rounder battle, this time between myself and Imran Khan, and though we won the first Test at Edgbaston by 113 runs, Imran certainly had the better of our private duel, with seven wickets for 52 in our first innings and knocks of 22 and 65. I took six wickets in the match, but two visits to the crease yielded only two runs, including a second innings duck. I did better at Lord's with 31 and 69, but though Imran's contribution was minor this time, Pakistan won by ten wickets thanks mainly to a superb double century by opener Mohsin Khan.

We went to the final Test at Headingley with the series in the balance and Imran and I both played blinders in a match that see-sawed one way and another. Imran scored 67 not out and I took four for 70 in Pakistan's first innings of 275, and I then hit 57 as Imran took five for 49 to leave us 19 behind on first innings. Second time around Imran was out one short of his half-century, but I collected five for 74 to reduce Pakistan to 199 all out. Set 219 to win, we almost contrived to throw it away, going from 168 for one to 198 for seven, with Imran claiming another three wickets, before Vic Marks and Bob Taylor got us home to clinch the series.

I'd had a second great summer in succession with bat and ball and, perhaps inevitably, I suffered a downturn in form during the following winter of 1982-83. Unfortunately it came during a disastrous Ashes tour Down Under, though the series began on something of a personal high for me. In the drawn first Test at Perth I scored my three thousandth Test run and then took my two hundred and fiftieth Test wicket when I got Allan Border out, but we lost the next two Tests, by seven wickets in Brisbane and eight wickets in Adelaide. I had to share responsibility for the Adelaide defeat. Bob Willis asked me what he should do if he won the toss and I told him, 'Put them in to bat.' He did just that, but as the temperature climbed above 100°

Fahrenheit we wilted in the heat. I did my best to compensate, taking four for 112 in 36.5 sweltering overs, but the Aussies piled up 438 and then bowled us out for 216. We followed on and could only set them 83 to win, which they knocked off before lunch on the last day.

We pulled one back in the traditional Boxing Day Test at Melbourne. Set 292 to win, Australia were 218 for nine when Jeff Thomson walked out to join Allan Border at the wicket. They survived until the close of the fourth day, but the Australian public's view of their chances was shown the next morning when the massive colosseum of the MCG, which could seat 100,000 people, was empty but for about forty spectators and a dog. However, as Border and Thomson kept surviving and whittling away the victory target, word spread and avalanches of people began to arrive in the hope of witnessing an unlikely Aussie victory. For some reason Bob Willis didn't turn to me until the game was just about up. He bowled everybody else in his attempts to break the partnership but when he finally threw me the ball, Australia only needed four to win. By then there must have been 60,000 people in the ground and the atmosphere was electric. One streaky four would have done it, and when I bowled a wide, full-length delivery, Thommo slashed at it. The ball took the edge and flew to Chris Tavaré in the slips. It was a regulation catch in front of his face but Tav could only palm it away. It ricocheted upwards and Geoff Miller, running round behind him, grabbed the rebound. What had seemed like a non-event of a last day had turned into one of the most exciting finishes to a game that I'd ever seen.

We needed victory in the final Test at Sydney to retain the Ashes but, set 460 to win, we could manage only 314 for seven and had to settle for the draw and a series defeat. The sight of the Aussies' celebrations at regaining the Ashes was one of the worst moments of my sporting life.

I'd not had a disastrous series, but I'd scored only 270 runs and taken eighteen relatively high-cost wickets, and despite finishing as our joint highest wicket-taker with Bob Willis, I was not happy with my bowling. Although I was barely aware of it, my back problem was beginning to have an impact on my flexibility, and that was inevitably affecting my pace and rhythm. Ever the optimist, I kept telling Bob that my bowling would come good and I'd blow the Aussies away, but it never happened, and with Bob also less effective than he had been in England in 1981, we were never able to exert the pressure that might have seen the Aussies crumble once more.

To make matters worse, I had also criticised the Aussie umpires, saying: 'We have had one poor decision after another. I hate to lose and, even less, I hate to moan after being beaten, but it has to be said the umpiring on this tour has not been very good. In fact it was so bad at times that you felt we had to get fourteen of their wickets and they only had to get seven of ours.'

I was only echoing the feelings of tour manager Doug Insole and captain Bob Willis. We had all thought that the umpiring was very poor, but the others were wise enough not to say so in public. My remarks were off the record, but they were reported anyway. I was immediately derided as a 'whingeing Pom', and after the Australian Cricket Board drew the attention of the TCCB to my comments, I was fined £200.

The British tabloids were looking for scapegoats and I fitted the bill nicely. The explanation that I had simply lost form was not the one they wanted to hear. There had to be another reason – sex, drink or drugs would have been ideal, but since they couldn't find any evidence of those, they settled for another form of overindulgence. An unflattering photograph of me chatting to Dennis Lillee by a swimming pool led Fleet Street's finest to declare that I had been playing badly simply because I was too fat. There was plenty of other 'knocking copy' going around as well. Before the tour I had signed an exclusive contract with the *Sun* for a ghosted column, giving the other 'red-tops' carte blanche to take a pop at me. Bizarrely, after this had been going on for a while, the *Sun* felt impelled to join in as well, trying to outdo the more sensational stories of their rivals. Bob

Willis advised me to sever my connections with the paper, but not for the first or last time in my career, I was given sound advice then chose to ignore it. My attitude was that the money was good and that no one cared what the tabloids said … another less than brilliant judgement on my part.

Things were no better back at home in the summer of 1983. We were hosting the World Cup and went into it with high hopes of lifting the trophy. We won our group in style, beating Sri Lanka and Pakistan twice and New Zealand once to canter into the semi-finals, but there we came up against India at Old Trafford. We won the toss and batted first, but never got on top of some tight Indian bowling on a slow pitch and only reached 213 all out in our sixty overs. Yashpal Sharma and Sandeep Patil then made batting look an awful lot easier. Sharma played the anchor role and Patil hit a brilliant 51 not out from thirty-two deliveries to see India home by six wickets with five overs to spare. I had a poor World Cup, and all of the other leading all-rounders performed significantly better than me, not least Kapil Dev, who helped India to an improbable success by beating the red-hot favourites, the West Indies, in the final.

I was also outshone by Richard Hadlee in the first Test of the series against New Zealand. That scarcely mattered as we won by 190 runs, but when I had another indifferent match at Headingley, where we lost the next Test by five wickets, Bob Willis, who had played a blinder himself, faced demands from the cricket press reporters for me to be dropped. When he asked, 'Which two players do you gentlemen suggest we should bring in to replace Ian?' the names of Trevor Jesty of Hampshire and Surrey's David Thomas were bandied about. When Bob pointed out that neither of them was enough of an all-rounder to step into my shoes on their own, a tabloid reporter immediately phoned the pair of them, told them 'Bob Willis says he doesn't rate you', and the paper ran that story instead.

Kath and I were also going through a rocky patch, the worst experience of our turbulent marriage so far. It should have been a very happy time for us, for Kath was pregnant again, but the constant hounding by the press was already affecting her badly and then, when I came home after the Headingley Test, she dropped a bombshell. She had been for a routine check at the hospital that morning and had been told by the gynaecologist that he could not hear the baby's heartbeat any more. He offered a few words of reassurance – 'This isn't by any means unusual, in most cases it's nothing to be alarmed about' – but told her to come back in a couple of days for a scan.

We both tried to be positive and hope for the best rather than fear the worst, but we weren't fooling each other or ourselves. We were both distraught. I felt utterly helpless but also riven with guilt, as I suppose all parents do at such times. Was there anything I could have done to prevent this unfolding tragedy? Had I allowed the pressure of my own situation to affect Kath's well-being?

The scan confirmed our fears. The baby was dead, and Kath was admitted to hospital immediately. It took us both, and Kath in particular, a very long time to get over the loss. When it was over – and the most heartbreaking part of the whole ordeal, as any parent who has had a similar experience would confirm, is that, even though the baby is dead, it still has to be 'born' – we decided that what had happened was private. It was our business and no one else's, but in order to ensure that the press did not get wind of it, we had to carry on as usual. If I missed games, questions would be asked and the whole story might come out, leading to yet more press intrusion and stress for Kath to deal with.

Somerset had a one-day match the next day and I organised a plane to fly me to and from it, so that I could be back with Kath as soon as possible. I have no recollection of the game at all, but our wicketkeeper, Trevor Gard, later told me that he had never seen me bowl as fast in my entire career. The game finished early and I was back with Kath that evening.

Unfortunately all our precautions were in vain. Someone, somewhere, perhaps someone at the hospital, had leaked the story to the media. The BBC led the *Nine O'Clock News* with the story that night and the next morning it was plastered all over the papers. Kath and I were furious at this intrusion into our private grief and it soured my relationship with the media even more. Bob Willis, a good friend to Kath and me, was as furious with the media over this as we were, and showed his displeasure during the next Test, at Lord's. As England captain, he was contractually bound to attend the press conference, but he gave one-word answers to every question from the assembled reporters. I wouldn't talk to them either, and back at Taunton I lost control one evening as I was walking around the outfield. Spotting the press box – mercifully empty at the time – I vented my frustration by throwing a deckchair straight through the closed window and would have demolished it altogether if some mates from the opposition team hadn't grabbed hold of me, calmed me down and steered me away.

Perhaps that gesture helped me to get something out of my system, because my form improved from then on. We beat New Zealand by 127 runs at Lord's. I took four wickets in the New Zealand first innings and scored 61 when we batted again, and I bettered that with 103 in the fourth and final Test at Trent Bridge, where we again came out on top, winning by 165 runs to clinch the series 3-1.

However, my best moment of that season came not in a Test match but in the semi-final of the NatWest Trophy. The Somerset captain, Brian Rose, was injured and I led the side against Middlesex at Lord's. I made a bit of a cock-up of my calculations when plotting who should deliver the final overs, meaning that Joel Garner, then probably the best fast bowler in the world, couldn't bowl the last of his twelve-over allowance – they didn't call me 'Bungalow' at school for nothing – and when we slipped to 52 for five in response to Middlesex's 223, the game appeared lost, but I then set myself to play a captain's innings to win the match. When the last over began I was still there on 96 and the scores were level, though I'd added insult to injury by running out Joel Garner for a duck the previous over. What happened next either baffled or outraged spectators, depending on which county they were from. I prodded and padded my way through the over, making no effort to score the winning run, because I had checked with the umpires and been told that as long as we did not lose another wicket, we would win. I decided to try and block out the final over, bowled by John Emburey, despite the close catchers clustered around the bat, although my heart was in my mouth when I padded up and survived a very loud shout for leg before. It may not have been exactly cricket, but I know that one of my Somerset mentors, Brian Close, would have approved. There were fewer dramas in the final, where we beat Kent by 24 runs and I raised a trophy as captain for the very first time.

England's tour that winter of 1983-84, calling at Fiji, New Zealand and Pakistan, looked like a good one to miss, but I ignored that premonition, made myself available and was picked. I was determined that the tabloids would not be able to get another picture of an overweight Ian Botham on this tour, so I went training with Scunthorpe United and did so well that I even got picked for the first team. The TCCB were rather less thrilled by this turn of events than me and notified me that they were unhappy to see me risking injury by playing football so soon before the tour. I wasn't quite sure why I was being singled out; Allan Lamb and David Gower were on a skiing holiday and Mike Gatting was also playing local football in London – why weren't the board on their case as well? I'd originally planned to pack the football in before Christmas but the TCCB got me so wound up that I carried on playing until the very last minute and told Scunthorpe that I would be available up to and including the Christmas holiday games. I'm glad I did; one of my greatest footballing moments was playing in the sold-out local derby against Hull City in front of a capacity 17,500 crowd. I had a real tussle with the Hull centre forward Billy Whitehurst, who went on to play for

Sunderland, and pretty much played him out of the game. Even though we eventually lost 1-0, I still remember that game with great pride and pleasure. I played the following day against Preston as well and then, still nursing my bruises, flew out with the England party for a warm-up match in Fiji two days later.

I had a good first Test in New Zealand, at Wellington, picking up five wickets for 59 in the Kiwi first innings and then scoring 138 and sharing a stand of 232 with Derek Randall, but we couldn't press home our advantage and had to settle for a draw. We disintegrated in the second Test in Christchurch, collapsing twice to be all out for 82 and 93, and losing by an innings and 138 runs in just twelve hours of actual playing time. I bowled a load of crap, and then in our second innings I was out first ball. I hit the ball smack off the middle of the bat but instead of a boundary to open my account I found myself trudging back to the pavilion after Martin Crowe pulled off a miracle catch. I gave a wry smile as I headed for the changing room, an acknowledgement that some days the force is just not with you, but the gentlemen of the press, never slow to stick the knife in when the going got tough, saw it in an entirely different light and decided I didn't give a toss about getting out for a golden duck.

Both myself and the team did better in Auckland – I scored 70 before being run out – but a drawn game gave New Zealand the series and the British press pack free rein to pull us apart. There were a lot of journalists on the tour who definitely weren't there to cover cricket. Most of the genuine cricket reporters used to cringe when they saw these other journalists flying in – 'the £30 suits' as I used to call them. I think the cricket writers resented them as much and maybe even more than we did. They'd scratch around for a bit of dirt, file the story and then fly out again, leaving their colleagues to carry the can. I was still 'writing' my column for the *Sun* and it was a strange experience to be working for a newspaper that also had a reporter out in New Zealand looking for ways to gun me down. I tried not to take it personally; it wasn't just me. The war between the tabloids was continuing, and anyone successful in any field – sport, music, entertainment – was fair game.

The reptiles had decided that our poor form was the result of our bad attitude and our off-field activities, and ever wilder rumours about what those activities might be were constantly doing the rounds. What happened on the New Zealand leg of the tour was no different from any other England tour; it's a stressful occupation and players need to relax after a day's play. Some do so with a few drinks in the bar, some go clubbing. As the most high-profile England player, the press were gunning for me more than anyone, and I didn't feel safe even going down to the hotel bar for a drink in case I was photographed and accused of being drunk. If I spoke to a barmaid or a waitress, I would hardly have time to leave the room before the reptiles were all over her demanding, 'Did he ask you for sex? Did he ask you for drugs?'

There were endless allegations about drugs and women. One paper claimed that several England players had been stoned on drugs at a concert by The Pretenders; another had a story about myself and Allan Lamb in a hotel bedroom with two women and a couple of bags of cocaine; and yet another claimed that during the Christchurch Test, the players had smoked pot in the dressing room and stuffed damp towels into the crack at the bottom of the door to stop the smell being detected. This was supposed to have taken place when rain had stopped play and the usual crowds of people were knocking on the door, asking for autographs. When Elton John turned up, that only added to the rumours flying around. The press saw his presence as further proof that we were all debauched, drug-crazed hippies, but, like Mick Jagger, Elton was a cricket fan and was there to watch a few games, not pass round the cocaine.

The stories grew progressively wilder and I continued to feature in most of them. One of the journalists covering the tour had brought his wife with him, who sold stories about the players to the other papers back home. Now, it wouldn't be tolerated for a moment. Then we just had to put up with it, one more stress in an already over-stressed tour.

All the allegations, no matter how wild, were fully investigated by the New Zealand police and, without exception, were found to be unsubstantiated, but that made no headlines in Britain and was of little comfort to those wives and families who, like Kath, were suffering the agonies of reading all those reports back home. She and all the other wives wouldn't have been human if they hadn't wondered if there could be quite so much smoke without any fire at all.

As if that wasn't bad enough, Liam then came home from school to tell her that one of his friends had been forbidden to play with him; his parents had told him to 'stay away from Liam Botham; his family are all drug addicts'. Kath was besieged by reporters trying to prise a response out of her about the stories of my alleged drug bouts and infidelities. In the end she took the kids and Jan and Gerry – who were also being besieged by reptiles – to stay with her sister Lindsay and brother-in-law Paul. When the *News of the World* then couldn't reach Kath or her parents for a comment, they tracked down Kath's grandmother and pressured her to say something herself, or to persuade Kath to make a comment.

The character assassination to which I was being subjected is a very British phenomenon. We're all for the gallant loser and the plucky underdog in Britain, but we don't seem to like winners very much. The sportspeople we really love always seem to be 'nearly-men', 'might have beens' and 'never-wases'. Eddie 'The Eagle' Edwards was the ultimate example. Although no doubt a very nice man and a real tryer, he was one of the biggest sporting non-events of all time. Yet he became a hero to millions of British television viewers. And even those who are genuine success stories are apparently loved as much for their failures as their victories. Henry Cooper was a fine boxer and ambassador for his sport, but he's most celebrated for the fight in which, though he did knock Muhammad Ali down, the champion then got up and wiped the floor with him. Frank Bruno finally achieved his ambition of winning one of the versions of the world heavyweight crown, but the public loved him as much – and probably more – for his ability to be a gallant loser. Tim Henman held British tennis together virtually single-handedly for a few years but it is his failure to win Wimbledon that apparently defines him in the public mind. And great driver though he was, Stirling Moss never won the world championship, yet is synonymous with motor racing for many Britons. You still hear people saying 'Who do you think you are – Stirling Moss?' to speeding motorists, whereas Nigel Mansell, who did win the world championship, and John Surtees, who was world champion both on a motorbike and a racing car, had far less popular acclaim.

I'm not denigrating the efforts of any of these men; I am pointing out the adulation they received despite, or possibly even because of, their lack of success at the very highest levels, whereas many of our few true successes in international sport have been pilloried for supposed personal failings. When it came to genuine success stories like Nick Faldo and Steve Davis, all the media apparently wanted to do was attack them. I was a cricketing success story and the same process was now being applied to me with a vengeance.

I injured my knee in the first Test of the Pakistan leg of the tour in Karachi and missed the rest of the tour, but I didn't know quite what to expect when I flew back alone into Heathrow. I knew that the tabloids had been running a few stories about me, but in those pre-Internet days I had not seen any and was quite unaware of how vitriolic they had been until I passed through customs and walked out into the arrivals hall. Suddenly a huge crowd of reporters and TV crews surrounded me, pushing, shoving and shouting. Kath and the kids were there to welcome me home but Liam took a pounding from reporters elbowing him aside to try and get to me and little

Sarah was reduced to tears. I was in such a state of shock that I'd passed right by Kath and the kids before I realised that they were there. I just wanted to get all the reporters out of my face and away from my family, and in answer to a barrage of questions about my alleged drug use, I said 'I've never smoked dope in my life.'

We dived into the car and as we drove away, with reporters still chasing after us and photographers trying to take pictures through the windows of the speeding car, the sheer absurdity of what we had just gone through reduced us to fits of laughter; but my mood soon darkened when Kath began to fill me in on the press stories that had been running and the pressure that had been brought to bear on her, our kids and our families. By the time we reached home, I was so furious that the first thing I did was to phone Alan Herd and get him to come up for a meeting the very next day. Yet like a complete idiot, I then proceeded to shut Kath out of our discussions completely. She told me later that whenever she entered the room, the conversation would die away and not start again until she left. I thought I was doing the right thing by trying to protect her but it would have done her – and me – far more good to have heard what was being said and been able to contribute. It heralded the start of the most difficult period of our marriage ... and there had been a few already. From then on, whenever the latest sensational allegation appeared, I shut her out of my life. Kath was not the only one I blanked – I became so paranoid that I treated almost everybody as if they were a potential traitor – but she suffered the most.

The worst and most inaccurate story of all about me had appeared in the *Mail on Sunday*. I was determined to sue for libel, whatever the cost, and I insisted that Alan Herd should fly out to Pakistan at once to get affidavits from the other England players. While he was out there, I gave a radio interview to the BBC's Pat Murphy. It actually took place in the recovery room at the hospital where I was coming round from the anaesthetic after the surgery on my knee. The interview lasted about half an hour and covered a whole range of subjects, including the pressures of touring; but I also made a feeble attempt at a joke. 'Pakistan,' I said, 'is the kind of place to send your mother-in-law for a month, all expenses paid.'

It was only a flippant remark, aimed as much at my mother-in-law, Jan, as at Pakistan, it wasn't even particularly funny, and it backfired big time. The staff at the Hilton in Lahore, where the England tour party was staying at the time, threatened to go on strike, and the legal clerks at the firm of Pakistani solicitors that Alan had employed refused to type up any more of the affidavits for my libel case. Alan, furious, sent a telex to his London office, which read simply: 'Tell our client to keep his bloody mouth shut'. Meanwhile the TCCB had convened a disciplinary hearing and levied a fine of £1,000 on me.

It was a relief to have something else to think about: another rebel tour to South Africa was being proposed and this time an offer was made to both myself and Viv Richards. Two South African businessmen had asked to see me about taking a multiracial side out to the Republic, and when I asked Viv what he thought, he just said, 'It's a short career, man. See what they have to say.'

After a twenty-minute presentation outlining all the lavish financial benefits that could be ours – and it was a hell of a lot of money – I said, 'What happens if Viv and I want to have a drink, or sit on the beach or play a round of golf together?'

One of them said, 'Oh, that's easy. We'll make him an honorary white man.'

I just laughed in their faces. 'When I go to Antigua to visit Viv, they don't have to make me an honorary black man. We're both members of the same race – the human race. Now piss off.' They were lucky that Viv was not present because he might have wanted to do more than just throw them out. The apartheid system they represented was the opposite of everything that my parents had brought me up to believe. If Viv and I had been born and raised in South Africa we could not have breathed the same air without risking arrest, let alone played cricket or shared a house, and the greatest friendship of my life would never have happened.

As I recuperated from the knee operation and worked on my fitness for the upcoming tour by the West Indies, I was told that I had been granted my wish of captaining Somerset in my benefit year. But just as the season was about to begin I lost a good friend in Peter 'Jock' McCombe, the liaison officer at the club, who died suddenly from a heart attack. He was not just a friend, but the man who sorted out the details of many of my events and engagements for my benefit season and, even more important, reminded me of where and when I was to appear. Without him, my diary was in chaos. I missed a couple of functions and had to issue profuse apologies for my non-appearance at an event that I had actually known nothing about. The press inevitably got to hear about this, and after I arrived a shade late at a benefit match after being delayed by road works, the *Sunday People* carried a story that I had refused to sign any autographs and deliberately got myself out so I could leave early. Neither was true, but the cumulative effect of all this bad publicity was overwhelming and it led to the cancellation of a few events.

Others did go ahead on schedule. At the close of play in one game at Taunton we were all in the bar having a drink when I glanced at my watch and told the players, 'I've got to go out on the pitch for a minute, lads. The Red Arrows are going to do a fly-past and give me a salute.' There was a stunned silence, a few disbelieving chuckles and one or two comments like, 'Whatever he's drinking, I'll have a pint too.'

Meanwhile, I wandered out to the middle of the square and stood looking expectantly up at the sky. Despite themselves, my teammates were soon lining the balcony. The barracking from them had just started again when, right on schedule, the Red Arrows roared in over the treetops and screamed across the ground, causing a few spilled pints in the bar as they passed fifty feet above my head. It caused them a bit of strife with the Ministry of Defence who were not best pleased at their impromptu detour from their authorised flight plan, but I appreciated it enormously.

The fly-past had come about after the leader of the Red Arrows, John Blackwell, invited me to go up with them. I'd learned to fly three years earlier at the Bristol and Wessex Club, but flying with the Red Arrows was something else. I was both excited and terrified when I arrived at RAF Kemble, the team's base, where they held a practice session to see if I would be able to cope with a full-on, top-speed flight. I was wearing a G-suit to protect me against the effects of the G-forces, but by the time we landed I was getting tunnel vision and feeling pretty queasy. When I said to them, 'Are you sure this suit's working right?' they gave me a few sideways looks, probably thinking I was just making excuses to cover the fact that I'd wimped out, but when they tested it they found that it was malfunctioning. Clad in a new suit, I went up again and enjoyed one of the most thrilling white-knuckle rides of my life.

It was the highlight of my benefit year, but inevitably there were more lowlights to come too. The most alarming came after hosting a day's shooting. I was relaxing in the pub where a dinner was to be held as the climax to the day, but halfway through a pint of the local brew, I started to feel queasy. As everything became a blur, I grabbed hold of my new PA, Andy Withers, and said, 'For Christ's sake, Andy, you've got to get me out of here now.' When we got out to the car park, I collapsed.

It was another non-appearance by Botham at a benefit event for the press to get their teeth into, but when we managed to piece together what had happened, we realised that someone had spiked my drink. Andy didn't want to call a doctor in view of the 'Botham out of it on drugs' headlines that would inevitably ensue, so he put me to bed and stayed up all night to make sure I was all right – above and beyond the call of duty, but mightily appreciated by me. Fortunately I had recovered by the next morning with no long-term ill effects, but it would be a very long time before I took a drink in public again.

During that summer's series against the West Indies, I passed four thousand Test runs and three hundred Test wickets, and didn't play badly myself, but we suffered a humiliating 'blackwash'. The pattern was set in the first Test at Edgbaston where I top-scored with 64 as we were bowled out for 191 and we then watched the Windies pile up 606 and beat us by an innings and 180 runs. At Lord's we managed to take a first innings lead of 41 runs as I achieved my best-ever bowling return against them – eight for 103 – and piled up a decent second innings total as Allan Lamb scored a century and I hit my highest-ever score against them. Frustratingly, with my first-ever century against them there for the taking, I was given out lbw to Joel Garner for 81. I didn't agree – it would have missed the stumps – but we've all had good and bad decisions against us and you have to accept them. Then the decision to declare at 300 for nine on the last morning, setting the West Indies 342 to win, proved to be over-generous. Although David Gower was the captain, he wasn't in any hurry to declare and it was the chairman of selectors, Peter May, who pushed very hard for it and eventually persuaded David to do so. It's easy to be wise with hindsight, but I felt and said at the time that after taking a beating in the first Test and with the wicket still playing well, we would have done better to bat out the innings and try to ensure that we couldn't lose, rather than chase an improbable victory that also gave the Windies a chance to win. In the event Gordon Greenidge simply took us apart, scoring a majestic 214 not out as they cantered to a victory by nine wickets, scoring the runs in just sixty-six overs. Inevitably, when it all went pear-shaped Peter May was already on his way back down the motorway, which left David to explain to a hostile press conference why he'd declared too early.

We improved slightly at Headingley – we only lost by eight wickets there – but there was another double century for Greenidge and another innings defeat for us at Old Trafford, despite a third century in successive Tests by Allan Lamb. Although I picked up another five-wicket haul and another half-century at The Oval in the final Test, we ended the summer as we had begun it, with an emphatic defeat, going down by 172 runs.

My growing disenchantment with the tabloid press rather than the on-field experiences against the Windies was one of the prime reasons for my decision not to make myself available for the winter tour to India. I also felt I owed Kath, and the kids, a bit of quality time. It would be the first winter we had ever spent at home together, and I was confident that, in my absence from the tour party, the tabloids would have no reason to bother us at all.

The first sign that I might have been over-optimistic came just before Christmas when I heard a rumour that some of the Humberside police were after me, apparently wanting to 'get even' for my acquittal on the assault charges after the Joe Neenan incident at Scunthorpe. If I was not already paranoid, I soon had even more reasons for it. As Christmas approached, I was sure that I was being followed whenever I went out in my car or on foot. I told Gerry, but left Kath in the dark about it because I knew it would upset her. I was sufficiently worried that I decided not to touch a drink if I was going to drive and it became one of the most sober festive seasons I've ever spent.

Christmas came and went and I was just beginning to relax a little and convince myself it was all in my imagination when, at six o'clock on New Year's Eve, as we were laying the table for a family party, the doorbell rang. Four policemen were on the doorstep. They came straight to the point: a substance had been found in the pocket of a pair of my trousers that had been taken to the dry-cleaners. I was lost for words, and Kath just said 'You must be joking.' They weren't, and they had a warrant to search the house. 'Help yourselves,' I said. 'I've got nothing to hide. Search away.'

I went round with them, sufficiently paranoid to think that if I wasn't watching them, they might 'plant' some drugs on me. As it turned out, they didn't need to. As they were searching the chest of drawers in our bedroom, one of them held up a small package and said, 'Excuse me, Mr Botham. Do you happen to know what this is?'

I certainly did – it was dope, and I could remember exactly how it came to be there. Years before, after a Test match at The Oval, some fan came up to me and gave me a small amount of dope. 'Have this for later,' he said, and disappeared back into the crowd. I found it in my pocket when I got home, shoved it in the drawer and then forgot all about it until now.

There was no point in lying, so I told them the whole story, but I knew they weren't going to let it pass. I would have to go down to the police station, make a statement and be formally charged with possession, and even worse, Kath would have to make a statement as well. The look she gave me as I got my coat and followed the police out to their car was not reassuring. I had smoked dope in my younger days. I was about eighteen when I first smoked it at a party, just to see what the fuss was about. It helped me relax and didn't harm anyone else. I'd seen businessmen, barristers, journalists and even senior police officers openly smoking joints at parties I had been to, and once I even shared a joint with a vicar in the vestry of his country church, but I never smoked at home. Kath never approved – to her, cannabis was illegal, full stop – so I never put her in an awkward position, nor risked her wrath, by smoking dope when she was around.

Yet she was now in the police station alongside me, being treated like the accomplice to a crime. We were released on bail, and while no charges were brought against Kath, she had to take the public opprobrium and the press intrusions – the tabloids fell on the story like starving men – after I was charged with possession of 2.19 grams of cannabis. Just like someone whose house has been burgled, Kath felt that her home had been violated by the police raid. She never felt comfortable there again and we moved not long afterwards. Kath was also convinced that her and the kids' reputations had been as badly damaged as mine, and when Sarah provided the proof, by coming home from school in tears after being taunted about her 'drug-addict dad', Kath lost control. Her anger with me for putting her and the kids in this situation erupted and she marched into the sitting room where I was lying down on the sofa, picked up the glass-topped table in both hands and hurled it at me. It missed, but I got the message.

On Valentine's Day 1985, Scunthorpe Magistrates Court duly fined me £100 for possession, but if I thought the case was now behind me, I was mistaken. The official conviction on drugs charges was now on my police record and to this day it causes me endless hassles and hold-ups at customs and immigration all over the world; I ceased even trying to go to the US for many years. The case also had some serious financial consequences for me. Saab cancelled a deal with me as a result of it, and a stationery firm also pulled out of negotiations and signed up the more wholesome figure of David Gower instead – and he didn't even give me a commission! – but some commercial partners like Nike and Duncan Fearnley, the manufacturer of my bats and pads, stayed loyal. Inevitably the TCCB was moved to take action as well; I was the first professional crick-eter ever to be convicted of drug offences and they were determined to make an example of me. Some of the more hard-core members were even demanding that I be thrown out of the game altogether, but eventually it was decided that, since I'd already been punished by the courts, it would be inappropriate and possibly illegal for the TCCB to fine or suspend me as well, and I was cleared to play.

Having opted out of the winter tour to India, I wasn't taking my Test place for granted, but with the Aussies arriving for an Ashes series I was dying for the chance to re-establish the dominance that we'd had at the end of the last home series, four years before. However, I soon heard rumours that my Test place might be in jeopardy. David Gower had led England to a shock series victory in

India, fighting back after losing the first Test by eight wickets, and there were suggestions – and it was impossible to verify how genuine they were – that some administrators and some players felt that both results and morale had been better as a result of my absence from the tour.

Fresh from their drugs orgy over my cannabis arrest, and fuelled by these new rumours, the tabloids were busy splashing headlines like BOTHAM AT THE CROSSROADS, but all of it only made me more determined to prove the doubters wrong. To suggest that I was a negative influence on the England team was farcical. I had practically carried the team on my back at times, but I hated the innuendo and endless sniping from the press and it had had an undoubted effect. I was no longer the relaxed character I used to be. I was discontented with my lot and looking for something, whether it was a new direction or merely a distraction, so I was ripe for the plucking when a larger-than-life character with a good line in flattery and plausible-sounding patter appeared on my doorstep.

Tim Hudson was an ex-public schoolboy who had played cricket for Surrey 2nd XI – not very successfully: he only appeared once and scored 1 and 0 – but then settled in California and made his fortune as a disc jockey and property developer. He was also the voice of characters in the Disney cartoons *The Jungle Book* and *The Aristocats*, and the self-proclaimed inventor of flower power and friend and confidant of rock stars … or so he said. It was often hard to decide what was real and what was PR in his utterances, but he was certainly rich and could turn on the charm like a tap. He also had a certain hippie-meets-Great-Gatsby sort of style with his trademark panama hat, rainbow-striped blazer and ponytail.

I had first come across him in the States at the end of the 1981 season, but by the time we bumped into each other again in 1984 he had established himself back in England with a stately home, Birtles Hall, in the Cheshire countryside, which had its own cricket pitch named 'the Birtles Bowl'. As part of our benefit seasons he set up a match between an Ian Botham XI and a Geoff Boycott XI. I didn't hear from him again until the following spring, by which time I'd gone through the drugs case and was feeling more than a little uncertain about my future. He called me from the States to say he had plans he wanted to discuss and invited Kath and me to meet him at Birtles as soon as he got back.

As we were driving to Birtles to meet him, Kath had told me some fabulous news, and when we got there, I said to Tim, 'Have you any champagne? We've got something to celebrate. Kath's pregnant.'

It was fantastic news for us, a chance to put all the traumas of the stillbirth behind us, but Tim and his wife Maxi looked like they'd just had news of a death in the family. I was far too happy to give it more than a moment's thought at the time and was soon lapping up buckets of Hudson's trademark flannel about what a great English hero I was and how he was the man to turn my fame into a genuine fortune. He had big plans, and a vision of me as an Englishman archetype with heroic overtones. Winston Churchill, Cary Grant and Horatio Nelson were mentioned; even I thought that was overdoing it.

Hudson's plans also embraced the way that cricket was played and promoted. The entire domestic cricket scene needed to be blown away. 'Let's have matches between teams captained by Eric Clapton and Elton John,' he said. 'We could put them on telly and the crowds would come flocking in. I'd love to see cricket totally orchestrated: Pink Floyd playing and the game going on. Start the day with a brass band, have Pink Floyd playing throughout the match and then a calypso band from close of play until the early hours.'

I'm embarrassed even to write this today, let alone admit that I was sucked in by it all. My only excuse is that I was at a very low ebb in my personal and professional life, besieged on all sides by hostile media and ready to clutch at any straw that was offered. The opulence of the surroundings also made his spiel easier to believe. He had obviously made a success of his life; something had worked for him, maybe it would work for me too.

Reg Hayter had always been my agent until then. A former cricket correspondent for Reuters, Reg had built on his friendships with the leading players of the late 1940s and 1950s by setting up a sports agency. He acted for cricketers like Denis Compton, Godfrey Evans and Fred Trueman, and later for sports stars like Basil d'Oliveira, Tony Greig, Henry Cooper and Malcolm Macdonald. However, he was now seventy years old and inevitably slowing down a bit, and though he showed no intention of retiring and was a friend as well as an agent to me, I did feel that I was missing out on financial opportunities.

Naively perhaps, I thought that Reg and Tim would be able to work together. Reg could continue to take care of the press leaving Hudson free to negotiate the commercial deals that would make my fortune. However, Tim was very definitely not Reg's type; Reg told me he couldn't work with a man like that, did not trust him and tried to warn me off him. It was wise counsel, but my track record in heeding good advice did not inspire confidence and, true to form, I rejected Reg's warnings in favour of my own – and Hudson's – pipe dreams. As a result I fell out with Reg and we parted company. My solicitor Alan Herd also saw through Emperor Hudson's new clothes, and Kath was never sucked in like I was, but they were in a minority. Most people, including me, swallowed the Hudson hype hook, line and sinker. Colin Cowdrey fell for it too. Even the canny Brian Close succumbed, and worked for Hudson as his cricket manager at Birtles.

Step One in Hudson's grand scheme was to use me to market a range of 'unique and classic' casual clothing. The theme was 'country-house cricket' and the predominant colours were the Rastafarian red, yellow, black and green. The fact that I am colour-blind may have had something to do with it, but I actually thought the clothes were great. I liked a lot of the other trappings too: the Rolls-Royce, the wild parties at Birtles, and most of all the endless flattery. I was a world superstar, not just a great cricket star but a sex symbol who would take Hollywood by storm.

Kath and I disagreed about Hudson, but one area on which we were in complete agreement was our home. We'd moved from Epworth soon after the police raid, and since Kath had always loved north Yorkshire and had spent many happy childhood holidays in the area around Thirsk and Northallerton, we started looking around there and eventually found an old coach house at Asenby. We converted it and lived there happily enough for a couple of years but, though it was a nice house, it was not the dream home we were looking for. Then one day I picked up a copy of *Country Life* magazine and saw an advertisement for a country estate in north Yorkshire. I said to Kath, 'Look at this, it's got the lot – a house, acreage, a lake, woodland, the works.' We rang up and fixed an appointment to view straight away.

The estate was in a pretty dilapidated condition. The house was a fine Georgian building, shaded by ancient trees and looking out over the village green, but it needed the works: rewiring, damp-proofing, woodworm treating and a total decoration job. One of the bathrooms was pink and lime-green, and even a man as colour-blind as me could see that the colour scheme in the rest of the place was similarly outlandish. The outbuildings were derelict, the walled garden was a weed-strewn wasteland, the fish were dying because the lake beyond the house needed draining, dredging out and starting again, and the woodland hadn't been touched in decades, but both Kath and I could see the potential in the place and we made up our minds at once to buy it.

When we'd finished looking around, the owner, a real old-fashioned gentleman, said, 'I can tell you now, I don't need to barter, so I won't be haggling over the price.' He looked somewhat taken aback when I said, 'Fair enough then. Done, you've got a deal,' and shook his hand.

I had reason to be grateful that he was a gentleman a couple of weeks later when I discovered that a flash 'loadsamoney' type from down south had made contact with the owner and tried to gazump my offer. Although he offered substantially more than we'd agreed, the gentleman said, 'No, I've shaken hands on it and that's that.' The gazumper then contacted me and offered me an instant profit of £70,000 if I'd sell the house to him, but I told him 'No', and when he persisted, I put the phone down on him.

It was the best money that Kath and I ever spent. We've renovated and extended the house and developed the estate a huge amount over the years and it's an ongoing project, a life's work. A lot of money and a lot of TLC has gone into it, but we've lived there for the past twenty years and loved every minute of it.

The house is comfortable and full of character, and the kitchen is the focal point, although it's often bedlam with phones ringing constantly and myself, Kath, Liam, Sarah and a rolling assortment of other people chatting, working on laptops and taking and making calls. Outside we've a courtyard shaded by a pergola where we can sit round the table in summer for a drink or an *al fresco* meal, there are beautiful grounds, a lake full of fish and waterfowl, and we're surrounded by woods and open country where we can walk our assortment of dogs – a bulldog, a fox terrier and an Irish wolfhound – and Ravensworth is a beautiful little village. We have some great friends there, and there are four or five pubs within easy reach that serve food as good as you'll get in most London restaurants.

The move, the time with Kath and the kids, and a winter off from cricket had done me a power of good. I scored a couple of quick hundreds for Somerset at the start of the 1985 Ashes season and was in prime form when, despite the rumours that I was to be omitted, I was picked for the one-day international series against Australia. I made 72 in the first game at Old Trafford, but after we lost by three wickets there were criticisms of the way I had got out. I tried to play the reverse sweep off Greg Matthews, missed and was bowled. The reverse sweep was unorthodox, but it wasn't my innovation. I remember seeing Mushtaq Mohammed using it years before and there were even hints that it might have been in use as far back as

1896, when *Wisden* noted that the Yorkshire opener John Brown was out for 107, 'in foolishly hitting back-handed at a lob'. I scored a lot of runs with it and it had become a favourite shot of mine, though as Peter May, now chairman of the England selectors, helpfully pointed out to the press, 'not one that you will find in the MCC coaching manual'.

The snipings from press and committee room did not affect my performances. Although we lost the one-day series 2-1, I was picked for the first Test at Headingley, took seven wickets in the match and, going in at 264 for four in our first innings, smashed 60 from fifty-one balls. We won that Test by five wickets, but Australia squared the series at Lord's. I took five for 109 and top-scored with 85 in our second innings, but Allan Border's brilliant 196 gave the Aussies the edge.

I was in good form, and the carping from the press and the committee room had almost fallen silent … until the third Test at Trent Bridge, when it all kicked off again. We'd posted 456 in our first innings with David Gower hitting a superb 166, but the Aussies then hit back with Graeme Wood leading the way with a big century. They were helped by injuries to our pace bowlers Arnie Sidebottom and Paul Allott, so by the Saturday afternoon I was the only fast bowler available.

The Aussies were on 300 for five, with Graeme Wood still there and Greg 'Fatcat' Ritchie beginning to build a partnership with him, when David Gower took the new ball and told me to let rip with it. I took him at his word and gave it the works; I can't remember bowling faster. The crowd responded, and the atmosphere was electric.

Graeme Wood faced my first ball and edged it to slip where Mike Gatting spilled the chance. Then I had Ritchie absolutely plumb lbw, only for umpire Alan Whitehead to shake his head and say, 'Not out.' He and I had never exactly seen eye to eye – he was always a stickler for the letter of the law and to hell with the spirit behind it – but a more prudent individual than I might have tried to keep on the right side of a man who could uphold or turn down appeals when I was bowling or batting. On this occasion, as on many others, we disagreed. I was absolutely convinced that Ritchie was out, but Whitehead indicated to me that the batsman had got an inside edge on the ball. I was far from thrilled, but next ball I dug it in short and Ritchie, trying to force it, got a top edge that flew to third man. Phil Edmonds made a lot of ground to pouch a great diving catch.

Honour was satisfied, but as I started to run towards Phil to cele-brate, I noticed out of the corner of my eye that Whitehead's arm was outstretched, signalling a no-ball. In the roar from the crowd neither I nor anyone else had heard the call. After the big problems I had with my run-up on the tour to Pakistan in 1977–78 I had resolved to eradicate no-balls altogether and had succeeded. I set my mark so that my delivery stride fell a few inches farther back than before, so I was never in danger of over-stepping; I just didn't bowl front-foot no-balls after that. In my entire career I was no-balled for over-stepping only a handful of times – all but two of them in Pakistan on that tour – but I was now called twice for it by Alan Whitehead. When I asked him to tell me how far over the line my front foot had gone – standard practice – he refused point-blank.

The batsmen had crossed while the ball was in the air and Ritchie was now at the non-striker's end, so I asked him, 'Did you get a touch on that one that trapped you in front?' He said, 'No mate,' and as I walked back to my mark I let fly with a mouthful. It wasn't aimed in Whitehead's direction, but you didn't have to be a genius to work out the reason for my outburst.

It didn't help when Graeme Wood then edged my next ball over the slips for four, so I let go with a bouncer, partly to let off some steam and partly because I felt it was the right ball to bowl, and I put everything into it. Whitehead then decided to issue a warning to me for bowling too many short-pitched deliveries. It was ridiculous. These weren't tailenders. Wood had already passed his century and

Ritchie was on the way to his. Straight afterwards Whitehead issued another official warning to me because he said I was deliberately running down the pitch in line with the stumps. By now I'd had more than enough of Whitehead for one day and I let rip with another furious mouthful as I walked away. Again I wasn't swearing at him, but I was certainly swearing about him, and any lip-readers watching the television coverage would have had no difficulty in getting the message.

At this point I asked my captain, David Gower, to intervene with Whitehead since I did not trust myself to speak to him without totally losing my rag. David soothed a few ruffled feathers on both sides and persuaded me to carry on bowling. I eventually did persuade an umpire to give Wood out, but he'd scored 172 by then and Ritchie went on to make 146 as Australia took a first innings lead. With the pitch still playing beautifully, the game petered out as a draw, but the repercussions of my exchange of views with umpire Whitehead took longer to fade away. TV news bulletins played and replayed the footage of my altercations with the umpire and my reactions as I walked away from him, and commentators, pundits and even MPs queued up to condemn me. John Carlisle, MP, opined that my 'disgraceful behaviour' had brought 'shame on the good name of sportsmen and cricket. It sets a terrible example … and could be a contributory factor to crowd misbehaviour.'

Once more the TCCB felt moved to take action against me, though in typical fashion, they did not get around to a disciplinary hearing for over six weeks, just before the sixth and final Test at The Oval. Perhaps they wanted to make sure we'd won the Ashes first.

Despite the row and the bad publicity, I was still revelling in a close battle with the old enemy. I took four for 79 as we bowled out the Aussies for 257 at Old Trafford and then took a first innings lead of 225 after a big century from Mike Gatting and good support from Graham Gooch and Allan Lamb, but an undefeated hundred from Allan Border steered Australia to the safety of a draw.

David Gower won the toss at Edgbaston and put Australia in to bat, and there were plenty of press critics of that decision as Australia reached 335 all out. However, David then put the Aussie innings into perspective by scoring a brilliant double century, and with Robinson and Gatting also making a hundred, we declared at 595 for five. I came in at 572 for four with a declaration imminent, so I decided to enjoy myself while I could. My very first ball, from Craig McDermott, went straight back over his head for six. I smashed the next one for four, blocked the third and then hit another straight six off the fourth. Commentators have often talked about my ability to empty the bars at cricket grounds, but this was the only time I was actually aware of it at the time; I could see spectators hurrying out of the bars and back into the stands. Unfortunately, they'd only just settled in their seats when I was out for eighteen, Jeff Thomson pouching another steepler off McDermott, but I hope they felt it was worth the effort.

We had plenty of runs in hand but the Aussies looked like they might hold out until a stroke of luck turned it our way. Wayne Phillips, who top-scored with 59, was leading the rearguard action when he cracked one away on the offside which had four written all over it. However, it struck the toecap of Allan Lamb's boot as he took evasive action at silly point, and ballooned up to give David Gower a catch that he took with his customary nonchalant ease. Richard Ellison completed a ten-wicket match as Australia crumbled to 142 all out, giving us victory by an innings and 118 runs and a 2-1 lead in the series.

All we had to do was avoid defeat in the final Test at The Oval and the Ashes were ours. Before that, however, I had a TCCB hearing to attend about my anti-Whitehead outburst at Trent Bridge. Greg Ritchie had volunteered to speak in my defence only for the Australian management to veto it, and I wasn't sure what line the TCCB would take, particularly after the drugs case earlier in the year. No one could have accused them of rushing into a decision – they deliberated for four hours – and in the end they decided that I had been 'guilty of dissent, likely to bring the game into disrepute', though they restricted themselves to imposing a fine and a warning about my future conduct, rather than a suspension. I was able to join the England team at The Oval where any Australian hopes of squaring the series and retaining the Ashes were blown away on the first day. Robinson went for just 3, but Gooch and Gower then added 351 for the second wicket, with Gooch hitting a brutal 196 and Gower – already with the highest-ever score in a home series against Australia – again setting a captain's lead with a brilliant 157, his third big hundred of the series. From 371 for one, 464 all out was something of an anticlimax, but it was still too much for Australia who were all out for 241 and had to follow on. I got rid of Wood and Wessels early on in the second innings, and with Richard Ellison producing another five-wicket performance, Australia collapsed to 129 all out, losing the match by an innings and with it the Ashes 3-1.

I also managed to put one over on the Aussies in another sport. I sometimes wonder what might have happened if someone had come along and put a seven iron in my hand when I was a youngster, because I think it's possible that I might have spent my time on the golf courses rather than the cricket pitches of the world. I can certainly hit the ball a long way off the tee, as I demonstrated during a game partnering Allan Border against Greg Ritchie and Craig McDermott at The Belfry in 1985. We were all square as we reached the tenth, a difficult hole, with a dog-leg to the right over water, and trees surrounding the green. It is 301 yards from tee to pin and the only golfers who had ever managed to reach the green with a drive at that time were Greg Norman and Seve Ballesteros. When I told Allan that I had decided that I was going to be the third one, he chewed me out. 'Forget that shit and concentrate on winning a hole for a change,' he said, not without some justice, since I was playing like a plonker and if it hadn't been for Allan we'd have been about five down by now.

'It's all right,' I said. 'You go first and just lay up, so we're covered if I blow it, but I am going to go for it.' He gave me a filthy look – and even when Allan is smiling he tends to look like he's scowling – but then went ahead and hit a nicely judged iron smack down the middle of the fairway. When my turn came I wound myself up and then smashed a booming drive that, by luck rather than management, faded at just the right moment to end up on the green. 'Told you,' I said to Allan, strolling nonchalantly off down the fairway. I then rather spoiled the effect by three-putting from thirty feet, while Allan chipped on to the green and holed his putt for a birdie. He may have won the hole but the commemorative plaque that still stands at the side of the tee carries the name of Botham, not Border.

Chapter 7

ONE FOOT IN FRONT OF THE OTHER

I'd done well for England that summer, but I'd taken my eye off the ball as far as Somerset was concerned. Under my captaincy, we were having a miserable season. Viv and I were scoring plenty of runs. I had my best ever season for Somerset with the bat, scoring 1,200 championship runs including five centuries, and averaging over 100 for the season for the only time in my career. The spectators would have enjoyed it too, for I struck eighty sixes in all competitions that season. But I knew that I was not making a captain's contribution in all areas of the game, on and off the field. Test calls and injuries meant that I was available for fewer than half of Somerset's county games, and when I wasn't away on England duty, I was spending far too much time listening to Tim Hudson's grandiose plans rather than taking care of business for Somerset. Even without that, the demands of my England career made it ridiculous for me to be trying to captain my county as well, and in September I agreed to relinquish the role, with Peter Roebuck taking over the reins.

If that was another low point for me, that autumn also brought one of the most fulfilling events of my life. In 1977, when I saw those tragic children whose lives were being destroyed by leukaemia at Musgrove Park Hospital in Taunton, I had just handed over £50 for a party. But as time went by, I started to think about how I could use my public profile to raise money for leukaemia research. I'd been making regular hospital visits to children suffering from the disease, but I felt there was so much more I could be doing. Above all, I wanted to do something dramatic that would bring in not just a few quid but a really substantial sum to help attack the causes of the disease. One Easter, on a walking holiday in the Lake District, Kath and I were agonising over the next move, when it hit me. 'I know,' I said. 'Walking. That's what I'll do.'

She gave me the tolerant smile she reserved for my more crackpot schemes. 'What do you mean?'

'I'll do a sponsored walk.'

'Good idea,' Kath said, probably thinking of a gentle afternoon stroll.

'Yes, that'll do it – a sponsored walk from John O'Groats to Land's End.'

Whatever the obstacles, I would not be deterred; I only had to think of those dying children at Musgrove Park Hospital. Planning the walk in itself was a case of the blind leading the blind. I didn't have the least idea of how to go about it, nor how many bureaucratic hurdles there were to clear, but I was determined to make it happen. I was greatly helped by Steve Andressier, who was just leaving Saab to set up on his own in marketing and promotions. I became his first client and he did a fantastic job for me as we planned the itinerary, negotiated our way through the minefield of regulations and restrictions and gradually won over to our cause the local councils, Department of Transport officials, police forces and the myriad other organisations that had to be consulted.

Of course there were cynics sniping from the sidelines and claiming that I was only doing it to restore my public image after the bad publicity of the drugs conviction, but I just ignored them and focused on the task in hand.

After all the administrative nightmares, I was expecting the walk itself to be a doddle, and even when I drove up to John O'Groats with Kath on Friday 25 October 1985, ready to start the walk the following day, I was still in a state of blissful ignorance about what such a long-distance walk would actually entail. I'd done no formal training, nor sought any advice from experienced road-walkers. Why would I bother? It was perfectly straightforward: just place one foot and then the other in front of you and keep doing so until Land's End comes into view – what could possibly be difficult about that? However, the last hours of the drive up there were a bit of a reality check, with sleet and horizontal rain lashing the car, and the realisation that there was an awful lot of very empty road up there and I'd soon be walking it.

I fortified myself with a few drinks that night and the first thing I did early the next morning was to saunter down to the harbour and dip a toe in the sea. My foot instantly turned blue with cold. I put my sock and boot back on, turned through 360 degrees and started walking south. I didn't lack for company as I was surrounded by a mob of people. Two men – John Border, the brother of Aussie Test cricketer Allan, and Phil Rance, a Manchester businessman whose father had died of leukaemia – were going to do the walk with me, and we had a back-up crew in a van blazoned with signs announcing the purpose of the walk. The back of the van also served as the works canteen – for the back-up crew; the walkers never even stopped for lunch – and as a temporary bank for the money we collected in plastic buckets along the way. To minimise the risk of traffic accidents we were escorted by police outriders and in and around them were a motley assortment of television crews, radio and press reporters, photographers, and a few Highlanders and their children come to see what all the fuss was about.

Most of the hordes had got what they wanted before we had gone more than a couple of miles, and after that, on that day and every subsequent day, we were down to the hard core: the walkers, the back-up crew and the police escort. I had no idea about technicalities like pacing myself, but I quickly learned not to run down hills but to walk down them, sometimes backwards, to ease the stress on the knees. It was also crucial that once I had established my pace I didn't deviate from it. The hardest part for me was breaking through the pain barrier. It took me a while to understand that no matter how much I was struggling and hurting, if I kept going long enough the pain would eventually disappear.

The first day was a bit of a breeze; it was all a novelty, there were no residual aches and strains and pains from the day before to deal with, and we marched along enjoying the scenery. Day two was the reality check; I nearly did myself so much damage that the walk might have finished there and then. I decided to run most of the thirty-six-mile stage and finished the day in agony, feeling like I'd been kicked in the shins all the way from John O'Groats. I discovered that 'shin splints' are a common problem for serious walkers. As rest was not an option, the best remedies were massage and elevation – sleeping with my feet propped up on pillows – but shin splints were a constant problem for the rest of the walk. I just had to put up with the pain, but I learned the lesson and stuck to a sensible, if brisk, walking pace from then on.

The climate of the north of Scotland is not the most gentle and welcoming at the best of times and the emptiness of the roads and the lack of human habitation was a psychological problem – sometimes the empty roads seemed to stretch away for ever – but while the TV crews and the press were showing some interest, we had to cash in; there was no knowing how quickly their editors would decide that the story, if not the walk, had run its course.

I was lucky that BBC TV, and in particular the *Breakfast Time* programme, decided to adopt the walk. They'd originally just planned to cover the start of the walk and do an occasional feature along the way, but they got such a positive reaction from their viewers that they decided to include a regular daily slot in the programme from then on.

That alone must have given a massive boost to our fund-raising, but even better, the tabloid war that had caused me such problems in the past now began to play to my advantage. The *Sun* and the *Daily Mirror*, the two biggest-selling tabloids, were rivals in everything they did, and when Chris 'Crash' Lander did a preview piece with Jimmy Savile for the *Daily Mirror* and followed it up by covering the start of the walk in John O'Groats, Alisdair Ross was also there to write a splash for the *Sun*. Alisdair then announced that he would walk the first few stages with me, and I struck a one-thousand-pound bet with him that he'd have to drop out before the end of the fourth day. Crash had not had the slightest intention of walking a step of the way himself; his idea was a few beers for old times' sake before the off, a quick colour piece to keep his editor happy, and then straight in the car for the journey back to civilisation. However, I then wound up him and his editor by telling him that if the *Sun* reporter could do it, a *Mirror* man could not lose face by dropping out before him. Crash still tried to wriggle out of it a few times. After a couple of hours on day one he said, 'OK Ian, I've got my story now and I've walked further than I've ever done in my life. Can I go home now, please?'

'Can you hell,' I said. 'If the man from the *Sun* can do it, then so can the man from the *Mirror*,' and I marched off before he could think of a reply.

When Alisdair Ross finally dropped out, Crash again tried to weasel out of it, but I told him, 'You can't quit now. There's even more reason to stick with it now you're the only national newspaper man still on his feet. Think of the kudos for the *Mirror*.' Crash's expression suggested that the *Mirror* and its precious kudos was the least of his worries, but he did keep going. He'd originally parked his car at John O'Groats expecting to pick it up the next morning. When he finally made it back there, it had been sitting in the car park for over five weeks. The battery was as flat as last week's pancakes and the parking fees were the equivalent of the national debt of a Third World country.

Crash's customary position on the walk was at the rear, some distance behind the rest of us, and we'd usually be on our second or third drink in the hotel bar before he finally limped in at the end of each day, but he did keep going. When we broke the hundred-mile barrier, I thought I'd give him a little added incentive, so I left a bottle of Scotch at the roadside with a note reading 'Only eight hundred miles to go. Man or mouse?' He made a nasty mess of the cheeseboard that night, but he never uttered another squeak of complaint on the walk and, like John Border and Phil Rance, he went every step of the way with me.

I had a very strict schedule so there was no question of taking a day off here and there; we just had to keep plugging on. The first week was particularly tough with endless miles of empty road – towns are fifty miles apart in some places – and although the scenery was breathtaking, we would sometimes have swapped it for the back streets of a rustbelt town, if that brought with it a bit of human company. What helped to get us through it was the staggering response from the people we did meet.

Lorry drivers would sound their horns as they passed us and we'd wave to acknowledge the greeting and watch each one disappear into the distance – just another person we'd never see again. Yet from a day to a week later, as they made their homeward return journeys, many of those same drivers pulled over with a hiss of air-brakes and handed over a carrier bag full of notes and coins that they'd collected for us from their workmates. The money went into the "bank" in the back-up van and we went on our way immeasurably lifted in spirits by the generosity of those people.

As we neared the English border the weather turned ugly with westerly gales blasting torrents of rain at us. The last leg in Scotland down to Gretna was particularly tough, the longest in miles – more than thirty-eight – and with incessant rain pounding down all day. It took thirteen hours' hard slog to get us to Gretna, and even though we'd set out before dawn, on those short winter days it was dark well before we reached journey's end. There was no pavement, so cars and lorries were zooming past inches away, and even though the road twisted, we always seemed to be walking straight into the weather.

Brian Close had volunteered to walk that leg with us and he arrived in totally unsuitable footwear, as if he was planning an amble round the corner to the pub instead of a route march. He had lost none of his skill in kidology, however. As we passed a milestone saying 'Gretna twelve miles', he snorted in derision and said, 'I know this road, it's nothing like as far as that.' As it turned out, it was every inch of that, but lessening the distance still to go was his way of convincing his mind and body that he could make it. He did of course, even though he was just about crippled by the time we got there. Not that we ever had any doubts about it: the idea of Brian Close ever dropping out of anything before the end was as ridiculous to him as it was to the rest of us.

Despite the pain and the exhaustion, we always managed to find time for 'light refreshments' at the end of each day's walk – as Jimmy Greaves said when he came to do a piece for Central TV, 'Christ, Beef, this is going to be the longest pub crawl of all time' – but the rest and recreation never got in the way of the serious business: raising money. The Leukaemia Research Fund people had told us that if we made £100,000 from the whole walk, that would be a great success. In the event, by the time we had crossed the border from Scotland into England we already had £100,000 in the bank and we were then only a third of the way to our goal. The Scots are supposedly legendary for their deep pockets and short arms, but if so, this cause had touched their hearts and opened their wallets.

People kept joining us and doing a section of the walk with us. The most welcome visitor was Kath, who, though very heavily pregnant, turned up north of Penrith and, though she hadn't intended to do any walking, got swept up with the sight of the Pied Piper's army of walkers, well-wishers and kids coming down the road towards her and fell into step beside me. Eight and a half months pregnant she may have been, but she was ready to do the whole seven miles into Penrith, and I had to half-persuade and half-order her to get in a car and just join us for the last mile or so into Penrith. Unknown to me, as we were doing the last few yards she slipped on some snow and fell over, landing right on her 'bump'. Kath didn't tell me what had happened and swore everyone else to secrecy as well, and luckily there were no apparent ill effects, though the birth of our youngest daughter, Becky, did come a couple of days early.

We parted company the next morning, as Kath went home to get ready for the birth. The next new arrival wouldn't be able to walk a step and I had to make a hasty detour to link up with her. When Kath went into labour, I kept walking for the moment, but received constant bulletins on how things were going at the Doncaster Royal Infirmary, and just north of Manchester I was told that the birth was now imminent.

A BBC guy who was walking with us tried to arrange a helicopter to airlift me to the hospital. He didn't quite pull it off but came up with an interesting alternative: a vintage white Rolls-Royce. I jumped in and out of a bath, threw on some clothes and, with Allan Border's brother John for company, headed for the hospital, travelling in the back of the Roller at a stately fifty mph.

When I got there, Becky had already been born, but I was able to take my first look at my beautiful daughter. I then lay down on the bed next to Kath and started to ask how she was, but I was so knackered that I'd fallen asleep before she'd even completed the answer. When I woke up again fifteen minutes later we talked for a while, then I said goodbye to all the family – Liam and Sarah were there as well, seeing their sister for the first time – and had to head back to Manchester, once more at a maximum of fifty miles an hour, ready for the next day's walk, though we did manage a couple of drinks that night to wet the baby's head.

During the regular BBC *Breakfast Time* television slot the next morning I did the usual interview with Selina Scott about the walk and about kids with leukaemia. Selina then asked me about the new baby and whether we had a name for her yet. 'No,' I said. 'Maybe we should call her "Selina".' I don't know what triggered it – maybe there were a lot of gentlemen of a certain age out there who were dreaming of making babies with Selina Scott, or maybe the arrival of a new Botham baby had melted the hearts of the nation's mothers – but such an avalanche of calls pledging cash to Leukaemia Research was made that morning that the telephone system at Great Ormond Street crashed. They raised £250,000 in credit-card pledges alone.

Kath was released from hospital the day after Becky's birth and, unknown to me, had gone to stay with her sister Lindsay and husband Paul in Worcestershire. The route of the walk passed through their village, and as I walked along, Kath suddenly appeared from the crowd, holding Becky in her arms, and joined me for a few yards. One of the press photographers didn't know who this strange woman was and convinced himself that he'd got a real scoop. He was probably already picturing the headlines – BOTHAM'S MYSTERY LOVE-CHILD – and the fortune he'd make in syndication rights when I introduced him to Mrs Botham.

Much of the success of the walk was down to the fact that we were literally taking our fund-raising campaign to the people. We were walking past their front doors, and though most people could not afford to give up a day's or even a few hours' work to come and find us, when we found them they were unbelievably generous. It wasn't just in the villages, towns and cities. On one quiet country road we came across a group of four farmers on their tractors who had collected money from every other farmer in the district. They climbed down, gave us the donation and then went back to their work in the fields.

That sort of experience always gave us a huge boost, but none did so more than the woman who suddenly screeched to a halt as we were walking along a dual carriageway. She was middle-aged and expensively dressed, but neither stopped her from hurdling the central reservation and running down the road after us. 'I've been phoning the police all morning to find out where you were,' she said. 'My husband died of leukaemia only six weeks ago.' I went to put my arms around her and started to stammer some condolences, but she waved them away. 'No, no,' she said. 'There's no need for sympathy. I was lucky enough to have twenty-five years of wonderful marriage with him, but I want to give you something for your campaign in memory of him, so please take this.' And she pulled off her diamond eternity ring and pressed it into my hand. Despite my protests, she then ran back up the road to her car and was gone. The ring was later auctioned and raised more than £1,000 for the Leukaemia Research Fund.

The media and public interest just seemed to keep growing all the way through the walk and we had some unbelievable experiences when we reached the south-west. In Bristol we were met by a ticker-tape welcome, bands playing and thousands of people lining the streets. We took over £40,000 in the collection buckets in just that one day and collected another £26,000 when we got to Taunton – the equivalent of 50p from every single man, woman and child in the town. Some of my fellow Somerset cricketers were among the bands of people stopping traffic on the A38 and charging drivers a 'Leukaemia Toll'.

There was another pleasant surprise at Okehampton, on the Devon/Cornwall border. A Rolls-Royce overtook us and then turned off into a side street. When we reached the corner, the driver was waiting for us. Elton John thrust a huge cheque into my hand and then waved and drove off, though he also joined us for a meal at the end of that day's walk.

There was a less pleasant experience as we passed through Cornwall. After the overwhelming warmth and generosity of the vast majority of the people we had encountered, it was a shock to find one or two whose motives were far less pure. A young freelance reporter joined us for a couple of days, claiming that he was doing a piece for a fitness magazine. He then went off and flogged a piece to the tabloids claiming we were smoking dope during the walk. To back up his claims to sceptical editors, he even reported it to the Devon and Cornwall police who investigated and dismissed it. How could we possibly have been smoking dope? We'd had an escort of police motorbike riders with us all the way, not to mention the tens of thousands of people we passed along the way.

However, I was lucky to avoid another bout of bad publicity and another appearance in court after a spot of aggro with a policeman on Bodmin Moor. The end was almost in sight but one of the three ever-presents with me, Phil Rance, was really struggling that day and dropping further and further behind. I wasn't in great shape myself – I was in so much pain from my back trouble that I'd been on painkillers for days – but Phil was even worse. A high-ranking police officer whom we'd never even seen before then turned up and told one of the police outriders that if Phil, who was about a mile and a half behind by then, didn't catch up he would be taken off the walk. The senior officer then swanned off again, without even the courtesy of speaking to me about it, leaving his men to cop the flak. One of the police escort riders – who had all been great to us all the way – broke the news to me. I knew him pretty well by now and said, 'Come on mate, this isn't fair on Phil when we're so near the end of the walk. He's been with us all the way from John O'Groats. Give him a break.' He just shrugged. 'I'm sorry, orders are orders.'

My feet and my back were killing me, I was close to exhaustion, and in my anger and frustration I turned and took a swing at him. It wasn't the smartest thing I've ever done for three reasons. First, it wasn't his fault, the senior officer was the one who was responsible; second, if it had connected properly, I might have been back in court on assault charges and looking down the barrel of a custodial sentence; and third, it was very poorly aimed. The punch landed on the side of his crash helmet, doing him no harm whatsoever, but breaking a bone in my knuckle. It was one of those things that I regretted the second it happened and not just because of the broken knuckle.

The policeman wasn't fazed at all and burst out laughing, saying, 'I bet that bloody hurt,' and eventually both Phil Rance and I were allowed to continue. But by the time we reached Redruth, the local radio station was running the story. With just one more day to go before the end of the walk, the last thing we needed was bad publicity, but luckily the officer I hit had decided it was all excusable on the grounds of fatigue and frustration. When I saw him the next morning I told him, 'I'm very sorry for trying to punch you; and since I broke my knuckle on your helmet, this really was a case where it hurt me more than it hurt you.' We both laughed about it, and he then said, 'I've got two days off today and tomorrow, but I'd like to help out on the walk.' In the circumstances it was a very noble gesture, and one I was delighted to accept.

Kath had recovered enough from the birth to join us for the final steps to Land's End. I wanted to end the walk in style, and having dipped a toe into the sea at John O'Groats I wanted to dive in at Land's End. Unfortunately, the cliffs made that a bit of a non-starter, so having popped into a pub to change into top hats and tails, we completed the last mile and then went down to the sea and hurled Crash into the breakers. It was a freezing cold November day, but by that time he'd ceased caring and would have put up with anything so long as I promised he didn't have to go back on the road the next morning.

It was a gruelling experience. We had covered the entire 874-mile walk in thirty-six days – almost a marathon distance every single day for five weeks – but in the process we had raised over £1 million for research into leukaemia. We ended with a lap of honour around London that added another £30,000 from a street collection. At Great Ormond Street Hospital, where the Leukaemia Research Fund had its office, there were people hanging from every window, and so many spectators, photographers and reporters that we could hardly make our way through. But it was a young girl in a car outside the building who held my attention. She was paralysed by leukaemia and unable to get out of the car to hand me a cheque for the money she had raised for the cause, so I pushed and shoved my way past everyone to spend a few relatively quiet moments with her. Accepting that donation meant more than anything. She represented the reason we had done the walk. The Leukaemia Research Fund received an immediate transfusion of funds, but it also gained in the longer term from the raising of its profile. People all over the country who previously knew nothing about leukaemia now understood more about the disease and the charity that was trying to counter it.

I felt strangely empty when the walk was finally over. It had been almost my sole focus not just for the five weeks we were doing it, but through the weeks of planning beforehand. Now it was over and I mooched around for a few days before Tim Hudson found a way of filling the void. He believed my time would be well spent schmoozing in Hollywood with the producers who, according to him, were clamouring for my signature, so we set forth on the yellow brick road with a reporter and photographer from the *Sun* in tow to document my honeymoon with Hollywood.

I'd seen films that portrayed Hollywood in what I thought was a tongue-in-cheek way, but when I actually got there I discovered that it wasn't an exaggeration at all – it was the reality. In Hollywood there were far more wannabes than had-beens; every waiter or taxi-driver I came across was either an actor 'between parts', a screenwriter working on a script or a would-be producer. The whole place seemed to be full of hustlers and bullshitters, and that was not a combination that had ever appealed to me. If I were a really successful actor, it would be the last place I'd want to live.

People-watching was very interesting, and I'm sure that if I'd told people I met that I was a casting agent looking for 'talent' for a British movie I'd have been bought endless drinks, dinners and anything else I wanted, but it was a very strange environment and, being a country boy, not one I'd ever have felt at ease with. In fact I don't like big cities full stop. I love Hobart, Adelaide, Brisbane, places that are a good size – you can cross them in twenty minutes and feel you know them – whereas huge cities like London and New York give me the creeps. I feel claustrophobic in them; they're just too vast and unknowable to me. There's no warmth in them, and I certainly found no warmth in Hollywood or Los Angeles.

Three days after we arrived, Hudson steered me into the offices of a Hollywood producer, Menachem Golan. Despite all Tim's previous claims about his bulging contacts book, the only producer he managed to get us some 'face time' with was Golan. Hollywood is built on bullshit, and Golan showed he was well capable of adding a few shovels-full with his statement before I'd even arrived in Hollywood that 'Ian Botham has got the looks, the build and the accent to be the next James Bond. I know they're looking around, because Roger Moore has hinted that he won't be in the next 007 film and Ian would be a genuine candidate if he takes my advice and puts his name forward.'

When we sat down at the other side of his five-acre desk, Golan got straight down to business. 'All I want you to do,' he said, 'is put me ten cents on every seat.'

'Botham will give you ten cents,' Hudson said. 'He'll give you a million kids in Britain, a million in Australia and even more than that in India and Pakistan.'

'Well, I'll tell you something,' Golan said, 'he's better looking than Tom Selleck' – talk about damning with faint praise. 'So Ian, all you've got to do for now is stay here in LA and take some acting lessons for six months.'

'Er … excuse me?' I said. 'I can't do that. What about the tour to the West Indies?'

Golan stared at me. 'The tour to the West Indies?'

'The England cricket tour. It starts in about three weeks.'

Golan's expression suggested that while he might just have heard of the West Indies, 'cricket' was definitely a new one on him.

The new James Bond now had an instant decision to make. It was clear that I couldn't do both; it had to be either a licence to kill or a licence to play cricket. There could only be one decision: I had unfinished business with the Windies, so Mr Bond would have to wait ... but if you're still out there Menachem, I'm ready for my close-up now.

There were no other producers to see and the boys from the *Sun* were getting earache from their editor about the size of their expenses claim in relation to the amount of usable copy and pictures – nil – that they had so far generated. 'When exactly will you be doing some screen tests, Ian?' one of them asked, as casually as he could manage. 'Only our editor would like to know.'

Hudson then had a brainwave. I had been on the Universal Studios tour a couple of times with Kath and the kids, so I knew all about 'The Wild West Shoot-Out', where any tourist with the requisite pile of greenbacks can dress up as a cowboy, walk into a plastic replica of Boot Hill or the OK Corral and have a pretend shoot-out with a gunman wearing a black hat and muttering 'This town ain't big enough for the both of us, stranger.' In the absence of anything better, I ended up taking part in a shoot-out, while the *Sun* photographer snapped away. My expression in the photographs showed my enthusiasm; I've seen roadkill with more animation. It was clear that, if ever, there could be no movie career while I was still playing cricket, but as soon as we got back to England, Hudson began issuing press statements about the 'major motion picture' deal I was about to sign.

My relationship with him was now putting immense strain on my marriage. Kath and I were having regular arguments about him. She didn't like him, didn't trust him and didn't believe his promises of jam tomorrow, and was furious that I seemed to spend as much time at Birtles as I did at home. When another celebrity cricket match at Birtles led into the traditional post-match party at which Hudson was spouting his usual stuff to anyone willing to listen, Kath had finally had enough. 'Ian,' she said, 'you're being played for a fool here. Can't you understand what is happening?'

I was in full party mode and in no mood to stop so I just said, 'Forget it Kath, you're making a fuss over nothing.'

It wasn't exactly the answer she had been hoping to hear. 'Right,' she said, 'that's it. I won't be a part of this any more. Either come with me now or we're through.'

In typical belligerent, boneheaded fashion, I elected to stay. Kath left with Jan and Gerry, and when we were finally speaking again she told me that the only reason she'd pulled back from the brink of divorce was because of the children. Not being the brightest bulb in the box, it took me a while longer before I finally realised that she'd been right about Hudson all along, after a conversation with Brian Close who told me that, not realising the relationship between Brian and Kath's father, Hudson had told him that Kath had no place in his plans. If I was to be marketed properly in Hollywood, it had to be as a sex symbol, and sex symbols are much less marketable if they're happily married men. So Kath and the kids were to be dumped; she'd be looked after financially, but she'd be out of the picture. I'd been so entranced by the Hudson tales of wealth and fame that I'd been on the brink of breaking up my marriage.

For the moment, I had enough on my plate without dealing with Hudson. Although I was approaching the tour of the West Indies in the right frame of mind, I was close to physical exhaustion. The John O'Groats to Land's End walk had taken its toll on me and then, forty-eight hours before I was due to fly to the West Indies, Becky, still only two months old, was rushed into hospital for an emergency hernia operation.

Kath had asked our nanny, Diane, to give Becky a bath. Moments later, Diane called out that she had found a lump in Becky's stomach. We took her straight to the doctor and she was then rushed to hospital and operated on that same evening. Fortunately she recovered so quickly that she was as right as rain again within days, but it was a very stressful send-off from the UK.

My last words to Kath as we parted at Heathrow in January 1986 were 'The tabloids won't be getting any headlines about me this time, because off the field they won't even see me.' I set off for the Caribbean in an upbeat mood about our prospects in the West Indies. We knew that it would take something special even to avoid defeat against a team that included four batsmen – Gordon Greenidge, Desmond Haynes, Richie Richardson and Viv Richards – who would walk into any team in the world, and a bowling attack that was the best I have ever seen. Michael Holding and Patrick Patterson opened the bowling, and if you survived their opening spells, Malcolm Marshall and Joel Garner were waiting in the wings.

However, having just won the Ashes, I and my team-mates were optimistic that at last we might be able to compete with, and even beat, the West Indies on their own patch for the first time in nearly twenty years. David Gower, Graham Gooch, Mike Gatting, Tim Robinson, Allan Lamb and myself had all scored plenty of runs against the Aussies, and we had a decent bowling attack as well.

The British media lost no time in stirring things up. The number of reporters had grown exponentially since my early tours with England, and most of them were news men, not sports reporters. They were there to dish the dirt and their first opportunity wasn't long in arriving. David Gower and I missed the first match of the tour, a loosener against the Windward Islands. As tour captain David had already been under a lot of stress, but shortly before we left for the Caribbean he also suffered a family tragedy. He was mentally worn out by the time we arrived and in need of a couple of days of rest.

So we took a relaxing trip around the island on a yacht, but when we switched on the radio to catch the score from the St Vincent ground, we discovered that England had been dismissed for 94 in their second innings – the lowest total ever recorded by England in the West Indies – and had gone down by seven wickets to what was, by common agreement, the weakest side in the Caribbean.

Unfortunately a cricket photographer had come along for the ride with us and his photographs of Messrs Gower and Botham basking on a yacht with a glass in their hands hit the picture desks of the English papers at the same time as the cricket correspondents were filing copy suggesting that instead of cruising on a yacht we should have been steadying the ship on the field.

The next match was a fortunate draw with the Leeward Islands in Antigua – we were hanging on at 94 for eight in our second innings at the close – but we then beat Jamaica by 168 runs in Kingston. So we approached the first one-day international in Jamaica in a reasonably positive frame of mind. The pitch didn't look too clever and if David Gower had won the toss he would have put the Windies in to bat; unfortunately, he lost it and we found ourselves making first use of it. Robinson and Gower were both out for ducks and Mike Gatting, who'd been in prime batting form in the opening games, found himself facing a pumped-up Malcolm Marshall on an extremely helpful pitch. Gatt had struggled his way to 10 not out when Marshall let go another flat-out delivery. The ball reared from just short of a length, and although Gatt was wearing a helmet, it had no protective grille over his face, and the ball went straight through the gap and smashed into his nose. I took a towel out to him on the pitch and it was one of the most sickening sights I have ever seen on a cricket field or anywhere else. They were still picking bits of bone and cartilage out of the ball and off the pitch some time later. When Marshall picked up the ball and found bits of Gatt still attached to it he went green and nearly threw up.

I was being rested to protect a slight injury and I helped physio Lawrie Brown look after Gatt in the dressing room. He always had a ton of guts – literally and metaphorically – and although badly shaken, after ice and cold towels had been applied, he asked casually, 'When will I be able to go out to bat again?'

'Sorry Gatt,' Lawrie said, 'that's not going to happen. Two reasons. One, when the ball hit you and you were staggering around, you knocked off your leg bail, so you're out. Second, your nose is such a mess that you're not going anywhere except straight to hospital.'

'You're kidding,' he said. 'It's not that bad is it? It doesn't hurt much.' He got up and set off for the dressing-room mirror to take a look for himself. 'Gatt,' I said, 'trust me, you don't want to bother having a look,' but it was too late. Things might still have been all right if he hadn't tried to blow his nose. The dressing-room attendant was kept busy for several minutes cleaning up the aftermath. With no further arguments from Gatt, we packed him off to hospital. They stitched him up and he was discharged straight away and came back to the hotel. By now the bruising had come out and he looked like he'd gone fifteen rounds with Muhammad Ali. He spent a terrible night back in the hotel suffering acute breathing difficulties as his nose and throat kept filling with blood. He told me that at one point he felt like he was drowning and was sure he was going to die. He was flown home for further treatment and when he arrived back at Heathrow, his nose bandaged and what could be seen of his face black and blue from bruising, he was asked one of the most stupid press questions of all time: 'Mike, where did the ball hit you?'

We lost that game by six wickets and three days later faced the West Indies again in the first Test, once more at Sabina Park on a pitch that was lightning quick and with a dangerously unpredictable bounce. One ball would come through at normal height, the next might keep low, and the next climb throat-high from a good length. John Woodcock of *The Times*, a man not noted for hyperbole, wrote, 'I never felt it more likely that we should see someone killed,' and it was certainly one of the most dangerous pitches I've ever played on. We were not helped by the infamous sightscreen in front of the George Headley Stand. It was just too low to give a batsman a sight of the ball when it was being bowled by the tall West Indian pacemen who were releasing the ball from a height of around ten feet. We had had trouble sighting deliveries from Michael Holding and Courtney Walsh in the game against Jamaica and had asked for the sightscreen to be made higher before the Test but we were told that it was impossible, because doing so would have obscured the view of spectators who had already bought tickets … so the only people who couldn't see the ball turned out to be the batsmen.

Given the problems in sighting the ball, it was unfortunate that we were coming up against a fast bowler making his Test debut, Patrick Patterson, who was described to us as 'the fastest bowler in the Caribbean, after Malcolm Marshall'. He came on as first change and by the end of his first over we had decided that the local pundits had got it wrong. 'Patto' was quicker even than Marshall. I doubt whether we would have played him with any confidence even if we had been able to spot the ball against the sightscreen. As it was we just had to hit and hope. He took four for 30 in eleven terrifyingly quick overs and most of the scoring strokes off him were involuntary ones. We were whipped out for 159, trailed by almost 150 on first innings and were eventually beaten by ten wickets inside three days, with only Peter Willey offering much in the way of resistance.

Fleet Street at once sharpened its axes. The obvious answer as far as the folks back in the UK were concerned was that either we weren't practising enough or we weren't trying hard enough. When Gower first used the phrase 'optional nets', he did so quite innocently – he had the same aversion to nets that I did, and for similar reasons – but the term was then constantly cited as proof that instead of busting a gut for England, we were just taking a winter holiday in the West Indies.

The issue of English players' cricketing links with apartheid South Africa, which had blighted the previous tour, soon became an issue once more. Pickets and protests aimed at Graham Gooch and the other players who had been on the rebel tour to South Africa in 1982 became so widespread and so serious that by the time we reached Trinidad for the second Test our hotel was under a twenty-four-hour armed guard. As the captain of that South African tour, Gooch was the principal focus of the demonstrators' anger, which was further fuelled by a statement from Lester Bird, the deputy prime minister of Antigua, that Gooch was not welcome in the West Indies. Gooch grew more and more withdrawn, brooding over it, and even threatened to quit the tour and fly home. It took the combined efforts of David Gower and A.C. Smith, who flew out from London to talk Gooch round, to finally persuade him to stay and tough it out.

He made the best possible response by hitting a superb undefeated century to steer us to a five-wicket victory in the second one-day international, but it was a rare triumph in an increasingly disastrous tour and we were hammered in the second Test at Port-of-Spain. Viv Richards won the toss and put us in to bat and only Gower with 66 and Lamb with 62 reached double figures as we were all out for 176. The West Indies then piled up 399 all out, a fine century from Richie Richardson the highlight, and although we managed 315 second time round, the West Indies then knocked off the 93 needed for victory, for the loss of three wickets.

Mike Gatting had returned to the West Indies as soon as he was given the all clear, and within twenty-four hours of his arrival he was back on the field in the game against Barbados, but he was struck on the hand as he fended off a short-pitched ball and broke his thumb, necessitating another lengthy lay-off. He did not play again until the final Test.

The third Test in Barbados was another shambles. This time David Gower won the toss and decided to give the West Indies a taste of their own medicine by putting them in to bat. The gamble failed. Greenidge went early but Haynes, who made 84, and Richardson, who scored his second successive century – 160 – then put us to the sword. The West Indies were all out for 418 and our response was no better than it had been in the first two Tests.

Dismissed for 189 and 199, we were thrashed by an innings and 30 runs. The series was over with the West Indians holding an unassailable 3-0 lead.

Off the field, things had also taken a decided turn for the worse. Our poor results were only further feeding the press pack's appetite for scandal. There were about sixty reporters tracking us, staying in the same hotels and flying on the same aircraft, and a large number were not there to watch cricket but to dish dirt. As a result, relations between us and them were absolutely poisonous.

The stories and the insinuations grew ever wilder and ever more unpleasant. At one press conference David Gower was asked if his apparent tiredness out on the field could be explained by the affair he was having with Paul Downton's wife. Apart from a peck on the cheek at the Downtons' wedding, David had never even touched her.

News at Ten got in on the act by running a story about drunken debauchery at our hotel and bottles being smashed on the tennis court. The story had the merit of being true in the sense that the incidents had indeed occurred, but none of the England players had anything to do with it. A bunch of drunken, rowdy hotel guests had caused the problems, but the clear implication of the story was that we were to blame.

Inevitably the reptiles were paying very close attention to me, and I was sure that some of them had been despatched from Fleet Street with one overriding aim: 'Get Botham'. The pressure was certainly not helping my form, and my paranoia about leaks to the press made things worse. I didn't know who to trust, kept newcomers to our circle at arm's length and was even suspicious of friends and fellow players, some of whom blamed me for the relentless press attention.

I spent hours brooding in my room and was so paranoid that I was even checking it for hidden 'bugs' and tape recorders. My moods most affected my roommate, Les Taylor, but other teammates grew increasingly concerned. John Emburey even got his wife to phone Kath to ask if she knew if there was anything physical or mentally wrong with me, because I never left my room. She was preaching to the converted because from the tone of my regular calls to her, Kath had already decided that something was seriously wrong.

My paranoia and my moods were now affecting the whole team. After getting out cheaply yet again, I stormed back to the dressing room, threw my bat on the floor and shouted, 'How the hell are you supposed to play that bowling on these wickets?' Gatt at once took me to one side and gave me a real tongue lashing. 'For God's sake Beef, stop whingeing,' he said. 'What sort of example is that for the other players?' He was absolutely right of course. Trying to blame the wickets or the conditions was the sort of loser mentality that infuriated me, and in normal circumstances I would have been the first to have stamped on that kind of behaviour in the dressing room, but these were not normal circumstances and press intrusion and my paranoia had locked me into an ever-deepening spiral.

Kath's father, Gerry, had flown out to Barbados to watch some cricket. We've always been mates as well as father-in-law and son-in-law, and he helped restore my sanity. He made me leave my room and get away from all the on- and off-field pressures. Whenever I was not on England duty we headed for the Oistins district, where we could sip a few rum punches and play a few quiet games of 'doms' with the locals.

I was back on a relatively even keel, but during the third Test I'd popped up into the stand to chat to two of England's celebrity supporters, Mick Jagger and Eric Idle. Mick asked me to dinner that evening and told me to bring a few friends along as well. I asked Gerry and my roommate Les Taylor, and since Bob Willis was nearby with his brother and his wife and an acquaintance of theirs called Lindy Field, I added them to the party list.

Ms Field gave me, Bob's brother and his wife a lift in her car while Les Taylor and Gerry drove behind us. Ms Field was a good-looking woman, an ex-Miss Barbados, but beyond a few bland pleasantries on the drive there I hardly spoke to her and spent most of the evening chatting with Mick about cricket. I went back to our hotel with Gerry and Les and forgot all about Ms Field.

I soon had plenty of other things to occupy my mind. A couple of days before the fourth Test in Trinidad, the *Daily Star* ran a story headlined BOTHAM DRUG SHOCK, the result of an 'off the record' chat between Tim Hudson and two English reporters in a bar in Santa Monica, California. Hudson had perhaps imbibed well and was clearly in expansive mood, because the *Star* had assembled a few choice quotes from him about me, including, 'I'm aware he smokes dope. Doesn't everybody?'

I was still in the process of suing the *Mail on Sunday* for libel over their 'sex and drugs' allegations about me in New Zealand in 1983–84. A few words out of place by my manager, Tim Hudson, could lose me the case and leave me with a costs bill of a million quid and change. When I finally tracked him down in Miami, the phone conversation was brief and to the point. 'If you do not at once put out a release through your lawyer threatening to sue the *Daily Star*,' I said, 'I will have no alternative but to sue you or sack you. Maybe both.' In the end I settled for the latter.

It had taken a while but I finally had my head on straight again. However, coupled with my earlier weird behaviour, my rage about Hudson led David Gower to wonder if the team would be better without my currently negligible contributions on the field and disruptive behaviour in the dressing room. There were whispers that I was close to being dropped for the fourth Test, something that had never happened to me in my entire cricket career, so I had very mixed feelings when David summoned me to his hotel room.

He told me that I was in the team, but made it clear that it had been a very close call – a split decision. David had backed me, he said, because he was reluctant to dispense with a player who could turn a Test with both the bat and the ball, but he'd had a struggle to convince the other selectors and he now needed me to justify the faith he had shown in me.

I thanked him for it, and it was a wake-up call that I was deter-mined to heed in the fourth Test. I still couldn't trouble the scorers to any great extent, but innings of only 38 and 25 still made me the second-highest scorer in both England innings. We recorded yet another disappointing total – 200 – after Viv Richards had again put us in to bat, and although I put in my best bowling performances of the tour so far, taking five for 71, it was in yet another lost cause. They totalled 312, dismissed us for 150 and knocked off the target of 39 runs without losing a wicket.

Just when I felt that I had at least got my own game back on track, there was another hammer blow. Straight after Mick Jagger's dinner party, Lindy Field had flown from Barbados to London with one aim in mind: to hawk around the London tabloid editors a story about a supposed night of cocaine snorting and wild sex with me. The *News of the World* had taken the bait and the story would be appearing in the paper the following Sunday. The story was complete fiction, but as long as Ms Field insisted it was true the paper would feel quite justified in running it, whatever I might say about it. It was a classic no-win situation for me. If I kept quiet, it would be taken as tacit acceptance that the story was true; if I denied it – well, I would do, wouldn't I? – the story would still be believed. I had only one ace in the hole and that was the fact that my wife's father was the prime witness for the defence. Gerry had been with me all evening, and while furious denials from me might or might not be believed, surely nobody and no court in the world would believe that my father-in-law would go out of his way to protect me if I really had been unfaithful to the man's daughter.

Kath was already due to fly out to Antigua before the final Test, but I now tried to get her to come out early with the kids so that they would not be exposed to the mob of door-stepping reporters who would be camping outside our home as soon as the story appeared. Unfortunately her flights could not be changed, but she also felt it would be foolish to fly out early and give the media the chance to run

BOTHAM'S WIFE IN FRANTIC DASH TO SAVE MARRIAGE
stories. In the event she stuck to her agreed schedule and the kids
went to stay with my mum and dad to keep them out of the way of
the media feeding frenzy that would inevitably erupt.

By the time she arrived, the *News of the World*'s scoop was out. I
could see why the paper's editors must have been salivating. It had
the lot: sex, drugs, an adulterous celebrity and a beauty queen: I
LAID OUT COKE ... BEAUTY QUEEN'S NIGHT OF
PASSION WITH BOTHAM ... TEST ACE IN SEX AND
DRUGS SCANDAL. One of the purported 'facts' that the *News of
the World* had used to back up the story was that so torrid was the
shagathon that Ms Field and I had allegedly embarked on in my
hotel room, we had broken the bed. The paper's reporters had even
interviewed a hotel maintenance man who was quoted as saying, 'I
didn't fix the bed myself, but all the guys were talking about it.' To
the *News of the World* this made it an open-and-shut case: Ian
Botham's bed was broken therefore he must have been having wild
sex on it. Had they bothered to ask me or my roommate, Les Taylor,
they would have discovered that it was actually Les who had broken
it, and not during a wild orgy but when slumping down on it to get
some sleep.

I was waiting for Kath when she came out into the arrivals hall at
the airport. As I kissed her, what seemed like a million photographers'
flashguns went off and the assembled slavering tabloid hacks started
bellowing questions at both of us. We ignored them and headed for
a back exit where Viv Richards had arranged to have a car waiting.
Kath and I spent the entire journey to the hotel in silence. I just
couldn't think of anything to say to ease the tension, and neither
could Kath. Only when we were safely in our hotel room did we talk
about the allegations.

Kath came straight to the point. 'Well, is it true?'

'Of course not. Gerry was with me all night. Ask him if you don't
believe me. She was at the party at Mick Jagger's, she gave me and

two other people a lift there, and that was it. She didn't come back to the hotel with me, we didn't have sex, we didn't snort coke and we didn't break the bed. She's just made up a plausible-sounding story to make herself a few thousand quid. End of story.'

That was as much of an inquest as we held into it. As far as I was concerned it was now ancient history, time to move on. But though she said nothing else at the time, Kath could not shake it off so easily. I've always had the philosophy that things happen for a reason; it's perhaps one of the things that enables me to move on without regrets and without looking back. If I've been out to a bad shot, I will analyse where I went wrong, but then I'll put it behind me and forget about it. I never brood about things. Sometimes that attitude of 'It's happened, OK, now let's move on' has brought me into conflict with Kath and others who are made differently and don't understand how I can so swiftly deal with and then forget events, however traumatic they might be, but that's the way I'm made and it's not something I can or would want to change.

It had a less appealing side – it was never my fault, someone else was always to blame – but it helped to make me successful in sport. I could never imagine, for example, admitting, as Steve Harmison did after his disastrous first day in the 2006-07 Ashes series in Australia, 'I froze.' I could never say that because it would send out the wrong message to my opponents. If I'd bowled a similarly wild opening spell, I'd have convinced myself and anyone else within earshot that it was all part of some fiendishly subtle tactical plan to lull the Aussie openers before I got them out.

I now tried to adopt the same tactic in relation to Ms Field's allegations, but it proved to be the wrong attitude entirely as far as Kath was concerned. Despite my denials and Gerry's reassurance that I was telling the truth, she was mired in a depression. She barely spoke, couldn't sleep, and the mere sight of a reporter or photographer was enough to send her stress levels off the dial. I was very concerned about her and began to worry that she might even be contemplating suicide. It was absurd, but it showed the mental stress we were both under. One morning, while I was at a team meeting, she went off alone to have a look at a holiday villa that we had been offered for a complete break at the end of the tour. When I got back to our room there was no message and no sign of her and I began to worry. The more time passed, the more frantic I became. I rang every person I could think of, then went out searching the island for her. Finally she walked back into our room, shocked to see the state I'd got myself into. I snarled at her for going out without telling me or leaving a note, she snapped back that I was being ridiculous, but eventually we calmed down and I suggested that we should go down to the bar for a drink to cheer ourselves up. A few of the boys were there, we had a few drinks and then we decided to go back to our room and watch a movie. Bob Willis was going to watch it with us, but set off to buy pizzas first.

While he was out, one of our friends told me some interesting news about Ms Field: it turned out that she had a very expensive cocaine habit to support. It was the best bit of news I'd heard in days, suggesting a strong motive for Ms Field to want to concoct a lucrative story for the press. I was delighted to hear it and I told Kath at once, thinking she'd be pleased too. Instead, she burst into tears. 'I never want to hear another bloody word about that woman,' she said. 'Can't you understand that?' Evidently not, because my next contribution to the conversation was, 'What the hell's the matter with you? Cheer up for God's sake.'

Kath stormed out of the bar with tears streaming down her face and greeted me with a stony silence when I got back to the room. Bob brought the pizzas shortly afterwards but, frustrated and angered by Kath's reproachful silence, I grabbed hold of mine and sent it flying, then went round the room overturning the ice bucket, including the bottle of wine it was cooling, smashing the bedside lamp and throwing a few other things that came to hand against the walls. Then I stormed out, slamming the door behind me.

I wound up throwing down rums in a beach bar, where Bob Willis found me a couple of hours later. He calmed me down, marched me up and down the beach for a while to try and clear my head, and then took me back to the hotel. I got back to the room blind drunk, and having delivered my pompous, drunken verdict – 'That's it. Our marriage is over. We have been trapped by the headlines' – I fell unconscious on the bed.

When I came round the next morning, the first thing I heard was Kath with a fit of the giggles. Opening a bleary eye and trying to ignore the pounding of hammers in my temples, I saw that a piece of pizza was dangling from the curtain rail with strings of melted cheese reaching almost to the floor. I started to laugh too, and it eased the tension between us. In that moment, I realised that if we could go through a night like the one we'd had and still wake up laughing, there might be a chance for us yet.

It was good to have something to laugh at, because in the fifth Test at St John's in Antigua we were hammered yet again. David Gower won the toss and put the Windies in to bat – there had probably never been a series where the side winning the toss had so consistently chosen to field – but yet again it didn't pay off for us. This time Des Haynes led the way with 131, and with the tail wagging as well we faced a West Indian total of 474. I bowled myself into the ground, sending down forty overs to finish with two for 147. Half-centuries from Gooch and Slack and a fine 90 from David Gower saw us total a semi-respectable 310.

By this time it was well into the fourth day, and if we had no chance of forcing a victory, we at least had hopes of getting a draw and avoiding a series whitewash; but we'd reckoned without the genius of Viv Richards. In just fifty-six balls and eighty-three minutes, Viv hit the fastest Test match century of all time, and I doubt if any batsman in the history of the game has ever played a better innings. He was not out 110 when he declared, setting us an implausible 411 to win or a more possible three and a bit sessions to bat to save the game. Against that West Indian attack it was never likely. At 33 for two overnight, we still had a fighting chance as long as Gooch was at the crease, but when he was out for 51, the innings folded and we lost by 240 runs. It was, I suppose, a fitting end to a tour that had started badly and got worse and then still worse, both on and off the field. In all we won just two out of the fourteen matches we played, and in the Test series our record was another 'blackwash': played five, lost five. Frustratingly for me, I didn't take a wicket in the West Indies' second innings, leaving me poised on 354 Test wickets, one behind Dennis Lillee's all-time record of 355. It was to be some time before I would have the chance to eclipse it.

While the rest of the tour party headed home to the inevitable press autopsy on the tour, Kath and I stayed on in Antigua. Viv had found us a secluded place to stay where we could take a break, safe from press intrusions and the long lenses of the paparazzi. Viv even got a couple of his mates to patrol the grounds to make doubly sure our privacy wasn't breached and I'll always be grateful to him and to Bob Willis for going out of their way to help us and give us time to put our relationship back together. We spent our time walking along the beach, scuba diving and sun-bathing, and just sitting by the pool talking everything through. Finally, several years too late, I began to realise just how lucky I was that Kath was still by my side.

By the end of our time there we were so relaxed that we could even laugh off yet another *News of the World* 'world exclusive', based on fresh allegations by the self-confessed heroin addict who was the wife of a cricket writer. Obviously stirred to action by the Lindy Field story, this fresh 'sex and drugs' story was impressively all-encompassing: I SAW BOTHAM TAKE POT, COCAINE, HEROIN AND PETHIDINE: TEST STAR TOOK THE LOT. When we got home, Kath and I discussed it with Alan Herd and decided that, with all the shit that was flying, a libel case against the *Mail on Sunday* was a risk that we could no longer afford to take. I still wanted to sue them, but if we went to court, a lot of other allegations would be made, the press stories from the Caribbean would be dusted off and given a fresh airing, and a jury might well decide that there could not be that much smoke without a bit of fire somewhere and find against me. It hurt like hell to give in without a fight, but it was time to call off the dogs and drop the case.

As part of the settlement with the *Mail on Sunday*, I had to agree to write an article for them. On 18 May 1986, they ran it as a front-page story. In it, as well as praising the honesty of the newspaper – 'the *Mail on Sunday* is not a paper which prints scandal for the sake of scandal' was the agreed form of words – which rather stuck in my craw, I also had to admit that I had smoked cannabis in the past, though I denied using any other drugs and all the other allegations that had been filling the tabloids over the winter.

I knew that the TCCB would take action against me, even though the article contained nothing new in terms of drugs admissions. I had already said the same things in an interview with Frank Bough – who would soon have drug-taking problems of his own – on breakfast television during the West Indies tour, but it wasn't too great a surprise when I was immediately withdrawn from the squad for the one-day internationals against India while the TCCB mounted a full investigation. This was all the tabloids needed to restart the 'Get Botham' campaign, rehash all the old stories all over again and seek out any old warhorses who might want to pontificate about the sort of punishment that would fit my crimes. Some of my fellow players joined in as well, a couple – hiding behind anonymity – saying I thought I was bigger than the game and deserved my comeuppance. Even the doves were advocating a fine and a one-year ban, and hawks like Denis Compton were demanding that I should be banned for life. Compton then saw John Emburey at Lord's and had a go at him for supporting me, but John just said, 'Ian's been a friend for a long time; you don't turn your back on your friends when the going is tough.'

The disciplinary hearing set for 29 May at Lord's – unusually quick by TCCB standards – went on for a bum-numbing seven hours. Alan Herd spoke on my behalf; the only time I opened my mouth was to correct TCCB secretary Donald Carr on a minor factual error. Finally, the committee retired to decide my punishment – the 'guilty' verdict had never been in doubt. Alan, a colleague and I went to wait in a nearby room. We played cards to pass the time but with one eye on the door to the committee room. I wasn't giving it my full attention, and was down about £375 by the time we were called back in. Donald Carr, looking suitably grave, read out their verdict and the punishment to be imposed. I had been found guilty of bringing the game into disrepute, first by using cannabis; second by admitting it in the *Mail on Sunday* after denying it previously; and third – possibly the most serious crime in the board's eyes – by not clearing the article with the TCCB in advance.

One of the committee had recommended a life ban, another a ban for ten years – effectively the same thing, since I'd be forty by the time the ban was up – but the eventual sentence was that I should be suspended from all cricket until 31 July of that year. I was so annoyed that for a while I gave serious thought to retiring from the game on the spot, but I stopped myself mainly because I thought it was exactly what some of them would have wanted and maybe even have been hoping for. To hell with that; I was damned if I was going to let an unholy alliance of tabloid journalists and a few backwoodsmen from Lord's drive me out of the game. I'd decide, not them, when my time was up and there were a few things I still wanted to do in the game before I was finished.

John Emburey drove me out the back way to avoid the press waiting outside the gates. Kath was waiting for me at the house of some friends, where – surprise, surprise – I started one of my great binges. I was well gone even before we got to the local pub and by the time we got back I was even more plastered than the night Bob Willis had rescued me from the beach bar in Antigua. I don't think I've ever been quite so drunk in my entire life.

The next morning I was woken by Liam.

'Morning Daddy,' he said. 'I had to put you to bed last night.'

I struggled to focus my bloodshot eyes on him. 'Why was that, Liam?'

'Because you were drunk.'

I was not proud of myself. Kath told me later that Liam, just eight at the time, had taken charge and told her, 'You just sit there, Mum, I'll take Dad to bed,' and had then steered me upstairs, taken off my shoes and left me to sleep it off.

Shamefaced, I saw that there was no alternative but to grow up, sober up and take my punishment like a man; but rather than sit around twiddling my thumbs for two months, I decided to do something positive with myself. So I set myself the challenge of learning to fly a helicopter, in three weeks, from a standing start. I did it, and given that I've always been afraid of heights, it probably ranks as one of my prouder achievements.

I almost managed to avoid getting into further hot water with the TCCB before the end of my ban, but perhaps that was a vain hope. When I was asked to be guest speaker at a fund-raising lunch in Manchester, I established beforehand that everything I said in a question-and-answer session would be in confidence. However, some charming person ignored that, smuggled in a tape recorder and caught me on tape describing the England Test selectors as 'gin-slinging dodderers'. The next morning a fresh Botham scandal was brewing as the tabloids splashed the story.

I immediately dashed off a letter of apology to all four selectors – Peter May, A.C. Smith, Phil Sharpe and Fred Titmus – but inevitably I was summoned to the TCCB to explain myself. Raman Subba Row, the chairman of the TCCB, heard me out and then accepted my apologies with no further action necessary, and the way was clear for my return to the Test side ... always providing the gin-slinging dodderers picked me.

After the blackwash in the West Indies, it had been hard to imagine how things could get any worse for the England team during my enforced absence, but somehow they had managed it. They were thrashed by nine wickets in the first one-day international against India and then beaten by five wickets in the first Test at Lord's. Since taking the Ashes the previous summer, England's record now read 'played six, lost six'. David Gower was struggling to exert his authority as captain and had even lost form with the bat – his three innings so far against India had been 0, 18 and 8. The selectors felt that David's laid-back demeanour showed he didn't care that England kept getting beaten. That was absolutely untrue, but it was a stick that had been used to beat David with ever since he started playing the game professionally.

The selectors wanted someone who would wear his heart on his sleeve and give blood for England, and since Mike Gatting had literally done that in the West Indies, they decided to sack David and appoint Gatt in his place. The change made little perceptible difference: although England won the second one-day international at Old Trafford, where David Gower took the man of the match award for a fine knock of 81, they were thrashed at Headingley in the second Test, bowled out for 102 and 128 to lose by 279 runs inside three and a half days, extending the losing streak to seven out of seven.

However, Gatt then played a captain's knock in the third Test at Edgbaston, carrying his bat for 183 not out in an England first innings of 390. India matched that exactly and England slumped to 235 all out in their second innings. With India at 105 for five, Gatt must have been sniffing a famous victory, but Azharuddin and More then shared an unbroken stand of 70 for the sixth wicket and Gatt was probably the more relieved of the two captains when the umpires finally called 'stumps'. The draw at least brought an end to the losing sequence, though India had taken the series 2-0.

The last Test during my ban was the first of the three-match series against New Zealand at Lord's, where batsmen dominated and there was never any chance of a result. I had served my ban, but the selectors were clearly in no mood to recall me until I had demonstrated some form in county cricket, because I was omitted from the side to face New Zealand in the second Test at Trent Bridge.

Some reporters and one or two selectors were already publicly doubting if I would be selected for the Ashes tour that winter, and if I needed any extra motivation, that certainly supplied it. When I walked out to bat in my comeback game against Worcestershire, urged on by Viv Richards – 'Beef, you're the man, now show them you're the man' – I made a century off sixty-five balls, the fastest of the season at that stage, to help Somerset win only their third County Championship game of the season. The following Sunday, Somerset played Northants in a John Player League match. It was one of those occasions when everything went right for me. We were 18 for two when I went in with just twenty-six of the forty overs remaining, but when I left the field unbeaten at the end of our innings I had made 175 not out, including thirteen sixes, a record for the competition.

Meanwhile, England were heading for defeat at Trent Bridge in the second Test. After making 256, they had the Kiwis on the ropes at 144 for five but then let them escape and a century from John Bracewell – a number eight batsman – took them to 413 all out. England's own number eight, John Emburey, then put on a batting show himself, top-scoring with 75, but 230 all out left the Kiwis needing just 74 and they won at a canter by eight wickets.

Gatt had already been pushing for my Test selection and now redoubled his efforts, and after the new England manager, Mickey Stewart, had checked if I was available for the Ashes tour – the answer was a resounding 'Yes' – I was recalled for the final Test at The Oval.

Batsmen I played against during my career often talked half-admiringly, half-scathingly about my 'Golden Arm', or sometimes, less politely, my 'Golden Balls': the ability to take wickets with deliveries that, if anyone else had bowled them, would have disappeared over the rope. My first Test wicket, when Greg Chappell contrived to be bowled by a wide long-hop that he edged on to his stumps, was one example. Bruce Edgar was about to provide another.

Gary Player made a famous comment when accused of being a lucky player: 'You're right, and know what? The more I practice the luckier I get.' I couldn't have used the same retort – everyone knew that there was probably no one in English professional cricket who practised less than I did – but it clearly wasn't all luck; no one who gets three hundred-plus Test wickets does it on luck alone. My own thoughts, for what they were worth, were that my success as a wicket-taker was partly down to my aggressive attitude. I was always looking to take wickets rather than just contain batsmen, and if the price of that was a few more boundaries conceded, I was also more likely to get them out. Mike Hendrick was a very fine seam bowler with a beautiful action who could and did drop the ball on a length all day, but he hated giving runs away.

I loved bowling in tandem with Mike, because he would frustrate the hell out of batsmen and when they got down my end and saw a nice juicy full-pitched delivery they were more likely to have a go at it. I'd happily bowl three away-swinging half-volleys outside off-stump in a row. The batsman might easily hit the first two for four but he might equally get an edge to the third and be out caught in the slips – often by Mike Hendrick, who was not just a fine bowler but a brilliant close catcher as well.

I could always swing the ball as well, but I also think there was a lot in a comment made by the great Australian fast bowler Glenn McGrath, just before his retirement. The gist of what he said was that people obsess too much about pace with fast bowlers. Pace wasn't important, he said; what was important was bounce. McGrath was quick, and because he had such a good clean action, people found it very difficult to pick up his variation in length, but he certainly had the ability to extract unexpected bounce from even the flattest track and I think I also had that knack. It surprised a lot of batsmen and got more than a few of them out.

Conditions at The Oval were just right for me on the first morning with a heavy, overcast atmosphere making the ball swing. Gatt didn't have to think about it when he won the toss and put the Kiwis in. He kept me waiting to bowl and gave Graham Dilley and Gladstone Small first use of the new ball, but the New Zealand openers survived without too many alarms and Gatt then brought me on as first change with the score on 17. For once my first ball, in my first over, in my first match since the ban was no loosener. I was so pumped up that I was determined not to bowl the usual 'floater' and I dug it in short of a length instead. That may have surprised Bruce Edgar; for whatever reason, he was a little late on it, and in trying to fend it off he only succeeded in edging it into Graham Gooch's hands at first slip. He juggled with it, then clung on, and as the crowd erupted and Edgar headed for the pavilion, I turned to where the England selectors were sitting and gave them a double clenched-fist salute. I'd never been so pumped up in my life. As I turned away, Gooch jogged up to me and said, 'Blimey, Beef. Who writes your scripts?'

That wicket not only announced that Beefy was back, it had also taken me level with Dennis Lillee's all-time Test bowling record of 355 Test wickets. I nearly overtook him with the next ball, which the new batsman, Jeff Crowe, edged just wide of John Emburey at third slip, but I didn't have to wait long. In the very next over I trapped Crowe on the back foot right in front of his stumps and the lbw verdict was a formality. As the loudspeakers broadcast the announcement that I was now the most successful bowler in Test match history and the England players and Kiwi opener John Wright offered their congratulations, the crowd went crazy. I'll never forget the ovation they gave me. Although I'd now headed Dennis Lillee's record, however, I never for a moment considered myself a better bowler than him. Dennis was the ultimate bowling machine, the best I've ever seen, and the fact that I'd taken more wickets didn't for a minute fool me into thinking I was his equal with a ball in my hand.

Gower and Gatting both scored hundreds as we declared with only five wickets down and a first innings lead of 101, leaving me on 59 not out with a comeback century there for the taking, though I did have the consolation of having scored one of the fastest fifties in Test history off only thirty-six balls. But there had been too many weather interruptions to achieve a result and the Kiwis only had to face one over in their second innings before the rain returned and the game was abandoned as a draw. We had lost a third successive Test series, but Beefy and England were definitely on the way back.

Chapter 8

THE REEK OF BETRAYAL

My Test career was back in gear, but events occurring at my county, Somerset, during that game left a bitter taste that no amount of passing years could erase. I'd joined Somerset at the same time as Viv Richards and, on Viv's recommendation, Joel Garner had come to the county a couple of years later. Together we had been loyal servants of the county for a decade, and if we'd been reasonably well paid for our efforts, we'd also played a huge part in Somerset's successes and generated a lot of additional income for the club. It wasn't egotism to suggest that the names Botham, Richards and Garner on the team sheet put an awful lot of bums on seats at Taunton and everywhere else we played.

After a century of failure, the county had enjoyed successes during our era that were absolutely unprecedented. That was partly a consequence of the work ethic, will-to-win and tremendous team spirit that had first been fostered under Brian Close and had carried on after his retirement. But success demands more than willpower and hard graft; sometimes you need sheer class and the flair that only a few special players possess, and Viv Richards and Joel Garner possessed those qualities in abundance. They won us countless games with their brilliance with bat and ball respectively, and if they were West Indian by birth, they had become as much part of the fabric of the Somerset side as any native sons. They both deserved the freedom of Taunton for what they'd done for the county.

There had been warning signs all season that all was not well within the club. The once unbreakable team spirit had started to fray around the edges and a few cliques and coteries had begun to form. The trigger for the unrest had been Somerset's attempts to re-sign Martin Crowe, the New Zealand Test batsman who had been our overseas player in 1984 while Viv and Joel were with the West Indies' tour squad in England. Essex had made Crowe an offer for the 1987 season and he had then gone to the Somerset committee to see if they'd go higher. New rules were being introduced from the start of the season, allowing each county just one overseas player. Because of their long service with the county, Somerset could have registered both Viv and Joel for the 1987 season, but if a new overseas player was signed, both of them would have to go.

The players tried to ignore the undercurrents and off-stage manoeuvrings as factions within the committee and the club jockeying for position, but the disharmony in the county showed in our results: after a decade of unparalleled success we were reduced to propping up the table.

If some at the club thought there should be a question mark over Joel, who had already made it clear that he only wanted to play for one more season anyway, there was no such convenient doubt about Viv. He had plenty of gas still in the tank and had already been told by Brian Langford, the Somerset chairman of cricket, that he would be given another one-year contract. When he was summoned to the club on that Friday afternoon, 22 August 1986, he thought he was going to sign that contract. Instead he sat outside Langford's office while Joel was called in and told he was being sacked. Viv went in next and got the same treatment.

My pleasure at breaking the all-time record for Test wickets was rudely shattered by the phone call I received from Viv just after close of play on the Friday. 'Have you heard?' he said.

I was full of myself. 'Heard that I've broken the record for the number of Test wickets? Yes, I've heard that one.' My smile faded as I realised the seriousness in his voice.

'Ian, listen, man. Joel and I have been sacked.'

'What?'

He had to repeat it; I couldn't take it in the first time. By the time he'd finished telling me what had happened I was white with rage, and in a bizarre reversal of roles, Viv finished up trying to calm me down. 'This isn't your fight, man. You don't have to sacrifice yourself for our cause. You've got to go on and there's no point in being side-tracked over something that doesn't directly concern you.'

It was typical of Viv to have said that, but he and I had been friends for a long, long time. When I'd been in trouble, not least on the last tour of the West Indies, he'd gone out of his way to help me. He'd stood up and been counted on more than one occasion when people willing to admit to being friends of Ian Botham were pretty thin on the ground. There was no way in the world that I was going to turn my back on him now.

'The hell it doesn't,' I said. 'If you're out, I'm going too.' Even if Somerset were ultimately forced to retract and reinstate Viv and Joel, I had decided in that moment that I was never going to play for the county again. I value loyalty above almost anything and I was not going to continue playing for a county that had shown such disloyalty to two of its finest servants. It reeked of betrayal, and I would neither forgive nor forget it.

Brian Langford had been the man to pull the trigger, but I had no doubt that Peter Roebuck, my successor as county captain, was the man behind the coup. He wanted a young side that he could mould in his image, and getting rid of Viv and Joel was an essential part of that plan. I'm sure he would have liked to get rid of me too, but the club officials would not have worn that; they knew that they could not afford to get rid of all their big draw cards at once, or it would have an impact on revenue and season-ticket sales.

Friday 26 October, 1985, John O'Groats – the start of a lifetime of charity walking. The smile was soon wiped off my face when I discovered the agony of blisters and shin splints.

The Leukaemia walk caught the imagination of the nation and attracted many guest walkers and well-wishers – of all shapes and guises.

© Getty Images

Never work with children or animals. The 1988 Hannibal charity walk was dogged by animal rights protests and European red tape. But what a time the elephants had!

Elton John and Eric Clapton were both huge cricket fanatics and followed every game. Elton even DJ'd for us between games on the 1986/87 Ashes Tour down under; while Eric once played an impromptu set at my Worcestershire local.

Below: Me sporting a Queensland cricket hat muc to the amusement of Allan Border and Greg Ritchie. I played a season for Queensland in 1987 and gre to love Australia as a place. I was always something of a *b noire* for Aussie teams, but tl also grudgingly respected an identified with my 'almost Australian' competitive natu

Above: Me telling Mike Gatting 'exactly how we won that one', with Phil DeFreitas looking on amused. We'd just triumphed in the Brisbane test in November 1986.

I had an occasionally fractious relationship with the press during my cricketing career. Here, the towel wrapped round my face is my personal protest, showing I've got nothing to say to them following the fourth day of the Headingly Test.

At other times, though, such as at the Sports Aid charity match involving West Indies vs. Rest of the World at Edgbaston, 1986, I was able to put my media profile to good use. Imran Khan sits beside me at the press conference.

Above: Receiving an early award from the Lord's Taverners in 1977 along with Paul Downton and Mike Brearley. Brears was a great captain and man-manager and one of the most astute observers of the game I know.

Right: Enjoying a glass of New Zealand wine with Graham Gooch after the Second Test in Auckland, 1992.

My great mate Allan Lamb and I enjoying net practice (if such a thing is possible!) in Sydney during the 1992 World Cup.

Robin Smith and I share a laugh as an Australian streaker takes to the pitch at Old Trafford during the fourth Cornhill Test in 1989. It was the start of a very long Ashes losing streak for England.

Pure joy at overtaking Dennis Lillee's record number of Test wickets. It was against New Zealand at the Oval, 1986, and all the sweeter for being on my return to Test cricket. Beefy was back.

My final professional innings was for Durham against Australia. I ended on 32, caught off Steve Waugh's occasional medium pace. I left the ground without a clue what I was going to do next.

© PA Photos

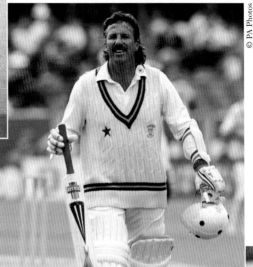

laugh with my best mate Sir vien Richards in a County hampionship match between urham and Glamorgan.

The charity work never ends. Here I am accepting a cheque from some Welsh school children for the Noah's Ark Appeal in 2002, and later flanked by two grown-up Welsh school girls Charlotte Church and Catherine Zeta-Jones supporting the same cause.

If you thought the mullet was bad, how about the mohawk? Getting my head shaved for charity on the pitch during a one-day international between England and New Zealand in Wellington, 1997.

Coming face to face with the Beefy of old outside Downing Street as I added my weight to a St George's Day campaign in 2005.

My long stint as a team captain on *Question of Sport*, opposite Bill Beaumont, gave me the opportunity to meet many great performers from other sports.

ILL CARLING　　SALLY GUNNELL

I've twice been honoured at the BBC Sports Personality of the Year Awards – once in 1981 and then in 2004 when I received a Lifetime Achievement Award. Here I am presenting Andrew Flintoff with the Sports Personality of the Year Award for 2005.

I now tour just as hard as I ever did, but as part of the Sky Sports commentary team.

On holiday with Mum and Dad.
Mum is still my biggest fan, but sadly
Dad died a couple of years ago.

Below: Kath and me at Buckingham
Palace after I was awarded an OBE. It
was one of the best moments of my life
… until the knighthood came along.

Above: Receiving an
honorary degree with
Kath at UMIST
university. I later added
to it with another from
the University of
Chester.

Viv could have scored more runs than Roebuck batting left-handed in a blindfold, but he had felt throughout the season that the ground was shifting beneath him. The younger players were easily convinced by Roebuck that Viv and Joel no longer cared about Somerset; some of them were even supporting the sackings because it improved their chances of first team cricket.

Yet Viv led by example, and if Somerset were not winning there were others, not least the captain, who should have carried the can, not the greatest batsman who had ever played for the county. He was a big match player but he delivered on the smaller stages too, and he was an inspirational figure on the field and in the dressing room. If some young players weren't interested in learning from a master of the game, they were the ones who should have been shown the door. If they weren't yet good enough and determined enough to fight their way into the team alongside Viv and Joel, then they should have been honing their skills in the Second XI, or joining the dole queue themselves.

I waited with mounting impatience while the Oval Test meandered to its conclusion – and I wondered just how coincidental it was that the sackings had occurred while I was safely out of the way on Test-match duty – but as soon as I returned to Somerset, I called my teammates and the club officials together. 'As things stand, you've left me no option,' I said. 'I'm shocked at what has been done and I'm resigning.'

For some reason they thought I was bluffing; after a bit of a stand-off, life would carry on as before. They obviously didn't know me very well. The dismissals were still not public knowledge, but the signs were there for those who cared to look. When Roebuck ordered the groundsman at Taunton to shave the pitch for the game against Surrey, Viv accused him in public of being afraid to face Sylvester Clark on a fast wicket. A few days later, Roebuck went round to Viv's house to talk things over 'man to man'. He threw Roebuck out.

Even when news of the sackings got out, Viv, Joel and I tried to carry on playing as if nothing had changed – and Viv gave the committee and the Taunton faithful a swift reminder of what they would soon be missing with innings of 53 and 94 in the next game against Essex. It was his last game for the club; neither he nor Joel featured in the remaining three championship matches. I went one better in the penultimate game at Old Trafford and scored 139, and perhaps as I was still scoring runs and taking wickets and giving no outward sign of any change, the club officials might still have thought I was bluffing as we went into our last championship match against Derbyshire at Taunton. It wasn't a glorious farewell – the first two days were washed out by rain, reducing the game to a one-innings match, and I scored 36 and took none for 48 as we went down to defeat by three wickets – but when I waved to all four corners of the ground on being given out before returning to the Taunton dressing room for the last time as a Somerset player, even the most obtuse committee man must finally have got the message. The public certainly did.

Viv and Joel had taken their sackings with great dignity – or perhaps they were both still in shock. In response, I hung a sheet of paper on Roebuck's peg in the dressing room. It contained only one word: 'Judas'. I would do the same now. Whatever success Roebuck had had was the result of being a member of a successful side, built around the professionalism, flair and star quality of Viv Richards and Joel Garner, yet he was quite happy to desert them in pursuit of his aims.

Such was my fury with him that I could quite happily have watched him drowning in the river behind the Taunton ground without feeling any need to pull him out, but the only emotion he inspires in me now is pity. He wanted to be a great captain but he couldn't inspire his own teammates, let alone frighten the opposition. He was aloof and distant when his team needed encouragement and active involvement, and he certainly couldn't lead by example because he wasn't a good enough player for that. His time as captain of Somerset was one of continuing failure. Somerset were back in the comfort zone, and no one was more comfortable than the opposition playing against them. The man brought in to replace Viv and Joel, Martin Crowe, could not step into their shoes. He lasted only one full season – not a happy one for him or Somerset – and just four matches of the next before a back injury forced him to quit. That was the last anyone saw of him at Taunton.

I never wanted to leave Somerset. The club had been a huge part of my life, I'd been a member of a great team and it meant an awful lot to me. Our outstanding success during the years I spent there was built on team spirit. We were from differing backgrounds – a few local lads, a couple of public school boys, two or three gnarled old pros, and Viv and Joel. It was a strange mixture, but our individual talents and personal ambitions were harnessed to a collective will to succeed. Closey taught us to be winners, and that spirit survived his retirement. The criticism in the dressing room could be fierce but it was always constructive, and we were mates on and off the field. During that great decade, we performed at the highest levels, became feared opponents for anyone, and won trophies. Now it was all over and Somerset was on course to return to mediocrity.

I was away on the Ashes tour when a special meeting was held at the Bath and West Showground to debate a vote of no confidence in the Somerset committee. The result was close but it went with the committee, though seven members then resigned. Nigel Popplewell had been expected to be a supporter of Viv and Joel. A fellow player, he had shared success with them and been to their houses as a guest and a friend, but when he spoke at the meeting he turned on them, accusing them of a 'lack of commitment'. It was a staggering attack on those he had called his friends and I think it hurt Viv and Joel more than anything else, just because it was so unexpected. We all knew what Roebuck was like, but Popplewell had shown no previous sign of dislike of or disloyalty to Viv and Joel and he has still never explained the reasons why he acted as he did.

Viv and I would never be teammates again but we would still be Test-match rivals, and though we were the best of friends off the field, we were both such super-competitive players that we were ferocious rivals out in the middle. There was no wicket I was more pleased to get than Viv's and there was no one that he hated getting out to more than me. But the fierce rivalry ended at the boundary edge. However competitive we might be during a game, we could always enjoy a laugh and a beer together after close of play.

In one game I got Viv out lbw to a very dodgy decision. I only appealed in a half-hearted sort of way and I was as surprised as Viv, though rather more pleased, when the umpire, Barry Meyer, gave him out. Barry later admitted that he realised he'd cocked it up and would have called Viv back if he hadn't already been well on his way to the pavilion. I could tell from the set of Viv's shoulders as he walked off that he wasn't exactly thrilled about it, and when I nipped into the West Indies' changing room to commiserate with him at close of play, he was still furious with me. He looked like he was going to chin me, but when I winked and said, 'Tsk, tsk, shocking!' he burst out laughing instead.

It would take more than the parting of the ways at Somerset to end our friendship. Our careers had run in parallel from the day we'd met. We'd progressed from unknown 'promising newcomers' in the Somerset dressing room to two of the leading players in the world game. We'd roomed together on the county circuit for a decade and knew each other inside out. Kath often said, only half-joking, that I'd spent more of our married life with Viv than I had with her, and certainly shared more confidences with him. She was probably right. If I had a problem with my cricket, it was hard to find someone to talk to about it, but because we were friends from way back, were playing at the same level and knew the pressures that could bring, we could always lend a sympathetic ear to each other and talk things over.

I knew that Viv would never bullshit me or say what he thought I wanted to hear. If I asked his opinion I'd get it: no frills, no flannel, just straight talk. He was unflinchingly honest in everything he did and said, and it did make him a few enemies along the way because not everyone wants to hear the plain, unvarnished truth, but that was his nature and he was not going to change it for anyone. We're similar in many ways. He's very dogmatic – and I should know. When he has made up his mind about something there is no changing it, come what may. I can go a year without seeing him, and he's hopeless with phones – I think he sends messages by carrier pigeon – but whenever we do meet, we pick up exactly where we left off the last time. He's godfather to Liam and their bond was so close that when I took Liam to the cricket with me he used to spend more time in the Somerset dressing room than I did, and whenever we played the West Indies he'd be in their dressing room, not England's, chatting to Viv.

Viv and I are more like brothers than friends; each of us would drop everything to help the other one out, if he needed it. We've only ever had one scrap, in a hotel room in Kuala Lumpur, of all places. A combination of fatigue and too much alcohol led us to fall out over a friend of mine, who was only trying to be funny, but Viv didn't see it that way. We almost came to blows that night, but when we met up the next morning we just burst out laughing and carried on as normal.

Viv had great natural ability, but so do many people who never reach the heights that they are capable of. Viv's talent was allied to an iron will and complete self-belief. He was also a man of high principle and great courage, and he'd stand up for himself and others, whatever the circumstances. There were racist morons at a few cricket grounds on the county circuit, the worst being in Yorkshire for some reason. He got a barrage of abuse from them in his first season with Somerset and the memory stayed with him. He scored a double century against Yorkshire in the first innings of a game at Harrogate, and when a travelling supporter of Somerset stood up to applaud Viv in, he was doused in beer by the cretins standing behind him. In the second innings, Viv pulled a hamstring, and as he limped back to the pavilion one of the Yorkshire morons shouted, 'Get a move on, you black bastard!' at him. Viv went straight over to where the culprit was sitting among a group of like-minded morons and challenged him to stand up and show himself, but the yob didn't have the guts for that. If he had, Viv would probably have flattened him and finished up on a disrepute charge from the TCCB.

The same sort of incident did happen at other county grounds, once even at Weston-Super-Mare, where Viv, Joel and I sorted out half a dozen drunks who were shouting racist insults. But Yorkshire had – and deserved – a reputation as the worst hotbed of racist so-called fans. It was something the Yorkshire committee should have dealt with years before, but they preferred to ignore it.

I was the son of Yorkshire parents and proud to live in the county, but I was shocked and disgusted by the intolerance and racism of some of my fellow Yorkshiremen, and after one match I spoke out about it. Instead of promising action, a Yorkshire committee man made a complaint to the TCCB about my comments. Luckily some more civilised and sensible Yorkshire committee men made him withdraw it. I hope that the selection of Yorkshire-born players of Asian descent signals the final extinction of a blight that has marred the county's reputation for many years.

Viv's been a fine friend to me and the family and I have nothing but admiration for him. It would not surprise me to see him going into Antiguan politics. He has strong beliefs and ideas, wants to do things for the island, and knowing the man as I do, the Antiguans could do a lot worse. And time has a way of healing wounds. Despite the acrimony of our parting from the club, Viv, Joel and I are now all honorary members of Somerset and proud of it, and one of the stands at the Taunton ground is even named after a certain England all-rounder who used to play there.

Chapter 9

CAN'T BAT, CAN'T BOWL, CAN'T FIELD

After all the problems and controversies of the preceding years, the Ashes tour to Australia in 1986–87 put me back on track. Both the England captain, Mike Gatting, and the manager, Mickey Stewart, sought me out before the tour and told me that as far as they were concerned, bygones were bygones and I started under them with a clean slate. They weren't expecting any trouble from me or because of me, and I was in full agreement with that. I'd already decided that I was not going to tour again without Kath by my side. The cost of flying her and the kids to Australia and accommodating them for the entire four-month tour was pretty eye-watering but it was a price well worth paying for the happiness and peace of mind that it brought me. My teammates saw and commented on how relaxed I was on that tour and that helped me make a real contribution to England's Ashes campaign.

I wasn't the only one who was relaxed. It was one of the happiest and most enjoyable tours I'd been on, and Gatt deserves a lot of credit for that. If hard work was needed, he wasn't afraid to ask for it, but for the most part he was content to let his senior pros choose their own workload in training and practice. We were all experienced professionals and Gatt reckoned that we knew better than anyone when we needed to step up the training or put in an extra session of bowling practice, and when we were in good shape and could take our foot off the gas. So he left us to keep ourselves in shape and in form, and it paid off in team spirit and results.

Kath and I made our own contribution to team spirit. She was with me for the whole tour and at each of our hotels I upgraded our room to a suite – at my expense – so that we could make sure we had some space and privacy from the media, and we held open house there every day for the rest of the squad, so that the suite effectively became the team room. Since one of the contracts I had at the time was with Lindemans, which always sent two or three cases of wine to each hotel for me, the players, wives and their friends were able to head up to our suite, drink some wine and relax without worrying about press and photographers catching us unawares.

We did not exactly get off to a flying start on the tour, losing the opening match to Queensland by five wickets, beating South Australia by the same margin and then hanging on for a draw against Western Australia, prompting Martin Johnson's famous lament in the *Independent* that there were 'only three things wrong with this team. They can't bat, they can't bowl and they can't field.' It was hard to argue with that assessment, but I had started in good batting form with scores of 86, 70, 48 and 40, and whatever our on-field troubles, off the field we could certainly party ... which, come to think of it, might have been part of the problem. The night before the game with Western Australia, a special match to mark Australia's defence of the America's Cup, a group of us were asked to a party in Fremantle with the British White Crusader team. It developed into a pretty big night and I had to be carried to the limousine for the trip back to our hotel. I woke up the next morning with one of the biggest hangovers of my life ... again.

David Gower had also had a big night. He managed to scrounge a lift back to the hotel with an Aussie who was only a little less drunk than David himself, and as they left Fremantle, he went through a 'Stop' sign without doing exactly what it said on the tin and was promptly flagged down by a police patrol car. The driver was thinking he'd waved goodbye to his licence and David was trying to make himself as unobtrusive as possible in the back seat – not easy with his distinctive blond curls – praying he wouldn't be spotted in case the tabloids got hold of the story. However, the driver jumped out and said to the policeman, 'You'll never guess who I've got in the back of my car.' To the relief of both parties the cop was a cricket fan, and having got David's autograph he waved them off into the night without issuing a ticket or reaching for the breathalyser.

I was still suffering badly when I got to the WACA ground the next morning and the thought of trying to run around in the broiling heat of a Perth scorcher did not appeal greatly to me. I plunged my head into a basin of cold water and ice to try and revive myself and I was so dehydrated that I even drank some of it. It didn't help much, nor did Mike Gatting's luck with the toss, which meant that if we lost any early wickets I'd be staggering out to bat before very much longer … but at least I didn't have to field.

Luckily the physio, Lawrie Brown, recognised my symptoms and with a nudge and a wink to me he told Mickey Stewart that I needed some intensive physio on a sore ankle. He then took me to a quiet and mercifully dark back room where he plied me with fluids and aspirins and walked me round the room to try and get the circulation going. Many of my teammates were in little better shape and my circuits of the room were punctuated by the sound of tumbling wickets outside.

Every now and again Mickey or Mike stuck their heads round the door to ask how the treatment on my ankle was going and whether I'd be able to bat soon. Each time Lawrie was able to put them off, but finally even that resourceful man had completely run out of excuses and I had to leave my cool and shady refuge and go out to face high noon at the WACA.

I'd originally been down at number five in the batting order, but Lawrie's manoeuvrings had managed to defer the awful moment for me until the fall of the sixth wicket. The score was 69 for six – I couldn't actually read the scoreboard but Gatt told me what it said – and my one consolation as I stumbled out of the dressing room was that, even if I was out for a golden duck, I'd scarcely stand out among the catalogue of England batting failures that morning.

To my surprise I didn't fall down the pavilion steps and was even able to walk an approximately straight line as I crossed the boundary rope and headed for the middle. I was starting to feel quite proud of myself until I felt a hand on my shoulder. I jumped a few feet in the air and turned round to see who it was. Our twelfth man was standing there with a curious expression on his face. 'Erm ... Beefy ... I think you might need this.' I looked down; I was empty-handed and he was holding my bat.

Mike Gatting was the not-out batsman at the other end and I avoided catching his eye as I made my way to the wicket like a French aristocrat on his way to the guillotine. In the hope of making contact with at least one delivery before I was out, I devised a *Blackadder*-style cunning plan: of the three balls coming at me, I would try to hit the middle one. Surprisingly, the plan worked, and I'd made 48 from thirty-eight balls before I finally chose the wrong ball and was out. As I meandered back to the pavilion, I had to wonder if my up and down batting form of recent years might have been because I hadn't been drinking enough ...

Once the serious cricket started, professional responsibility put an end to the wild nights, though our suite continued to be used as a players' lounge where we could all relax after a day's play, safe from press intrusions, paparazzi and cricket bores, and have a few beers with people we could trust. Elton John was out there to watch a couple of Tests and he often came up and played the role of disc jockey – we christened him 'EJ the DJ' as a result. I really valued his company and it was great to be able to talk things over with a man whose experiences at the hands of the media made mine seem like a Sunday School picnic. He was a true friend to Kath and me and he even baby-sat the kids for us so that we could go out for a candlelit dinner for two together. The kids loved him – the fact that he fed them copious quantities of jelly and ice cream and read them stories probably helped – and he even tucked them up in bed.

Like any England cricketer, I always revelled in an Ashes series, and beating Australia was as good as it got for me. I always felt that I was more Australian than the Australians in the way I approached the game – ruthless on the field, but good mates in the bar afterwards – but I drew the line at 'sledging' – vilifying opposition players in an attempt to put them off their game.

First under Ian Chappell and then Allan Border, Australia's sledging had grown so vicious and so widespread that it was in danger of destroying the friendly relations between opponents that was one of cricket's most cherished characteristics. I'd certainly had my share of free and frank 'exchanges of views' with opponents in my time, but there's a world of difference between letting rip in the heat of the moment and a cold, calculated campaign to intimidate and unsettle opponents. Under Allan Border's leadership it had got completely out of control, and I was horrified by it.

After the pounding the Aussies had taken from us last time around, they needed a good start to the series, but we got the drop on them in the first Test at the Gabba in Brisbane. Allan Border won the toss and put us in, but his bowlers couldn't take advantage of the early help in the wicket and we piled up a big first innings score. I scored 138, including thirteen fours and four sixes, and was belting the ball to all corners of the Gabba, including 22 from one over bowled by the new Aussie fast bowler Merv Hughes. I shared a century stand with David Gower who came down the wicket at one point and said, 'I should be telling you to calm down, but I'm having much too much fun myself.' After he was out, I found another good partner in Phil DeFreitas. He was batting at number nine and Allan

Border kept setting fields to give me a single, thinking that his bowlers could then get to work on Phil, but I knew that he could play and was happy to take the offered singles. The scoreboard kept ticking along and we added 92 together before I – not Phil – was out. We eventually totalled 456, with Phil scoring a valuable 40.

At close of play Merv Hughes came up to me and said, 'G'day Ian, remember me?'

I looked at him – and with his big moustache and Desperate Dan chin, Merv was a pretty distinctive-looking guy – and I said, 'No, I don't think we've ever met before.'

'Yeah we have,' he said. 'Ten years ago in Melbourne when I was a kid, I came up to you and said, "G'day Mr Botham, I want to be a quick bowler. Got any advice for me?" and you said, "The best advice I can give you is to take up tennis or golf instead."' He fixed me with the trademark Merv Hughes stare and said, 'What do you reckon now?'

'Know what, Merv?' I said. 'Considering I've just been smashing you all over the Gabba, I'd say it was pretty good advice, wouldn't you?' For a moment it looked as if he was going to take a swing at me, but then he burst out laughing, slapped me on the back and bought me a beer instead.

Graham Dilley took five wickets as the Aussies were all out for 248 – nine short of avoiding the follow-on. John Emburey did the damage in the second innings with five for 80, and set only 75 to win, we cruised to victory by seven wickets. I took the Man of the Match award in Brisbane but was brought down to earth with a bump in Perth where I was out for a duck. However, big centuries from Chris Broad and David Gower and a rare century from Jack Richards took us to a massive 592 for eight declared. This time Australia just avoided the follow-on by nine runs and we ran out of time to force the win, but it was a moral victory.

While bowling during their second innings I tore an intercostal muscle and had to leave the field mid-over. Lawrie Brown, the England physio, took a look at it and said, 'It's going to be a long time healing and it's going to hurt.' When I sneezed a few minutes later, I saw what he meant. It was absolute agony, the most painful injury I ever had. Lawrie set me a punishing schedule to speed my recovery and gave up huge amounts of his time to help me through it. Kath had flown out to be with me, but I saw more of Lawrie than I did of her, going for treatment six times a day and exercising in the swimming pool in between. Lawrie always made a point of giving me one final dose of treatment every evening after he'd finished with the other players and, a true Scot, he always had a dram and poured one for me too. I did once ask him for a drop of water with it but he gave me a pitying look and said, 'Nay lad, it's got enough water in it already.'

Despite our best efforts, I missed the next Test in Adelaide with my injury, where Australia had the better of another high-scoring draw, but I was back for the traditional Boxing Day Test in Melbourne, though I was nowhere near fully fit. I probably shouldn't have played – I couldn't bowl above half-pace – but the Aussies didn't know that and a bit of kidology saw me through. After Gatt won the toss and put Australia in, Gladstone Small and I – even at half-pace – took full advantage of some helpful conditions to take five wickets each as they collapsed to 141 all out. Chris Broad then hit his third hundred in successive Tests to anchor the England innings of 349 all out. Needing 208 to make us bat again, the Aussies fell 14 short, with Phil Edmonds and John Emburey wrapping up the tail.

Our crushing innings victory ensured that we retained the Ashes, and the party in the team suite at the hotel got going straight away. EJ the DJ was there to play some music, we ordered up plenty of food from room service, and Lindemans sent us some extra cases of wine, which was a very generous gesture from an Australian company after we'd just hammered their team. Nine-year-old Liam and seven-year-old Sarah were pressed into service as waiters, which created its own problems. Chris Broad came up to me after the party had been going a while and said, 'Beefy, I think you need to take a look at your son.' When I did so, I discovered that, egged on by a couple of the younger players, Liam had decided to join in the celebrations himself and was now a little worse for wear. I had to take him off to the bathroom and give him the cold shower treatment – Liam's first experience of a technique that had sorted out his father on more than one previous occasion. The next morning, showing no more ill effects than his father, Liam demolished a large cooked breakfast.

With the Ashes and the series already in the bag, we perhaps let our guard drop a little in the final Test in Sydney where Dean Jones scored a brilliant 184 not out in Australia's first innings total of 343. We got off to a bad start for the first time in the series and trailed by 68. Set 320 to win, wickets fell at regular intervals and a certain Ian Botham did not help the cause by getting out for a duck. We were still in with a shout while Gatt was at the crease, but when he fell caught and bowled to Steve Waugh for 96, the task was beyond us and we fell short by 55 runs. The Aussies had saved some face, but we had the Ashes. It completed a clean sweep – we also won the America's Cup Challenge competition and the one-day series against Australia – and Mike Gatting deserved the lion's share of the plaudits because he captained us brilliantly, did not miss a trick in the field, and his man-management was spot on.

Back in Britain, I'd found myself a new day job. I had quit Somerset at the end of the previous domestic season but, as it turned out, I was not out of work for long and signed for Worcestershire for the 1987 season. I already had links with the county through their chairman, Duncan Fearnley, who had furnished me with my bats ever since I left the Lord's ground staff. I knew him and trusted him, and though a number of other counties were chasing me, I was very happy to shake hands on a deal with him. The Carphone group were sponsoring me and Graham Dilley, who moved to New Road at the same time, and the double signing proved good business for them and for Worcestershire, where applications for membership rose by 100 per cent. There was such demand for tickets for our opening game of the season that the club had to erect temporary grandstands to accommodate all the people who wanted to be there.

I was keen to avoid tabloid hacks camping on my doorstep if possible, and as part of the deal with Worcestershire they had undertaken to find me a house in the back of beyond. They were as good as their word, sorting me out with a rambling old farmhouse in deepest, darkest rural Worcestershire. It was so far off the beaten track that I had to go back twice for improved directions before I actually managed to find it, but as far as I was concerned that just made it an even more desirable residence; if I couldn't find it, what chance did the tabloid reptiles have? The approach was through an orchard full of gnarled, ancient apple, pear and cherry trees, and a salmon river, the Teme, meandered through the bottom of the valley a hundred yards away. I was in my element there, and it was also a great place for parties. All the Worcester boys would come for a barbecue and we'd drive golf balls off the lawn, trying to land one in the river.

I was joining a club that was a similar type of county to Somerset, with a homely, almost family atmosphere, but it was also full of hope for the future with a core of very good players like Tim Curtis, Graeme Hick, Richard Illingworth, Phil Newport and Steve Rhodes. Phil Neale was also a very astute captain and a great motivator of his players.

Worcestershire's ground, New Road, was also one of the most beautiful settings for cricket, with the cathedral rising majestically beyond the tree-lined banks of the River Severn. On the cathedral side was a beautiful copper beech planted to commemorate Don Kenyon, who led the county to its first ever championship in 1964, and then repeated the feat the following year – the club's centenary. Among the chestnut trees on the other side there was a rare black pear – the club's crest is three black pears. Whenever cricket-lovers start arguing about the perfect ground, New Road is always one of the first to be mentioned, and the cakes and scones produced from the Ladies Pavilion weren't bad either. I was so keen to do well for my new county that during a spell when I was not getting as many runs as I thought I should, I actually spent two days in the nets. I could not have found a better place to land on my feet. I had a great set of teammates, I was living in a beautiful old house, and the local pubs and the fishing were both excellent too.

Worcestershire were being talked up as hot favourites for the championship that year, but because of Test calls and injuries, Graham Dilley and I missed a lot of matches and the one-day competitions became our best chance of a trophy that first season. How I enjoyed myself in the Sunday League. The rib injury that had kept me out of the Adelaide Test in Australia kept flaring up again, and with my back problems as well I was never able to bowl flat out, but I turned myself into a poor man's Tom Cartwright and bowled such a miserly line and length that the lads even took to calling me 'Tommy'.

In the Sunday League I took to opening the batting with Tim Curtis and we formed a hugely successful partnership, racking up a stream of century stands. I claimed that he only outscored me because he'd been to university where they'd taught him to count to six so that he could pinch the strike off the last ball of an over. When we beat Northants by nine wickets in the last game, the title was ours. It was the first of several trophies in the time I spent at Worcestershire. We were a good side and a very happy one, and after the traumas of my last years at Somerset, it became a pleasure just to play the game again ... though it was even more pleasant that we were a winning side as well.

The summer Test series against Pakistan was less enjoyable. Although I was out in single figures only twice, I threw away a series of good starts and my highest score was only 51 not out. My pleasure at passing the milestone of five thousand Test runs in the final Test at The Oval was also diminished by the series result. The first two Tests were rain-ruined draws, but we then lost the third at Headingley by an innings. We were tantalisingly close to a victory at Edgbaston that would have levelled the series, but needing 124 for victory in eighteen overs, we suffered three run-outs in rapid succession and were 109 for seven from 17.4 overs when we were forced to settle for the draw. Pakistan only needed to draw the last Test at The Oval to take the series, and after they won the toss on a real featherbed of a wicket, Javed Miandad scored 260 as they batted for two and a half days to total 708 and kill the game. We collapsed to 232 all out, but following on we batted out time quite comfortably, finishing on 315 for four with Gatt and I sharing an unbroken century stand.

I found a new way of spending the winter that year. I'd always wanted to play in the Australian Sheffield Shield – the toughest domestic competition in world cricket – and after discussing the situation with Allan Border, I opted out of the England tour to India that winter and joined Queensland for the Australian season. I was looking forward to playing Sheffield Shield cricket, and it turned out to be fantastic, really tough and uncompromising, but hugely enjoyable too. After England's Ashes success, my signing created a big stir, and Queensland had a surge of membership applications and greatly increased gates. The downside for me was, once more, the media. Taking a leaf from the book of their English counterparts, a number of Australian tabloid journalists set out to 'get Botham' and one or two members of Queensland who had opposed signing me went out of their way to help them nail me.

When I cleared customs and walked into the arrivals hall at Brisbane Airport I was met by a barrage of photographers' flashguns and a mob of journalists and had to stage an impromptu press conference before I could even leave the airport. If I was not already aware that my signing by Queensland was a very big story, it was confirmed by the fact that, while chasing me through the arrivals hall, the press pack completely ignored Lindy Chamberlain, the defendant in the notorious 'dingo baby' trial, who was in the airport at the same time.

Queensland was the only state in the competition never to have won the Sheffield Shield since its inauguration way back in 1892. Every year the supporters would dream about that elusive first title and every year they were disappointed, but this time things really did look as if they were going to be different. We were top of the table going into the final rounds of matches, but with this burden of history and expectation to carry, the tension was escalating fast, and our captain, Allan Border, was almost permanently sunk in one of the black moods to which he was prone. Far from just being happy to see us in contention, some of the Queensland committee members were also keeping up the sniping from the sidelines and complaining that I was acting as if I was the sole reason for our success.

It was a disgraceful slur, but I tried to ignore it and concentrate on the cricket as we went 'on the road' for our last couple of games. First we flew to Launceston to play Tasmania. We were hot favourites, but after being dropped at slip by Border off the third ball of the match, Tasmanian opener David Boon went on to score a century in each innings and we slid to a shock defeat by 94 runs. Dennis Lillee was playing for Tasmania that season and he came into our dressing room afterwards to help us drown our sorrows. After a few beers, the two of us had an impromptu competition, tossing empty stubbies (beer bottles) at a target chalked on the wall, while our teammates took bets on the result. The Launceston ground authorities then slapped a huge bill on us, claiming that we had completely wrecked the dressing room. That was rubbish. We'd certainly broken a few bottles but nothing more than that, and the Launceston dressing room was a cross between a dungeon and a toilet anyway. It was about to be demolished and replaced, and as

Dennis said, 'You could have driven two steamrollers through the place and ended up with a smaller bill than we did.' We paid it anyway, but when the news got back to Queensland, it provided fresh ammunition for the Botham detractors on the committee.

We were still in with a great chance of the title, and if we could beat Victoria in our next match it would guarantee us home advantage in the final. His moods growing filthier by the day, Allan Border tried to ensure that we did so by imposing a curfew and an alcohol ban on the team as we arrived in Melbourne. I don't know what the rest of the team said, but when he told me this, I just laughed and said, 'Forget it. If I don't have a drink, I can't get to sleep, and if I don't sleep, I'll be no good for the team.' I saw no reason to alter a personal regime that had stood me in perfectly good stead over the years, and had done so all season for Queensland as well, but my defiance caused a serious fall-out with 'AB'. The Queensland coach, Greg Chappell, was soon on my case as well, wanting to know why I wasn't attending nets. I hadn't been doing so for ten years so why he would have expected me to start now, I don't know. It all contributed to a growing feeling that if Queensland did fall at the final hurdle, the team's expensive Pommie import was being set up to be the scapegoat.

The match against Victoria saw another defeat. We were on the back foot throughout, with Allan Border's decision to field backfiring on us, and my back injury worsening so much that I was unable to bowl at all in Victoria's second innings. On the last day we were set a near-impossible target of 376 off sixty-four overs and fell short by the whopping margin of 207 runs. I also found myself hauled up before the Australian Cricket Board and fined five hundred dollars for swearing. Pom-baiting is practically the national sport in Australia, but a group of half a dozen morons in the Melbourne crowd went well beyond the norm. I like a bit of banter from a crowd – it gees me up – but this was just mindless, vicious, foul-mouthed, personal abuse. I put up with it for a while, but in the lunch interval

I complained to the umpires, the ground authorities and the police about it. Nothing was done, and the more drink the morons took on board the louder and the worse the abuse got.

With about fifteen minutes to go, I snapped, walked over to the boundary edge and gave them a mouthful back. When I was summoned to appear before the Australian Cricket Board, I told them, 'The ground authorities and the police had all day to do something about it and just sat on their hands. I put up with it for hours and yet as soon as I open my mouth, I'm up on a disrepute charge?'

The chairman of the ACB said, 'But the point is that you shouldn't have sworn at them.'

'I accept that entirely,' I said. 'I was in the wrong, but what about the ground authorities, don't they have a duty to the players and the cricketing public not to allow cretins like that to mouth off with impunity? They should have controlled their own back yard.' They smiled, nodded and fined me anyway, though they did tell me that, had I not been provoked by the crowd, the fine would have been higher.

After two successive defeats, we had now lost home advantage in the Sheffield Shield final, and Western Australia, who now led the table, hosted the final in Perth. If we could win, we would all be given the freedom of Queensland, but it was a big ask, because as the current holders of the title, WA only needed a draw to retain it.

Another defeat had not done anything for Border's sour state of mind, and as we flew to Perth, he and Greg Ritchie started a furious argument. We'd barely taken off when Ritchie began complaining to Allan about being dropped from the Aussie Test team for being unfit and overweight. 'Listen Greg,' Allan said, 'you've got to stop moaning about it and take a good, hard look at yourself instead. You're a good player, no doubt about it, but you are overweight, but all you've got to do is lose a few pounds and you'll get back in the side. It's all down to you.' That didn't help at all, and after putting up with their bickering for half an hour, I left them to it and went off to have a drink with 'the bowlers' club' at the back of the plane.

They kept it up all the way from Brisbane to Melbourne, where we were changing planes, and almost as soon as we had taken off again from Melbourne it all kicked off once more, even worse than before, with the two of them having a real go at each other. By now all the players were telling Ritchie to belt up and they weren't mincing their words, but the swearing was too much for some of the other passengers. Ritchie stomped off to the loo, and while he was gone I tried to get Border to let it go in the interests of team harmony. All that achieved was to give him a fresh target for his foul temper and next minute he was having a huge go at me.

There was a bit of 'serve and volley' between us, and then someone in the row of seats in front of us turned round to complain about our language. My own temper was thoroughly up by now and, annoyed at the interruption, I said, 'Oh, mind your own business,' placed my hands on his shoulders, and turned him round to face the front again. I shouldn't have laid hands on him, and as we got off the plane at Perth I sought out the man and apologised for my behaviour. He seemed happy enough and I set off for the team hotel, but as we were checking in the police rolled up and put me under arrest. The man on the plane had evidently been persuaded by one of his fellow passengers that my apology was not good enough and had then gone to the police station to complain that he'd been assaulted. I could already imagine the tabloid frenzy in Australia and back at home: BEEFY BANGED UP – MAN ASSAULTED etc, etc.

When I reached the police station, the duty officer asked me to sign a cricket bat for him and then charged me with assault, which hardly seemed a fair exchange. Kath and my solicitor Alan Herd had flown in from England that day to watch the final, and straight off the plane, jet-lagged and sleepy, Alan had to come to the police station to try and bail me out. It had been a very minor incident and it seemed I would be given bail without too much trouble – despite our differences of opinion, Allan Border was even happy to stand surety – but Western Australian law required two landowners from the state to stand bail. I was left in the police station with the duty officer while Herdy went off to round up two locals to stand bail. Having tried and failed to find Rod Marsh, Herdy finally tracked down Dennis Lillee, who had been down the coast, a couple of hours' journey away. He came down to the jail with his son as co-signatory to bail me out and brought some emergency supplies – a six-pack of beer – to ease my trauma.

It wasn't exactly ideal preparation for the most important match in the history of Queensland cricket, and the game did not go our way. Western Australia won the toss and put us in to bat, and though we totalled 289, Graeme Wood hit a fine 141 to give his side a useful first innings lead. We slumped to 88 for five in our second innings, but Trevor Hohns and I then put together a decent sixth-wicket partnership. I passed 50, and with Trevor also going well we looked to have given Queensland a fighting chance, but I was out soon afterwards, and though Trevor remained undefeated on 59, the tail barely wagged and WA, needing only 162 to win, got home by five wickets.

Our season had ended with three successive defeats and my bickering teammates flew back to Brisbane without the Sheffield Shield … once they'd found a plane to take them. After the swearing and ructions on the flight out, Ansett Airlines had announced they would not fly any of the Queensland party anywhere again. Greg Ritchie then said, 'In that case I'll walk back. We'll all walk back.' It was a noble statement, if a bit implausible: Perth to Brisbane is over two thousand miles. Ansett finally relented, but I didn't fly back with my teammates; I couldn't leave Perth until my case had been heard by the magistrates' court. The magistrates didn't give the impression that they thought the case really required the full majesty of the law, but I had laid hands on a man, so I was technically guilty of assault and had to swallow my pride, plead guilty and pay a thousand-dollar fine.

I left Australia to fly home confident that as well as making some lifelong friends I'd also more than paid my way at Queensland. I'd played well: I'd made 646 runs, including seven fifties, and averaged 34, and I led the Queensland bowling averages with twenty-nine wickets at 27.75. I'd also gone out of my way to encourage the younger players at the club, even if some of the encouragement took fairly unorthodox forms like always getting a carton of stubbies of beer for them after each game we played, and I also did good business for Queensland at the turnstiles. Their average attendance went up by 6,500 that year and crowds were much higher than normal wherever we played throughout Australia.

We had come very close, though not close enough, to winning the precious Sheffield Shield. It's all very well believing in the law of averages, and saying that if there are only a handful of sides – six – playing in the tournament, things must turn in your favour at some point, but you still have to do something to make it happen. That's what I was there for, and I feel that, on the field and off it, I succeeded. I gave them the belief and the buzz, and my figures for that season spoke for themselves, but clearly some Queenslanders weren't listening because the Queensland Cricket Association decided not to offer me a contract for the following season. That was surprising, but it didn't bother me because I'd already decided that I wouldn't be returning the next year. It had cost me money to play for Queensland, who only paid me their normal match fee, leaving me to earn any extra income through endorsements and personal appearances. I'd enjoyed the experience, but it wasn't one I could afford to repeat, and Queensland didn't find it any easier to win the Sheffield Shield without me. Their long drought did not end until 1994-95.

If the way things ended left a bit of a sour taste in my mouth, that didn't spoil my affection for the state or the country, nor for the great Australian outdoors, though I do draw the line at some of the wildlife. Along with a fear of heights, I'm also petrified of snakes, sharks and crocs. When playing golf in Australia, if I hit a ball even one yard into the rough, I'll take the penalty and get another ball out of my bag rather than go into the bush looking for it. Australia is home to some of the world's most aggressive and venomous snakes, and even though cold logic tells me that the chances of encountering one when armed with nothing more than a seven-iron are pretty remote, I'm still not going to chance it. Sharks are another phobia. I can be swimming in the sea – very gingerly – but if anyone so much as mentions the word 'shark' I'll be on the beach towelling myself dry before they even get past 'sh'. Crocs are a similar no-go area.

If the cricket was ultimately disappointing, away from the game I made some great friends while I was in Queensland, not least Ken Brown, universally known as 'Brownie'. My mates there all seem to be colour-coded, because another great mate, Peter Green, is known by everyone, perversely, as 'Blue'. I met Brownie for the first time when I chartered his boat to go marlin fishing off Brisbane. We had a great day, and caught a marlin, a couple of tuna and a big sailfish. At the end of the day, as we tied up at the jetty, I tried to pay him. He just said, 'No mate, I want to do something for you in appreciation for the pleasure I've had watching you play cricket over the years.'

Some people come out with that sort of stuff and you can tell that there's another agenda, but I didn't get that feeling with Brownie at all. I argued with him, because it was a large amount of money and I could see he wasn't a wealthy bloke, but he was absolutely insistent. He loved his life, he had his house, his boat and his fishing, and there was nothing else he wanted. He didn't want my money, nor to be seen around town with 'a celebrity'. Even though I was a Pom, he'd simply enjoyed watching me play cricket and this was his way of saying thanks.

So in the end I said, 'OK Brownie, thank you very much, but if we're going to be mates then you're going to have to let me pay the proper rate next time.'

I've chartered his boat many times since then and sent a lot of other people his way when they wanted to try marlin fishing, but first and foremost, we're good mates. Brownie's one of the most genuine guys I've ever met and I can sit down with him and chat about anything ... and the one thing we don't talk about is cricket because I'd far rather be talking about fishing.

While Kath and I were away one time, Brownie and a mate of his were staying in our rented house in The Gap outside Brisbane. They were unmarried at the time, and after a big night out they brought a couple of 'pretty ordinary girls' – his description – back to the house for a nightcap. They couldn't find anything to drink anywhere, but after ferreting about in various cupboards Brownie finally found a case of wine in the cellar. He opened it, pulled a cork and decided it was 'a pretty decent drop', so over the next couple of days he and his mate and their new best friends drank eleven of the twelve bottles. When I got home he said, 'Oh, by the way, we drank some of your wine, Beefy. Tell me how much it cost and I'll replace it.'

'Where was it?' I said.

'Oh, down in the cellar in a box.'

The colour drained from my face. 'You can't replace it,' I said. 'It's bloody irreplaceable. It was Grange Hermitage, 1974.'

'Lucky we drank it then,' he said. 'If it was that old, it must have been nearly out of date.' It's an old joke, but he told it very well ...

He owed me one for that, but he repaid me many times over when I was playing for Queensland. I was a bit worried about Liam at the time. There was nothing wrong, he was ten years old and a lovely kid, but I was away an awful lot, and even though I had the family with me I had so many promotional duties for the club that even when I wasn't playing cricket I was still very tied up. So Liam was spending most of his time with Kath, his sisters and the nanny we had, and I really wanted him to have some time to do the bloke things that he loved – fishing, shooting, and so on – that the girls wouldn't do with him. So I said to Brownie one day, 'Would you do something for me? Liam needs to be around men more. He's ten years old, going on seventeen, and I just don't have the time to spend doing that stuff with him. He's on an extended holiday from school, he loves hanging around with you and going fishing with you. I've known you a long time, I trust you completely, would you take him fishing with you for a while?'

'Of course I will,' Brownie said, 'but there are a few ground rules. I'll make him work and I will not ever compromise a charter for him. If he's seasick, he'll have to put up with it all day – and we're out there for twelve hours in a small boat. And, mate? There's no way he can do this and keep living up at The Gap with you. I'm heading out to sea at six in the morning. I haven't time to drive up and down to The Gap every day to pick him up.'

I said, 'That's fine. I want him to live with you for a while.'

Brownie still took a little bit of convincing. He was single, sharing a house with the deckhand on the boat and living the bachelor life to the full – clothes everywhere, washing-up stacked up in the sink and no shortage of beer and girlfriends – but eventually he agreed and Liam duly moved in for a few weeks.

When I took Liam down there, Brownie gave him the hard word straight away. 'OK Liam, when we're out on the boat, here are the rules. If you give me lip, I'll break your nose. Disobey me and I'll break your arms.'

I shot a glance at Liam at this point to see how he was taking it. He just nodded. 'Don't worry about it, Brownie,' he said. 'You'll have no problems with me, I'll fit right in.' Not for the first time, I marvelled at my son's maturity and confidence – he was only ten, after all.

That was the start of a *Boys Own* adventure for Liam. Brownie phoned me up every night to let me know how things were going, and after a few days he said, 'Jeez Beefy, that kid's tough. He's been sick as a dog every time we've been out so far, but never once in seven days has he laid down, shirked a job or asked to go home.'

In the end Liam conquered his seasickness, and over the next few weeks he was transformed. He broadened out, he was tanned, he had the marlin fisherman's swagger about him, he looked great and he was loving what he was doing – in fact, he was having the time of his life. He was developing in other ways too. He was always a bit of a slow starter in the mornings – Brownie tossed him in the swimming-pool a few times to get his eyes open first thing – but once he was up and running, he was ready for anything. They stopped at a bakery every morning and Brownie sent Liam in to pick up the bread rolls for the day. He ambled across the road, got the rolls and came back. One morning he was ages, and when he came out he was with a girl whose mother was looking daggers at Liam as she and the girl got back into their car.

'Liam,' Brownie said, 'where the hell have you been?'

'I've pulled, Brownie.'

'Pulled? She must be three years older than you. You're ten years old, for Chrissake.'

Liam shrugged. 'We've all got to start some time, Brownie. I want to take her for a Chinese meal tonight, but her mother won't let her. Would you go and talk to her?'

Brownie looked across at her mother, who was still glowering at them from her car across the street, and then sighed. 'OK Liam, I'll do what I can.'

He went over and tapped on the window. The woman rolled it down with an expression like she was sucking lemons.

'Excuse me,' Brownie said. 'My young friend Liam there – he's a good lad and he comes from a good family – has taken a bit of a shine to your daughter and wants to take her for a Chinese meal tonight. Now I know they're both a bit young for this sort of thing, but I wondered if you'd be willing to let them do it if I chaperoned them, and of course, if you wanted to come along yourself as well, that would be fine too.'

There was no reply. The woman just put the car in gear and took off in a cloud of dust. 'Sorry Liam,' Brownie said as he got back in the car. 'I think we can take that as a "No".'

When he wasn't trying to pull, Liam had palled up with a boy called Chad who was about the same age and they played a bit of backyard cricket together and talked about marlin fishing for hours. When Chad went back to school, he told his mates, 'I've got a new friend, Liam Botham.'

The other kids said, 'What, Ian Botham's son? Bullshit. You don't know him.'

'I do, I do,' Chad said. 'I've met his dad as well, he goes fishing on Brownie's boat.'

The other kids didn't believe him, and when Chad persisted with the story he was picked on and beaten up by a couple of the bigger boys. When I heard about it, I said to Brownie, 'What time does Chad do his cricket practice at school?'

'After school on Thursdays, about three-thirty.'

'OK, can you have Liam there?'

He wasn't going fishing that day, so that wasn't a problem, and we didn't have a game, so I met them outside the school. We waited a few minutes as the boys started their net practice and then I told Liam to go over and say hello. Brownie and I watched as Liam walked over and introduced himself and we could see some of the boys still going, 'You're not Ian Botham's son, you don't look anything like him.'

Then I got out of the car and walked over to them. They were all standing there saucer-eyed, but I ignored all the others, made straight for Chad and said, 'Hi Chad, how's it going? How's the fishing coming on? I had a great time last time we were out on the boat together. Now, why don't you grab a bat and I'll bowl a few balls at you.'

Chad could hardly speak but his eyes were shining. I said hello to the other boys, bowled a few at Chad – nothing too heavy, so he could hit a few – and then wandered off. Brownie told me that Chad didn't have any more problems at school after that.

When he was out on the boat with Brownie for the first few weeks, Liam worked as number two to the 'Deckie', the deckhand who plays a vital role on the marlin boat. While the skipper steers the boat and finds the fish, the Deckie is baiting the hooks – and they have to be done in a very special way to lure the marlin – looking after all the rods, helping the clients to catch and land their fish, and he is also the front-line safety man if anything goes wrong or a client gets a line tangled round him.

Liam has always had an uncanny ability to watch someone doing something and then be able to replicate it. It was to stand him in good stead in his sporting career, because he could learn from the skills of others, and I suspect that I had the same knack myself. In my case it showed itself mainly in impersonations of Jeff Thomson's bowling action, but perhaps when I was younger, I was able to improve my cricket by subconsciously absorbing the skills and techniques that others used.

However, there is no doubt that it was a skill that Liam had in spades, as Brownie was about to discover. He had a charter of six going out one day – an unusually large number of people, since four is the norm – but his Deckie phoned him that morning to say he'd crashed his car and couldn't make it. When the clients turned up, Brownie had to say, 'I'm really sorry guys, but I can't take you out today. My Deckie's been in a car crash and I've no one else I can use.'

Liam stepped in at once. 'No problem, Brownie' – the old Botham self-confidence again – 'I'm a Deckie, I can do it.'

Brownie said, 'Yeah, but you're just a little Pommie squirt number two Deckie, you can't handle this.'

'I'm a Deckie,' Liam said. He turned to the clients and said, 'Tell you what, I'll make a deal with you. If I stuff up and you don't get a fish because of me, I don't get paid. And if I really stuff up badly, the whole trip's free. What do you say?'

Liam clocked that Brownie had gone a bit pale at the mention of a free trip, so he hastily added, 'Or rather, you just have to pay for the fuel. OK?' It was a question directed at Brownie as much as the clients, but he eventually got the nod from all of them.

I could still hear the surprise in Brownie's voice that night as he told me the story. 'It wasn't a good deal for me really, Beef, because if they didn't catch any fish I was goneski, but I thought what the hell – let's play the kid's game. So I said, "OK Liam, mate, I want forty baits made before we hit the point at the end of Moreton Island — twenty swimming mullet and twenty skipping garfish."' It takes exactly an hour to get there from the jetty, before they head out to the open sea, and they are not easy baits to make. They have to look like they're alive when they're in the water, so you have to fix sinkers underneath them and put little stitches in the neck to get them looking just right. If they're not realistic the marlin and sailfish won't take them and the clients won't get any trophy fish. A layman would struggle to make one in an hour and he certainly wouldn't get anywhere near forty.

Brownie left Liam working on the bait table on the deck and took the boat out. They'd been going about forty minutes when Liam came up on the fly-deck and flopped down. 'What the hell are you doing?' Brownie said. 'Get your arse back down and make those baits.'

'They're done.'

Brownie did a double-take. 'They'd better swim, Liam.'

'Don't worry about that, Brownie,' Liam said. 'They'll swim.'

When they got to the fishing-ground, Brownie looked down at the deck and saw Liam ready to go with the Deckie's wire-cutters and knife in his belt – because if you get wrapped up in the wire with a big marlin on the other end of the line, you've got to cut yourself out in a hurry. The regular Deckie, Brad, was a very slick operator, and by the time Brownie had the boat down to trawling speed Brad would have the outriggers out and four lines in the water fishing. When Brownie looked down, Liam had done exactly the same. Half an hour later they caught a big sailfish. Liam kept talking the angler through it, saying, 'Wind. Lift your rod. Get up on the transom,' and so on.

The angler has to get it within thirty feet of the boat and then the Deckie has to get a wire round it and haul it in with the wire wrapped around his hands until it's close enough to tag it with the tag-pole. Like me, Brownie doesn't believe in killing the game-fish we catch; we do it purely for the thrill of the pursuit. They're caught, tagged – which helps with conservation and scientific research into their migration routes, etc – and then released. It's why I always like to charter my own boat if I'm going fishing with people I don't know – my boat, my rules, and if there are trophy-hunters among them, they leave disappointed.

The tag-pole is fourteen feet long, so Brownie was ready to do that bit for Liam and shouted down to him, 'When you get it up to the side, shout and I'll come down and tag it for you.' As he was talking, he could see Liam doing exactly the same things in exactly the same way as Brad the Deckie, tapping his clippers and his knife handle two or three times in rapid succession, to make doubly, trebly sure they were there if needed.

Brownie finished up standing there, watching Liam still doing everything in an identical manner to Brad, wiring the fish, bringing it in, tagging it with the tag-pole and shaking the hooks out of its mouth, just like Brad did. And then, when the fish was safely returned, Liam was shaking the angler's hand, congratulating him, writing out the tag card and then shouting up to Brownie, 'Come on Brownie, let's get another one.' All this from a ten-year-old kid …

In the end Liam spent four months with Brownie. We couldn't prise him away. Brownie even had to drop him off at the airport to meet us on our way home because Liam didn't even want to waste one day's fishing to come back to the house at The Gap a day early. When we saw him, he was as brown as a berry and he'd filled out and grown up; the transformation was amazing. I said to Brownie,

'You've done us proud. He looks a proper bloke now, no doubt about it.'

As I did so, Liam looked across at Brownie and said, 'Fuck it, Brownie, the party's over, eh?'

Kath did a double-take and said, 'Liam, where did you learn to swear like that?' But, like Captain Pugwash's cabin boy, Brownie just smiled and said nothing.

When you've looked after someone's child for a few months like that, the bonds of friendship are even deeper, and one of the things I like about Brownie is that we can sit there on the boat, looking at the ocean, the birds, the dolphins and anything else that comes along, taking it all in, and not feel the need to say a word to each other.

While we were in Queensland, I'd taken the first tentative steps towards a life after sport, doing my first bit of public speaking. I'd accepted an invitation to do a talk in the small town of Bury in South Australia, and I travelled up there with David 'The Loon' English – even my children call him by his nickname – a friend I'd known since I was seventeen, who was also the creator of *The Bunbury Tales* book and songs, who was going with me to compere the night. We made the journey in a small light aircraft – more common than taxis in the Outback – but we'd somehow forgotten that it would help if one of us knew the way. Since I had both a pilot's licence and 'more front than Selfridge's', as a Cockney mate used to say, I managed to persuade the pilot to let me take over the controls and I then flew low enough so that we could read the road signs as we went along. When we got to Bury – surprisingly intact – and found the venue, The Loon did an introduction and then I told a few stories, answered questions from the floor and signed a few autographs. It went pretty well and we made up our minds to do more of them elsewhere in Australia and then back in England.

My Australian agent, Rod Loader, was only working as an agent in a fairly small way when I first met him, but I liked him at once. He ran a 'Beefy and Friends Tour' for me, along with Dean Jones, Allan Border, the rugby league legend Wally Lewis and a celebrated Aussie Rules footballer, Dermot Brereton. We were on the road for three weeks doing venues all the way from Tasmania to Brisbane, and by the end of it we had a pretty good relationship, so I said to him, 'I haven't got an Australian agent at the moment, why don't you see how you get on?'

Like my English agent Adam Wheatley at Mission Sports Management, Rod has done a great job for me, and even though I've since been approached by some far bigger agents who've said to me, 'Come to us and we'll do this, that and the other for you, far more than Rod Loader can do,' I've always said, 'No. Why would I want to do that to Rod?' I've stuck with him, and partly through me but mainly through his own hard work he's now representing cricketers like Viv Richards, Michael Holding, Sir Richard Hadlee, Wasim Akram and a whole host of other major sports stars. I'm not the perfect client in many ways because if I want to fly somewhere I won't be told that it can't be done, even if it's in the middle of a hurricane. However, although I can be demanding, I am very loyal.

The weakness of the Aussie dollar means that I tend to treat the money I earn over there as 'play money' to pay for a few expensive 'boys' toys' and some fine Australian wine and food while I'm there. I get great pleasure from taking a group of friends out for dinner, or chartering a boat to take us all deep-sea fishing. I was trying to get my mate Brownie to come up to the Barrier Reef with me to go fishing for black marlin, and he said, 'Beefy, this may be news to you, but I don't get paid hundreds of thousands of dollars a year. I can't afford it.'

'Brownie,' I said, 'it's the trip of a lifetime, the boat's already hired, you're coming.' He kept protesting that he couldn't freeload on me, and I said, 'Brownie, what good is money if you don't share the good times with your mates? You charter your boat to an awful lot of rich men. How many of them come on the boat on their own? I'll tell you: most of them. That's not what life's about. If you've got it, share it with people you care about: your friends and your family.'

When I'm covering an Ashes tour, Kath always flies out to be with me over Christmas, and we rent a house on the Mornington Peninsula. During the traditional Boxing Day Test match in Melbourne, I have a Harley-Davidson on standby outside the Melbourne Cricket Ground and a helicopter waiting at the Melbourne helipad a couple of miles away. We've got it down to such a fine art that, exactly seventeen minutes after the umpires have removed the bails to signal the end of the day's play, while my Sky colleagues are still making their way out of the ground or looking up and down the road for a taxi to get them back to their hotel, I'm already sitting down with Kath on the terrace outside the house with a glass of wine in my hand.

Back in England The Loon and I took our 'Evening with Beefy' show on the road, and the first one was in Stourbridge. The Loon made the introduction and ran a short video of some of my career highlights and lowlights, and I then did my bit. To save time waiting for someone with a microphone to reach the questioners from the floor, we'd asked people to write out their questions on slips of paper and deposit them in a box. Loon then pulled them out one at a time, as if he was drawing the prizes in a raffle. He pulled out the first question and read it out. 'My name is Kate. I live just above the chip shop in the High Street. Is it true you are hung like a rhino?' You'll never know, Kate.

In company with any or all of Viv Richards, Allan Lamb, my friend Jeremy Atkinson and David English, we have now done around two hundred shows around the world. Viv and I are best friends, but having two such self-willed and opinionated characters in close proximity for a long time can lead to an occasional flare-up, and The Loon has always been brilliant at damping down the fires.

He was also the man who introduced me to Eric Clapton. Eric's a keen fisherman as well as a 'rock god' and we've fished together on a few occasions. He's also a cricket fanatic, both as a spectator and a player, though his playing career was abruptly terminated by his management after an unfortunate incident in a charity match. Eric was fielding in the gully when the batsman flashed hard at a wide delivery and edged it straight at Eric. He stuck a hand out by instinct as much as design, and dislocated one of his fingers ... even worse, he dropped the catch. As Eric walked off, nursing his finger, a bee landed on the other hand and stung it. Eric finished up with both hands plunged into ice-buckets, trying to bring the swelling down so that he wouldn't have to cancel his impending tour of Japan.

From then on, at his management's insistence, Eric confined his cricket activities to spectating, and he was a regular visitor to New Road. During a match against Essex, he challenged me, 'Score a hundred and I'll play in your local tonight.' I duly called his bluff by scoring 125, and Eric promptly set off into Worcester to try and find an amplifier – not an easy task on a Sunday afternoon, but he managed it somehow.

That night, we swarmed into my local, deep in the Worcestershire countryside. It wasn't a big night until that point, just a few customers playing doms and darts, and a dog sleeping by the fireplace. Eric strolled up to the bar and said to the landlord, 'I'm Eric Clapton. Would it be OK if I plugged in my amp and played a few songs?'

When he'd recovered the power of speech, the landlord said that on the whole he thought he could probably allow that, and Eric got set up. The Worcestershire and Essex players all turned up as well, and as the news got round that Eric Clapton was playing for free in the taproom, other people came running in from all over the place, including the bride and groom and their guests from a wedding reception just up the road. At the end of the evening I gave Eric a signed and inscribed bat with which I'd hit 80 first class sixes in a season and he handed me his Fender Stratocaster inscribed 'To brother Beefy'. I did also suggest that one of his songs would be much improved with 'Beefy' as the title, but he stubbornly insisted that 'Layla' worked much better.

Chapter 10

PLAYING ON BORROWED TIME

When I got back to Europe in the spring of 1988, I barely had time to turn round before I was off on another charity walk for leukaemia research. I wanted to do something high-profile enough to attract media attention and generate another huge return for the Leukaemia Research Fund, and had toyed with the idea of following the route of Napoleon's retreat from Moscow, but instead Kath and I came up with the Hannibal Walk, crossing the Alps with a troupe of elephants as Hannibal had done in his attack against Rome in 218 BC. It was a relatively high-risk, high-expense project, but the potential publicity benefits seemed to far outweigh that: history, legendary military campaigns and commanders, foreign travel, Alpine scenery and, above all, elephants – what was not to like?

The omens did not seem to be favourable. I flew into Perpignan to start the walk just as the news was breaking that I had been sacked by Queensland, generating the usual media circus. It was a bad start to the walk, and things soon took several turns for the worse. The local people in the towns and villages we passed through took us to their hearts, but from officialdom we met only a blank wall. They had no idea what we were trying to achieve – elephants and cricket were equally alien to them – and attempts to explain about the LRF and its research only led to looks of bafflement and much Gallic shrugging of shoulders.

Even worse, we weren't allowed to collect money en route. A law prohibits the collection of money on any street in France. Its original purpose had been to drive vagrants off the streets, but it was now stopping me collecting money for charity. Although we begged and pleaded, the French authorities were immovable – 'The law is the law, monsieur' – and they made it clear that there was not the slightest chance of a blind eye being turned.

We were also under fire from a few animal lovers who accused us of cruelty to elephants, even though one of Britain's leading vets, David Taylor, was with us to monitor the elephants' condition. The elephants, borrowed from a circus, were used purely for their publicity value and we had David there to keep them in mint condition. Each morning we'd set off with the elephants and walk a mile or so out of town, and then, while I kept walking, they were loaded into huge air-conditioned transporters and driven to the day's destination for some food and r'n'r in a field until it was time to rendezvous with me for the brief stroll to the day's finishing line.

Since this was always in a town or village, it brought its own problems: the elephants would make a beeline for the fruit and vegetable shop and hoover up the entire contents of the displays outside. One of our back-up team had a near full-time job walking behind and paying out compensation for all the stuff that the elephants had eaten. In one place it was market day and all these old French ladies were trying to shoo the elephants away from their stalls with brooms.

The elephants and I got to know each other pretty well and, since I used to fill my pockets with fruit, they followed me wherever I went. When I took Becky – who was eighteen months old at the time – down to see them in the morning, they'd smell the fruit and be all over me, and one used to pick her up in its trunk and put her gently on his back. I really grew to love them. When we went over the top of the Alps, it was the first time in their lives that these elephants had ever seen snow. Normally I never stopped the walk for anything, but this time, the sight of those elephants playing like puppies in the snow, rolling in it, picking it up in their trunks and spraying it over each other, and over me – and I threw it back over them – was so moving that I stopped the walk for half an hour and we all just stood and watched.

One of the elephants had a heavy cold one morning, maybe from playing in the snow for too long. The thought of a cold in the nose when you've got one as big as an elephant was pretty terrifying, so I said to the vet, 'How do you treat an elephant with a cold?' expecting the answer, like the one for porcupines making love, to be 'Very carefully.' He just said, 'Like this,' walked over to it and poured half a bottle of brandy into its mouth, which, though it probably wasn't on the RSPCA's recommended treatment list, seemed to do the trick.

With or without a shot of brandy to speed them on their way, those elephants were having the time of their lives, but one British paper decided that it was cruel to make them walk all that way. They weren't, they were only doing one or two miles a day, but the reporter never bothered to check his facts, he just wrote the story. They then got Brigitte Bardot wound up to make some critical comments and I challenged her to come and look at the elephants for herself. She didn't take up my invitation, but another paper flew out Bill Travers, the actor who had played George Adamson in the film *Born Free* and who now worked with Zoo Check, in the hope that he would find that the elephants had been maltreated.

We also had to fly another vet out to corroborate David Taylor's assessment of the elephants' condition, and he reported that they were absolutely in the pink. Some members of the French Animal Liberation Front also came to see for themselves and were so impressed that they gave us a donation.

There were no more allegations of animal cruelty, but had anyone pilloried us for cruelty to pilots we wouldn't have had a leg to stand on. Alan Dyer, my pilot friend, had been in a horrific car accident that left him with five broken ribs, a broken pelvis, a collapsed lung and pneumonia. However, he was still desperate to make the walk and began walking round and round his home with the aid of a walking stick, getting a little bit further each day. He flew out to join us with the aim of doing one day but finished up walking every inch of the whole walk.

Fund-raising improved dramatically after we crossed the border into Italy, where red tape and laws about street collections were brushed aside with an expansive wave of the hand. We collected most of the money there, the Italian Cricket Association gave us whole-hearted support, and the Mayor of Turin even held a reception in our honour, but sadly the damage had already been done. The press allegations about animal cruelty undoubtedly affected the success of the walk, especially the level of donations from England. We only made £300,000, which, considering the work and effort that went into it, was a disappointingly small amount.

There were more problems after Benson & Hedges ran a Hamlet cigar advert using my picture and, at my request, donated the fee to Leukaemia Research. It was the cue for yet more media outrage: how could a cancer charity accept tainted money from the tobacco industry? It baffled me. If I'd trousered it myself, I'm sure there would not have been a word of complaint, but when I gave it to charity instead, the media went crazy.

As soon as I'd completed the Hannibal Walk, I went straight into training for the new English cricket season, and in contrast to Queensland, my time at Worcestershire continued to be hugely successful. In the five years I spent with the county we won the championship twice, the Sunday League twice and the Benson & Hedges Cup as well. The one thing that shone through above all else – just as it had done in the golden era at Somerset – was the tremendous team spirit.

There was one potential problem. Ever since I'd first injured my back way back in April 1980, I knew I was playing on borrowed time. I had continued to play – and to bowl – through the pain but just after the start of the 1988 season, during a county match against my former team Somerset, it finally gave out. It was the second morning of the match and I had just taken my first championship wicket of the summer when I dived for a catch in the slips and fell heavily. At first I thought I'd just strained a muscle in my back, but as we sat around in the dressing room after rain stopped play I soon discovered that this was much more serious than that.

I'd sat down on the floor, and when the rain stopped and the umpires called us out again, I found that I couldn't stand up. My back had locked up and a couple of teammates had to lift me on to my feet. I was in absolute agony, but somehow the Worcester physio and the twelfth man got me out of the pavilion and down the steps to the car park. They then manoeuvred me into a car and out of it again at the hospital, where the surgeon, John Davies, looked at the X-rays and then told me that if I had the back operation that had been so long delayed I had an 80 per cent chance of making a full recovery, but only a 50 per cent chance of playing top-class cricket again. I was encased in plaster from neck to waist to immobilise my spine and I had the weekend to make my mind up whether to have the operation. It was career-threatening, but if that operation would sort out my back problem for the rest of my life, I felt it would be well worth the risk, and three days later I went under the knife.

The operation proved a success, but recuperation was painfully slow. For two weeks I just had to lie there, and every couple of hours the nurses would come in and turn me over. After that I was allowed up and began to take my first tentative steps. I was so weak and unsteady and so nervous about my 'new' back that I could hardly put one foot in front of the other. When I was finally allowed home I spent six months virtually immobile – mental torture for someone who had always been constantly on the go – and with nothing else to do, I ate and drank to excess and piled on the beef as a result.

I told anyone who asked that I'd soon be back playing cricket for Worcestershire and England again, but in my heart I wasn't even sure that the odds were as good as the fifty-fifty chance the surgeon had quoted me. I always felt that there were other avenues in life I could have followed, but I hadn't finished with professional cricket yet. There were things I wanted to do, goals I had set myself – win a World Cup, score a century against the West Indies – but I had to face up to the possibility that my career might be over, the fact that this could be the end.

Slowly I became more mobile and could walk myself around the garden. I was too impatient to wait any longer. I had to see for myself what I could and could not do from now on, so every morning I got up at dawn, took our boxer dog Tigger in the car, drove to the nearby army range and then walked slowly over the moor. I couldn't do more than fifty yards at first, but I pushed myself on and every day I got a little further – a hundred yards, two hundred, five hundred, half a mile and then a mile. Eventually I could walk for miles, but I still had no real idea of what would happen if I picked up a bat or tried to run in and bowl again. As I walked, I ran through every conceivable possibility in my mind, so absorbed in my thoughts that on one occasion I even wandered into the path of a Chieftain tank that suddenly came rumbling over the brow of the hill. I scrambled out of the way just in time. I had to smile at the thought of what the headlines would have been if I'd gone under the tank tracks: BEEFY – TANKS A LOT.

I spent a lot of time at New Road as I was recovering. I felt I could help build morale in the dressing room and guide and advise some of the younger players, though what I wanted most of all was to be back out there, leading from the front. When I was finally pronounced fit enough to start light training I had tremendous help from the Worcestershire physio, Dave Roberts. Over the endless months of training, despite the verbal abuse that I often dished out in my pain and frustration, he gave me encouragement when I was down, bullied me when I needed it and urged me always to be positive. It might be hard, it might take a long time, but I would get back on the field. It was a huge blow when I discovered that I would never regain all my old strength and flexibility, but once more Dave encouraged me to be positive: Beefy at 90 per cent efficiency would still be better than many players at a hundred; I had to keep going, keep believing.

Kath was fantastic as well. She never pressured me to quit or to keep going, but supported me wholeheartedly. 'You know what's best for you, Ian,' she said. 'Whether you decide to retire or to play on, I'll do all I can to help you.' My drive to succeed, to be the best, had also not left me, and I decided very early on that there was no point in making a comeback if all I was going to do was make up the numbers. I didn't want to be just another run-of-the-mill county player; I had to be good enough to play for England again. I knew I wasn't going to be able to bowl fast ever again, but guile and experience could substitute for sheer pace and energy.

At the start of the 1989 season I felt fit and ready, and hungry for the chance to prove myself again. Australia were that summer's visitors and I was determined to show that I was still worth my place in the England side to face the old enemy. I had to prove my fitness first, but providing there were no injury alarms, England captain David Gower intended to bring me straight back into the Test side.

I made my comeback at the end of April in Worcestershire's opening championship match against Notts at Trent Bridge. I was pretty nervous waiting to take the field and then getting ready to bowl my first ball in county cricket for a year, but it passed off without incident, and if it was a fairly sedate spell of medium pace to start with, I was pleased to get through it safely and bowled well enough to pick up two for 37 in sixteen overs. Over the next few games I got my bowling right back in the groove, and if I was a little short of runs, I felt that I was just coming into form when I missed a hook shot against a short ball from Glamorgan's Steve Barwick and fractured my cheekbone. My Test comeback had to be delayed and my name was not on the team sheet for the first Test at Headingley.

Ted Dexter, the new chairman of selectors, and the manager Mickey Stewart had originally wanted Mike Gatting to captain the side but the chairman of the TCCB, Ossie Wheatley, vetoed their choice on the grounds that Gatt had not spent sufficient time in the wilderness as punishment for various on- and off-field crimes and misdemeanours. Dexter and Stewart's second choice was David Gower, but they seemed strangely reluctant to back his judgement. Dexter, in particular, was continually interfering.

Before the start of the Headingley Test, Dexter persuaded David that a forecast of bad weather – which turned out to be inaccurate – meant that he should put Australia in. David duly won the toss and put Australia in, but the toss was the only thing he did get right. They batted all the first day, all the next and into the morning of the third day before declaring at 601 for seven with Mark Taylor making a hundred and Steve Waugh a brilliant 177 not out, and went on to win the match by 210 runs. David then won the toss again at Lord's and this time batted first, but it made no difference to the result. Australia bowled England out for 286, piled up 528 in reply, with Steve Waugh again the chief scourge, 152 not out, and, despite Gower's captain's century, won the match by six wickets. Already two down in the series, no one in the England camp, including the captain, seemed to be sure who was in charge: David Gower, Mickey Stewart or Ted Dexter.

I returned for Worcestershire at Yorkshire in late June, scored a few runs in that game, and against Middlesex in the next, and then took eleven wickets in the match as we thrashed Northants in early July. That was probably the clincher as far as the England manage-ment were concerned, and when David Gower asked me if I felt I was now fit and in form enough to play in the third Test at Edgbaston, my answer was an emphatic 'Yes'.

I had been playing fairly well in a fine Worcestershire side, and having largely missed out through injury on the county's championship-winning season the year before, it was great to be playing a part in the winning run that would lead to our second successive championship that year; but Test cricket was the ultimate, and I was both excited and nervous as I prepared for my comeback. Even at the height of my powers, I never took my Test place for granted. Now, in the quiet hours of the night, there were moments when I wondered if I still had what it took to succeed at the very highest level.

However, before I could establish that, I first had to come to terms with the weird and wonderful world of Ted Dexter. He had taken over as chairman of selectors with a pledge to bring a new professional approach to English cricket, but when we arrived in Birmingham for the traditional pre-match meal and team talk, I discovered that his definition of professionalism was an unusual one. As we entered the hotel conference room where the team meeting was being held, Dexter was standing in the doorway handing out songsheets.

It turned out that one of Dexter's ideas of the professional way for us to approach the game was for us all to learn the new lyrics he'd composed to the tune of 'Onward Christian Soldiers' – in future to be known as 'Onward Gower's Cricketers' apparently – and then, as Ted himself told us, 'When you get in the bath tonight, I want you to sing this at the top of your voices.'

I smiled politely, took the proffered lyrics and then started looking round for the nearest wastepaper bin. Some of the younger players looked a bit puzzled but perhaps assumed this sort of thing went on all the time in the England dressing room, and David Gower, the team captain, who perhaps felt that he had to go along with Dexter's Looney Tunes idea if he wanted to keep his job, looked like he'd just been invited to a ritual disembowelling. Suffice it to say that as we settled down for the night at our hotel, I didn't hear anyone singing in the bath.

Dexter often complained that every time he opened his mouth the press were lying in wait to 'harpoon and lampoon' him; with raw material like that to work on, it must have been like shooting fish in a barrel for them. I never understood what the point of Ted Dexter actually was, as far as the England team was concerned. His tactical input was practically nil, his judgement of players was often awry and he couldn't even manage to identify them half the time. Devon Malcolm became transposed to Malcolm Devon in Dexter-speak, and although he managed to get Jimmy Cook's name the right way round, Ted was so busy singing his praises as a future England opening batsman that he neglected to notice that Cook was actually South African. His lack of knowledge of those who really were qualified to play for England was equally alarming. John Morris and Jonathan Agnew first realised they had no chance of going on the tour to the West Indies that year when, on their way to the Cricket Writers' Club annual dinner, they were hailed by Dexter. 'Excuse me, chaps, you two look like cricketers. Do you know where this dinner is taking place?'

For the high priest of a new professional approach, such rank amateurism in his own work made Dexter a bit of a music-hall joke to some of us, and whatever he was being paid – and it was probably plenty – he wasn't remotely earning it. If anything, English cricket was going backwards on his watch.

It felt like forever until we took the field on the opening morning of the Edgbaston Test and, just as on my Test debut all those years before, I was delighted when Australia won the toss and chose to bat. Fielding first, I had an early chance to get in on the action. I had to wait a bit longer than usual to make my mark as Geoff Marsh and Mark Taylor put on 88 for the first wicket on my return to the England side, but finally, in my thirteenth over, I beat Marsh's defensive push and had him plumb lbw. It was to be my only wicket in the innings, but after twenty-three months' absence, I was back. With Dean Jones this time hitting a big century – 157 – Australia totalled

424, and it was a familiar tale of an England collapse as I walked out to bat at 75 for four, which then became 75 for five. Slowly, in partnership with Jack Russell, we got ourselves back into the game. It wasn't a typical Beefy knock – I batted for two and a half hours to make 46 – but Jack and I put on almost a hundred for the sixth wicket, enough to help us avoid the follow-on, and with rain intervening, we salvaged a draw.

Before the next Test at Old Trafford I had to decide whether I could play at all, and it had nothing to do with form, fitness or on-field events. I and my family had been the target of plenty of cranks and sick bastards in the past. Some charming soul once sent human excrement through the post to my mother, and someone else sent me some pubic hair and invited me to 'Smoke this, you bastard'. I'd also had letters aplenty from National Front yobs calling me 'nigger-lover' and threatening to 'do' me because of my friendship with Viv.

I usually put them straight in the bin, but just before the Test I received a series of threatening letters that I had to take seriously. They were coherent and convincing and showed an alarming knowledge about my movements, and they contained the threat that I would be assassinated. I took the letters straight to the police who told me I was right to be worried by them. Special Branch officers then briefed me and my 'minder', Andy Withers, about security precautions we should take, including checking my car for concealed explosive devices and varying our routines and the routes we followed when driving to the cricket ground. They also detailed some undercover plainclothes officers to carry out counter-surveillance around me and bodyguard me at particularly vulnerable locations.

Luckily Kath was away in Portugal at the time and I felt that there was no point in her worrying as well, so I didn't tell her about the threats until months later, and meanwhile I decided that I had to carry on as normal. Nothing happened – the writer had either been just another crank or had thought better of the idea – but the thought that it conceivably might added another layer of stress and tension to an already over-stressful existence.

The Test results weren't helping my stress levels either. I was out for a duck at Old Trafford after missing with a particularly wild 'yahoo' at Trevor Hohn's gentle spin, and though Steve Waugh was out for a relatively modest 92 this time, Australia batted well all the way down the order and then rattled us out again, with only Jack Russell showing much resistance with a fighting 128 not out. We lost that Test by nine wickets and with it the Ashes, and then subsided to another humiliating defeat at Trent Bridge. After Marsh and Taylor put on 329 for Australia's first wicket, they piled up 602 for six, declared, and beat us by an innings. I dislocated a finger and did not bat in the second innings, but that didn't make me feel any better. We were now 4-0 down in the series and I couldn't point to a single decent innings I'd played or a good bowling performance. If the 1981 Ashes had been 'the Botham summer', this was looking like the Botham winter. My injured finger meant that I missed the sixth and final Test at The Oval, where even with only pride left to play for England didn't show too much of it, Australia having much the better of a rain-affected draw. Indeed they could have argued that but for bad weather they would have finished the series with a 6-0 clean sweep.

England's form all summer had been dismal, but apart from the Dexter follies, behind the scenes a fresh intervention by the South Africans had undermined team spirit. Dr Ali Bacher, Clive Rice and Mike Procter had been in England recruiting players for another 'rebel tour' to be played that winter while the England Test side was taking on the West Indies in the Caribbean. The England dressing room was rife with rumours of the money on offer, who had signed and who had not. The England selectors had also heard the rumours and began requiring players to sign a declaration that they would be available, if selected, for the tour of the West Indies.

The South Africans had also approached me, and I was certainly willing to at least hear what they had to say. I'd discussed it with Viv and he just said, 'Go and talk to them. You can't play for ever, man.' We all understood – and if we didn't, the noises emanating from Lord's made it crystal clear – that anyone joining the rebel tour would be banned from Test cricket for several years, which in my case effectively meant that I would never play for England again. I also knew that the loss of my England status and my involvement with the apartheid regime would jeopardise my existing commercial contracts. But my Test and indeed my first-class career might be coming to an end anyway. My back could have given out again at any time.

If I were to go, my motivation, like that of all the English crick-eters who went there, would be purely financial. The South Africans were not offering jam tomorrow, they were offering jam, and plenty of it, today. I still had a visceral dislike of the apartheid system, but I also had a duty to do the best I could for the financial well-being of my family. I talked to other players, including my Worcestershire teammate Graham Dilley, who had been to South Africa in the recent past, and was reassured by what they said about the changes taking place in the country. I made up my mind that any deal I signed would have to include provision to coach and promote the game in the black townships.

When the South Africans came calling on me, they told me to name my own price to join two rebel tours. I pulled a figure out of the air and said, 'It would have to be an absolute minimum of £500,000, tax-free, and I'd also need compensation for any commer-cial endorsements and contracts that are cancelled as a result.' I waited for the jaws to drop, but they didn't even blink. 'We'll discuss it and get back to you,' was all they said.

Clive Rice and Mike Procter had conducted the first negotiations, but Ali Bacher, the chairman of the South African Cricket Board, took over to thrash out the final details. He also arranged for their accountants to meet my advisers to sort out the question of compensation for lost income. The offer he ultimately came up with was a three-year contract. In the first two years I'd commit to a five-week rebel tour, and in the last year I'd play for one of the South African provinces in their domestic competition. In return I would be paid an absolutely eye-watering amount of money – well in excess of the minimum I had set.

Ali spent a lot of time telling me how South Africa was changing, the progress being made in involving black people in what had formerly been bastions of all-white sport. He even acknowledged that the apartheid regime had deserved its long sporting isolation, but insisted that the best way to further the process of reform was now to rebuild sporting contacts. I repeated the question I had asked about Viv the last time they had come to make me an offer and he insisted that there was no longer any question of Viv needing to be made an 'honorary white man', but despite his reassurances, I was still not completely convinced.

The money was certainly tempting, but having talked it over with Kath and my solicitor and long-time friend Alan Herd, I saw it as no more than an insurance policy for me. The England selectors had been trying all summer to get me to confirm my availability for the Caribbean. Mickey Stewart kept telling me that he and Dexter were going to pick a new side for the tour, but they wanted Mike Gatting to lead it, with me as senior professional. He begged me to make myself available and made it clear to me that if I did so I was more or less guaranteed a place on the tour. I had no reason at that stage to question whether the offer was genuine or merely a device to stop me from giving the South Africans the publicity coup that my signing would represent.

The rumours about the identity of the England players committed to the rebel tour had a big impact on the dressing room with the team splitting into two factions – the putative rebels and the rest. The atmosphere was absolutely poisonous during the Old

Trafford Test when the news at last broke about the rebel tour and an initial squad was released. Neither my name nor that of Mike Gatting was mentioned at that stage, but it was common knowledge in the game that we'd both received very large offers.

I finally reached my decision during the fifth Test at Trent Bridge and told Alan Herd to call the South Africans and thank them but reject their offer. This was probably going to be my last chance to prove myself against the West Indies and score that elusive century against them. I was sure that I'd made the right decision for both financial and playing reasons, and I still felt that I had the ability and the hunger to do well in the Caribbean, and even if any more Lindy Fields came crawling out of the woodwork I was confident that this time, with Kath at my side, I could take even that in my stride.

In my opinion that West Indies side, led by Clive Lloyd, was the greatest side that had ever played the game in the entire history of cricket. I felt then and still feel now that their combination of a quartet of world-class fast bowlers and brilliant, free-scoring batsmen would have been a match even for the greatest sides of previous eras. Their pace attack was no longer quite so terrifying – Roberts, Holding and Garner had now retired from Test cricket – but they were still formidable opponents. I had never scored a Test century against the West Indies. I'd had a few sixties, seventies and eighties, but had never reached three figures, and I wanted another crack at testing myself against the best. I'd always tried to lead from the front against them and really challenge them, and perhaps that was one reason for my relative failure against them – maybe I had tried too hard to take the battle to them, played too aggressively. But you have to measure yourself against the best, and without doubt that was the West Indies. So I reconfirmed my availability to Mickey Stewart and he expressed his delight.

Then, the night before the tour squad was due to be announced,

Ted Dexter called me at home. 'Hello Ian,' he said. 'I'm afraid we're not taking you to the West Indies.'

'What?' I said. 'You begged me to make myself available for the winter tour and I told the South Africans where to go as well. And now you're saying you've changed your mind?'

'Er, well, I personally didn't ask you,' he said.

I gave him a mouthful and then slammed down the phone. I was so enraged that if I'd still had the South African contract in front of me, I'd have signed it there and then. Mike Gatting did so, after being left in the wilderness by them. When they were asked by the press to comment on my omission, Mickey Stewart and Ted Dexter then denied that they had ever persuaded me to make myself available for the tour.

I've never been given a satisfactory explanation, but I was told by one person that it was Graham Gooch, who had replaced David Gower as captain when he was sacked at the end of the Ashes series, who did not want me on the tour. It was not without irony that Gooch was now the England tour captain, since he had, of course, gone to South Africa on the first rebel tour.

The hurt at being dumped from the tour was all the more intense because of everything I'd gone through to regain my place after my back injury. The realisation that I might never be selected for England again made me feel as if it had all been a huge waste of effort. It was no real satisfaction to me to note that David Capel, the player who had been picked as all-rounder in my place, averaged 13 with the bat and 48 with the ball during that tour. Had the figures been the other way round, they would have been quite impressive.

I was in a filthy mood for much of the winter. I was furious at how I had been treated by Mickey Stewart and Ted Dexter, and since they weren't around to act as punchbags, I took things out on Kath and the kids instead. I was also drinking too much, which wasn't helping either. Things finally came to a head on Valentine's Day, 14 February 1990 – we certainly pick our days. In honour of the occasion I'd had thirty-six hand-tied red roses delivered to Kath and we'd been out for a meal with some friends. So far, so good, but Kath had been brooding about my behaviour to her and the children for some time, and on the way home she reached a conclusion, turned to me and said, quite matter-of-factly, 'I'm sorry, Ian. I just can't go on living like this. We've got to sort things out.'

As usual, I tried to defuse an awkward situation with a joke but it was no laughing matter and Kath was in no mood to be jollied along. When we got home, I poured a couple of glasses of wine and sat down and let her talk. She told me she was at the end of her tether, unhappy with me and with the life she was leading. She was fed up with my moods, my selfishness, my habit of venting my anger at others by picking on her and the kids, and sick to death of the constant rows between us. The rows had also had an effect on the kids. Sarah had even asked the question all parents dread to hear: 'Are you and Daddy getting divorced?'

For once I did not interrupt, become angry or stomp out in a huff. I sat quietly and listened as she went through a litany of complaints that in some cases went back years. Finally she issued an ultimatum to me. Unless I could promise her that things would be different from now on – and then prove it by my actions – she was going to leave me and take Liam, Sarah and Becky with her.

I just sat there in silence. I realised that she was right. I had been a stupid, selfish idiot, and was close to losing the most important people in my life. It was the first time in our life together I had ever heard her talk this way, but then it was probably the first time I had ever given her the chance. Throughout the whole time we were talking – and it must have been a couple of hours at least – we never raised our voices or lost our tempers with each other. We were calm, methodical and considered, and, perhaps for the first time in my life, I was able to take a completely dispassionate look at myself, Kath and our life together. On the previous occasion when we had almost split up, after the row at Birtles four years before, Kath had backed down because of the children. It was now my turn, and I made a solemn promise to her that I would do everything in my power to make it up to her. I've done my best to do so. I'm still a hard man to live with at times, but our marriage, our children and now our grandchildren as well are the most important things in both our lives.

Chapter 11

THE NEW JAMES BOND

The West Indies were not quite the power they had been a few years earlier. A pace attack picked from Bishop, Ambrose, Moseley, Marshall, Walsh and Baptiste was still not to be taken lightly, but it didn't compare with the great quartet of Holding, Roberts, Marshall and Garner. Perhaps as proof of that, the tour of 1989-90 was different in one respect: England did win a Test, the first one, by nine wickets. They held on to that series lead after the second Test was abandoned without a ball bowled and the third Test was drawn, but after that normal service was resumed and the West Indies won the last two Tests by huge margins to take the series 2-1.

Over the course of the year that followed, as England played home series against New Zealand and India, and were thrashed 3-0 on another Ashes tour of Australia, I was forced to sit on the sidelines as a succession of players were tried in my position as Test all-rounder, without any conspicuous success. I was reduced to the role of an onlooker, playing my county cricket for Worcestershire – and hugely enjoying it – during the summer and then spending the winter appearing in pantomime. I actually earned more from a season in panto than I would have done for a winter tour with England.

I first persuaded Max Boyce, who I'd known for a long time, to let me appear in his show *Jack and the Beanstalk*. Max wasn't exactly keen at first, I suspect because he thought I wasn't serious. Anyone who visited my dressing room might have got a similar impression because there was a huge pile of condoms on my make-up table. My singing voice is so terrible that the producer banned me from singing, but he didn't want me to mime either, so we reached a compromise. I stuck a couple of the condoms over the radio microphone clipped to my costume; I could then sing along with the songs in my happy tone-deaf way without the audience noticing anything amiss. According to the critics, the thespian talents I displayed were about on a par with my singing, suggesting that Menachem Golan's estimate of six months of acting lessons for the new James Bond was a considerable underestimate. One critic said that 'the only thing more wooden than the beanstalk was Ian Botham', but at least the audiences seemed to enjoy it.

My season in 1990 was disrupted by injury – a knee injury meant that I missed the early part of the season and a torn hamstring curtailed the end – but in between I scored centuries in the championship and Benson & Hedges Cup, always a favourite competition since my first appearance against Andy Roberts all those years before.

I started with a bang in 1991, however, and if the Test selectors needed a reminder of my abilities, I provided it with a century for Worcestershire against Lancashire in the first week of May. The following week we were facing the West Indies. Viv Richards took centre stage first, murdering our bowling as he raced to a magnificent 131 from 153 balls. The Windies declared on 409 for seven, and just before I went out to bat I took a call from Lord's informing me that I was being recalled to the England one-day side to be announced at noon that day. I was in the mood to celebrate, and as I got to the wicket I decided that anything that Viv could do, I could do better, and took just eighty-three balls to reach my first-ever century against the West Indies. I went on to make 161 from 139 balls, including one six and thirty-two fours.

I took four for 45 in the first one-day international against the Windies, but I then tore my hamstring again and missed the rest of the one-day series and was left out of the first four Tests as well. Finally, two years after my previous Test match, all my rivals for the all-rounder role having fallen by the wayside, I was recalled for the final Test against the West Indies at The Oval. I was doubly determined to show the selectors what they had been missing. It was also to be Viv Richards' last Test in England and his last as West Indies captain. Before the match I told Viv, 'You know what I'd like? You to score a hundred and us to win.'

I'd probably never have another chance to score a Test hundred against the West Indies, but after I'd made 31 in our first innings I managed to find a new way to get out. I overbalanced as I tried to hook a short one from Curtley Ambrose, tried to hurdle the wickets and finished up knocking off my leg bail with my pad. Viv then scored a fine second innings 60, and when England batted again I had the pleasure of scoring the winning runs – from the only ball I faced – as I cracked Clayton Lambert's long hop for four. It was a doubly sweet moment for me, the first time I had ever finished on the winning side against the Windies in more than twenty attempts.

The domestic season saw a double triumph for Worcestershire as we beat Lancashire in both the Benson & Hedges and the Refuge Assurance League. Had our County Championship season not been badly hit by the weather we might even have added a third championship to the two I had already won with the county. It was my best ever season with Worcestershire, fittingly perhaps, as it was also to be my last with them.

I hadn't set the world ablaze on my Test comeback, but I'd done well enough, scoring 35 runs and picking up three wickets, and I was duly selected for the World Cup in Australia and New Zealand, immediately following the England tour of New Zealand. On that tour I came up against the fabled realities of the Gooch/Stewart regime. I had already heard rumours and anecdotes about the new training and playing regimen the two sergeant-majors of English cricket had adopted that made me unsure whether to laugh or cry. Now I was to experience it for myself. I was not exactly an objective witness because their treatment of David Gower had shocked and angered me as much as it did most English cricket-lovers. Gower had been our best player on the Ashes tour of Australia the previous winter, but he and John Morris had fallen foul of the England management after they overflew the Carrara Oval on the Gold Coast in a vintage Tiger Moth aircraft. It was done for the right reasons: Robin Smith had been struggling for runs and they waited at the airport until he was approaching his hundred and then took off, ready to overfly the ground as soon as he got his hundred to salute him. I would have thought you would have to be a pretty dumb manager not to see the value to team spirit in gestures like that, and as David said to them, 'You can either be heavy about it or you can treat it as harmless prank.' Clearly they preferred the former option because both men were fined £1,000. If senior members of management had had their way, the two players would have been sent home as well.

It was a complete overreaction and showed that they were already gunning for David, yet he was one of the most talented batsmen we've ever produced and a great fielder. Yes, he would far rather have a glass of vintage wine and a damn good lunch than a five-mile run – so would I for that matter – but he did score an awful lot of runs.

I soon had my own first taste of the new management approach. Just after the Oval Test against the West Indies, Graham Gooch was one of the guests on *Question of Sport*, the long-running BBC TV quiz on which I was a team captain at the time. As we were chatting before the programme Gooch asked me what I was doing about training. I told him I was a professional cricketer who'd been playing even longer than he had at Test level and I wasn't going to let him, England or myself down. As a joke, I added, 'Anyway, it's too late to worry about that now, Goochie. I'm on the plane, mate.'

He didn't even crack a smile. 'We can soon see about that.'

I had great admiration for the way Gooch had disciplined and reinvented himself after his portly early days in the game. On his Test debut, against Australia at Edgbaston in 1975, he was out for a pair, and took some stick for being overweight. His training regime dated from then, and to his considerable credit he had fashioned a prolonged and great Test career, maintaining and even improving his standards well into his thirties. The physical preparation of his players on his first tour as captain, to the West Indies in 1989–90, must also have contributed to their relative success, but when results and performances deteriorated, as they did in Australia the following winter, the only answer that Gooch and Stewart could come up with was to step up the training, even though it was clear to any onlooker that it was now proving counterproductive.

Gooch had a 'one size fits all' approach – if it worked for him, it must work for everyone else – but that simply wasn't the case, and the most high-profile victim of his approach was David Gower. A 'touch' player, a thoroughbred of incomparable talents, Gower was treated like a reluctant carthorse and worked into the ground.

On the previous occasion I had toured under Mickey Stewart's management, in 1986-87, he had been fine, but then he had just been feeling his way into the job and his captain, Mike Gatting, ran the show pretty much his way. Now Mickey and Graham were equal partners, and as well as driving the players on in training, Stewart also filled their heads with meaningless jargon and 'business-speak' like the 'corridor of uncertainty'. Mickey also spent hours analysing the opposition batsmen and lecturing me and the other bowlers on what not to bowl to them ... but in my experience, most Test bowlers tend to be aware that bowling accurately to a good length is quite a good idea and that it's best not to bowl too many half-volleys, long-hops and full tosses.

Gooch and Stewart's obsession with keeping the squad constantly together so that every available minute was spent either playing, in the nets, training or talking about cricket also caused major problems. Human nature being what it is, among a sixteen- or seventeen-man squad each player is bound to have a few close friends, a few nodding acquaintances and one or two that he really doesn't like. If you're constantly forced to spend all your time in each other's company, the inevitable results are going to be boredom and friction between players, and if all your time is spent training, practising and playing, staleness and fatigue will result, none of which is exactly good for team morale or results. In all the England tours I had been on, I had never heard so many complaints like 'Oh no, not bloody nets again' and 'God, I'm knackered'.

I arrived in New Zealand towards the end of January 1992 and was straight in the tabloids again. I had overdone the Christmas pud before I came out and put on a bit of weight, but it was nothing serious and Mickey Stewart obviously wasn't unduly concerned because he told me to acclimatise myself with an afternoon on the golf course. However, a photographer then took a few pictures of me enjoying myself out on the golf course, a reporter added some copy suggesting that I had skipped nets, and the 'red tops' had a nice picture story. My new tabloid nickname was clearly 'Fatty' not 'Beefy' from now on. As one paper put it: BOTHAM PUTS HIS GUTS INTO PUTTS.

The original plan had been for me to sit out all the matches in New Zealand, keeping me wrapped in cotton wool for the World Cup, but injuries to Chris Lewis and Derek Pringle meant that I had to be called into the side for the third Test at Wellington. Derek broke the news to me the night before. 'I'm struggling with a back injury, Beef, so don't go out on the lash till five a.m. tonight... best be in bed by three!' The match was a memorable occasion for me as, albeit by default, I collected my hundredth Test cap. My overriding memory of the game was not of that personal milestone, however, but of a horrific injury to fast bowler David 'Syd' Lawrence. The game was ambling towards a draw but Syd never gave it less than everything he'd got, and as he came charging in to bowl, making the ground shake, he hit his delivery stride, and then there was a sound like a pistol shot and he collapsed. I knew at once that he was in big trouble; Syd never made a fuss about anything, yet he was now screaming in agony. I'm not surprised – his kneecap had broken in half. I could see both parts below the skin and they were three or four inches apart. We got him on a stretcher, off the pitch and away to hospital as quickly as possible. We were all tremendously upset; he was a very popular character and a good player, and his career had now been ended by a freak injury. A press cameraman – and they can be real ghouls at times like these – was actually trying to get into the ambulance to get some pictures. I manhandled him out of there and then got in trouble with the England management for doing so. I just said, 'You saw how much pain Syd was in. Now you just back off,' and for once they did.

The next casualty of the trip was less severe: Allan Lamb's dodgy hamstring went in the final one-day international at Christchurch, and ruled him out of all our World Cup matches until the last two qualifying games. I'd played in the last two one-day internationals, opening the batting at Christchurch, where I'd hit 79 from seventy-three balls, and we were in good shape, winning the one-day series 3-0 and the Test series 2-0, putting us in good heart for the World Cup, but it had also taken a lot out of us. We should have had some time off for r'n'r, but instead we kept playing one practice match after another. I tried to tell Gooch and Stewart that they were over-doing it and wearing everybody out, but they just didn't want to know. Part of the problem might have been that Gooch appeared to have no interests or hobbies outside cricket. He didn't play golf, he didn't go fishing or sailing, all he wanted to do was train and play. His fitness regime left him so tired that he frequently fell asleep at the dinner table, and it wore out his players too.

The next month or so was highly successful on the field but murder off it, with constant travelling between games and Gooch and Stewart pushing us to the limit on the training ground. We began in Perth against India, where we won a tight game by nine runs, and then beat the West Indies in Melbourne, restricting them to just 157 all out, which we knocked off for the loss of four wickets.

Next came Pakistan, on an overcast day in Adelaide. Our seamers exploited the English-style conditions to the full and the Pakistanis just couldn't break the stranglehold. Derek Pringle took three for 8 in eight overs, I took two for 12 in ten, and they were hustled out for just 74 – their lowest-ever one-day total and the lowest ever recorded by a Test-playing side in the World Cup. Victory was guaranteed, and it would have sent us into the next round and eliminated Pakistan from the tournament, but when we had reached 24 for one from eight overs the heavens opened and washed out the rest of the match.

The game was declared void and all we could claim was a moral victory, but it did strengthen our belief that we were the best team in the competition, and our next match against Australia under the floodlights at the Sydney Cricket Ground confirmed that. We bundled the Aussies out for 171 and cruised to victory by eight wickets. I had a great night, taking four for 31, including a spell of four wickets for no runs in seven balls, and then scored my first ever half-century – 53 – in the World Cup, sharing an opening partnership of 107 with Gooch. I nearly added another one against Sri Lanka but was out for 47. It didn't matter; we batted well all the way down the order to total 280 and then bowled them out for 174.

Apart from the bad break with the weather in Adelaide, everything had gone perfectly for us so far, but the wheels began to come off when we returned to Melbourne to play South Africa, now returned to the fold after their exile in the sporting wilderness. The endless round of training and playing was beginning to take its toll. Gooch had already strained his hamstring in the game against Sri Lanka and missed the South Africa game, and Phil DeFreitas pulled a muscle, limped through his ten overs and then had to leave the field. Dermot Reeve only managed two and a bit overs before a back injury ruled him out. We ended up using seven different bowlers and did quite well to restrict South Africa to 236 for four, but we were in real trouble at 166 for five. Neil Fairbrother hit 75 not out, and with a rain interruption reducing the target to 226 from forty-one overs, he and Phil DeFreitas saw us through with a ball to spare.

We had now qualified for the semi-final stages, but our injury worries were growing. Derek Pringle was added to the sick list after straining his ribs in our next match against New Zealand. That game saw our first defeat in the competition. Our total of 200 never looked enough and the Kiwis passed it for the loss of three wickets. Worse was to follow in our next game when, exhausted, injury-hit and perhaps over-confident, we slumped to a humiliating defeat against the minnows of Zimbabwe. They were on an eighteen-match losing streak and entertained no hopes of beating us. Their number eleven, Malcolm Jarvis, said that the theme of each Zimbabwean team talk before their previous matches had been 'We can beat this team', but before the England game the theme was 'Let's see how long we can last'. Long enough, as it turned out.

We put them in to bat, hoping for a low total and a quick finish, and bowled them out for 134 – first part of the mission accomplished. However, when we batted we lost Graham Gooch to the first ball of the innings. Allan Lamb and I then added 32, not altogether comfortably – my two boundaries both came off inside edges that whistled past leg-stump – but we then lost four wickets in rapid succession and at 43 for five – four of them to a chicken farmer, Eddo Brandes – we were staring at a defeat. Neil Fairbrother and Alec Stewart then seemed to have got us out of jail with a fifty partnership, but the Zimbabweans weren't finished and broke through again. We began the last over still needing 10 runs, and with our last pair at the wicket, Gladstone Small chipped the first ball to mid-wicket to give the Zimbabweans the greatest victory in their cricket history. To add insult to injury, Zimbabwe's coach, Don Topley, was one of Graham Gooch's teammates at Essex. After the game he told Gooch that he'd remind him of the game every single day of the coming English season. 'No you won't,' Gooch said, showing that at least his sense of humour was relatively intact, 'because I don't expect I'll be coming to too many second-team matches!'

Although we had already qualified for the semi-finals, the defeat was hardly ideal preparation for the match against Zimbabwe's neighbours, South Africa, and we won through as a result of the tournament's arcane rules. We were put into bat and despite again losing Gooch early we batted pretty well to a total of 252 for six, though Kepler Wessels' tactics were an irritation. Since his bowlers couldn't get us out, he indulged in so much time-wasting that they only completed forty-five overs in the allotted time. South Africa's batsmen all made a few runs and either side could have won as we entered the closing stages, but an interruption for rain and bad light brought the calculators out and exposed the stupidity of the tournament's rain rules. Requiring 22 from thirteen balls, the South Africans were then told they needed 22 runs from seven balls, and then, farcically, 21 from one ball. As I walked past Brian McMillan, who was facing the next ball, I said, 'Bloody hell, Macca, you aren't half going to have to hit this one a long way.'

It wasn't really amusing though; the target was impossible to achieve, and the situation was infuriating for the South Africans, embarrassing for us and baffling for the crowd, whose boos and catcalls showed what they thought of it. Even though it could have been seen as payback for Wessels' negative tactics, no one really wants to win a game like that. The South Africans took it pretty well in the circumstances, but it was clearly a ridiculous situation for either side to have been in. Nonetheless, we were now in the World Cup final, facing Pakistan at the Melbourne Cricket Ground.

The night before the final we had to attend a banquet. When the meal finished, a drag artist took to the stage and started to take the piss out of the Queen. Dame Edna it definitely wasn't. It was crude, rude and deeply offensive to any patriotic Englishman. I took it for a couple of minutes and then I got up and made for the exit. Graham Gooch joined me and Mickey Stewart was on the point of doing so as well when he thought better of it and sat down again. I knew there would be repercussions, and sure enough the next morning the papers were full of the story and the airwaves were humming with it. Paul Keating, the Australian Prime Minister, got in on the act, describing me as 'precious', so I snapped back, 'No I'm not, I'm just very, very proud of my heritage ... and, unlike Mr Keating, I actually have one.'

I put it all to the back of my mind as we took the field. It was my second appearance in a World Cup final; the first had been in 1979 when one of Viv Richards' greatest innings had given the West Indies the trophy. Back then I had swallowed my disappointment, knowing that I was still young enough to win a World Cup medal in the future, but now, as I looked around the packed tiers of the MCG, I knew it was the last-chance saloon for me. It was one of the biggest games of my entire career and I was determined to finish on the winning side this time. Had the final come a couple of weeks earlier we would have been the unbeaten favourites for the title, but now, injury-hit, fatigued and fresh from two defeats and a victory that was at least in part engineered by the competition's rule-makers, we looked there for the taking.

We weren't just taking on Pakistan in the final, it seemed that the whole of Australia was against us as well. Even in Ashes series I had never known such a level of vitriol to be directed at us before and during the game. It was much more than the usual Aussie Pom-bashing, it was pure hate-filled abuse, delivered in foul language. Kath was watching the game from the stands and she told me the swearing was horrific and not confined to adults; even quite young kids were joining in.

Imran Khan won the toss and decided to bat, but we had a real stranglehold on them early on. Derek Pringle took two early wickets and then had a huge shout against Javed Miandad turned down. Derek was convinced that Miandad was plumb lbw, but the umpire disagreed. Imran Khan promoted himself to speed up the run rate, but he then struggled himself and had made just 9 from sixteen overs when he tried to drive a slower ball from Phil DeFreitas and skied it to mid-wicket. Goochie had to make a lot of ground but got under it in time. What happened next was reported by a radio commentator: 'Imran is out. No, Gooch drops him.' He would have held that catch nine times out of ten, but on this crucial occasion, it didn't stick. Reprieved, Imran began to accelerate and made 72 in a stand of nearly 140 with Javed. Inzamam-ul-Haq then smacked 42 from thirty-five balls and Wasim Akram 33 from eighteen. In the last twenty overs, Pakistan had put on 153, including a vital 52 in the last six. Their total of 249 for six, although by no means out of reach, was now a very stiff one.

I opened the England innings again with Goochie, facing Wasim Akram and Aqib Javed, who were moving the ball about a lot. Akram came round the wicket to me and it was an eventful first over. He bowled a no-ball, then struck me high on the pad. He appealed, but it was way too high. Next came a very wide wide, but the next one was straighter, and with some sharp late movement away from the bat. I played and missed outside the off-stump but the ball flicked the upper shirtsleeve of my right arm as it flew through to the keeper.

I knew at once that, even though I hadn't edged it, the amount it had deviated and the faint noise as it flicked my sleeve would make it easy for the umpire to think I'd got a touch on it. TV replays showed that the ball was nowhere near my bat or hands and only caught the upper part of my sleeve, but Kiwi umpire Brian Aldridge couldn't see those and he gave me out, caught behind for a duck. Heart-sick and seething with anger that my last chance on the biggest stage in world cricket had been ended so unjustly, my mood was not helped by one of the Pakistan fielders, Aamir Sohail, who, recalling my ill-advised comments of a decade before, said, 'Why don't you send out your mother-in-law now? She couldn't do any worse.'

When I stormed into the dressing room, my teammates took one look at my face and gave me plenty of elbow-room. I vented my anger on the nearest inanimate object, taking my bat and smashing it into little pieces. It was childish, I know, but it was the only way I could think of to relieve the tension and frustration without generating a fresh wave of newspaper headlines. When I'd calmed down a little, I had a shower and went to join the rest of the players on the balcony. Whatever happened now was out of my hands. I could only sit and watch.

Gooch had been going well, but when he was fourth out at 69, we were struggling. Neil Fairbrother, who scored a fine 62, and Allan Lamb then swung the balance back our way a little as they put on 72 in fourteen overs, but Wasim Akram then produced two astonishing deliveries, clean-bowling Lamby for 31 and then doing the same to Chris Lewis the next delivery. The first one, bowled from round the wicket, was going well down the leg side when suddenly, about two-thirds of the way down the wicket, it began to swing and moved so far to the off that, having beaten Allan all ends up, it clipped the off bail. The next one, to Chris Lewis, did the reverse, starting well wide of off-stump but then suddenly swerving in to hit the stumps. I just sat there open-mouthed; I had never before seen a cricket ball behave like those two deliveries, and I couldn't think of a single batsman who would have managed to even get a touch on either of them.

It was the decisive moment of the match, and we eventually lost by 22 runs to a team that, had it not rained in Adelaide, would not even have reached the semi-finals. As I watched the last rites of the match, I knew that I would never have another chance. The World Cup had been there for the taking and now it had gone. The dressing room is never a happy place after a defeat, but this was as bad as I had ever seen it. Nobody spoke; everyone was lost in their own private thoughts. Goochie had now lost in three World Cup finals and was absolutely inconsolable. I felt that the endless training, nets and playing for months on end had ground us down and perhaps cost us the World Cup, but I kept those thoughts to myself. I could see how very much this game had meant to him, and, like me, he would now never experience the feeling of winning a World Cup. It remains a competition that England has never won. To his credit, Goochie later admitted to me over a drink, that he felt he'd got it wrong and overdone the training.

On my return to England in the spring of 1992, I changed county for the second and last time in my career. I had achieved real success in my five years with Worcestershire; it was a great team with a fabulous team spirit, and my decision to give that up in exchange for a move to Durham was one of the worst mistakes I ever made. On the surface there were great attractions in going there. Durham was a new side in the County Championship and full of ideas and ambition, and the prospect of playing home matches only an hour's drive from where I lived was extremely appealing; it felt like I was finally playing at home for the first time in my career. I had actually been offered the captaincy as one of the inducements to join the county in the first place, but when I later met Geoff Cook, the director of cricket, to confirm the details of my move, he told me that he had already promised the captaincy to David Graveney. I was not happy, but there was nothing I could do about that decision, so I shrugged my shoulders; but it became more and more obvious to me that Cook had never wanted me at the club in the first place. His big idea was that there should be no star system at Durham. It was his dream to build a kind of 'socialist cricket republic' where all the players would be equal.

I enjoyed my cricket at Durham but I didn't enjoy the office politics that went with it. I never stopped trying – I've never given less than my best in my life – but there was a lot of internal wrangling that didn't make it a happy experience for anyone. As a new club, it was inevitably feeling its way to an extent, but there was also an internal power struggle going on that the players found themselves dragged into. That had an inevitable effect on team morale, and the more games we lost, the worse that became.

Even more depressingly, I was out of favour with the England selectors, and after playing in the first two Tests against Pakistan that summer I was omitted from the last three and from the tour of India and Sri Lanka that followed it. I did play a full part in the one-day series against Pakistan, however, filling in as a temporary opener – and scoring 40 – in the fourth ODI at Lord's, though that was the only one of the five-match series we didn't win.

However, the game was notable for another reason: the use of ball-tampering by the Pakistani team. Not long after I was out, and just before the lunch interval, I saw Allan Lamb do a double-take as he looked at the ball, then pick it up and hand it to umpire Ken Palmer. He in turn showed it to his fellow umpire John Hampshire and they immediately concluded that the ball had been tampered with. The ball was replaced but, to avoid a scandal, the England players were ordered not to discuss what had happened with anyone.

Ball-tampering was already a hot issue for us; we believed that some Pakistani players had been doing it since the tour began. Others, including BBC commentator Richie Benaud, had noticed it as well. I fundamentally disagreed with covering up cheating in the game so I got hold of Chris Lander as soon as play had finished and told him what had happened, so that he would run a story in the newspapers about it.

The story then acquired legs of its own as Sarfraz Nawaz began court proceedings against Allan Lamb – subsequently dropped – for accusing him of ball-tampering. Lamb's reward for raising an issue that Lord's wanted swept under the carpet was never to be picked for England again. The one umpire, Don Oslear, who had the courage to stand up and confirm that ball-tampering had taken place was treated in the same way: he was removed from the umpires list and never stood in another Test.

However, Lord's could not put the genie back in the bottle, and as the controversy grew, discussion turned again and again to those two extraordinary deliveries by Wasim Akram in the World Cup final. Although ball-tampering became a huge issue in world cricket in the coming months, in my opinion Wasim and Waqar Younis, another player who was under something of a cloud of suspicion, were such talented players that they certainly had no need to resort to ball-tampering. Wasim was one of the greatest fast bowlers who ever lived – an amazing cricketer – and Waqar was hugely talented too.

However, ball-tampering was certainly a charge that could be levelled against Imran Khan, because he publicly confessed to doing it, but then went on to claim that it wasn't cheating. In his authorised biography he admitted to occasionally scratching the side of the ball and lifting the seam, usually with his nails. Only once, he said, did he use an object: 'When Sussex were playing Hampshire in 1981 the ball was not deviating at all. I got the 12th man to bring on a bottle top and it began to move around a lot.' Having made these admissions, Imran shortly afterwards resigned as Pakistan's representative to the ICC, a decision applauded by the ICC chief executive David Richards as 'entirely appropriate'.

Imran even went on a television programme to demonstrate exactly how he used the bottle-top, but he continued to insist that he had done nothing wrong, and certainly nothing that could be construed as cheating. That's not what the laws of cricket say and it was not what I felt – and said – about it. I'd never tampered with the ball, and when Imran was quoted in the *Sun* claiming that 'the biggest names in English cricket have all done it', I felt it was time to set the record straight. The situation was further inflamed by an interview with Imran, published in *India Today*, claiming that 'the English media and a section of cricketers' were blowing the row 'out of all proportion', and having suggested that English complaints were based on racism, the article went on to say that people who agreed with Imran's views were 'educated Oxbridge types' like Christopher Martin-Jenkins and Tony Lewis. 'Look at the others,' Imran was quoted as saying, 'Lamb, Botham, Trueman. The difference in class and upbringing makes a difference.'

Imran would later claim, like so many other sportsmen when

embarrassing quotes are published, that he had been misquoted or his remarks taken out of context. He also wrote me a letter to put the record straight, claiming that he had never 'called anyone lower class or under class'.

It was not enough. Comments about me had appeared under his name in the *Sun* and *India Today* implying that, like the other biggest names in English cricket, I had been guilty of ball-tampering and that my criticisms of Pakistani players for doing so were motivated by racism and class hatred. I've been called a lot of things in my life, many of them justified, but to call me a racist shows such a profound ignorance of me, and was so deeply and grievously insulting, that I could not let it pass. Had Imran thought for a moment about me and about the people who are my friends, he would have known how inaccurate and how wounding such a comment would be. I had fierce on-field rivalries with many players, including Viv Richards, Javed Miandad, Wasim Raja and Aamir Sohail, but off the field there was no edge at all; we were very good friends and remain so to this day.

I instructed Alan Herd to start libel proceedings against Imran. Allan Lamb also sued him. I wasn't motivated by a desire for revenge for our World Cup defeat, nor by the chance of a quick buck, as some observers suggested. All I wanted was a clear public apology for the allegations that I was guilty of ball-tampering – cheating – that struck at the heart of my standing as a professional sportsman, and that I was motivated by race and class hatred. The closest Imran would come to that was an offer to write an open letter to *The Times*, but the draft he produced suggested that he was going to hide behind the claims that he had been misquoted, and not just once, but three times: by his official biographer, by the *Sun* and by *India Today*. It was laughable, and I turned it down.

No apology was forthcoming, and the libel case eventually went to court. Imran was represented by George Carman, the larger-than-life libel QC with a reputation for winning improbable cases for his clients, and he certainly justified his reputation and his enormous fees on this occasion. Even after Imran was forced to withdraw in court his allegations of ball-tampering against me and apologise for doing so, Mr Carman planted enough doubt and innuendo in the jurors' minds that when the verdict was announced they had found for Imran, a decision that left the judge visibly stunned and angered. Over ten years have passed since then and I still cannot understand how the jurors allowed themselves to be persuaded to vote that way. It may be that it was a mistake for Allan Lamb and me to take joint action against Imran – perhaps that appeared to be two white guys ganging up on a Pakistani one, though that was emphatically not the case.

I'm full of admiration for Imran's work in establishing a cancer hospital in Lahore, but I don't suppose that he and I will ever be sharing a dinner table again and that's not something that keeps me awake at night.

There were an awful lot of other allegations of ball-tampering over the succeeding years and I've got my private opinions about who has done it and who hasn't, but the one consolation is that, in the modern era when TV cameras now cover every move on a cricket field, it's not that hard to detect and police. The umpires can check the ball whenever they want – every over if they wish – and tampering is not hard to see. You hear of it very rarely now and I hope that the authorities have at last got the problem under control.

David Gower played his last Test for England in the final Test of that contentious 1992 series against Pakistan. Although I didn't know it at the time, I had already played my last one earlier in the series at Lord's. I had decided that 1993 would be my last season as a professional cricketer anyway, but I wanted to go out at the very top and I was determined to win back my place in the England team to face Australia for the Ashes. I felt I still had plenty to offer, and what had gone on in India and Sri Lanka, when they had been thrashed in all four Tests, suggested that England needed some inspiration from somewhere.

Graham Gooch had passed David Gower's record as England's highest run scorer in Test cricket during the tour, a fitting reward for having kept himself fit enough to play Test cricket for twenty years, but as England captain – and I should know, since I suffered from a similar complaint – he had never understood that what worked for him was often the wrong thing for someone else.

Gooch hadn't even wanted to go on the winter tour but then allowed himself to be talked into it. He was by no means the only one on that tour who looked and played as though they didn't want to be there, yet the man who might have made a difference and had genuinely wanted to go, David Gower, wasn't there because Gooch had dumped him from the tour squad for reasons that I'll never understand … if I didn't know better, I'd say it was to ensure that he'd pass David's Test match run record!

The team that Gooch did take seemed – admittedly from a few thousand miles away – to lack motivation, will to win and any pride in their own and their team's performance, and when things started to go wrong they gave up without a fight as the tour dissolved in a fog of excuses and mutual recriminations. Sending out a 'pastoral counsellor', the Reverend Andrew Wingfield Digby, instead of a team doctor showed that Lord's was as dazed and confused as the players … or perhaps, by that stage of the tour, prayer really was the only answer.

Even with the England team ripe for changes, I knew how hard it would be for me to claim a place. I had apparently been written off by the selectors and the media, but I had come back before and I could do so again, especially with the prize of a chance to face Allan Border's Australians at stake. It hurt my personal and professional pride to see an England team performing so badly and I knew that, even at my age and with my back problems, I could do better, a lot better, than the all-rounders who were being picked ahead of me.

My record against Australia was as good as anyone's and I still held a psychological edge on them. I was delighted to be picked for the Duchess of Norfolk's XI at Arundel in the traditional opening fixture of an Australian tour and I was genuinely excited about the match. So were the public: the roads were so choked with traffic that it took us an hour to travel the short distance to the ground, and the 'House Full' signs were up with 16,000 people packed inside.

The Australians were certainly not taking the game lightly, and nor were their fans. When I was hit for four in the opening over I heard an Aussie voice yell out, 'It's '93 now mate, not '81.' I didn't hear too much more from him after I had Damien Martyn caught by Joel Garner, and I then took the prized wicket of the Australian captain, clean bowling Allan Border through the gate as he tried to push the ball on the offside – a weakness of his that I'd managed to exploit before. I finished with two for 29 in ten overs.

As chairman of the selectors, Ted Dexter was there to run the rule over the England candidates on view, but he clearly wasn't impressed. When asked by Mark Saggers in a BBC radio interview what he thought of my bowling, Dexter said, 'Are the Australians trying to play him into the side?' Saggers thought Dexter must have been joking, but when he said, 'But seriously though ...', Dexter refused to say anything else at all.

A couple of journalists told me about it at once, but wanting to avoid yet another run-in with the TCCB for talking out of turn, and perhaps scuppering my already thin Test chances for good, I decided the best thing to do was just go home. It was probably a wise move, but when I read the newspapers the following morning, my anger bubbled up. How dare Dexter suggest that the Aussies would throw their wickets away against me to con the selectors into picking me. The last thing any Aussie wanted to do, especially Border, for whom Headingley 1981 was a permanent scar on his playing career, was to get out to me; his aim would have been to hit me out of the attack to establish a psychological advantage.

I was so angry that I phoned the TCCB and told them that I wanted an immediate, unconditional apology from Dexter. It took him two days but he finally phoned me at home and told me, 'It was just a throwaway line I came up with, because I wanted to avoid the interview being all about Ian Botham. And after all, you're the master of the one-liner, Ian; look at what you said about Pakistan being the kind of place you would send your mother-in-law for a paid holiday.'

'True enough, Ted,' I said. 'And the board fined me one thousand pounds for that one. How much are they going to fine you?'

I'd been around long enough to have a pretty good idea of the answer to that, but I wasn't ready to let him off the hook just yet. 'I'm not happy about what you said and I'm not going to back down,' I said. 'If someone in your position behaves like that then it's up to you to explain yourself and apologise for it.' In the end he did manage to bring himself to apologise, which was all I wanted. It was no great surprise when the TCCB let it pass without any official comment or reprimand for Dexter, whereas if a player – especially me – had come out with those kind of comments about another player – or, perish the thought, a TCCB official – there would have been hell to pay.

After that indication of the way the wind was blowing, I never expected to get picked for the first Test that summer. I still felt I was better than all the other all-rounders – Chris Cowdrey, David Capel, Phil DeFreitas and Chris Lewis – who had been tried in my place, but when Lewis picked up an injury and was ruled out of the third one-day international at Lord's, he was replaced by Dermot Reeve. I was now not even the fifth best all-rounder in England in the selectors' eyes, yet I could not imagine the Aussies quaking in their boots at facing Reeve or any of the others, whereas the name Botham on the team sheet would certainly have given them pause for thought. They were privately delighted, if a little puzzled, that I was not being picked.

The late Kenny Barrington had once told me that Dexter was a hell of a player, but could be something of a weirdo. He would wander about in a dream, even during a match, and he was renowned for reacting to pressure by practising his golf swing in the slips. It had its amusing side, but he was way too eccentric to be running English cricket. I wasn't picked for the first two Tests, both of which Australia won, and I didn't hear from Dexter again until a few days before the third Test at Trent Bridge. When the phone rang I was stunned to hear Dexter's voice. Was there a chance of a recall to the England team even at this late stage? Was there hell. 'Ian,' Dexter said, 'I was wondering, would you be interested in taking the England A team to Holland as captain?' I could hardly believe my ears. I couldn't decide whether this was supposed to be some sort of consolation prize after my exclusion from the Test side, or some warped public relations exercise. Either way, I wanted nothing to do with it, so I just said, 'Sorry, prior engagements and all that,' and put the phone down.

England was 2-0 down after two Tests. If ever a side needed stiffening with experience, this was the moment, yet when the team was announced, it contained five uncapped players. I knew then that even if every other all-rounder in England was struck by lightning, I'd never play for England again. If Dexter didn't want me to be part of the new set-up, why didn't he have the guts to say so to my face? In the back of my mind I can't help wondering whether the real reason why Dexter, Gooch and the other selectors did not want David Gower, Allan Lamb or me back in the side was that if we had succeeded they would have been left looking pretty stupid for leaving us out in the first place.

I went back to county cricket with Durham but it remained a troubled, unsuccessful team, and the atmosphere off the field was not designed to improve matters on it. I wasn't enjoying playing very much and I was glad of a break of five days after our game against Glamorgan at Cardiff in the second round of the NatWest Trophy. I flew down to our holiday home in Alderney to join Kath, who was already there with the kids. We had started going to Alderney in the first place because of John Arlott, who had moved there some years earlier for the good of his health; he suffered from emphysema and the clean air and sea breezes helped it. We fell in love with the place ourselves and, having stayed with him on our first few visits, we eventually bought our own holiday home there.

John and I shared many a glass of wine together on Alderney; I would see him virtually every day when we were there. He had an unbreakable routine. He would wake up at 6.30 every morning, listen to the *Today* programme on Radio 4, then turn off the radio and make two phone calls. The first was always to his doctor – also a close friend – and the second call of the day was always to me. Kath and I reckoned we could set our watches by him, because the call would come in at exactly six minutes past nine every morning. The phone would go and when I picked it up, the voice with that famous Hampshire burr would say, 'What time are you coming round?'

'What time would you like me, John?'

'As soon as possible, and bring your thirst with you.'

I wandered up to his house at about 9.30, by which time the day's wine deliveries had arrived – and there were always plenty because John was as prolific, knowledgeable and well regarded a wine writer as he was a cricket commentator, and one of the few British wine experts whose opinions were as respected by the French as by his fellow Britons.

So my first job when I arrived was to sort out the new deliveries and take them down to the cellar for him. He had a lovely little wicker basket that held six bottles of wine and I'd then fill that with the wines that he'd chosen to drink that day – and he had a magnificent cellar. As my knowledge of wine grew under John's tutoring, I'd try to tell him about New World wines. He was very sceptical at first but, though he would never publicly admit it, he did come to enjoy some of them in the end. We'd sit and chat, and though his emphysema made his conversation slow as he paused every few words to catch his breath, he was a remarkable raconteur and what he said was always spellbinding.

What always struck me about the man was his generosity of spirit. That is not to say he never had a bad word to say about anyone, but those who got it in the neck generally deserved it; to those fortunate enough to win his respect, he was a fiercely loyal friend. The generosity showed in the way that he treated everyone alike; he was one of the few people I met over the years to whom a person's essential humanity meant more than any status, wealth or fame. When asked to fill out an immigration form on entering South Africa for the first time he was appalled to be asked to what race he belonged. He thought for a moment and then wrote 'human'.

Kath and John's wife Pat usually joined us for lunch and we'd drink our wine from the antique glasses that John collected; he had a huge collection of corkscrews too. Kath and I might then disappear for an hour or two to go swimming or take the boat out, but I'd come back at four o'clock prompt and take him for a drive around the island. We always went in his car but I drove while John sat in the passenger seat, taking in the views. We maintained a pretty stately pace of about five miles an hour, which must have driven anyone behind us demented if they were in a hurry, though Alderney wasn't the sort of place to be in a rush about anything. I once accelerated to about nine miles an hour and John glanced across at me and said, 'What's your rush?'

He would always find something new to tell me about every place we passed, even though we had done so many, many times before. We had a couple of regular watering holes where someone would already be waiting with a couple of glasses of wine on a tray as we crawled slowly into sight. We'd pull over and enjoy the sea views for a while and then make our slow way back to John's house.

His wife Pat and I always tried to persuade him not to go down into the cellar at his house, because he wasn't a well man by then and the steps were steep and narrow, but one day he got it into his head that he had to go down to check on something and fell, then had a heart attack. He was rushed to hospital in Southampton, and when I went to see him I took along a half-bottle of cognac because John always liked a brandy when he was in hospital. I showed it to his doctor who said, 'A shot of brandy – just one mind – will do him no harm at all.'

I found John sitting up in bed and champing at the bit to get back to Alderney. Though I was heartbroken when he died, I was glad that his last days were spent in the home on Alderney that he loved. He died there on 14 December 1991, at the age of seventy-seven. I was one of the pallbearers at his funeral. He was a great friend to me and I miss him still.

Whenever we were in Alderney after that, Kath's dad Gerry and I would always go to John's grave with a bottle of wine. We'd have a glass or two each and then put the cork on the grave. We did it for years and we obviously weren't the only ones because each time we went there were more and more corks – dozens – on the grave, in tribute to that remarkable man.

When I got to Alderney on this occasion, it was beautiful, hot, dry weather, the Channel Islands at its best. We had a wonderful few days together, but when I woke up early on the last morning – I had to catch a flight back to Durham for our game against the Australians – I was so stiff and sore that it literally took me five minutes to get out of bed. As I was lying there, I did a quick mental check of my body: the shoulder operation that hadn't worked; the back operation that had, but who could say if and when that might give again; and the knees, hips and ankles, sore from all the pounding they'd taken on wickets all over the world. By the time I finally managed to get out of bed, my mind was made up. I'd always set myself high standards; if I could no longer match those standards, I didn't want to keep on playing any more.

From the moment I had my back operation in 1988, I had known that the clock was ticking and that one day time would run out. I made the most of the extra time that the surgeon John Davies had won for me with his skill, but I had now reached the end of the road. If I played on I risked embarrassing myself and my colleagues by failing to play to the standards I had always set myself and I might even do further damage to my back that could leave me crippled for life. Whatever else happened, I didn't want that. Physically it was all starting to fall apart, and mentally I'd had enough; I was just worn out from head to toe. Sitting on the edge of the bed that morning, I realised that my body was sending me a message that I'd have been mad to ignore.

After twenty years as a professional cricketer, I'd had enough. I was a physical wreck, tired and disillusioned, and I was no longer even enjoying playing the game. It was not fair to me, my teammates or the public to carry on playing. Many sportsmen find it hard to face the moment when their career is over and they often dread what will come next. I had no worries on either count. I'd enjoyed every moment of my career as a cricketer – well, almost every moment – but cricket wasn't the only thing in my life and I had a whole stack of other things I wanted to do. As far as accepting that it was time to go, I'd always said to Kath, 'When I wake up one morning and think "I don't want to do this any more", that's the day I'll retire, and I'll accept it without making things any more difficult for myself and those around me.'

I ran over everything again in my mind, wanting to be doubly sure. I knew where I stood with England, but I wanted to be sure that I was doing the right thing by Durham as well. I could see no point in playing any more championship cricket for them. We were near the bottom of the table anyway and the county needed to rebuild for the future. Although I could still score a few runs and take a few wickets – I'd hit a century against my old mates from Worcestershire earlier in the season – in our last match against Surrey at The Oval I had batted twice, faced eight balls, and made 8 runs as we lost in two days by an innings and more than 200 runs.

I knew I was not going to be playing next season so it made sense to retire now. A few players were out of contract at the end of the season and my going would give one of them a chance to stake a claim to my spot, and Durham the chance to assess their own priorities and the talent available to them. It would also save the club a few quid on my wages.

There was one other plus in quitting now. In every walk of life, dads want to see their sons doing better than they did; it's human nature. I was no exception. I'd never pushed Liam into professional sport. I was there to help, encourage and advise him if he needed it, but it was his choice what he did with his life. However, he had natural ability as a sportsman, determination and a strong will to win and was now on the verge of a professional career either in cricket or rugby. His talent and temperament were not at issue, but no one, including Liam, was under any illusions about the problems lying in wait for him, just because his surname was Botham.

He had already played for England Under-15s – one up on his father – and on the strength of his displays for England had been snapped up by Hampshire. When he made his Second XI debut against Worcestershire, the county ground at Southampton was besieged by reporters and photographers. Liam took the whole thing in his stride and even told them that he planned to be even better than his dad, and then went on to back it up by taking four wickets.

However, the paparazzi had already been targeting him, and a couple of weeks later there was 'an incident' in a nightclub. I was getting the strangest sense of déjà vu...

Liam had been playing for Hampshire Seconds against Warwickshire, and he went with some of the players to a nightclub that evening. He was smart enough to stick to soft drinks, but even so someone told the manager that Liam was underage. The manager told him that, even though Liam was doing nothing wrong, if there were any more complaints, he'd have to leave. Half an hour later there was another and Liam left without making any fuss about it, but the 'story' duly appeared in the *Sunday Mirror*: Liam Botham, son of cricketing legend Ian, kicked out of a nightclub, together with a lot of 'like father, like son' copy. It was clear to Liam and me now that while cricket fans might want to see if Liam was as good as his dad on the field, the tabloid reptiles would be out to prove he was as bad as me off it as well.

I'd love to have played with or against Liam at county level – and it would have been quite a battle if we'd been opponents, because we're both ferociously competitive, especially with each other. I'd had the next best thing when he played alongside me as a last-minute replacement in a charity match between the Rest of the World and my own England XI at Hove, and did pretty well, but I knew that it wasn't going to happen any other way now, because by the time Liam was a first team regular, I'd be out of the game. By announcing my retirement at once, rather than hanging on to the end of the season, I felt I could deflect some of the media pressure from him as he made his way in the game.

I never had any doubts that Liam was good enough to make it. His performance on his first class debut for Hampshire against Middlesex at Portsmouth, when two days short of his nineteenth birthday, proved 'Golden Balls' were hereditary. Summoned from a Second XI game at five minutes' notice when a player dropped out injured, Liam didn't arrive until after the game had started, but at once made an impact, dismissing Mike Gatting with the first ball of his second over and finishing with five for 67.

Had he had any other father and any other surname, he might well have been an England all-rounder like his dad; he really was that good. He could have gone all the way. However, having weighed up all his options and the career opportunities in his two preferred sports, he opted for a career in professional rugby. The media pressure was one, but only one, of the reasons he made his choice; it was also based on how he thought the two sports would develop and what the opportunities would be for him in each of them. Neither of us is the type to spend much time pondering on 'what might have been'. He made his choice, did well in his rugby career, and I'm as proud of him and his achievements as I am of my daughters Sarah and Becky.

Having made up my own mind about my future sporting prospects, I packed my bag, went downstairs and said to Kath, 'Right, I'm off. I'll see you in three days.'

'What?' she said. 'You're not due back for another three weeks.'

'No,' I said, 'three days. I'm retiring.'

Cliff Morgan, who had come over to record an interview with me, was staying with us and he guessed at once what was on my mind. When I got to Newcastle airport, Dean Jones picked me up and as soon as he saw my face he also said, 'You are, aren't you?'

I gave him a blank look. 'What are you on about?'

'You're throwing the towel in, aren't you?'

'How do you know that?' I said.

'Because I've never seen you look so happy on your way to a game of cricket. Jane and I were talking about when you might quit only last week.'

When I arrived at the Durham University ground, I told Geoff Cook, the director of cricket at Durham, and the club captain, David Graveney, straight away. Geoff agreed that I was doing the right thing and David, though shocked at first, soon came round and accepted it. We still had a mathematical chance of the Sunday League title at that stage and I told them that if they wanted me to play the last few games, I would, but in the end we decided it was better to make the clean break at once.

I left them to notify the other people at the club and break the news to the dressing room when they thought it was appropriate, but the Durham chairman, Don Robson, then got very upset with me because I hadn't notified him in person. It all became very petty. The club officials were straight on the phone to say that someone would be round to collect my sponsored car that day and that my medical insurance would be cancelled with immediate effect.

My last game would be against Australia. I couldn't have found a more appropriate way to bow out than against the old enemy, but the circumstances surrounding my final game of professional cricket have left me with a tinge of guilt. Although I was more than happy to be bowing out against the Aussies, it was such a spontaneous decision to go then that I didn't tell my parents about it until it was too late. I felt bad about that because my dad would probably have wanted to be there at the finish, as he was at the start, and I still regret not giving him that chance.

I had decided to keep the news quiet and, apart from Geoff Cook and David Graveney, Dean Jones was the only one of my teammates who knew in advance. None of the other players knew until the following day, when the *Mail on Sunday*, which had managed to get wind of it somehow, ran the story. Geoff then felt that he had to confirm it, but I kept silent until I had given Chris Lander the exclusive that our personal friendship merited and my contract with the *Daily Mirror* required.

My last innings in first class cricket ended on 32 when I was caught off Steve Waugh's occasional medium pace. We piled up 385 for six declared, shot Australia out for 221 and made them follow on, but rain interruptions and some good batting by the Aussies removed any possibility of a last victory over them to end my career. The final day's play didn't start until the afternoon because of rain, but I'd been kept busy all day. A retirement press conference went on for fifty-five minutes, probably the longest one of my career. When we eventually took the field we went through the motions as the game meandered towards a draw. I bowled six overs for 21, but didn't take one last wicket as David Boon and Matthew Hayden took the chance for some extended batting practice.

In my final over in first class cricket, bowled to 'Boonie', I decided to bowl a few balls in the style of Jeff Thomson, and then for my last ever ball in top-level cricket I upped the ante another notch. There were no TV cameras at the ground, the press photographers, bored out of their wits, had downed telephoto lenses and gone off in search of liquid refreshments, and the crowd was too far away to be able to see enough to get upset, so as I turned at my mark to run in one last time, I unzipped my fly, hauled out the 'meat and two veg' and ran in to bowl with my old man dangling free.

Boonie took one look and burst out laughing. 'Beefy,' he said, 'what are you doing? Jeez, no, you can't do this to me.'

By the time I got to the wicket he was almost crying with laughter, and if I'd managed to get the ball on target it would prob-ably have got him out, which might not have amused him quite as much in retrospect as he was battling to win a place in the Australian Test line-up at the time and needed to be the straight man in a comedy routine about as much as a hole in the head; he'd probably never have spoken to me again. However, Boonie survived, and with the old man safely restored to my flannels, I turned to David Graveney and said, 'Thanks David, I think that will do.'

It was quite a moment. I'd bowled my last ball as a professional cricketer, and as I went to take my position in the field, the reality of what I was doing suddenly hit me. In twenty years as a professional cricketer I'd scored almost twenty thousand runs, taken nearly twelve hundred wickets and 350 catches. Now it was over: no more bowling, no more batting, no more fielding, no more anything. The pavilion clock showed there was still half an hour to go, but my time was already up.

Boonie was out for a well-crafted century soon afterwards, but I can't remember that or anything else that happened until just before stumps when, minus pads and gloves, I made an appalling attempt to keep wicket for the final over of the match. As the umpires removed the bails – the last time I would ever witness that ritual end to the day – both batsmen, Matthew Hayden and Steve Waugh, came down the wicket to shake my hand. I waved to the sparse remnants of the crowd as I made my slow way off the field. It wasn't the end I would have chosen for myself – a century in each innings and a hat-trick to win the final Test against Australia at The Oval would have been more the mark – but it would have to do.

A small crowd of well-wishers and autograph-hunters had gathered by the pavilion steps. There were a few reporters' questions to answer as well, and then I went and had a quick beer with the Aussies in their dressing room. By the time I went to clear my locker, I discovered that there was nothing left to clear. My 'coffin' – my cricket bag – was there but there was nothing in it. The boys had already pinched the lot: gloves, bats, boots, the works. When I asked 'What's happened to my stuff?', one of them just said, 'Well, you won't be needing it any more, so we thought we'd have it.' They were right. I left the coffin there as well and set off out of the gates for the very last time.

Chapter 12

WHO THE HELL DID THEY
THINK THEY WERE?

I hadn't really given much thought to what would happen next. There had always been a vague plan to get into TV work at some point, though I'd never even had a preliminary discussion with anyone about it, but as soon as the news of my retirement broke, Sky TV's senior cricket producer got straight on the phone. He flew down to see me the next day, told me what they'd pay me and a contract was agreed without even specifying what I would do for them in return. As it turned out, working for Sky couldn't have suited me more. I have been fortunate to be part of their cricket commentary team ever since then, covering English cricket at Test, one-day international and domestic level. The people at Sky are great and have always looked after me very well. I really enjoy the work and the banter with the other geriatric cricketers in the commentary box, Athers, David Gower, Michael Holding, David Lloyd and all the other boys – the party hasn't stopped yet.

The only problem I've had has been with my colour blindness. I never found it the slightest handicap during my playing career, but now, when I'm looking at a graphic of the 'ball-spotter' or the 'pitch-planner' with different coloured spots to represent the result of each ball – boundary, wicket, dot-ball, one run, two runs, three runs – they all look the same colour to me and I have to give one of my colleagues a nudge and get him to fill in for me and interpret the images. Sky are so progressive in their coverage of all sports, always looking to innovate, and to be part of that has been really exciting. I'm not just saying this because I work for them; I really do believe that Sky's innovations such as super slo-mo cameras and Hawkeye have revolutionised the televising of the game worldwide. The next step must be for TV umpires to rule on more and more decisions. Whatever the purists may say about human error adding to the glorious uncertainty of sport, the fact is that livelihoods are at stake. It must be wrong when a cricketer's career is adversely affected, or even damaged beyond repair, by a decision he knows to be wrong, yet is powerless to overturn or even appeal against. When the technology exists to make absolutely certain whether a batsman is out, to put a player's job at risk for the sake of some nebulous notion about taking the rough with the smooth is merely perverse. The best technology is never 100 per cent; there will still be a place for human judgement. In the end, the principle that the batsman will always receive the benefit of the doubt will still remain intact, yet umpires will be allowed to get on with their main job of making sure the game runs smoothly without the intolerable pressure of being proved wrong by the cameras.

Not everyone is happy about Sky's involvement in cricket of course, but there's always been snobbery in the game and there's a bit of snobbery about the criticism I hear of Sky, much of which is hopelessly ill-informed. I heard one radio commentator complaining on air that 'Sky's footage of the Barmy Army is inflaming the situation on the Ashes tour'. I hate to rain on his parade but if he'd done the smallest amount of research he would have known that it wasn't Sky's footage anyway. We just take a feed from the host broadcaster, like the BBC used to do in the days when they bought the rights to televise cricket for almost nothing at all. Sky's involvement has not only revolutionised coverage of the game, it has also put a huge amount of money in cricket's and cricketers' pockets. If anyone thinks that

Test players are going to accept a 70 per cent wage cut just so that coverage can be given back to the BBC or one of the other terrestrial channels on the cheap, then they're living in a different world from the rest of us.

The transition from player to commentator has been an interesting one and obviously it has changed my relationship with the people who are playing the game now. I'm being paid as a TV pundit to express my opinion, and that's all I'm doing, but players – or often their wives – can take it very personally. I can understand that. When I was a player I used to take offence at some of the things that were written about me, but as you get older, you realise that's just the commentator's job; that's what he's being paid to do. When I'm commentating or summarising, I'm simply stating things as I see them – that was a magnificent innings, that was a poor shot, the wrong bowling change, and so on – and sometimes I'll express those opinions in fairly colourful terms. However, anything I say about a player I'm happy to repeat to his face. I don't hide from them and I will justify what I've said to them.

On one tour of the Caribbean I thought the England bowling attack was a bit toothless. It was a pretty average West Indian team, and we regularly had them five or six wickets down but then couldn't knock them over. I made the comment that the England attack had all the killer instinct of the Teletubbies. A couple of them took offence at that, but I said to them, 'OK, hold on, which one of you can tell me to my face now that I'm wrong?' They started saying, 'Well, we're trying our hardest ...' and I said, 'I never said you weren't. I said you had the killer instinct of the Teletubbies and I'll stand by it.'

I am paid to express an opinion, and it isn't an uninformed one; like Brian Close all those years ago at Somerset, I'm not asking the current England players to do anything I wouldn't, couldn't and haven't already done myself. I try to keep it balanced and I try not to target particular players, because if they're that bad they'll do it by themselves, but some things really get my hackles rising. I sit in the Sky commentary box and watch a bowler who's trying his guts out. If a regulation catch goes to slip and he drops it, the bowler then calls out 'Well tried' or 'Bad luck'. Bad luck? If it was me, I wouldn't be consoling him, I'd be calling him a bleeding idiot, and I'd expect my teammates to do the same to me if I dropped a catch or got myself out with a wild slog. Yet the 'never mind, well tried' attitude seems to pervade every aspect of our society now. I've watched my grandchildren at primary school, where all the games they play are non-competitive and their teachers keep telling everyone that 'there are no losers here, everyone's a winner'. But what happens when they grow up and go into the big world outside the school gates, because life is competitive, make no mistake about that.

One thing hasn't changed for me having made the transition from player to commentator: I still hate to see England lose. So the 2006-07 Ashes tour was a pretty unpleasant experience for me, as it was for the players and everyone involved with the England team. I got a sense of déjà vu reading the criticism of 'Freddie' Flintoff. His team was under-performing and he was struggling for form with the bat, and the press comments were the same as the ones I used to get when I was England captain: he'd lost form because of the pressures of the captaincy. I didn't believe it was true of me back then and I don't believe it was necessarily true of Freddie either, but a lot did go wrong on that tour. It was a humiliation for the England team and for English cricket in general. It would be easy to blame the coach – he's always a convenient scapegoat – and there's no doubt that Duncan Fletcher got a few things wrong, both on the Ashes tour and in the World Cup that followed it, with equally disastrous results, but the coach doesn't go out on the pitch. The players are the ones who go through the gate on to the field of play, and they're the ones who have to carry the can if they don't deliver.

There were clear errors in selection, and I do think it was a mistake to allow Duncan Fletcher a role in picking the team, though in fairness to him he did offer to stand down as a selector the previous summer and was turned down. Fletcher answered criticisms of the apparently incomprehensible decisions to prefer Giles to Panesar, Anderson to Mahmood and Jones to Read in the first two Tests by using the royal 'we' and saying it was a collective decision by him and Andrew Flintoff. Perhaps it was, but I believe that a coach should either be solely responsible for selection or should have no say in it whatsoever. You can't have a middle way where the coach can pass the buck to others. Either he does it all and stands or falls by his results, or he coaches what he's given and someone else picks the team.

My personal preference is for the latter. If you were a batsman, say, and were having a problem playing Shane Warne – and most people did – and you said, 'Coach, I've got a problem with this,' what happens when it's time to pick the team? Maybe the coach thinks, 'I know that guy's got a problem with Warne; I'll pick someone else in his place.' So players have to have complete faith and trust in their coach and that doesn't always work if he's a selector as well.

I'd much rather see a three- or four-man selection panel. It's a system that has worked very well for the Aussies. John Buchanan, the Australian coach in 2006-07, had no say in selection whatsoever and he managed to turn out a pretty successful team. Similarly, if you're going to pick the strongest England team, you want a chairman of selectors who's an outsider looking in. By all means let him consult with the captain and the coach and the senior players – and the captain will always have a strong input and will often get his way – but then the chairman has to go away, discuss it with his fellow selectors and come up with the team that they feel is best equipped for the task. Once they've done that, then the coach can get involved and start doing what he does best – coaching the players and preparing them for the Tests.

Having got the selection right, then you have to get the physical and mental preparation and the itinerary right as well. Yet we failed on all those counts. I honestly don't think some of those English boys knew what they were going to be in for when they got to Australia; they didn't look ready for it in any way. They deserved to enjoy their victory over the Aussies in 2005 and the plaudits that came their way, but some of them still seemed to be living off that success when they got to Australia sixteen months later. While they were polishing their MBEs, the Aussies were being put through hell, working their guts out at a training camp in the Outback and psyching themselves up for the battle to come

The itinerary was also badly flawed. Tour itineraries are planned years in advance, so there's no excuse for not getting them right. It was a huge mistake to fly the players back to England for a few days after the ICC Trophy in India and then fly them all the way back to Australia. And then, having finally got them to Australia, whoever came up with the bright idea of having a couple of meaningless tip-and-run warm-up games and then going straight into the first Test in Brisbane should have been fired instantly. The top six in our batting order had very little experience in Australian conditions; two or three of them had never batted there at all. Some of our bowlers were similarly inexperienced. To take on Australia on their own turf you need a minimum of four weeks' preparation, including four-day games against the top state sides, whose fringe Test players will be busting a gut to impress against you. Batsmen, bowlers and fielders would then have reached the first Test having adjusted to Australian conditions – the heat, the light, the pace of the wickets and outfields – and the intensity of the opposition.

Instead we went into that first Test woefully under-prepared both physically and mentally, got hammered and never recovered from it. You'd have to be very naive to imagine that you could come straight off the plane and successfully take on an Australian side that was smarting, hurting, cursing after the defeat in 2005. They were the first Australian side in twenty years to lose the Ashes and they had to fly back home and cop the flak from that. Did the English blokes think that they were in for a stroll in the park after that? Who the hell did they think they were?

I guarantee that, as they watched England at The Oval in 2005, every single Australian player would have been saying to himself, 'I don't like having to watch those Poms celebrating; I'm going to make damn sure I don't have to see that again next time.' From the moment they got on the plane to come home in 2005, the Aussie coach John Buchanan, the captain Ricky Ponting and all the players were focused on the 2006-07 series. They wanted revenge. They didn't just want to scrape a win, they wanted to rub English noses in it, and that's exactly what they achieved. They paid minute attention to every single part of their preparation, they picked the right team and they were willing to sweat blood for the right result. You only had to see the difference in fielding between the two sides to recognise that the intensity levels of the Australians were far above ours.

We looked like schoolboys playing against the world's best, never more so than on that last morning in Adelaide. What was going on in that dressing room? What on earth had been said, so that when the English batsmen came out they scored just 30-odd runs in the whole of the thirty-over morning session? What were they thinking? But it wasn't just in Adelaide. Every single pressure session was lost right through the series. Whenever the pressure was on, the Australians came to the party and the England players stayed at home. I can't think of a single crucial passage of play where we came out ahead. Many of the same players were on the winning side against Australia sixteen months previously, but Australia learned lessons from that and England did not.

Even the ways the two teams went to the ground for each game pointed up the difference in attitude and work ethic. Every morning, the Aussie players carried their own bags out to the three minibuses they used, hopped aboard and took it in turns to drive to the ground. One day you'd see Shane Warne in the driving seat, cigarette in one hand, the next day it would be Matt Hayden, Adam Gilchrist or Glenn McGrath. When they got to the ground, they'd pick up their bags, push their way through the crowds queuing to get in, go to the dressing room and get ready to go work. When England travelled, it was like a rock group on tour: a luxury coach with flunkeys to carry their bags for them and security men holding back the crowds behind a rope whenever they were getting on or off the coach, so that the England superstars could disappear into the dressing room without being troubled by any human contact. For God's sake, this was Sydney and Melbourne, not Baghdad and Kabul. They didn't need security men, they should have carried their own bags, and who knows, they might have benefited from a little closer contact with the England supporters; it might have made them more aware of what the fans thought of their performances.

I counted twenty-five people wearing England shirts out in the middle before the start of one Test – who the hell were they all? As well as the players, the coach and the physio, England had a batting coach, a bowling coach, security men, flunkeys of one sort and another, a dietician to tell them what to eat and even a team psychologist to motivate them. Since when did you need a psychologist to play cricket? I never took any notice of those idiots – how many overs have they ever bowled? From the results the team achieved, the psychologist obviously did a great job.

Maybe next time we can take a few less passengers and a few more players with the hunger for victory and the guts to fight it out – 'the ticker', as Brian Close used to say. But the first thing we need to do is to ensure that we're not going to Australia straight off the back of the ICC Trophy. Why the hell people didn't object to that I'll never know. When the ICC Trophy was first proposed it was as a competition to aid the developing cricket nations – the first one was in Kenya – and the aim was that it would be played in those countries. Yet the last two have been played in England and India, a decision that was all about making money and not at all about developing cricket in the emerging nations. We don't need the ICC Trophy. It's a non-tournament, a nuisance that neither players nor spectators really want. We should have just turned round to the ICC and said, 'Sorry, we can't play, we're preparing for the Ashes.'

Given that they had to play the ICC Trophy on this occasion, I would have wanted to go straight to Australia from India after the ICC Trophy, not fly all the way home for a few meaningless days and then fly all the way out to Australia; I just don't see the logic of that. Much as we all love having our wives and families around, I don't think the players needed to spend a handful of days with them before heading for Australia. I won't accept that argument that they were spending so much time away from their families that they had to have some time at home first – that's bullshit. I counted 103 members of the England party in Melbourne at Christmastime – wives, children, parents, brothers and sisters. Players can have their wives out for as long as they want; some of them had them there for almost the entire tour. So the idea that they had to go home for some family time first just doesn't stack up. Wives are flown out and put up in luxury hotels, all at ECB expense.

It's a great contrast to my own playing days, but good luck to them, nice work if you can get it, and that's not why I have an issue about this. What does concern me is the failure of those England players to deliver. They are picking up around half a million pounds a year in basic pay to represent their country and I don't think it's unreasonable to say that in return for that very substantial amount of money they should be willing to do whatever it takes to be successful on the field. The concept of central contracts from the ECB for Test players was a great thing but I think we've leaned too far now towards what the players want. Sometimes you have to say, 'No, this is the way we're going to do it.'

I'm all in favour of central contracts but the balance has to change a little. Players need to play; that's how they develop and improve.

Whether you're a Botham or a Boycott in your attitude to the nets, there is still no substitute for cricket out in the middle, and I don't think that the centrally contracted England players play enough county cricket at the moment. Past greats like Fred Trueman would bowl twelve hundred overs or so a season; his modern descendants like Steve Harmison don't bowl anywhere near that number, and for me, our top-flight bowlers don't bowl enough. Like our batsmen, they certainly looked very under-cooked at the start of the last Ashes tour. So I'd like to see them playing more games, bowling more overs and getting some more batting time in the middle, so that they're fully match-fit before beginning any series, let alone an Ashes one.

I was well known for my aversion to net practice, not to mention Graham Gooch's fitness regime, but I made sure that I delivered on the field by putting in the work when it was needed, whether by training with Scunthorpe FC or bowling enough overs to get myself in the groove. However, you can't always rely on players to get themselves to the right peak of condition. Some will do so, but a lot of them have to be pushed, and that needs to be addressed. If the coach won't tell you, then you need to have the guts and the honesty to say to yourself, 'I need more work than this, I need to bowl twenty overs an innings for a couple of games to get myself in the groove,' because if those players thought they were match-fit when they began the last Ashes series, God help us all.

The 2006-07 Ashes was a huge wake-up call for the whole England squad and the interesting thing for me will be to see how they respond to it. We'll see between now and 2009, when the Aussies are next due here, who's got the ticker, who's prepared to go out and fight. Those English cricketers were humiliated in Australia and if they don't hurt all the way to the core of their bodies, if they're not burning for a chance to avenge that, then they don't deserve to be in the England squad at all.

How do those players think the English supporters feel, waking up early in a cold and grey Britain to listen to the cricket from

Australia as they're getting ready to go out to work? It's freezing cold, it's foggy, it's dark. They're going to be working long hours on a production line, or in a warehouse, factory or office, and they're listening to some pampered England player complaining that after staying in five-star hotels, eating fine food and playing cricket in the sunshine for seven weeks, he's tired and needs to go home to recharge his batteries ... get a life, boys.

The 2006-07 series ended in early January, and the one-day-games – for those who stayed for them – went on till mid-February. The English county season didn't begin until the end of April and the first international match wasn't until mid-May. Was that enough of a break, lads? Was that enough time to charge your batteries? How about your hearts? How long will it take to get them pumped up enough to play for your country? You're being paid to play cricket for God's sake, you're not having to lay bricks, assemble computers, operate a checkout till or stack shelves in Tesco all day long. You should have such enormous pride in that England shirt that you're willing to play all day, every day, if that's what it takes.

Despite those comments I do get on very well with some of the current England players, particularly Freddie Flintoff, a fellow member of the 'All-Rounders' Club' and a player in whom I see a lot of similarities to myself in his positive attitude, will to win, and ability to turn a game, but I don't go in the dressing room now. That's partly because I don't want to make players uncomfortable, feel they have to guard what they say, but mainly because I feel the dressing room is their sanctuary. It's the place where team talks are held, decisions are made and where players can get away from the pressure, from the well-wishers and backslappers, the people who want to have a go at them, the press and everybody else. It's the place where you can be quiet if you want to, lie down and have a sleep, talk things over with your teammates, have a game of cards, or whatever you want to do, and I think we should respect that and leave that sanctuary undisturbed.

I adopt the same attitude towards other sports. Ian Woosnam is a very good friend of mine and I went to the last Ryder Cup as a guest of the PGA, enjoyed every moment of it and soaked Woosie with a magnum of champagne on the last green after Europe's magnificent victory, but then I left them to it, because that was the players' time. They'd earned the victory and the right to celebrate it and enjoy it among themselves. I did the same when Sam Torrance was captain, although on that occasion, just as I was getting ready to go to bed because I had an early start the next morning, the phone in my room rang and there was Sam saying, 'Where the hell are you? Get yourself up here now!'

In one respect my life now hasn't changed that much from when I was playing. Even though I'm long retired from the game, my personal appearances, advertising work and my duties as a commentator on Sky TV still see me away from home for days, weeks and months on end. When Sky's football commentator Andy Gray, a good mate of mine, goes to a game, he's back home twenty-four hours later. I can be away for three months on an Ashes tour, but it's the life I chose and one I love, and at least now Kath and I, not the England selectors, decide when she can come out and join me.

Looking back over all that we have been through together, I realise how lucky I have been to have Kath at my side, and it's a tribute to her that despite all the upheavals, trials and tribulations that life with me has brought, our children, Liam, Sarah and Becky, are so self-sufficient and well adjusted. She shielded them so well from all the pressures of 'celebrity kid syndrome' that Sarah told me that, though she was obviously aware that people often recognised me in places we went to, it wasn't until she was in her twenties and working for Sky TV that it really hit home how much of a public property I was. We've worked together for the last eight years and we've a great relationship now, better than we've ever had.

Liam's success in professional sport and in his business is nothing to do with his father, it's all down to his own talent, determination and sheer hard work, and Sarah and Becky have also made their own way in the world and can look anyone in the eye and be proud of who they are and what they've achieved. Becky is building her own career and she has shown huge courage in battling the chronic brittle diabetes that affects her. It's a horrible form of the disease. She has to inject herself with insulin four times a day, and even then, she can be fine one minute and then her blood sugar level can suddenly go through the roof. Our worst moment came when she was in her early teens. She began complaining of a sore throat and headaches and feeling sick. We'd been through similar alarms before but this time she ended up in intensive care on a ventilator. The doctors told us it was touch and go whether she would pull through. It was the longest night of our lives, but she got through it and made a full recovery.

Although Liam lives next door, Becky is living and working in the north-east and Sarah now lives in Spain, where she has built up her own business, but they come home regularly and the family reunions are the highlights of my year.

Being away so much has made me appreciate my home life all the more. The general consensus among my family, friends and fellow players was that I wouldn't handle retirement very well. Throughout my life I've never been able to sit still for long, but when I get home now, I don't even want to go out. There is nothing nicer for me than sitting in my house, with my wife and my grandchildren, Regan (thirteen), James (nine) and Imani (six), playing with my dogs and enjoying some nice wine from my cellar. It's lovely to have my grandchildren wandering in from time to time. Liam and his dog Lulu tend to drift in and out as well; you can tell that they've been because they're usually both covered in mud from wandering down the fields and you can spot Liam's boot marks and Lulu's muddy footprints right across the kitchen floor. They both have a snack from the fridge and then wander out again.

I'm enjoying life even more now than I was twenty years ago. We take my grandchildren skiing every winter and we go on safari once a year. I'm lucky that I have the income to be able to do it, I know, but it's a great way to teach kids about the natural world. Try and get kids out at five in the morning normally and they'll just mumble something and go back to sleep, but on safari my grandchildren are ready to rock and roll at five in the morning because they want to see what's happened overnight. Have the lions made a kill? Is there an elephant at the waterhole? We've even had a leopard and its cub sleeping on the thatched roof of our lodge. During the night Kath woke up and accused me of snoring, but I was already wide awake, listening to the sound myself, the low rumble of a leopard purring as it groomed its young. In the morning, the two leopards jumped down from the roof, strolled through the compound, took a drink from the spa pool and then disappeared into the bush. It took my grandchildren a few hours to get their eyeballs back into their heads after that.

I've always said that the great thing about having money is that it gives me the opportunity to share great experiences with friends and family. I can charter a boat and take a bunch of my mates out deep-sea fishing for marlin off the Queensland coast in Australia, or hire a yacht to cruise Sydney Harbour and watch the fireworks bursting over the Harbour Bridge and Opera House on New Year's Eve. Kath and I also took all our families – our parents, brothers and sisters and their families, twenty of us in all – to Africa for our joint fiftieth birthdays. We went to Cape Town, went on safari in a game reserve and then finished off at Sun City.

We sold our holiday home in Alderney about seven years ago. We all had a great time there and the kids used to love it, but the island has changed quite a bit now and we felt it was time to move on. We now have a place in Spain, purely for holidays and weekends away. It's easy to get to – we can fly there from our local airport – and is a nice place to escape to. It's also good to be somewhere where I'm not continually recognised and approached. We really enjoy the lifestyle there too, but we'd never move there permanently. We like our Yorkshire home too much ever to leave it.

My retirement from professional cricket has given me plenty of time to reflect on the game that brought me fame and fortune. It has moved on since then – it's never static, always developing – but some things have remained constant ever since the game was born. Cricket is played by individuals who come together in pursuit of common ambitions, and more than any other sport, a single individual can change the outcome of a game, almost irrespective of what his team-mates are doing around him. In my view, individuals who have that ability are born, not made. Coaching can improve them and refine their skills, but it can't turn a cricketing frog into a prince. Like any sport at the very highest level, there has to be something in the genes – there from the start.

If you're playing quick bowling, you have four-tenths of a second between the bowler releasing the ball and you playing the shot. That's not something you can learn; you either have that innate quickness of mind and eye that enables you to play a ball travelling towards you at ninety miles an hour, or you don't. I was lucky, I did. I can remember looking at some of my schoolmates playing cricket and football and thinking 'How crap is he'? or 'God, he's uncoordinated.' They weren't, of course, it was just that they didn't have the gift, that natural ability that I'd been lucky enough to be born with. My son Liam had it too, and when I look at my young grandsons now I can see that they've inherited that same gift. I believe that at least one of them could go on to make a successful career in professional sport.

That ability can extend even into old age. Jeff Thomson told me that he went to Don Bradman's house with a bunch of other cricketers when 'The Don' was eighty. They played a bit of cricket in the indoor nets and though Thommo wasn't going flat out, he wasn't bowling gentle long-hops either. Yet at eighty years old, with no pads, box or even gloves, Bradman flicked him off his legs a few times. There are good cricketers a quarter The Don's age who would struggle to do that.

So it begins with your natural ability, but having the right genes and some innate skills are only a part – and a small part at that – of what's needed to be successful in any sport. It's then down to the individual to develop and hone that ability, and there are many, many naturally talented sportsmen who never make the grade and fall by the wayside for all sorts of reasons. Some don't have the desire, the drive to succeed, some just don't have the bottle when the pressure's on. The process begins at a very early age and obviously your parents and teachers can play a crucial role in that, but at some point you have to take it over yourself. There's a saying in sport: 'You have to ride the torpedo to the end of the tube.' Once you've taken the first step on the path, you either follow it where it leads until you reach the end, or you fall by the wayside.

A lot of things can get in your way and they can be psychological problems as much as physical problems and injuries, but you have to overcome them if you want to be an elite sportsman. They're a special breed, and whatever differing individual talents they may have, one thing they all share is self-discipline and self-belief. If you don't have enormous self-confidence, you simply won't make it, and if that sometimes comes across to others as arrogance, it's usually backed up by results. At junior school – Under-11s – where 20 was a very good score, I was regularly making hundreds. Most other top-level players can tell similar stories. We can't all be sports stars of course, but most people do have a talent in whatever area it might be, though it often remains unfulfilled. It's a matter of unlocking it; you've got to let the animal loose.

I held on to the tail of my own personal tiger and it took me on an extraordinary ride. When I look back now, I have only my memories to guide me because I have absolutely no memorabilia from my career at all. Souvenirs and mementoes didn't matter to me then and they still don't. Nor did I study my stats. People ask me how many Test runs I scored and I can't tell them; I have to go and look it up. Yet I know batsmen who can tell you every single shot they played in any particular innings. There really ought to be more to their lives than that. A lot of golfers do the same thing, but at least they have the excuse that they've got to keep their own score: if they get it wrong, they're disqualified.

I couldn't understand kids of my age who would collect programmes or go and watch the local football team rather than play a game themselves. I've never had that mindset. What was important to me was always being there in the moment, doing it, not watching it or analysing it eternally, or collecting stats or souvenirs about it. I've never kept anything at all from my career, not even from the 1981 Ashes series.

I never play social cricket these days, but my main pastimes are golf and angling. I've played golf on some of the great courses of the world, and though my physical powers are waning, my competitive spirit remains undiminished by the passing years. But my great passion is fishing, particularly for salmon and sea trout; I would go to the ends of the earth for a good stretch of salmon river. Once more, my colour-blindness can be a problem, because I can't tell the difference between one fly and another, which is not a great help, because the fish certainly can. So when I go in a tackle shop, I either have to get the assistant to distinguish them for me, or I just buy a few of each of them and then sort it out later with someone. I find fishing so therapeutic – simultaneously relaxing and challenging. I can look at my watch and find that two or three hours have passed without me even being aware of it. There's no fast lane, no car waiting, no helicopter or plane to catch; there's just me and the river, and it's heaven for me.

I also watch an occasional game of football. As a lifelong Chelsea fan, one of the great nights for me was when I was invited to play in Ron Harris's testimonial game at Stamford Bridge. It's probably not how professional footballers should prepare for a game, but we all got together at lunchtime, had a nice meal and a few wines or beers, and then went out to play football in the evening. It was a fantastic feeling to be on the same field as some Chelsea legends – Peter Bonetti, Eddie McCreadie, Dave Webb, Marvin Hinton, Alan Harris, Ron Harris, Tommy Baldwin, Charlie Cooke, Alan Hudson, Jimmy Greaves, Peter Osgood and Ian Hutchinson.

It's now almost fifteen years since I ceased to be a professional cricketer and became a pundit … and a few other things instead. The television advertisements I've done – Shredded Wheat and English meat – Beef and Lamb – with Allan Lamb, and many others – have kept me in the public eye, and it's surprised me that the 'Ian Botham brand', as marketing people like to say, has proved to be so durable and long-lived. A whole new generation has grown up who don't associate me with cricket at all; I'm either Mr Shredded Wheat or the guy who does those charity walks, or they see me on TV with Sky. The news that I was also once a cricketer comes as something of a surprise.

Success on and off the cricket pitch has opened doors that would have otherwise have been closed to me, but even so, you still have to want to go through them. The most high profile of my many extracurricular activities was *Question of Sport*. Bill Beaumont and I co-captained the teams for more years than either of us care to remember and I couldn't have worked with a nicer guy. Bill and I were both out of the country so often on overseas tours that we'd often record four or five programmes together in a block. I once had to fly home from Australia in the middle of a tour, record a few programmes and then fly straight back again. One of the golden moments I can remember was when my mate Ian Woosnam was on the panel and miraculously managed to identify that week's mystery guest – a near unidentifiable figure posing with a fishing rod and dressed in a plastic mac that covered him from head to foot. 'That's Greg Norman,' Woosie said at once. When he was asked how on earth he'd managed to guess it correctly, he just smiled. 'Oh, it was easy,' he said. 'I saw your lot shooting the film at Gleneagles a few weeks ago!' I was always trying to get them to let me have golf as my 'home' sport, because I watched a lot of it and I hardly used to watch cricket at all – least of all the games in which I was playing. So I'd always get the cricket questions wrong, much to the amusement of everybody else, whereas Bill always got them right, because he loved to watch the game.

I wasn't allowed to ski until I'd retired from cricket – the risk to my back was too great – and Bill had never done it either, so while we were recording one programme I said to him, 'Why don't we give this skiing lark a go?' He was all for it, so off we went. The sight of us in our skiing gear reduced our family and friends to hysterics, and things didn't improve out on the slopes. We couldn't even stand up when we started. I'd never seen Bill lose his temper before – he's a big, big unit, but he's a real gentle giant – but while we were struggling along trying to do what the instructor was telling us and falling over again and again and again, a British tourist kept shoving a cine camera in our faces. Knowing the shortness of my fuse, Kath kept saying to me, 'Ignore him, Ian, it's not worth it,' but then he suddenly disappeared. 'Where did he go?' I asked Bill. He smiled. 'I told him that if he didn't disappear, his camera would be disappearing to somewhere where the sun doesn't shine.' I met top sportsmen – in every sport – from all over the world while I was doing the programme, and our paths would otherwise not have crossed, so I've always been grateful for that.

My Sky TV work, the advertisements and my personal appearances and speaking tours give me a comfortable income and I really enjoy doing them, but the twin pillars of my life now are my work for the Leukaemia Research Fund and my family. I still regularly do a charity walk for the LRF and Kath is now as much a part of the walks as I am. She throws herself into the organising and even into the walking, so we have been able to share the highs and lows together. There were plenty of both to come as at ten a.m. on Monday 11 October 1999, fourteen years after I first walked the 874 miles from John O'Groats to Land's End, I set off to do it again.

My final preparation had not been exactly by the book. On the eve of the first leg from John O'Groats to Occumster, I went on the booze with a few of the usual suspects. Aged forty-three, I then found the walk even tougher than the first time and the weather on that first day was terrible, as bad as on any of the walks. By the time day one was over I was beginning to wonder if there would even be a day two. Thanks to the care and attention of physio Dave Roberts, the teamwork and friendship of my fellow walkers – Dave 'The Bet' Chisnell, David Parker from the British Diabetic Association and Stuart Watson – the support of Duncan March and the back-up crew, and the incredible, inspirational generosity of the public, I made it to the end of the day – and thirty-three days later, the end of the walk as well.

Tom Moody, the Worcester coach, brought a couple of the young lads from there to do part of the walk with me. They were all young, fit lads but by the end of the day – twenty-six miles – they were absolutely knackered, hobbling along, feet blistered, the works. Tom reckoned it took them a month to recover, but he felt it was well worth it, for the lesson behind it: if you want to succeed you have to be willing to suffer. It takes determination, and if you don't have that, not only will you not complete a twenty-odd-mile walk for charity, you won't be a successful cricketer either.

The best moments of the walk came as we arrived at Bridgnorth in Shropshire. As we crossed the finish line for the day, I racked up my four thousandth mile and raised my four millionth pound on the Leukaemia Research walks. At three-thirty on the afternoon of Saturday 13 November, I reached Land's End once more, and the pleasure of doing so was doubled by the knowledge that I would never have to pound down that long stretch of road again. I intend to continue doing what I can to further the cause of leukaemia research, including any number of shorter charity walks, but the body is the best judge of what it can and cannot do, and mine left me in no doubt that twice from John O'Groats to Land's End was more than enough for my lifetime.

When I started the walks all those years ago, raising money in this way was something I wanted to do for its own sake, but the experiences I've had and the people I've met as a result of those walks are beyond price. Often I'd feel that I simply couldn't go another step, but I only had to think of those kids in the Leukaemia Unit at Taunton all those years ago and I'd be off and striding towards the finish again. What were a few niggles, blisters, aches and pains compared to what those kids had to go through?

When I look back now at everything we have achieved, it fills me with tremendous pride. From a personal point of view, I have the satisfaction of knowing that if I can get through one of these walks and survive the pain, I can get through anything; but that's nothing compared to the satisfaction I have about the money we have raised for leukaemia research, and the good use to which it has been put. What was meant to be a routine hospital trip in 1977 changed the focus of my life, though there was no way I could have guessed how my involvement in the fight against the disease would develop. Over the years we have raised more and more money for the Leukaemia Research Fund, and I was profoundly honoured when the LRF laboratories in Glasgow were named after me.

I see it as a lifetime commitment. People who know me well know that when I start something then I usually finish it, one way or another. I got started with the LRF, got involved, and now I want to see it through to a finish … and the only one that would satisfy me would be the complete eradication of the disease, so there's a long way to go yet before I can think about hanging up my Nike trainers next to my cricket ones.

The walks have changed a bit over the years. I don't tend to do such marathons as I used to and we do choose the routes with more care now, so that we spend as much time as possible in built-up areas – not because I like the pollution, but so that we can raise the maximum amount of money. In the early days, walking from John O'Groats to Land's End, there'd be hours when we were just walking through open country with hardly a house or a person to be seen. Beautiful though that often was, the object was, and is, not to appreciate the British countryside but to raise cash. As well as the John O'Groats to Land's End walks, I've done the East Coast from Aberdeen to Ipswich; the West Coast from where I was born to Yeovil; the South Coast; Belfast to Dublin; the Channel Islands; the Alps; and many others. Still more are planned.

If the Hannibal walk was the least rewarding financially, the East Coast walk was the most painful. We were nearing Ipswich when we encountered a group of children on mountain bikes. One of them ran over my already blistered heel and the thick, hard-tread tyre caught me in just the wrong place, ripping away all the skin from my heel. The pain was excruciating, but luckily it was raining and there were few onlookers to see a grown man cry. I pulled down my hood, gritted my teeth and marched on. It was four hours of agony.

That was the time I was most grateful for the efforts of Dave 'Rooster' Roberts, the England physio who came with me on that walk and many others. Not only is he good at his job but we share the same sense of humour, and like me, he never knows when he's beaten. The wound got so badly infected that Rooster had to cut away lumps of flesh from the heel, and it was sore for weeks, but Rooster knew better than to try and persuade me to quit and his skill and encouragement kept me going through the pain till we reached the finish of the walk.

I confine my walks to the UK these days, but to my delight, mates of mine like David Boon, Allan Border and Dean Jones in Australia have taken up the idea there. Allan and Dean were sitting with me in the Brisbane Broncos Leagues club one night talking about the walks I'd done for the LRF and I just said, partly as a wind-up and partly as a genuine challenge, 'Why are you blokes just sitting there talking about it? Why don't you get off your arse, do something to help the community and do one of your own?' They both did exactly that. Allan Border walked from Sydney to Brisbane and raised $850,000 for leukaemia research, Dean walked from Sydney to Melbourne and raised $1.3 million, and David Boon walked round the coast of Tasmania and raised $550,000.

Once you get your teeth into these things, you just keep going. It's very much a family business. Kath did all the administration for years, and when she took a step back because of other commitments, Sarah took over and effectively ran the last walk that I did, in 2006. My grandchildren are also very keen to be involved, especially if it gets them a day off school, so they come along and help with the collection buckets and things.

I try to make myself available whenever possible for the Leukaemia Research Fund. There has only ever been one occasion when I wished I hadn't, and the reasons for that were nothing to do with the LRF. I was the guest of honour at a Christmas Carol Service at the Royal Albert Hall way back in 1988. The whole thing went really well and we then went on to a party hosted by *TV Times* at a West End hotel. Afterwards we stood outside on the hotel forecourt to wait for a taxi. We hung about for twenty minutes, and I'd twice asked the doorman to get us a cab. Finally, when I again asked him 'Are the cabs coming?', he just said, 'No, we're not getting any.'

'So we've been standing here for half an hour for nothing?'

He just shrugged and walked away. I told him what I thought of him, but that was as far as it went. I was on crutches from my back surgery so I was hardly in a position to do anything else about it. By this time there was quite a queue of people waiting, but eventually someone else in our party went round the corner and found a taxi and we piled in for the short journey back to our own hotel.

I became aware of a police car following us, lights flashing, and as we stopped on our hotel forecourt, a dozen or so police officers leapt out of several vehicles and stormed our taxi. Despite my protests about my back injury – and I had the crutches to prove it – I was dragged out and hurled into the back of a police car.

I was taken to Chelsea police station, where I was told, 'The police doctor is seeing the other man.'

'What other man?' I said. It turned out that, seeing the chance of a nice little nest-egg from the tabloid newspapers, the hotel doorman had accused me of head-butting him. However, when the police doctor examined him, he could not find a mark on him. The attitude of the police then became all sweetness and light and suddenly nothing was too much trouble for them. A senior officer appeared from nowhere and started to apologise profusely for the inconvenience. When I told him that I was far from happy, he drove me back to my hotel himself. I was furious at my treatment, particularly as the arrest outside the hotel had taken place in front of my family, including Sarah, who was nine at the time and deeply upset by what she'd seen happen to her daddy.

By the time I got back to the hotel it was two in the morning, presumably after final deadline for the newspapers, because the *Sun* splashed the head-butt allegations on their front page the following morning. It was a very expensive story for them, because when the police refused to press charges, the *Sun* was forced to make an out-of-court settlement, so at least the Leukaemia Research Fund benefited from an ugly incident, but once again the headlines had been hijacked by a ridiculous allegation. I was angry at my treatment, but even more furious because so much of my work for leukaemia research has been overshadowed by this kind of nonsense.

I still do a charity walk every twelve to eighteen months and we have many other fund-raising activities like sporting dinners, corporate events and golf days, but the walks are the flagships of the whole operation. They keep the awareness of the LRF high, and that leads to all sorts of spin-offs, not just in direct donations at the time but in bequests in wills, the involvement of large companies who make us their charity of the year, and so on. We've now raised £12 million or so directly through the walks, and though it's impossible to say precisely how much money has also come in through donations and bequests as a result of that, I'm sure that the amounts are very, very significant – perhaps as much as twenty or thirty times that figure.

As I found out more about leukaemia and the research efforts that are going into developing a cure, my interest grew stronger and stronger, and I became so closely involved that I'm now president of the LRF. But Douglas Osborne, the chief executive for many years, is the man who deserves the lion's share of the credit for the charity's growth. Douglas is a remarkable guy who has done so much work for the LRF and always took particular pride in the fact that it has the lowest ratio of costs to funds distributed of any charity in the UK. Of all the money donated to the LRF, ninety-odd pence in every pound goes where it's meant to.

I'm also very proud that none of my back-up team on the charity walks – around twenty people – claims a penny in expenses, even though they all take time from their jobs and busy lives to help, some even deliberately saving a couple of weeks of their holiday entitlement. So our running costs on the walks are minimal. Each one takes around twelve months to organise, and though we've got all the experience from previous ones to help us – fourteen of them in all – negotiating the red tape, the permits, permissions, securing the co-operation of councils, police, etc, etc, is still hugely demanding of the time that Kath, Sarah and many other helpers put in.

The LRF leads the world in research into leukaemia. When I started raising money for them, there was a 20 per cent chance of survival for sufferers; that is now an 80 per cent chance – an astonishing rate of progress. But there are still some very deadly strains and there is an awful lot more to do. We won't be satisfied until the success rate is 100 per cent, and, proud though I am of my achievements as a cricketer, without question the work I've done for the LRF is the most satisfying and worthwhile thing I have ever done in my life.

These are the special people who have helped me on the walks and they deserve special thanks.

Chapter 13

A LONG ROAD BACK

We never give our parents the thanks and credit they are due when we are young. We're all so busy growing up and then finding our own way in the world that it's perhaps only when we have children of our own that we really begin to appreciate how much our parents have done for us. My mother is still alive and thriving at eighty-one, but my father died two years ago. It was heartbreaking to watch him deteriorate; he didn't recognise me or my mother for the last two years of his life. As someone once said, you start life as a child and you end it as one, but it was horrendous to watch. I wouldn't wish that on anyone. My sister Dale and her husband Pete were big supports to my mother through that awful time, and we remain very good friends. There are only fourteen months between us and when we were young Dale and I used to fight constantly, as only siblings can, but now I see Dale, her husband Pete and their family whenever I'm near Taunton.

My debt to my family is enormous, and I've been fortunate to have had their support not just in my childhood but throughout the twists and turns of my adult life as well. It's a lasting reproach to me that, because of the demands of my cricket career, I was rarely able to be there for Liam, Sarah and Becky when they were young, in the way that my dad and mum had been for me, and that Kath was for our children. Kids take things as they find them; they grew up used to the fact that I was away a lot of the time, just like the kids of people in the forces. It was just the way things were, but it's something I now regret, though with the career I followed, I really had little choice about it. I've tried to make sure that I don't make the same mistake with my grandchildren. I love spending time with them, and whenever Liam is away playing rugby or running his business I've made a point of filling the gap with his children as much as I can, in the way that Kath's dad, Gerry, so often did for me. I also do a lot of things with Liam, Sarah and Becky now. I know you can never compensate for the years that you've missed, but in whatever time I've got left to me, I want to enjoy my family, Kath, my children and my grandchildren to the full.

I make no apologies for what I've done nor the way I am, but I'm certainly not blind to the fact that I have made plenty of mistakes. I have tried to be true to myself and my principles at all times, but those around me, particularly Kath, have often had a high price to pay for that. We have been together now for the best part of thirty years and she has suffered more aggravation and heartache along the way than anyone deserved. Women who marry cricketers know that their life is hardly ever going to be normal; the demands of the profession see to that. I'm sure she was also aware of what a selfish person I could be – if she wasn't, she soon found out – but in that respect I was probably not much different from others utterly focused on reaching the top in their sport. There are times when you simply have to acquire a kind of tunnel vision because you just cannot afford to allow that focus to be blurred by anything. I also saw nothing wrong in spending more time with my teammates in the pub than I did with Kath. It was more careless immaturity than malice, but it upset her greatly.

Throughout my cricket career, I was also the subject of endless tabloid allegations about 'romps' with a succession of women. These were just the usual tabloid fabrications, except on one occasion when it was true. It began in 1998, long after my playing career was over. There's no excuse really I suppose it was the sort of menopausal madness that seems to affect quite a few men in middle age.

I was in Australia without Kath, commentating for Sky. On New Year's Eve lunchtime, I went to a harbourside restaurant in Sydney, got talking to the waitress, Kylie Verrells, who was serving me and ended up asking her out. It was the beginning of a sexual relationship that lasted almost two years. I saw her when I was in Australia and I even brought her to Europe on one occasion.

Kath suspected that something was going on but when she challenged me, I denied it. I kept on living the lie until 13 January 2001 when a telephone call told me that my double life would be exposed in the *News of the World* the next day. Kylie had sold her story.

I'd not had the guts to confess to Kath before; now I would have to. She was out shopping with Becky. When she got back I took her through to the lounge and said, 'I've got something to tell you.' I told her the whole story. I admitted I'd been infatuated with Kylie, but it was over now. I told her I wanted to stay and try to repair the damage to our marriage that I'd caused, but I'd understand if she wanted me to go. She was white with anger but she didn't shout or scream, or cry. As she later told me, 'I'd done nothing wrong and I wasn't going to show a weakness.'

She just heard me out in silence, asked one or two questions and then told me that I'd have to tell the kids as well before they found out. Liam's wife Sarah-Jayne had just given birth to their daughter, Imani, four days before – my timing was better on the cricket field – and I hated myself for taking the gloss off their happiness. Liam told me that if he hadn't been holding the baby at the time, he would have flattened me. Becky was very upset, and Sarah – who I had to tell by phone, because she was working away – was so furious with me that she wouldn't even speak to me for a long time, and when she phoned home it was always to Kath's mobile, in case I answered our home phone.

When the story broke the next day, I put out a brief statement to the press: 'This is obviously a very difficult time for my family and friends. I am extremely sorry for the distress and embarrassment I have caused, in particular to my wife. I would like to take this opportunity to apologise to them all and would request that members of the media leave them alone.' Then I shut the door on the world and started trying to repair the damage that I'd done. We'd had some difficult times during our marriage, but these were the most difficult of them all, and no one was to blame for that but me.

I was due to fly out to do some work in Australia soon afterwards, but that was obviously a non-starter now and Kath reinforced the point by saying, 'I'm not asking you, I'm telling you that you're not going. If you do, that will be it.' The hardest thing for her to forgive was the deceit and the betrayal of trust.

A few days later, Kath and I went to a lunch – our first public appearance together since the story broke. It was a long-standing commitment but it wasn't the most comfortable occasion to begin with. Everyone there obviously knew what had happened and the conversation around us was pretty strained. A very good-looking waitress was serving us our lunch, and desperate to break yet another growing silence, without thinking I said to Kath, 'She's beautiful, isn't she?'

She gave me a sideways look. 'She certainly is, Ian, and as we all know you're an expert on waitresses.' There was a pregnant pause, then Kath burst out laughing and everyone else joined in. It broke the ice at the lunch and between Kath and me as well. That was only the beginning. It was a long road back for me, but we came through it in the end and, strangely, I think we're now stronger together as a result.

Only she and I know how close she came to leaving me not once, but twice. She had taken a cool look at the marriage and weighed up her options carefully. Life on her own would have meant an end to the newspaper headlines, the whispers, the verbal battles with me; an end to the sleepless nights she had suffered for years, the terrible feelings of insecurity and loneliness, and the constant need to defend me and our relationship; an end to my stubbornness and selfishness and the long silences when I fell into one of my darker moods. She discussed leaving me with her mother, but Jan said to her, 'Is your life and that of the children going to be better, or is it going to be the same or worse? You should only leave him if it's definitely going to make your life a lot better.' In the end Kath decided to stick with the marriage for the sake of the children, and we've come through those sometimes turbulent years to a time when we are both genuinely content in each other's company.

Bearing in mind my upbringing and the character and personality of my mum and dad, there was never any danger of me becoming a librarian. I'm certainly not academic, though unlike many observers I don't consider myself to be thick, but I really do believe that I'm one of those who has simply been blessed with the ability to turn my hand to anything I choose. So I've learned about life by doing it rather than reading about it.

I've never been one for compiling stats about myself or anybody else, but on the rare occasions when someone brings them up, I am proud of what I achieved. None of the present crop of England cricketers has got three hundred Test wickets or is going to get three hundred Test wickets ... with the possible exception of Monty Panesar. I've got five thousand Test runs and fourteen Test centuries to my name as well, but those bald statistics don't show the way I made those runs and played the game, and I hope people will remember me as much for that – a ferocious competitor certainly, a man who never gave less than 100 per cent to whatever I turned my hand to, a hard opponent, but above all an entertainer. I hope that those who know me well will also remember me as a true friend. But my finest testament and greatest hope is that I might be remembered as one of the men who helped pave the way for a cure for leukaemia.

Whatever I'm involved in, I want to try and squeeze the last drop out of every experience, always pushing the boundaries to discover what I'm capable of. That pattern has been consistent throughout my life and I'm not going to change now. I'm just a country boy from Yeovil who knew what he wanted from life and went for it. I wouldn't change a thing, good or bad, because it's all combined to bring me to the place I am now, and it's a great place to be. I couldn't be happier with my wife, my family, my work, my home and my life, and I wouldn't trade places with anyone. It's been a fantastic life and there's plenty more to come before I'm through.

Postscript

There have been some spectacular highlights in my life so far but nothing has compared to the moment in May 2007 when I received a letter telling me that I was to be knighted in the Queen's Birthday Honours List 'for services to cricket and charity'. There had been whispers and rumours of a knighthood in the offing for years, with people tapping the side of their noses and murmuring things like 'It's definite this time; I heard it from a friend of a friend who works at the Palace', but each time the rumours turned out to be false and, to be honest, I'd pretty much given up on the whole idea when the letter finally arrived.

As soon as I saw the official crest on the envelope my hands started shaking and I nearly tore the letter in half getting it out of the envelope. It arrived a month in advance of the official announcement but I was warned to keep it in 'strict confidence' and say nothing to anybody else about it – and they are ultra-strict on secrecy – so, although obviously I told Kath, or 'Lady Botham' as she will now be known around the breakfast table, straight away, I had to keep the news from the rest of the family until the news was made public on 18 June, the Queen's official birthday. It was torture to keep quiet about it but finally we called all the kids and grandchildren together the evening before it was officially announced and told them and, since it coincided with my mum's eighty-first birthday, we had a double celebration that night.

As a patriotic Englishman, nothing compares with having my

work recognised by Her Majesty the Queen and it is an honour and an occasion that I'll never forget. It eclipsed great events in my life like my first Test match, Ashes victories and even Headingley 1981. I was particularly pleased that my work for leukaemia research had been recognised and though the award was made to 'Sir Beefy', I accepted it on behalf of the countless people who have helped me over the years in the fight against that terrible disease. The knighthood won't make any difference to who I am and the way I am, but I will always treasure the honour bestowed on me and I hope the publicity and prestige that goes with it will help us to raise even more money for the fight against leukaemia that is my life's work.

Acknowledgements

To all my family and friends – without them life wouldn't have been half as exciting.

Index

Adelaide 186–7, 270, 319, 324, 350
Agnew, Jonathan 303
Akram, Wasim 290, 323, 324, 326–7
Alam, Intikhab 38
Alderman, Terry 160, 161, 163, 165, 167–8, 170–2
Alderney 333–6, 357
Aldridge, Brian 323
Ali, Liaqat 106
Ali, Muhammad 54, 196, 234
Alley, Bill 49
Allott, Paul 172, 210
Altrincham Football Club 135
Ambrose, Curtley 312, 314
America's Cup Challenge 265, 271
Amiss, Dennis 182
Anderson, James 348
Andressier, Steve 217
Andrews, Eamonn 176
Ansett Airlines 279
Antigua 145, 148–9, 198, 233, 236, 240, 244–5, 247, 262
Arlott, John 36–7, 334–6
Arlott, Pat 335
Arundel 331
Ashes Test series 112–18, 204, 291, 312, 315, 322, 329, 345, 355
  1977 80–1
  1981 153–4, 162–74, 180, 360
  1982 186, 187–8
  1985 209–14
  1986-87 111, 250, 259, 264–71
  2005 349–50
  2006-07 242, 347, 353–4
  and the legend of the burning of the bails 129
Ashman, Ron 135
Athers 344
Athey, Bill 74, 138
Atkinson, Jeremy 291
Auckland 104, 193
Australia 74–8, 280–91, 314, 318–25, 357, 365–6
Australian Cricket Board 188, 276–7
Australian cricket team 76, 86–94, 107, 108, 112–18, 122–3, 127, 134–5, 151–2, 153, 154, 159–74, 186–7, 204, 209–14, 267–70, 300–1, 303–5, 316, 319, 330–1, 336, 341–3, 348–51, 353
Australian Sheffield Shield 274–81
Australian tours 108, 112–18,

122–3, 125, 127, 186–8, 264–71, 315, 349
Azharuddin, Mohammad 249

Bacher, Ali 305, 306–7
Bairstow, David 119–20, 134
Bakht, Sikander 106
Baldwin, Tommy 361
ball-tampering 326–9
Ballesteros, Seve 214
Bangalore 179
Baptiste, Eldine 312
Barbados 144–5, 146–8, 236, 238
Bardot, Brigitte 296
Barrington, Ann 148
Barrington, Kenny 25–6, 89, 90, 138–9, 141, 143–4, 147–8, 174, 178, 332–3
Barwick, Steve 301
Bath grounds 66–8, 69
Bath League 40–1
Bath and West Showground 259
Beaumont, Bill 361, 362
Bedi, Bishan 119
Bedser, Alec 129, 141, 142, 155, 159
'Beefy and Friends Tour' 290
Belfry, The 214–15
Benaud, Richard 163, 181, 326
Benson & Hedges cup 43–9, 55, 59, 297, 313, 314
Berbice 143
Bird, Dickie 135, 170–1
Bird, Lester 236
Birtles Hall, Cheshire 205–6, 207, 230–1, 311
Bishop, Ian 312
Blackwell, John 200
Bligh, Ivo 129
Bombay 122, 123, 181
Bond, James 229–30, 313
Bonetti, Peter 361
Bonham, John 61
Boon, David 275, 341–2, 365–6
Border, Allan 116, 122, 153, 165–7, 170–1, 173–4, 186–7, 210, 212, 214–15, 218, 223, 267–9, 274–9, 290, 330–1, 365–6
Border, John 218, 221, 223
'Botham barbecue' 160–1
Botham, Becky (Ian's youngest daughter) 223–4, 231–2, 295, 310, 340, 355–6, 370, 372

Botham, Dale (Ian's sister) 9, 12, 13–14, 370
Botham, Ian Terence
  Alderney holidays 333–6, 357
  Asenby house residence 208–9
  birth 7
  celebrity troubles 57–9, 98, 129, 136–7
    court appearances 136–7, 204
    drugs allegations 194–5, 197, 202–4, 226, 239, 240–4, 245–7
    sex scandals 194–5, 240–4, 371–4
  charity work for children with leukaemia 94, 362–9
    Hannibal Walk 294–7, 365
    John O'Groats to Land's End walks 216–28, 363–4, 365
  childhood 7–20
  claustrophobia 23–4
  colour-blindness 15, 344–5, 360
  cricketing career 19–20, 22–42, 68–94, 96, 97, 112–21
    assassination threats against 304–5
    association with Tim Hudson 205–8, 216, 228, 229, 230–1, 239
    awarded 1st county cap 71
    bats 25–6
    BBC Sports Personality of the Year 182
    on central contracts 352–3
    considers South African rebel tour 305–9
    on the contemporary England team 346–54
    on cricketing ability 358–9
    debut 25–6
    dressing-room habits 83–4
    plays for Durham 325, 333, 336, 337–8, 340–3
    on the England selection committee 125, 137–8
    and the England team 63, 70–4, 76, 96
    captaincy 125–9, 134–58, 169
    debut 72–3
    maiden Test hundred 101
    uniform 82
    see also Botham, Ian Terence, cricketing career, Test cricket
  experiences paranoia and mood swings 237–8, 239

fines 188, 198, 279, 332
inability to shoulder blame 242
injuries 46–9, 93–5, 96, 113–14,
185, 196–7, 199, 269–70, 273,
298–300, 313, 336
lack of career memorabilia
359–60
as Lord's ground staff 30–6, 38–9
money issues 82, 91–3, 178, 180,
189, 306, 345–6
named one of *Wisden's* Five
Cricketers of the Year 112
and the NatWest Trophy 191–2
nicknamed 'Golden Arm/Balls'
250–1
player of the match awards 48–9
playing history 359–60, 374
plays for Queensland 274–82,
294
retires from professional sport
336–7, 339, 340–3, 344–7,
355–8, 360–1
plays for Somerset 28–30, 36–40,
43–51, 54–68, 70–1, 74, 80,
105, 120–1, 127–8, 152–3, 173,
185–6, 190–2, 199, 209, 216,
225, 250, 254–63
sues Imran Khan for libel 327–9
superstitions 83–4
Test cricket
1970s 79–81, 82–94, 98–107,
112–19
1979–80 122–6, 128–9, 131–5
1981 137–55, 158–75, 177–82,
184
1982 184–8, 191
1983–4 192–5, 201–2, 204–5
1985 209–14
1986 232–9, 244–5, 252–3,
264–71
1987 273–4
1989 300–9
1991 313–14
1992 326
bans 247–8
captaincy 129, 131–58, 169
centuries 106–7
double centuries 185
on training 98–9
Whitbread young player scholarship, Australia 74–8, 96
plays for Worcestershire 271–3,
292, 297–8, 299–302, 312, 313,
314, 325
World Cups 118, 120, 189, 314,
317–25
Young Cricketer of the Year
1977 94
education 14–20, 29–30
and Eric Clapton 291–3
family
birth of his daughter Becky 223
birth of his daughter Sarah 118
birth of his son Liam 95–6
grandchildren 356–7, 366, 371,
372
and his father's death 370

and football 22–3, 135–6, 192–3,
353, 360–1
and girls 21–2, 58
on his selfishness 371
hobbies
fishing 360
flying 200–1, 248
love of good wines 37, 334–5
shooting 21
in Hollywood 228–30
illnesses
childhood 12
deformity of spine 128
dysentery 99, 104
food poisoning 114–15
jobs 12, 31–2, 62
life beyond sport
advertising work 361
Beefy shows 290, 291
pantomime 312–13
public speaking 289
and a *Question of Sport* 361–2
Sky TV commentary 110, 291,
344–7, 355, 361, 362, 372
Sun column 188–9, 193–4
marriage to Kath 59–66
early married life 66–7
marital problems 80–1, 96–8,
104–5, 153, 156, 157, 189–90,
231, 243–4, 309–11, 371,
372–4
marriage and honeymoon 64–5
proposal and engagement 61–4
media interest in 114, 118, 154,
175–7, 183, 188–91, 193–9,
202, 205, 220, 237–43, 245–8,
271, 274, 317, 322, 367, 371–3
Spanish holiday home 357–8
teenage years 21–42, 43–51,
56–66
This is Your Life appearance
175–6
Botham (née Waller), Kathryn (Ian's
wife) 59–66, 74–5, 80–2, 91–2,
94–8, 104, 153–4, 161, 202–4,
232, 237–8, 247–8, 260, 278,
282, 289, 300, 304, 307, 308,
322, 337, 355, 357, 366, 370–1
and the birth of Becky 223
and the birth of Liam 95–6
buys Asenby house 208–9
and the England wives club 130–1
first pregnancy 75–6, 88
fourth pregnancy 206, 222–3
as grounding force for Ian 129–30
holidays on Alderney 333–4, 335,
336
and Ian's appearance on *This is
Your Life* 175–6
and Ian's charity work 217, 218,
222–3, 224, 227, 294, 362–3,
368
and Ian's retirement 340
and Ian's sex scandals 240–4, 371,
372–4
marital problems 80–1, 96–8,
104–5, 153, 156, 157, 189–90,

231, 243–4, 309–11, 371,
372–4
and the media 114, 176–7, 190–1,
195, 196–7, 240–3
runs the 'Botham' business 97–8,
130
second pregnancy 112
and the South African rebel tours
178–9
third pregnancy, looses the baby
190–1
and Tim Hudson 206, 207–8, 230
on tour with Ian 112–14, 115, 147,
240–4, 245, 264–5, 268, 270
Botham, Les (Ian's dad) 7–8, 10–13,
17–18, 21–3, 25–7, 29–30, 62,
80–1, 241, 341, 370, 374
Botham, Liam (Ian's son) 95–7,
104–5, 115, 176–7, 195–6, 209,
223, 247–8, 261, 270–1, 282–9,
310, 338–40, 355–6, 358, 370–2
Botham, Marie (Ian's mum) 7–13,
17, 18, 21–3, 30, 41–2, 50, 80–1,
157, 241, 341, 370, 374
Botham, Sarah (Ian's daughter) 118,
176–7, 197, 204, 209, 223, 270,
310, 340, 355–6, 366–8, 370,
372
Botham, Sarah-Jayne 372
Bough, Frank 246
Bournemouth Football Club 135
Boyce, Max 312–13
Boycott, Geoffrey 25, 52, 83, 89, 91,
93, 98, 100–4, 116–18, 120, 122,
128, 131, 133–4, 139, 146–7,
149, 152, 154, 160–1, 174,
177–8, 180–2, 206
Bracewell, John 250
Bracknell, Lady 164
Brad (Deckie) 287, 288
Bradman, Don 358–9
Brandes, Eddo 320
Breakfast Time (TV show) 219,
223–4
Breakwell, Dennis 39, 40, 50, 58–9,
85
Brearley, Mike 83, 86–7, 89, 91, 93,
98–100, 104, 106, 115–20, 122,
125–7, 129, 145, 151, 158–9,
162–3, 166, 170–1, 173–4, 177
Bridgetown, Barbados 144–5, 146–8
Bright, Ray 93, 154, 164, 167–8,
171
Brisbane 114–15, 186, 268–9, 278,
279, 349
British Broadcasting Corporation
(BBC) 191, 197, 326, 345, 346
radio 36, 331, 334
TV 219, 223, 315
British Diabetic Association 363
British White Crusaders 265
Broad, Chris 269, 270–1
Brown, John 210
Brown, Ken 281–9, 290–1
Brown, Lawrie 233–4, 266–7,
269–70
Bruno, Frank 196

Buchanan, John 348, 350
Burgess, Graeme 44
Bury, South Australia 289
Buss, Mike 37, 71
Butcher, Roland 137–8

Calcutta 181
Canada 118
Capel, David 309, 332
Cardiff 333
Carlisle, John 212
Carman, George 328–9
Carphone group 271–2
Carr, Donald 74–5, 112–13, 114, 247
Cartwright, Tom 29, 30, 37, 45, 51, 54, 55, 57, 174, 273
Centenary Test
  Lord's 134–5
  Melbourne 73, 77
Central TV 222
Chad (friend of Liam's) 285
Chamberlain, Lindy 275
Chappell, Greg 86, 87–8, 122–3, 135, 250–1, 276
Chappell, Ian 77, 123, 267
Chappell, Trevor 166
Chatfield, Ewen 102–3, 107
Chelsea Football club 23, 360–1
Chisnell, Dave 'The Bet' 363
Christchurch 101, 120, 193, 194, 318
Churchill, Winston 206
City of London School 34
Clapp, Bob 48
Clapton, Eric 206, 291–3
Clark, Sylvester 257
class hatred 327–8
Close, Brian 36, 38, 43–4, 49, 51–7, 59–66, 69–70, 72, 80, 86, 92, 95, 97, 118, 126–7, 144, 150, 155–6, 174–5, 185, 192, 207, 222, 231, 254, 259, 351
Close, Vivienne 69, 97, 118
Collins, John 35–6
Collins, Phil 61
Compton, Denis 207, 246
Constant, David 135
Cook, Geoff 177, 325, 340, 341
Cook, Jimmy 303
Cooke, Charlie 361
Cooper, Henry 195–6, 207
Cope, Geoff 103
Cosier 115
Country Life magazine 208
County Championships 250, 314, 325
  1974 43, 57, 61
Cowdrey, Chris 332
Cowdrey, Colin 52–3, 57, 75, 207
Creed, Len 40
Cricket World Cup 299, 347–8
  1979 118, 120
  1983 189
  1992 109, 314, 317–25, 326–7
Cricket Writers' Club 94, 303
Croft, Colin 131, 139, 149

Crowe, Jeff 252
Crowe, Martin 193, 255, 259
Crusaders' Union National Sports Day 17
Crystal Palace 22
Cup Final 1970 23
Curtis, Tim 272, 273

Daily Mirror (newspaper) 220, 341
Daily Star (newspaper) 239
Daniel, Wayne 53
Davies, John 298, 337
Davis, Steve 196
DeFreitas, Phil 268–9, 319, 320, 323, 332
Delhi 181
Denning, Peter 'Dasher' 56, 60, 64, 70
Derbyshire cricket team 70, 258
Dev, Kapil 120, 184–5, 189
Dexter, Ted 301, 302–3, 305, 307, 309, 331–3
Diane (Botham's nanny) 156, 231
Digby, Reverend Andrew Wingfield 330
Dilley, Graham 147, 161–3, 166–7, 252, 269, 271–3, 306
Disney 205
d'Oliveira, Basil 207
Doshi 185
Downton, Paul 237
Dredge, Colin 121
Duchess of Norfolk's XI 331
Duncan Fearnley 204
Durham cricket team 325, 333, 336, 337–8, 340–3
Dyer, Alan 297
Dymock 122
Dyson, John 159, 166, 167, 170

East Yorkshire cricket team 13
Edgar, Bruce 251, 252
Edgbaston 73, 96, 106, 134, 170, 179, 186, 201, 213, 249, 274, 301, 303–4, 315
Edmonds, Phil 101, 102, 107, 211, 270
Edwards, Eddie 'The Eagle' 195
Elizabeth II 88
Elliott, Charlie 96
Ellison, Richard 213, 214
Els, Ernie 168
Emburey, John 116, 117, 139, 170–1, 173, 182, 192, 237–8, 246, 247, 250, 252, 269, 270
England 351–2
England cricket team 29, 52–5, 63, 70–4, 76–94, 96, 248–9, 291
  charity matches 339
  contemporary 346–54
  'Three Gs' 107–8
  World Cup 1992 314, 317–25
  see also Ashes Test series; Test cricket
England Schools 20
England Under-15s 26–7, 28, 73–4, 338

England and Wales Cricket Board (ECB) 104, 106, 352
English, David 'The Loon' 289, 291
Essex cricket team 258, 292, 320
Evans, David 92
Evans, Godfrey 207
'Evening with Beefy' show 291

Fairbrother, Neil 320, 324
Faldo, Nick 196
Fearnley, Duncan 271
Field, Lindy 238–9, 240–3, 245, 308
Fiji tours 192, 193
Fletcher, Duncan 347, 347–8
Fletcher, Keith 177
Flintoff, 'Freddie' 84, 137, 347, 348, 354
Football Association (FA) Cup 135
Fredericks, Roy 72
Fremantle 265–6
French Animal Liberation Front 296

Gabba, Brisbane 268–9
Gandhi, Indira 177–8
Gard, Trevor 190
Garner, Joel 56, 120, 121, 128, 131, 191–2, 201, 232, 254–60, 262–3, 308, 312, 331
Gatting, Mike 74, 79, 108, 110–12, 134, 152, 166–7, 171, 180, 192, 210, 212–13, 232–4, 236, 249, 252–3, 264–5, 267, 270–1, 274, 301, 307–9, 316, 339
Gavaskar, Sunil 119, 120, 181, 185
Georgetown 144
Gilchrist, Adam 351
Giles, Ashley 348
Gillette Cup
  1974 56–7
  1979 120
Glamorgan cricket team 33, 40–1, 54, 65, 301, 333
Gleneagles Agreement 142, 177–8
Gloucestershire cricket team 43, 65, 71, 84
Golan, Menachem 229–30, 313
Gomes, Larry 146
Gooch, Graham 107–9, 112, 123, 140–1, 147–9, 152, 154, 159–60, 182, 212, 214, 232, 235–6, 244–5, 252, 309, 314–25, 330, 333, 353
Govind (baggage master) 181
Gower, David 72, 79, 106–12, 118–19, 123, 132, 139, 148–9, 170, 173, 180, 192, 201, 204–5, 210, 212–14, 232–3, 235–7, 239, 244, 249, 253, 265–6, 268–9, 300–2, 309, 315, 329–30, 333, 344
Grant, Cary 206
Graveney, David 325, 340, 341, 342
Gray, Andy 355
Great Ormond Street 224, 227
Greaves, Jimmy 222, 361
Green, Peter 281

Greenidge, Gordon 131, 139, 147, 201–2, 232, 236
Greig, Tony 38, 72, 73, 78, 79, 83, 92, 107, 207
Griffith, Charlie 52
Grimsby Crown Court 136–7
Guyana 140, 142–4, 147

Hadlee, Sir Michael 290
Hadlee, Richard 100, 101, 189
Hall, Wes 52
Hampshire cricket team 43–9, 173, 327
  Second XI 338, 339
Hampshire, John 326
Hannibal 294
Hannibal Walk 294–7, 365
Harmison, Steve 242, 353
Harris, Alan 361
Harris, Ron 360, 361
Harrogate 262
Hayden, Matthew 341, 342–3, 351
Haynes, Desmond 131, 132, 139, 232, 236, 244
Hayter, Reg 179, 180, 183, 207
Headingley 93, 107–8, 119, 134, 152, 158–69, 170–2, 186, 189–90, 201–2, 210, 249, 274, 301, 331
Hendrick, Mike 83, 85, 99, 106, 159, 182, 251
Henman, Tim 196
Herd, Alan 136, 179, 180, 197, 198, 207, 245, 247, 278–9, 307, 308, 328
Herman 48
Hibbitt, Richard 14, 15–17
Hick, Graeme 272
Hilton, Lahore 198
Hinton, Marvin 361
Hogg, Rodney 76, 115, 116–17
Hohns, Trevor 279, 305
Holding, Michael 53, 72, 131, 132, 139, 146–7, 232, 235, 290, 308, 312, 344
Hove cricket ground 37–8, 71, 339
Howarth, Geoff 56–7, 104
Hudson, Alan 361
Hudson, Maxi 206
Hudson, Tim 205–8, 216, 228, 229, 230–1, 239
Hughes, Kim 115, 134, 152–4, 159–60, 164, 166–7, 170, 174, 268–9
Hull City 192–3
Hussain, Mahmood 106
Hutchinson, Ian 361

ICC Trophy 349, 351–2
Idle, Eric 238
Illingworth, Ray 158
Illingworth, Richard 272
Ilminster Town 22
Independent (newspaper) 265
India 351–2
India cricket team 53, 118–20, 181, 184–5, 189, 249, 312, 318–19

India Today (newspaper) 327, 328
India tours 76, 177–8, 181–2, 202, 205, 274, 326, 329, 349, 351–2
Indian Golden Jubilee Test 122, 123–5
Insole, Doug 188
International Cricket Council (ICC) 327
  see also ICC Trophy
Inzamam-ul-Haq 323
Italian Cricket Association 297

Jack and the Beanstalk (pantomime) 312–13
Jackman, Robin 142, 143, 177
Jagger, Mick 194, 238–9, 240, 241–2
Jamaica 233–5
Jamaica cricket team 233
James, Jimmie 36
Jardine, Douglas 117
Jarvis, Michael 320
Javed, Aqib 323
Jesty, Trevor 44, 189
John, Elton 194, 206, 225, 267–8, 270
John Player League 250
Johnson, Martin 265
Jones, Allan 44, 52, 54, 55
Jones, Dean 271, 290, 303, 340, 341, 365–6
Jones, Geraint 348
Joyce, Mrs Olwyn 14–15

Kallicharran, Alvin 131
Karachi 110, 196
Kaye, John 135
Keating, Paul 322
Kent cricket team 57, 192
Kent, Martin 171
Kenya 351
Kenyon, Don 272
Kerslake, Roy 30–1
Khan, Imran 186, 322–3, 327–9
Khan, Mohsin 186
King, Collis 118
Kingston, Jamaica 233
Kitchen, Merv 29, 44, 52, 55, 57
Knott, Alan 55, 72–3, 91, 131, 173, 174, 182

Laker, Jim 107
Lamb, Allan 185, 192, 194, 201–2, 212–13, 232, 236, 291, 318, 320, 324, 326–9, 333, 361
Lambert, Clayton 314
Lancashire cricket team 43, 313, 314
Lander, Chris 'Crash' 124–5, 220–1, 227, 326, 341
Langford, Brian 255, 256
Lansdowne Cricket Club 40
Laughlin, Trevor 76
Launceston 275–6
Lawrence, David 'Syd' 317–18
Lawson, Geoff 152, 160, 164, 167
Led Zeppelin 61
Leeds United 23

Leeward Islands 233
Leicestershire cricket team 59
Leukaemia Research Fund 222, 224, 225, 227–8, 294–5, 362, 364, 365–9
Lever, John 182
Lewis, Chris 317, 322, 324
Lewis, Tony 327
Lewis, Wally 290
Lillee, Dennis 122–3, 134, 160, 162, 163, 167, 171–2, 174, 188, 245, 252, 275–6, 279
Lindemans 265, 270
Liverpool 26–7
Liverpool Football Club 135
Lloyd, Clive 54, 131, 133, 134, 139, 146, 308
Lloyd, David 43, 344
Loader, Rod 289–90
London 31
Londonderry 8–10
Lord's 30–6, 38–9, 52–3, 74, 78–9, 89, 98, 104, 106, 108, 118–20, 126, 128, 132–5, 141, 143, 151–2, 154, 156, 158, 160, 169, 184, 186, 191, 201, 210, 246–7, 249–50, 271, 301, 306, 313, 326, 329–30, 332
Nursery End 107

Macdonald, Malcolm 207
MacLaren, Archie 28
Mahmood, Sajid 348
Mail on Sunday (newspaper) 197–8, 239, 245–6, 247, 341
Malcolm, Devon 303
Mansell, Nigel 196
March, Duncan 363
Marks, Vic 56, 128, 186
Marsh, Geoff 303, 305
Marsh, Rod 88, 93, 160, 167, 171, 279
Marshall 312
Marshall, Malcolm 111, 131, 232, 233, 235, 312
Marshall, Roy 42
Martin, Charlie 175
Martin-Jenkins, Christopher 327
Martyn, Damien 331
Matthews, Greg 209
Mattis, Evertorn 139
May, Peter 201, 210, 248
MCC 35, 53, 79, 87, 89, 135, 143, 154–5, 210
McCombe, Peter 'Jock' 199
McCosker, Rick 86–7
McCreadie, Eddie 361
McDermott, Craig 213, 214
McGrath, Glenn 251, 351
McMillan, Brian 321
Melbourne 116, 123, 129, 187, 269, 270, 276–7, 278, 291, 319–20, 321–5, 352
Meyer, Barry 260
Miandad, Javed 274, 322–3, 328
Middlesex cricket team 129, 191–2, 301, 339

Miller, Geoff 116–17, 141–2, 187
Ministry of Defence 200
Mission Sports Management 290
Mohammed, Mushtaq 209–10
Moody, Tom 363
Moore, Roger 229
More 249
Morecambe, Eric 54, 98
Morgan, Cliff 340
Morris, John 303, 315
Moseley 312
Moseley, Hallam 45, 47–8
Moss, Stirling 196
Motspur Park 17
Mr Khrushchev (Ian's teddy bear)
    12
Muhammad, Anwar 33
Muncer, Len 30, 31, 34–5, 36, 39
Murphy, Pat 197–8
Murray, Deryck 131, 139

National Front 304
NatWest Trophy 191–2, 333
Nawaz, Sarfraz 326
Neale, Phil 272
Neenan, Joe 135–7, 202
Nelson, Horatio 206
New Road ground 271–3, 292, 299
New Zealand 314, 317–18
New Zealand cricket team 100–4,
    107, 118, 189, 191, 193, 249–50,
    252–3, 312, 320
New Zealand tours 96, 99–104,
    120, 192, 193–5, 314
Newport, Phil 272
News at Ten (TV news programme)
    237
News of the World (newspaper) 195,
    240–1, 245, 372
Nike 179
Nine O'Clock News (TV news show)
    191
Norman, Greg 214, 361–2
Northamptonshire cricket club 120,
    250, 273, 301
Northern Ireland 8–10
Nottinghamshire cricket team 52,
    71, 300

O'Keeffe, Kerry 79
Old, Chris 73, 98, 100, 104, 106,
    125, 144–5, 150, 164, 166–8,
    182
Old Trafford 53, 107, 133, 171–3,
    184–5, 189, 202, 209, 212, 249,
    258, 304–5, 307–8
Ontong, Rodney 33–4
Osbourne, Douglas 368
Osgood, Peter 361
Oslear, Don 326
Oval, The 94, 119–20, 133–4,
    173–4, 185, 202–3, 212–14, 250,
    252, 257, 274, 305, 314–15, 337,
    350
Oxford University Cricket Team
    128

'Packer Affair' 78–9, 122
Packer, Kerry 78, 79, 92, 107, 115,
    117, 123, 126
Pakistan 177, 197–8, 332
Pakistan cricket team 53, 105–7,
    108, 110, 118, 186, 189, 273–4,
    319, 321–4, 326–8, 329
Pakistan tours 96, 99–100, 104, 125,
    192, 196, 211
Palmer, Kenny 49, 326
Panesar, Monty 348
Parker, David 363
Parks, The 128
Pascoe, Len 122–3, 134
Patil, Sandeep 189
Patrick (sports equipment specialist)
    179
Patterson, Patrick 232, 235
Paul (Kath's brother-in-law) 195,
    224
Perth 108, 112, 122, 186, 266, 269,
    277, 278, 318–19
Pete (Ian's brother-in-law) 370
Phillips, Wayne 213
Pink Floyd 206
Player, Gary 251
Ponting, Ricky 350
Popplewell, Nigel 259–60
Port-of-Spain, Trinidad 139–40,
    236
Pretenders, The 194
Pringle, Derek 317, 319, 320, 322
Procter, Mike 305, 306
Professional Golf Association
    (PGA) 355
Public Schools XI 26

Qasim, Iqbal 106
Queensland Cricket Association
    280
Queensland cricket team 265,
    274–82, 294
Question of Sport (TV show) 315,
    361–2

racism in sport 59, 261–2, 327–8
Radio 4 334
Radley, Clive 103–4, 106
RAF Kemble 200
Raja, Wasim 328
Rana, Shakoor 111
Rance, Phil 218, 221, 226, 227
Randall, Derek 'Arkle' 91, 102, 115,
    119, 184, 185, 193
Read 348
Red Arrows 199–200
Reeve, Dermot 319, 332
Refuge Assurance League 314
'Rest of the World' (charity team)
    339
Reuters 207
Rhodes, Steve 272
Rice, Clive 305, 306
Richards, Barry 44
Richards, David 327
Richards, Isaac Vivian Alexander
    40–2, 50, 56, 59, 105, 109, 118,
    120, 131–2, 133, 139, 143, 148,
    149, 156–7, 182–3, 198–9, 216,
    232, 236, 240, 241, 244–5, 250,
    254–63, 290–1, 304, 306–7,
    313–14, 322, 328
Richards, Jack 260
Richardson, Richie 232, 236
Ricky (England dressing room
    attendant) 168
Ritchie, Greg 'Fatcat' 210–12, 213,
    214, 277–8, 279
Roberts, Andy 45–7, 49, 53, 55, 71,
    72, 106, 131, 132, 139, 308, 312,
    313
Roberts, Dave 'Rooster' 299–300,
    363, 365
Robinson 213, 214
Robinson, Peter 29
Robinson, Tim 232
Robson, Don 340
Roebuck, Peter 56, 121, 216, 256–9
Romaine, Paul 28
Roope, Graham 104, 107
Rose, Brian 56, 138, 191
Ross, Alisdair 220
Row, Raman Rubba 248
Royal Albert Hall 366–7
Royal Navy 7–8, 13
Fleet Air Arm 7, 10
rugby 339–40
Russell, Jack 84, 304, 305
Ryder Cup 355

Saab 204, 217
Sabina Park, Jamaica 149, 234–5
Saggers, Mark 331
Sainsbury, Peter 46
St John's, Antigua 244
St Vincent 139, 232–3
Savile, Jimmy 220
Scarborough cricket ground 72
Scott, Selina 223–4
Scunthorpe Football Club 135–6,
    192–3, 353
Scunthorpe Magistrates Court 204
Selleck, Tom 229
Sharma, Yashpal 120, 189
Sharp, Harry ('The Admiral') 34, 35
Sharpe, Phil 248
Shastri 1840–5
Sidebottom, Arnie 210
Singh, Yajurvindra 120
Sky TV 110, 344–7, 355, 361, 362,
    372
Slack, Wilf 244
Slocombe, Phil 56
Small, Gladstone 252, 270, 320
Smith, A.C. 141, 142–3, 144, 147,
    236, 248
Smith, Robin 315
Snow, John 55
Sobers, Gary 55, 175–6, 181
Sohail, Aamir 323, 328
Somerset County Cricket Club
    28–30, 36–40, 43–51, 54, 55–60,
    61–8, 70–1, 74, 80, 105, 120–1,
    127–8, 152–3, 173, 185–6,

190–2, 199, 209, 216, 225, 250, 254–63, 298, 346
First XI 68
Second XI 257
Somerset Schools Under-15 side 25–6
Somerset Schools Under-25 side 40–1
South Africa 335
South Africa cricket team 319–20, 321
South African Cricket Board 306
South African rebel tours 109, 111–12, 177–83, 198–9, 235–6, 305–9
South Australia cricket team 265
Southampton ground 338
Special Branch 304
Sports Illustrated magazine 175
Sri Lanka cricket team 189, 319
Sri Lanka tours 326, 329
Stamford Bridge 360–1
Stevenson, Graham 27–8, 74, 77, 145
Stewart, Alec 320
Stewart, Mickey 250, 264, 266, 301, 307–9, 314–18, 321–2
Stovold, Andy 71
Sun (newspaper) 50, 188–9, 193–4, 220, 228, 230, 327, 328, 367
Sunday League 37, 80, 121, 173, 273, 297, 340
Sunday Mirror (newspaper) 158, 339
Sunday People (newspaper) 199
Surrey cricket team 38, 56–7, 70, 257, 337
Second XI 205
Surridge, Stuart 25
Surtees, John 196
Sussex cricket team 37–8, 43, 71, 327
Sydney Cricket Ground 116, 117, 122, 187–8, 271, 319

Tasmania cricket team 275
Taunton ground 16, 25, 28–9, 36, 43, 44, 67–8, 80, 121, 129, 157, 173, 199, 254, 257–9, 263
Tavaré, Chris 84, 128, 172–3, 174, 187
Taylor, Bob 55, 101, 103, 117, 161, 166, 167, 171, 186
Taylor, David 295, 296
Taylor, Derek 44, 54, 55
Taylor, Les 236, 238–9, 241
Taylor, Mark 301, 303, 305
Test bans 177–80, 182, 246–50, 306
Test and County Cricket Board (TCCB) 74, 78, 92, 112–14, 136, 141, 152, 177, 179, 182, 188, 192, 198, 204, 212–14, 246–8, 262, 301, 331–2
Test cricket 39, 79–94, 98–119, 316–17
1932-33 ('Bodyline' series) 117
1963 52–3
1966 53

1976 72, 77
1977 79–81, 82–94, 98–105
1978 107–8, 110
1979-80 122–6, 128–9, 131–5
1981 137–55, 158–75, 177–82, 184
1982 184–8, 191
1983-4 192–5, 201–2, 204–5
1985 209–14
1986 232–9, 244–5, 249–50, 252–3, 264–71
1987 273–4
1989-90 300–9, 312
1991 313–14
1992 326, 329–30
1993 332, 333
2005 349–50
2006-7 349, 350–1, 352–4
see also Ashes Test series
Thomas, Bernard 99, 114–15
Thomas, David 189
Thomson, Jeff 79, 88, 108, 122, 187, 213, 286, 342, 385–9
Times, The (newspaper) 234, 328
Titmus, Fred 248
Today (radio programme) 334
Topley, Don 320–1
Torrance, Sam 355
Travers, Bill 296
Trent Bridge 52, 71, 80, 83, 84, 89, 92–3, 107, 121, 131–2, 153, 191, 210–12, 213, 250, 300, 305, 308, 333
Trinidad 139–40, 236, 239
Trueman, Fred 207, 327, 353
TV Times magazine 366
Tyson, Frank 75

Underwood, Derek 'Deadly' 123–4, 182
United Nations (UN) 142, 177
Universal Studios tour 230
US Open 168

Vaughan, Michael 137
Vengsarkar, Dilip 119, 120, 184
Venkat 120
Verrells, Kylie 372
Victor Ludorum cup 17
Victoria cricket team 276
Viswanath 119, 181

WACA ground 266
Walcott, Clyde 107
Walker, Max 88, 108
Waller, Gerry 59, 61, 62–3, 66, 195, 202, 231, 238–9, 240, 241–2, 336, 371
Waller, Jan 59–60, 61, 62–3, 66, 95, 195, 198, 231, 374
Waller, Lindsay 59–60, 195, 224
Walsh, Courtney 235, 312
Walters, Doug 88
Warne, Shane 348, 350–1
Warwickshire cricket team 29, 158, 186, 338
Watson, Stuart 363

Waugh, Steve 271, 301, 305, 341, 342–3
Webb, Dave 361
Weekes, Everton 107
Wellington 100, 101, 317
Wesley, John 65
Wessels, Kepler 214, 321
West Indies 177
West Indies cricket team 52–4, 71–3, 105, 108, 118, 126–8, 131–4, 139–40, 143, 146–9, 152, 189, 199, 201–2, 234–7, 244–5, 255, 261, 299, 305, 308, 312–15, 319, 322, 346
'Three Ws' 107
see also Young West Indies
West Indies tours 137–45, 146–51, 229–30, 231–45, 246, 303, 308–9, 316, 346
Western Australia cricket team 265–6, 277, 279
Westland Helicopters 10
Second XI 17, 26
Weston Gazette (newspaper) 26
Weston-super-Mare ('Dogshit Park') ground 67–8, 262
Wheatley, Adam 290
Wheatley, Ossie 301
Whitbread young player scholarship 74–8, 96
Whitehead, Alan 210–12, 213
Whitehurst, Billy 192–3
Wigan Football Club 135
Willey, Peter 128, 132, 133, 140, 149, 150, 152, 154, 161, 168–9, 170, 182, 235
Willis, Bob 83, 85, 101, 103, 106–7, 115, 119–20, 131–3, 139–40, 142, 158–9, 164–70, 172, 174, 186–9, 191, 238, 243–5, 247
Wiltshire Under-15 side 25
Windward Islands 139, 232
Withers, Andy 200, 304
Wood, Graeme 134, 152, 154, 166, 210, 211–12, 214, 279
Woodcock, John 234
Woolmer, Bob 93, 131, 173, 182
Woosnam, Ian 355, 361–2
Worcestershire cricket team 250, 271–3, 292, 297–8, 299–302, 312–14, 325, 337, 338, 363
World Series Cricket 78–9
Worrell, Frank 107
Wright, Bob 101
Wright, John 252

Yallop, Graham 76, 115, 117, 166, 167, 170, 173
Yeovil 10–33, 42, 61, 375
Yeovil cricket club 26, 31–2
Yorkshire cricket team 261–2
Young West Indies 139
Younis, Waqar 327

Zimbabwe cricket team 320–1
Zoo Check 296